Southeast Asia in the Age of Commerce 1450–1680

Southeast Asia in the Age of Commerce 1450–1680

Volume One
The Lands below the Winds

Anthony Reid

Yale University Press
New Haven and London

A portion of chapter II previously appeared in *Death and Disease in Southeast Asia,* published by Oxford University Press, copyright © 1987 by the Asian Studies Association of Australia.

Designed by James J. Johnson and set in Trump Mediaeval Roman types by Keystone Typesetting Co., Orwigsburg, Pennsylvania.
Printed in the United States of America by Edwards Brothers, Inc., Ann Arbor, Michigan.

Library of Congress Cataloging-in-Publication Data

Reid, Anthony, 1939–
Southeast Asia in the age of commerce, 1450–1680 / Anthony Reid.
p. cm.

Bibliography: p.
Includes index.
Contents: v. 1. The lands below the winds
ISBN 0–300–03921–2 (v. 1 : cloth)
0–300–04750–9 (v. 1 : pbk.)
1. Asia, Southeastern—History. I. Title.
DS526.4.R46 1988
959—dc19 87–20749
CIP

The paper in this book meets the guidelines for permanence and durability of the Committee on Production Guidelines for Book Longevity of the Council on Library Resources.

10 9 8

for
Wang Gungwu

Contents

Illustrations

MAPS

FIGURES

Preface

The history of man is a seamless web. No part of it can safely be treated in isolation, and certainly not a part as bound up with international commerce as the "lands below the winds." We who study this region have not found it easy, however, to recognize the interconnectedness without losing the Southeast Asians from the centre of their own historical stage. During the first half of this century colonial history reduced them to an undifferentiated backdrop for the great sweep of Western expansion. Much nationalist history has extended the problem by treating Asians as powerless victims rather than actors, or trying to correct this by isolating the region of study from international forces and comparisons. It fell to orientalist scholarship to begin the heroic task of recovering and making accessible the written record of Southeast Asians themselves, though this erudite tradition offered little guidance on how court chronicles, religious exegesis, or lyrical poetry could be brought to bear on the world of production and exchange.

The omnivorous approach to theme and source material I have attempted in this book is not new. Before colonial history, orientalism, and ethnography created such unfortunate fragmentation of the field, Marsden, Sangermano, Raffles, Crawfurd, and Pallegoix, and even such pioneers as Galvão, La Loubère, and Valentijn, covered every aspect of the life of their subjects by using literature, language, travel accounts, trade statistics, and above all their own firsthand knowledge. In that primitive era of scholarship it seemed possible to write the "total history" of a region or people. How can similar goals be pursued in our age of specialization, when no one person can hope to command the dozens of languages and other skills which have rightly come to be expected of professional researchers in this complex region?

The risks are certainly great that such a broad approach will lead to the superficial or the obvious. Yet to remain confined in the specialisms for which we have been trained also involves risks, and perhaps more serious ones, of excluding those dimensions of history most vital to most of the population. Modern geographers, anthropologists, demographers, and environmental scientists have been more successful than conventional historians in exploring many of the constraints under which the "little people" of the region lived. Making use of their findings offers one way for the historian to extend the limits imposed by the tales of travellers and the chronicles of kings. I am also convinced that treating Southeast Asia as a whole makes it possible to describe a number of areas of life which would otherwise remain in the shadows. For each separate cultural area the sources are frustratingly fragmentary. When we study them together, a coherent picture begins to emerge of the ways of life of the region as a whole. Even if enormously varied in language and culture, this region was subject to many of the same climatic, physical, and commercial pressures and thus developed a very similar set of material cultures.

Finally, Fernand Braudel's call for "historians who are ambitious" (Braudel 1966: 22) has been a great inspiration to me. His remarkable success in drawing on various disciplines, particularly geography, to show both the "collective destinies" of a broad region and its splendid variety provided me with the courage to believe that also in the lands below the winds such methods would yield worthwhile results. In Southeast Asia we have far fewer data and far fewer research monographs on which to base a study than does the Mediterranean world. On the other hand, the region was manifestly better integrated by the warm and placid waters of the South China Sea than were southern Europe, the Levant, and North Africa by the Mediterranean. Moreover, the interdisciplinary approach exemplified by Braudel and the *Annalistes* is especially rewarding in Southeast Asia because of the relative richness of its anthropology, orientalism, and even archaeology, as compared with the poverty of the strictly historical sources.

The aim of this study is to suggest how total history can bring important issues into focus in the two centuries before the establishment of a Dutch commercial hegemony in Southeast Asia. As far as the sources allow, I have concentrated on those features and changes which most affected the population at large, rather than on the rulers and foreigners who play such a large part in the published record. These are frequently long-term changes discernable only by looking at a canvas which is broad in both space and time, with one eye always open for comparable developments in other parts of the world. These priorities determine that we should begin with the structures and constraints which made Southeast Asia a region, and then move to the changes which made what I have labelled the age of commerce so critical a period below the winds, as indeed in most other parts of the world. This volume is devoted to the physical, material, and social structures of Southeast Asia in this period; a second volume will address what the Annalistes would call the *conjonctures* and *événements* which occurred within that context.

Even in this volume, however, the importance of change is everywhere apparent. As capitalism and the Renaissance were transforming Europe, extraordinary forces were also at work in Southeast Asia. The greatly increased tempo of trade magnified the size and role of cosmopolitan cities and their contacts with each other and with the world outside. Islam, Christianity, and (over a longer period) Theravada Buddhism established and strengthened their hold first in these trading cities. States formed and strengthened around the cities, and more secular forms of thought and culture flourished in them. Eventually, in the seventeenth century, European commercial penetration established an efficient monopoly, the effect of which was no longer to strengthen but to suppress indigenous urban and commercial life, so that many of the above processes went abruptly into reverse. Even in this volume, therefore, the reader is urged to shun stereotypes of an "unchanging east," still more of a declining one. The age of commerce brought as much change to Southeast Asia as to Europe, though by no means in the same directions.

The sixteenth and seventeenth centuries have certain advantages in terms of sources. This is the earliest period for which there is a substantial body of surviving indigenous writing—either repeatedly copied because of its sacral character or picked up by early European visitors. This writing is crucial for an understanding of ideology, law, religion, and ceremonies. The chronicles were not, however, concerned with the "obvious daily things," as a Burmese historian has pointed out (Kaung 1963: 33). For the life of ordinary people we are especially reliant on the rich descriptions of the first generation of European visitors—Portuguese from 1509, Spanish from 1523, English from 1579, and Dutch from 1596. The accounts of Chinese, Arabs, and other Asians are also useful, but as they were in much longer contact with Southeast Asia their writings do not always show the same astonished interest in the life-style of the people they encountered.

Having conceded that no scholar is equipped with all the languages and skills which a study of this breadth would ideally require, I should clarify my own limitations. Malay/Indonesian is the only Asian language I command sufficiently for scholarly purposes. For sources in other Asian languages I have depended on translations into one of the European languages (or occasionally into Indonesian). Where English or French translations of Spanish and Portuguese sources have been conveniently and reliably published, I have made use of these. I wish to declare here my gratitude to all those whose labours have made these sources more accessible. In citing the original author and date of composition of a source rather than the edition used, it is not my intention to minimize the contribution of the editors and translators without whom I could not have undertaken this task. My purpose is to keep references as concise and helpful as possible, banishing all publication details to the reference list. Manuscript sources from Dutch and English archives also give only the author and date in the text. This procedure should make clear to the reader which sources date from the period and which are later ethnographic or secondary works. In a further bid for economy, "cf." has been used in citations to mean "see also."

This book results from interactions with Southeast Asia during more than two decades. My considerable debts cannot be expressed by listing names. To those with whom I have worked most closely at the University of Malaya, Hasanuddin University, and the Australian National University, and to numerous other friends who have tried to explain to me something of their culture and history, I remain deeply indebted. The ANU has supported me generously in all my research. In the lengthy preparation of this manuscript I have been especially aided by Jennifer Brewster and Takeshi Ito, who provided or located valuable material; by Jennifer Brewster (again), Tony Diller, Robert Elson, Anthony Johns, Margaret Kartomi, Ann Kumar, Norman Owen, Lenore Manderson, David Marr, Robyn Maxwell, Anthony Milner, and Baas Terwiel, who commented on sections of the draft; by Lio Pancino and Keith Mitchell, who drew the maps; and by Dorothy McIntosh, who typed most of the text and introduced me to the mysteries of word processing. My wife, Helen, as always, made life both possible and agreeable despite the importunate claims of this book.

Southeast Asia in the Age of Commerce
1450–1680

Volume One
The Lands below the Winds

I

Introduction: The Lands below the Winds

Most of "Below the Winds" enjoys a continual spring season. . . .
As is always the case in "Below the Winds," the posts which exist are not based on any power and authority. Everything is simply a show. . . . The natives reckon high rank and wealth by the quantity of slaves a person owns.

—*Ibrahim 1688: 174–77*

Southeast Asia as a Physical Unit

Few major areas of the world have been so spectacularly demarcated by nature as has Southeast Asia. Apparently formed by the pushing together of the Pacific and Indian ocean plates, its southern rim is a massive geological arc, or rather series of arcs, pushed up by the advancing Indian Ocean plate. Most obvious is the volcanic arc formed by the Sunda Islands of Sumatra, Java, Bali, Lombok, and Sumbawa; but outside these is another largely submerged arc, showing itself only in the chain west of Sumatra, with a characteristic deep trench beyond it. On the eastern perimeter another such spectacular arc of volcanic activity is formed by the Philippines, again with a deep trench lying outside it where the Pacific plate appears to be folding down as it expands. The northern boundary of Southeast Asia is formed by the almost impenetrable mountain complex of the eastern Himalayas, where the region's greatest rivers begin.

Within these boundaries lies what paleogeographers know as Sundaland, and marine geographers as the Sunda Shelf, the shallow waters from the Gulf of Siam to the Java Sea. As recently as fifteen thousand years ago water levels were two hundred metres lower and this whole shelf was a land mass uniting Sumatra, Java, Bali, and Borneo to the Asian mainland. The dominant flora and fauna of the region made their way to these larger islands prior to their separation from the

Mainland. Even now, when submerged, the Sunda Shelf plays a central role for the people of the region as one of the world's most abundant fishing grounds.

Water and forest are the dominant elements in the environment of Southeast Asia. Though very difficult of access by land, the region is everywhere penetrated by waterways. Thus on the one hand it has been relatively free from the mass migrations and invasions from Central Asia which affected India and China, while on the other it has always been open to seaborne traders, adventurers, and propagandists in more moderate numbers. Not only were the sea-lanes ubiquitous; they were also remarkably kind to seamen. Winds were moderate and predictable, with the monsoon blowing from the west or south in May–August and from the northwest or northeast in December–March. Except in the typhoon belt at the eastern periphery of the region, storms were not a major hazard to mariners, who on the whole had more to fear from swift currents in certain channels. Water temperature was uniform, with the result that vessels which could not survive a voyage to Europe or Japan could operate successfully for years in Southeast Asian waters. All of these factors made the mediterranean sea of Southeast Asia more hospitable and inviting a meeting place and thoroughfare than that deeper and stormier Mediterranean in the West. Add to this the abundance of wood at the water's edge, suitable for boat building, again in sharp contrast with the Mediterranean during the sixteenth and seventeenth centuries (Braudel 1966: 140–43), and we have a region uniquely favourable to maritime activity. A boat was a normal part of household equipment.

The other element, forest, owes its dominance not to the soils, which share the relative poverty of most tropical regions, but to the reliably high temperatures and rainfalls. Southeast Asia benefits at once from average year-round temperatures as high as any in the world and from higher overall rainfall than any other region of comparable size (Fisher 1966: 41–42). Except at the southeastern and northern extremities of the region (the Lesser Sunda Islands and northern Indochina and Thailand), where there is a marked dry season, rainfall is dependable throughout the year, providing a luxuriant cover of evergreen rain forest. Although a large proportion of the trees are dipterocarps, the Southeast Asian forest presents "an abundance and diversity of forms which are without parallel anywhere else in the world" (ibid.:43), including many economically valuable species. Even today, industrialization and a twentyfold increase in population have not succeeded in taming this forest as sixteenth-century Europe or China had done theirs. Four centuries ago the areas of permanent cultivation were but tiny pockets in an otherwise forested region. More widespread was the exploitation of the regenerative powers of the forest itself through shifting cultivation and the collection of forest products. Even the largest urban centres appear to have enjoyed such an abundance of wood, bamboo, and palm as building materials that these are never recorded as significant items of expenditure or maritime trade. On the edge of such cities and agricultural pockets the forest remained, a common resource and a common danger—home to bandits as to tigers, elephants, and game.

Southeast Asia as a Human Unit

The bewildering variety of language, culture, and religion in Southeast Asia, together with its historic openness to waterborne commerce from outside the region, appear at first glance to defy any attempts at generalizations. Yet as our attention shifts from court politics and religious "great traditions" to the popular beliefs and social practices of ordinary Southeast Asians, the common ground becomes increasingly apparent.

For rather more than half of the people with whom we are dealing—those speaking the closely related Austronesian languages which then covered what are now called the Philippines, Malaysia, Indonesia except its easternmost extremity, and southeastern Vietnam (the Cham group)—this can be partly explained by common ancestry (see map 1). These languages are thought to have sprung from a common parent (proto-Austronesian) about five thousand years ago, with the more widely spoken languages diverging much more recently than that. The Mon-Khmer group of languages still spoken in Pegu and Cambodia in historic times had previously been even more widespread in at least mainland Southeast Asia. The tones which Vietnamese and the Tai group (Thai, Shan, Lao, and others) share with Chinese once caused linguists to classify these languages as Sino-Tibetan, but recent work (Haudricourt 1953, 1954) has established that Vietnamese is an Austro-Asiatic language related to Mon-Khmer, and that its tones have developed relatively recently. Benedict's attempts (1942, 1975) to show that the Tai family belongs with Austronesian in an Austro-Thai group have been less widely accepted. It seems increasingly probable that the numerous common elements in all Southeast Asian language families should be explained in terms of intensive interaction between the southward-moving speakers of Vietnamese, Tai, and Burmese languages on the one hand and the longer established Mon-Khmer and Austronesian speakers on the

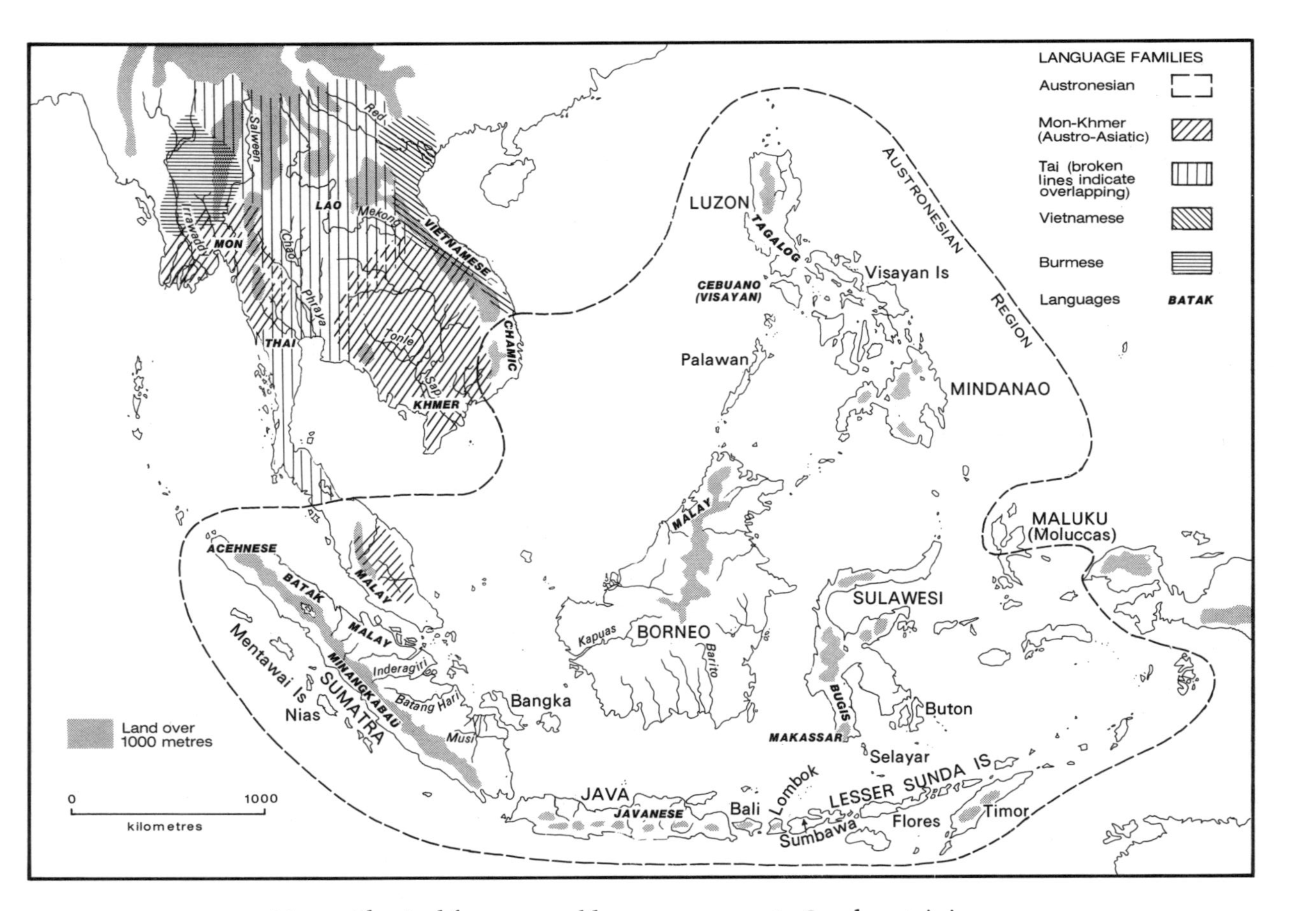

Map 1 Physical features and language groups in Southeast Asia

other. This same borrowing from longer-established Mons, Khmers, and Chams must explain many other sociocultural similarities between the relatively recent migrants and other Southeast Asians.

Two other factors have given this region a common character. The first is adaptation to a common physical environment; the second, a high degree of commercial intercourse within the region.

The common environment was responsible for a diet derived overwhelmingly from rice, fish, and various palms. Southeast Asia has no substantial grasslands, no pastoral tradition, and therefore a very limited intake of animal proteins. Rice is probably indigenous to Southeast Asia and has been for millennia the basic staple of the great majority of its people. In areas as far dispersed as Luzon, Sulawesi, Java, Sumatra, and parts of Siam and Vietnam, harvesting was done by women using not a sickle but a characteristic Southeast Asian finger-knife, which honoured the rice-spirit by cutting only one stalk at a time.

The dominance of rice and fish in the diet, and the small part played by meat and milk products, was characteristically Southeast Asian. So were the half-fermented fish paste which provided the major garnish to the rice, and the palm wine which constituted the favourite beverage. Palm trees provided much of the flavour of Southeast Asian diets, as of life-styles. In a few areas the sago palm was the staple source of starch, but everywhere coconut and sugar palms provided sugar and palm wine, as well as the fruit itself. The areca palm, probably also native to the region, furnished the vital ingredient of betel, which was throughout Southeast Asia not only the universal stimulant but also a vital element in social relations and ritual transactions.

The predominance of forest and water over a relatively thinly peopled region accounts for much else in the life-styles of Southeast Asians. Wood, palm, and bamboo were the favoured building materials, seemingly inexhaustibly provided by the surrounding forest. By preference Southeast Asians lived in houses elevated on poles, whether on the coastal plains, as a precaution against the annual floods, or in the most remote highland villages, where security against human and animal predators may have been the major motive. Much of the characteristic architecture, domestic pattern, and even sociopolitical structure characteristic of Southeast Asia can be derived from the ease of building and rebuilding such elevated wood-and-thatch houses.

Not all the common features of Southeast Asia, however, can be explained by a common environment. The universality of betel chewing cannot have derived from similar spontaneous responses to the existence of areca palm in the region, since the three ingredients of areca, betel leaf, and lime have to be brought together in a complicated operation before the desired effects are experienced. Similarly, the dispersal of the finger-knife, the piston bellows, and such characteristic sports as cockfighting and *takraw* (kicking a basketwork ball in the air), of musical patterns dominated by the bronze gong, or of similar patterns of body decoration and of classification has little to do with the environment. Fundamental social and cultural traits distinguish Southeast Asia as a whole from either of its vast neighbours—China and India. Central among these are the concept of spirit or "soul-stuff" animating living things; the prominence of women in descent, ritual matters, marketing, and agriculture; and the importance of debt as a determinant of social obligation.

Whether such common phenomena should be explained by prehistoric migration patterns or by continuing commercial and political contacts lies beyond this study. What I wish to stress here is that maritime intercourse continued to link the peoples of Southeast Asia more tightly to one another than to outside influences down to the seventeenth century. The fact that Chinese and Indian influences came to most of the region by maritime trade, not by conquest or colonization, appeared to ensure that Southeast Asia retained its distinctiveness even while borrowing numerous elements from these larger centres. What did *not* happen (with the partial exception of Vietnam) was that any part of the region established closer relations with China or India than with its neighbours in Southeast Asia. The Chinese continued to see Southeast Asia (minus the special case of Vietnam) as a whole—"the Southern Ocean" (Nanyang). Indians, Persians, Arabs, and Malays named the region "the lands below the winds" because of the seasonal monsoons which carried shipping to it across the Indian Ocean. Both terms stress the fact that it had to be reached by sea, by a journey substantially more difficult than that which Southeast Asians themselves required to reach such central marketing points as Sri Vijaya, Melaka, or Banten. As one observer noted about 1600, speaking primarily of the Archipelago, "these people are constrained to keep up constant intercourse with one another, the one supplying what the other needs" (Pyrard 1619 II: 169). Until the trade revolution of the seventeenth century, when the Dutch East India Company established an astonishingly regular and intensive shipping network to take a large share of the region's export produce around the Cape of Good Hope, coinciding with an increase in Chinese shipping to the Nanyang, the trading links within the region continued to be more influential than those beyond it.

The period which I have designated "the age of commerce," from the fifteenth to the seventeenth century, was one in which these maritime links were particularly active. I will argue that the interconnected maritime cities of the region were more dominant in this period than either before or since. The most important central entrepôts had, moreover, for some time been Malay-speaking—first Sri Vijaya and then its successors, Pasai, Melaka, Johor, Patani, Aceh, and Brunei. The Malay language thereby became the main language of trade throughout Southeast Asia. The cosmopolitan trading class of many of Southeast Asia's major trading cities came to be classified as Malays because they spoke that language (and professed Islam), even when their forebears may have been Javanese, Mon, Indian, Chinese, or Filipino. It was possible for Magellan's Sumatran slave to be immediately understood when he spoke to the people of the Central Philippines in 1521 (Pigafetta 1524: 136–37), and almost two centuries later for Dampier's Englishmen to learn Malay in Mindanao (southern Philippines) and use it again at Poulo Condore, off southern Vietnam (Dampier 1697: 268). It was during this period that hundreds of Malay words in commercial, technological, and other fields passed into Tagalog (Wolff 1976); that the major trading centres of Cambodia came to be known by the Malay-derived term *kompong*; and that the Vietnamese adopted such words as cù-lao (from Malay *pulau*, for island). Similarly, Malay words such as *amok*, *gudang* (storehouse), *perahu* (boat), and *kris* were noted by Europeans in Pegu and even in the Malabar coast of India, as if they were local words (Bausani 1970: 95–96). At least those who dealt with matters of trade and commerce in the major ports had to speak Malay as well as their own language.

In defining any region there are peripheral zones whose position is problematic. In the first place, I am consciously defining a maritime region linked by waterborne traffic, so that the hill peoples of the northern mainland will not play a large part in my story, even though many of them were linked by culture with the Thai of the coast and the central plain. At the opposite extremity of the region, I am inclined to draw a boundary between Maluku (the Moluccas) and New Guinea, across which the level of maritime exchange and cultural similarity (although it cannot be ignored) becomes of a much lower order than that which linked Maluku with the islands to the west and north.

Vietnam, incontestably a major actor in Southeast Asia as we define it today, presents much more of a problem. Here alone I cannot say with confidence that the common Southeast Asian elements outweighed the factors which linked Vietnam to China, and particularly to the southernmost provinces of China. In their diet and many of their pleasures—betel chewing, cockfighting, a type of *takraw*—the Vietnamese clearly shared in a common Southeast Asian culture, as indeed did some of their neighbours in South China. Their women were markedly freer, their manufacturing less developed, than was the case in China. Yet the political and intellectual life of Vietnam, and even such basic habits as the manner of eating (with chopsticks), had already borrowed deeply from China by the fifteenth century. Moreover, the population of the Red River delta was already closer to China's dense pattern than Southeast Asia's dispersed one. This may have been the reason why Vietnamese abandoned at some time in the first millennium A.D. the Southeast Asian pole house, just as the Javanese and Balinese were to do as their populations increased several centuries later. It was too demanding of wood.

Cambodia and Champa, which shared the southern half of the Indochina peninsula until the fifteenth century, were unquestionably Southeast Asian in commercial orientation and culture. Vietnamese expansion at their expense, which was very rapid during the period we are considering, was a two-way process, in which the conquering Vietnamese by no means obliterated the existing culture in the south. Until the eighteenth century, central and south Vietnam (then the Nguyen-ruled kingdom known to Europeans as Cochin-China—see map 2) continued, for example, to prefer the elevated style of Southeast Asian pole house (Borri 1633 III: D; La Bissachère 1812 I: 246). Although the southern Vietnamese state was somewhat more closely bound in commerce as in culture to the rest of Southeast Asia than was its northern Trinh-ruled rival, it would be absurd to draw a line between the two. Both were essentially Vietnamese, and both looked to China as a cultural model. Although the Vietnamese appear to have traded with the south in the twelfth to fifteenth centuries, at least to judge from the dispersion of "Annamese" ceramics, they did not do so in the sixteenth and seventeenth centuries: "They do not sail to Malacca, but to China and to Champa" (Pires 1515: 114; cf. Dampier 1699: 46; La Bissachère 1812 I: 212–19).

In short, the role of Vietnam is as a frontier between Southeast Asia and China, and a critical one. Had Vietnam not learned so well the lessons of Chinese bureaucratic and military practice, and fought so hard to maintain its equality and independence from the Middle Kingdom, Chinese political influence would certainly have spread

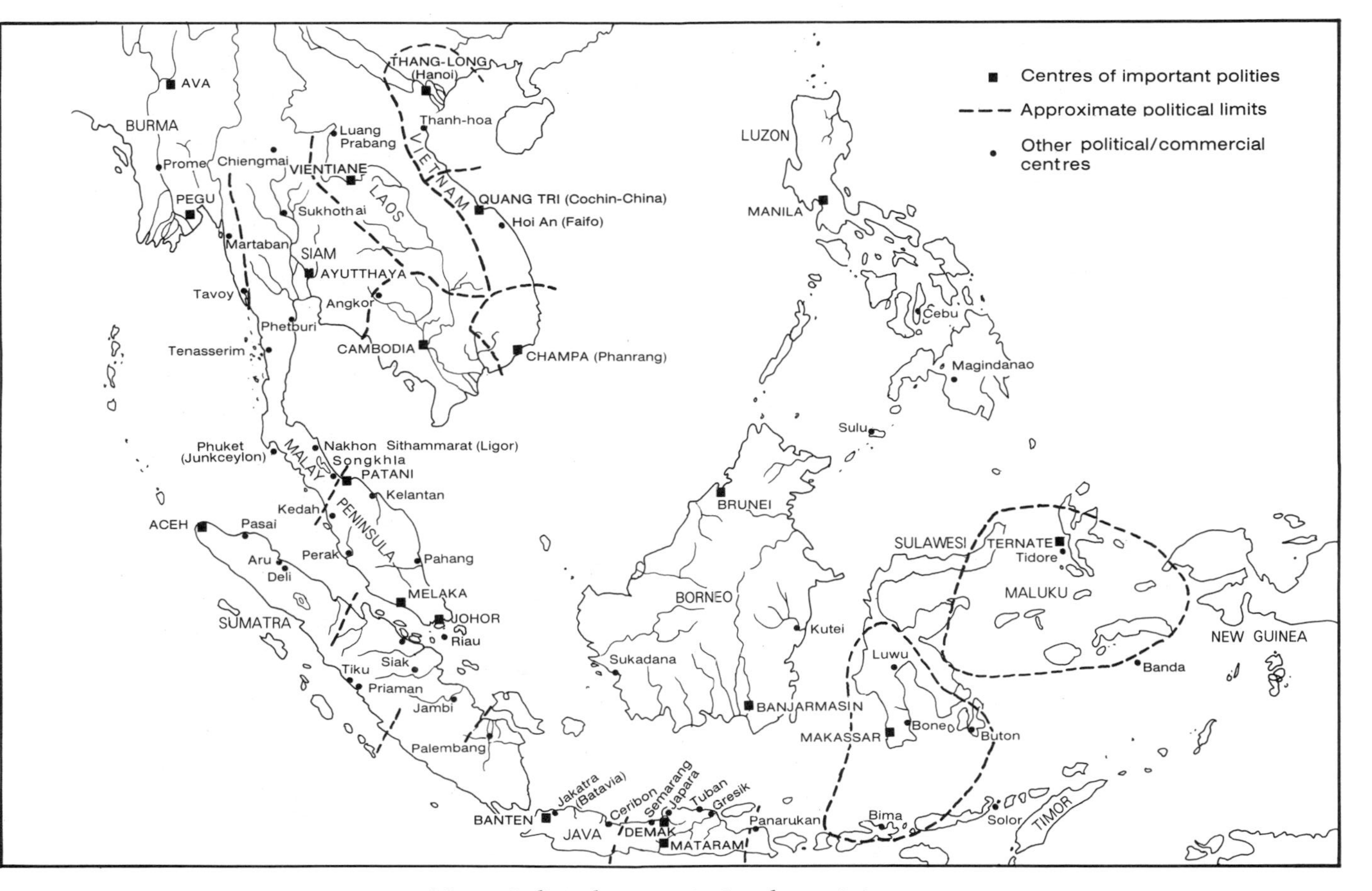

Map 2 Political centres in Southeast Asia, c. 1600

further south, using land as well as sea routes. As it was, Vietnam forced the Chinese to reach the Nanyang only by sea, and almost exclusively as peaceful traders. In some important respects Vietnam will appear as part of the Southeast Asian maritime world. In most it will not.

2

Physical Well-Being

Historians have an understandable reluctance to draw statistics of misleading exactness from the extremely unsatisfactory sources with which we have to deal in precolonial Southeast Asia. Yet without some degree of quantification it is impossible to compare one period or one region with another, or to relate the Southeast Asian data to the increasingly sophisticated social history of such better-studied regions as Europe and China. The hazards of conjuring a specific figure out of partial and contradictory evidence are great, and the margin of error relatively high. Yet the problems of premodern European social historians are different in degree rather than character (they have *more* contradictory sources to handle), and no one would now question the advances that have been made after hesitant beginnings there. After cautioning the reader against giving any absolute value to the figures which follow, therefore, I will begin with the most important and perhaps the most difficult problem of quantification—that of population.

Population

Java, Siam, Burma, and Vietnam all had a tradition of counting households within their kingdoms for purposes of taxation and manpower mobilization. "The Siamese," La Loubère asserted (1691: 11), "keep an exact account of the Men, Women and Children . . . in this vast extent of Land," recalculating the numbers every year. Unfortunately, very few such enumerations have survived, and fewer still have been analysed by modern scholars. Those exempt from corvée were, moreover, not enumerated—such people as slaves, religious functionaries, and "outlaws" outside the areas of permanent settlement. Where these estimates have come down to us in indigenous archives or through the enquiries of foreign visitors, they nevertheless provide a helpful indication of rises and falls in population. In addition, the Spanish in the Philippines provided periodic estimates of the number of taxpayers *(tributos)* under their sovereignty from 1591 onwards.

One way to use the earliest estimates is to compare them with what appear to be comparably based estimates in the eighteenth or early nineteenth century, just prior to the great modern takeoff in population, in order to arrive at long-term rates of population change (see table 1).

The most spectacular rate of change in these figures is the apparent sharp *reduction* in population in Central and East Java. This has to be explained by the lengthy wars of succession prior to the Dutch-guaranteed Gianti peace of 1755, even if some of the war-affected population may simply have migrated to more peaceful areas. All the figures suggest extremely low population growth, contrasting markedly with the rapid growth in all Southeast Asian societies once conditions of internal peace were established, usually by colonial intervention. Continuous rapid growth began in the Spanish Philippines, with average growth rates well over 1 percent from 1735 onwards. Then came Java, which must also have grown at over 1 percent per year after the 1755 peace, to reach ten million in 1845 and twenty million in 1880 (Ricklefs 1986: Owen 1987A). In most other parts of Southeast Asia, the establishment of colonial rule at some time in the nineteenth or twentieth century appears to have initiated the extraordinarily rapid growth rates of the modern "demographic transition" (between 1 and 3 percent). The Cakri dynasty in Siam was also able to preserve conditions of relative internal peace from about 1800 onwards, which is probably the reason that Siamese numbers also grew rapidly in the nineteenth century, though not so rapidly as the colonially ruled areas.

Despite these high modern growth rates, the uniformly low or negative rates for the seventeenth and eighteenth centuries illustrated in table 1 require us to assume very low growth for the whole area before 1800. I conclude that 0.2 percent per annum should be taken as the basis for extrapolating backwards from 1800 for the populations of

Table 1 Population Growth in Southeast Asia, Seventeenth–Eighteenth Centuries

Country or Region	*Population Estimates in Thousands*				*Growth Rate p.a.*
	Earliest Estimates		*Latest Pre-modern*		
Siam	1687 (La Loubère 1691: 11)	1,900	1822 (Crawfurd 1828: 452)	2,790	+0.28
Kedah (Malaya)	1614 (Beaulieu 1666: 246)	60	1837 (Newbold 1839 II: 20)	50	−0.08
Banten (West Java)	1696 (Pigeaud 1968: 64)	191[a]	1815 (Raffles 1817 I: 63)	232	+0.16
Central Mataram (Central and East Java without coast)	1631 (van Goens 1656: 114, 225)	3,000[a]	1755 (Ricklefs 1974: 71–72, 159)	1,035[a]	−0.85
Bali	1597 (Lodewycksz 1598: 198)	600	1815 (Raffles 1817: II ccxxxii)	800	+0.13
Luzon and Visayas (Philippines)	1591 (Dasmariñas 1591: 8)	668	1735 (Church figures in Le Gentil)	837	+0.16

[a]These figures are based on multiplying by 6 the number of *cacah,* or taxable households. A Mataram census in 1631 is described as yielding a population of 2.5 million (*Dagh-Register* 1631: 37), but I take this to be the same 500,000 cacah figure as that of Van Goens, multiplied by a factor of 5 rather than 6. Historians of the seventeenth and eighteenth centuries persistently take a minimal reading of the cacah estimates (Schrieke 1942: 139; Ricklefs 1986), whereas demographers reading back from the high populations of the late nineteenth century believe them too low. The higher factor of 6, preferred by eighteenth-century Dutch observers, has been used here because Javanese households were often large and some allowance must be made for the nontaxable part of the population. My assumption that these 500,000 cacah excluded the north coast (*pasisir*) and the far east is based on Van Goens (1656: 225). Ricklefs (1986) has recently shown that the 1755 figure is derived from estimates made earlier, but his conclusion is that it should, if anything, be lower still.

those areas for which we have no better data. In some areas which suffered exceptionally high levels of warfare and internal disruption in the seventeenth and eighteenth centuries, such as Cambodia, the Malay Peninsula, and Sulawesi, a still lower growth rate of 0.1 percent or zero seems more appropriate. In table 2 I have attempted to calculate probable populations for Southeast Asia in 1600 by first making the best estimate possible for 1800, on the basis of numerous nineteenth-century estimates and censuses of questionable reliability, and then calculating backwards to a 1600 population figure in those cases where contemporary estimates (see table 1) do not take precedence.

Taken as a whole, Southeast Asia was sparsely populated in 1600,

Table 2 Population Estimates for Southeast Asia in 1600 (in thousands)

	Estimate for 1800	*Corresponding Percentage Growth p.a., 19th Cent.*[a]	*Estimate for 1600*	*Corresponding Percentage Growth p.a., 1600–1800*	*Density p/km², 1600*
Burma	4,600[b]	0.83	3,100	0.2	4.6
Laos (incl. Northeast Thailand)	1,200[c]	low	1,200	0.0	2.9
Siam (minus NE)	2,800[d]	0.8	1,800	0.22	5.3
Cambodia-Champa	1,500	1.3	1,230	0.1	4.5
Vietnam (North and Centre)	7,000[e]	0.34	4,700	0.2	18.0
Malaya (incl. Patani)	500	1.56	500[f]	0.0	3.4
Sumatra	3,500[g]	0.49	2,400	0.2	5.7
Java	5,000[h]	1.72	4,000	0.11	30.3
Borneo	1,000	0.83	670	0.2	0.9
Sulawesi	1,800	0.45	1,200	0.1[i]	6.3
Bali	700	0.25	600	0.08	79.7
Lesser Sunda Is.	900	0.54	600	0.2	9.1
Maluku	400	0.41	275	0.2	3.7
Luzon and Visayas	1,800	1.30	800	0.4	4.0
Mindanao and Sulu	230	0.98	150	0.2	1.5
Approx. total Southeast Asia	33,000		23,000	0.2	5.7

[a]Calculated to the first reliable census, which is not before 1920 in the cases of Borneo, Sulawesi, Maluku, and the Lesser Sunda Islands (Reid 1987: 47).
[b]Burney (1842) calculated on the basis of a Burmese enumeration of 1783 that there were then about 4,209,000 people (including 830,000 "wild tribes" and 1,069,600 Shans) in Burma excluding Arakan. An 1826 enumeration showed a very marginal increase. Details from the same two surveys are set out in Trager and Koenig 1979: 400–06.
[c]The high estimate for Laos (Lan Sang) is based on enumerations of 1376 and c. 1640—see Wyatt 1984: 83,121.
[d]The nineteenth-century estimates are conveniently summarized in Skinner (1957: 68).
[e]Compare Woodside (1971: 158–59) with Crawfurd (1828: 526–28). Even allowing for a million Montagnards outside the tax rolls, other Western estimates appear much too large.
[f]The presumption of a population as high in 1600 as in 1800 is based on high contemporary estimates for the population of Kedah, Johor, and Pahang prior to the devastating Acehnese raids of 1618–19 (Reid 1980: 244) and on a large urban population in Patani around 1600.
[g]A relatively low nineteenth-century growth rate is explicable in terms of internal warfare in West Sumatra, Tapanuli, and Aceh.
[h]Both Nederburgh's 1795 estimate of 3.5 million and Raffles' 1815 census of 4.6 million are probably underestimates, but not of the magnitude argued by demographers such as Durand (1967) and MacDonald (1980), who believe the high nineteenth-century growth rates inherently improbable.
[i]A below-average growth is premised on a high outflow of migrants and slaves, in addition to the usual factors.

especially in comparison with its immediate neighbours. Its overall density of about 5.5 persons per square kilometre contrasted with densities for South Asia of about 32 and for China (excluding Tibet) of about 37 (after McEvedy and Jones 1978). Further away, Europe had roughly double the Southeast Asian population density. A surprisingly high proportion of the population, moreover, was concentrated in a number of large trading cities and in pockets of intensive wet-rice cultivation—in the Red River delta, parts of Upper Burma and of Central and East Java, in Bali, South Sulawesi, and Pampanga in Luzon. Outside these areas Southeast Asia presented the appearance of a vast tropical jungle, upon which the impact of man was largely limited to shifting cultivation in isolated hillside patches and gathering the varied products of the forest for export. Tigers were a threat even to those who lived on the outskirts of the great cities, such as Melaka, Banten, and Dutch Batavia (Ma Huan 1433: 113; Fryke 1692: 76–77; Bontius 1629: 177–78). An envoy to Ayutthaya from Golconda in South India is said to have quipped that though Siam's territories were vaster, "the King of Golconda is a king of men, while that of Siam is king only of forests and mosquitoes" (Gervaise 1688: 26).

The most extraordinary feature of Southeast Asian population, however, was the very slow rate of growth in the seventeenth and eighteenth centuries, even if compared with that of China, India, and Europe, followed by exceptionally high growth in the nineteenth and twentieth centuries, especially where European colonial rule was established. It does not seem possible to explain this contrast by any improvement in health introduced by Europeans. Southeast Asian health struck early European visitors as relatively good, and it was only in the nineteenth century that negative contrasts began to be made.

In comparison with Europe, moreover, marriage occurred early and almost universally, while parental affection for children was often remarked on. Although Gervaise (1688: 112–13) claimed an exceptionally high infant mortality in Siam because of parental neglect, his testimony is contradicted by the great majority of observers. John Anderson (1826: 207–08) insisted that none of the "positive checks" to population expansion listed by Malthus seemed to apply to his healthy Sumatrans, who nevertheless seldom bore more than six children. Similar conclusions have been drawn by a modern historical demographer of the Philippines (Ng 1979: 150–52).

It may be that some of the specific features of Southeast Asian sexuality and childbirth customs had a marginal effect in lowering the birthrate in this period (see chapter 4; Reid 1987). The important changes between then and now in terms of the great modern boom in population, however, can be reduced to two—religion and warfare.

Religious conversion is associated with changes in a number of other areas, so that it cannot be isolated as a factor in any narrow sense. We have seen, for example, that the transition to rapid population increase begins first in the Philippines, in the mid-eighteenth century. Is this a consequence of new Christian values, of the "Spanish peace," or of changes in agriculture, hygiene, ritual, or taxation introduced by the Spanish regime? That there was a change in values does seem to be clear in this case, since pre-Christian Visayan women, in particular, were reported to abort their third and subsequent children deliberately to keep their families small (Dasmariñas 1590A: 413; Loarca 1582: 119). By contrast, later Spanish reports after Christianization had taken hold are full of admiration for the Filipina's "fertility that causes our wonder" (San Agostin, 1720: 237; cf. Ortega 1594: 103; Bobadilla 1640: 292).

Twentieth-century census figures also show a remarkable contrast between the exceptionally low birthrates of animists in the Mentawei Islands, East Sumba, Central Sulawesi, upland Borneo, and the Luzon Cordillera and the exceptionally high ones of recently Christianized peoples such as the Toba Batak, Nias, and Sa'dan Toraja (*Volkstelling* 1930; Reid 1987). In the twentieth century, as in the seventeenth, Christianization was frequently encouraged by grouping the new converts in accessible, settled communities on the valley floors, and this in turn often entailed a change from shifting to permanent cultivation. Since ploughing was a male task, and such valley-floor settlements were likely to be much closer to both the cultivation area and the water source than the former hilltop villages, the work load of women was substantially reduced. This, and the greater security which went with it, may well have encouraged larger families.

At least where it was associated with such a complex of changes, conversion from the Austronesian variant of animism to Christianity does appear to have encouraged a rise in fertility. It does not necessarily follow that the much more widespread process of religious change from animism and Indian-influenced syncretic faiths to an already Southeast Asianized Islam or Theravada Buddhism brought similar results. This process was in an early and dynamic stage in the age of commerce and has continued at a variable pace up to the present. Although often associated with absorption into a more settled, valley-floor agriculture and a monarchic state, conversion to Islam or Buddhism was usually so gradual and piecemeal that its impact on population cannot be assessed even as roughly as in the above cases of Christianization. The most I can say is that changes in religious belief may have been one of the factors stimulating population growth, especially when associated with movement towards larger polities and permanent agriculture.

A much more important factor was the instability created by constant low-level warfare. Southeast Asian wars caused relatively few battle casualties. It was a primary objective of war to increase one's own manpower, either directly by seizing the enemy's subjects as slaves or captives or indirectly by so devastating his country that its inhabitants were obliged to move to one's own. Lives were not therefore wasted in fighting. By contrast, the disruption and uncertainty caused by war was a critical demographic factor. The larger states mobilized a substantial proportion of their male population into vast, ill-organized armies, without providing adequate supplies either for the soldiers or for their families left behind. Thousands of captives were marched back home by the victorious armies of Burma and Siam, or shipped home by Aceh and Makassar, with incalculable losses on the voyage. Perhaps an even more important factor demographically was the need to be constantly ready for flight in troubled times. This probably meant avoiding further births at least until the older children were able to run by themselves.

As shown in table 1, a remarkable decline in population in Central and East Java occurred prior to the Gianti Peace of 1755, which put an end to eighty years of almost constant warfare between rival claimants to the throne of Mataram. That warfare was the primary cause of this decline was borne out by numerous contemporary observers. In the interior regions, the Javanese rulers reported to Governor-General Mossel that "not a quarter of the families which were there before the disturbances are left now" (Mossel 1757, cited Schrieke 1942: 152), while in the coastal areas "half the people who were there before the Chinese revolt are no longer there, as the precious, deserted coconut groves along the coast witness" (Hartingh 1759, cited ibid.; also Ricklefs 1986: 9–10; Stavorinus 1798 III: 336–40).

In densely settled wet-rice areas much of the loss of population was caused by destruction of food crops—either as a tactic of war or as a result of the passage of thousands of troops. In Sultan Agung's campaigns in 1620–25 against the coastal regions of East Java and Madura, eighty thousand troops besieged Surabaya and its nearby towns off and on for five years, devastating all the rice crops and even poisoning and damming up the river water of the city (de Graaf 1958: 77–97). The *Dagh-Register* recorded that after these campaigns "in Surabaya not more than 500 of its 50 to 60,000 people were left, the rest having died or gone away because of misery and famine" (cited Schrieke 1942: 148). Even on the side of Mataram there must have been enormously heavy losses, not only from the famine and disease that beset the unsuccessful besiegers of Batavia in 1628–29, but also from "the lack of men, so that they had not been able to bring the water to the rice fields" during the wars against Madura in 1624, with the result that the major rice-growing areas of Mataram itself were barren (cited de Graaf 1958: 90, also 151).

The demographic pattern of precolonial Southeast Asia, it would appear, was far removed from the smooth but shallow growth curve resulting from backward projections. When conditions of reasonable stability prevailed, the combination of early marriage, abundant food, and relatively good health probably gave rise to rapid population growth, at least among the wet-rice cultivators and urban traders of the lowland and coast. Population must have declined equally sharply when these areas were laid waste by the movement of armies, however. Java probably underwent several such periods of population decline in the three turbulent centuries before 1755, and certainly did so in 1675–1755. Siam must have lost a large portion of its population when it was laid waste by the Burmese in 1549–69 and again in the 1760s, resulting in terrible deaths from famine and disease as well as in deportation (Wood 1924: 146; Turpin 1771: 156–78; Wyatt 1984: 99, 136–37). Lower Burma was twice severely depopulated after the Mons of Pegu suffered terrible defeats at the hands of Burman kings in 1598 and 1757, respectively (Jarric 1608: 618–26; Lieberman 1984: 45, 248). Similarly, Malaya lost much of its population as a result of the campaigns of Aceh in the period 1618–24.

Southeast Asia in its age of commerce was a sparsely populated region of little more than twenty million people, unevenly distributed over a vast forested region. A majority of these people clustered in pockets of relatively intensive wet-rice agriculture and in maritime trading cities which were surprisingly large in relation to the overall population (Reid 1980). Population was kept low primarily by the insecurity of life in conditions of frequent raiding and warfare, but it rose quickly, by migration and natural increase, wherever conditions of stability were assured.

The Agricultural Pattern

> *What should be planted and grown assiduously are rice, maize, yams, red yams, taro and bananas . . . so that the country will be prosperous and everything will be cheap.*
>
> —Hikayat Banjar: 374

Rice was the overwhelmingly dominant food staple and agricultural product of Southeast Asia. Other staple foods such as taro, yams, sago, and millet appear to have preceded rice at least in the Archipelago (Ishige 1980: 331–37), but by the fifteenth century rice had become the preferred crop wherever it could conveniently be grown. Only in the dry or infertile islands of the east, such as Timor, the northern Moluccas, the Aru Islands, Buton, and Selayar, was the population obliged to depend on sago (the pith of the sago palm, *Metroxylon*, growing naturally in the forests of the Archipelago) or tubers for its primary source of calories. When maize was introduced from Mexico in the sixteenth century, such areas quickly added that valuable dry-land crop to their list of staples. It was already established in Maluku by 1540 (Galvão 1544: 132), perhaps brought by the Saavedra expedition of 1527–28.

For a larger number of more marginal areas of shifting cultivation dependent on uncertain rains, eating rice was frequently a luxury of the harvest season. "Rice is the main article of food in these [Philippine] Islands. In a few of them [Central Luzon, Panay] people gather enough of it to last them the whole year. In most of the islands, during the greater part of the year, they live on millet, *borona*, roasted bananas, certain roots resembling sweet potatoes and called *oropisa*, as well as yams" (Artieda 1573: 201–02).

Dampier (1697: 213–14) similarly noted that the poorer people of Mindanao had to eat sago for three to four months of the year. Sago, which yields almost pure starch after being boiled, strained, and dried, was available in most swampy areas to all who needed it, while various types of breadfruit were a frequent alternative along the coasts and on small islands. Marsden (1783: 64) noticed that Sumatrans resorted, if their rice crops failed, "to those wild roots, herbs, and leaves of trees which the woods abundantly afford in every season. . . . Hence . . . failures of crops or grain are never attended with those dreadful consequences which more improved countries and more provident nations experience." Except as a consequence of war, famines do not appear to have devastated Southeast Asians as they did Indians and Chinese in the same period.

Since the affluent always ate rice by preference, however, reliance on other staple foods was looked down upon. In deriding the Butonese enemies of Makassar during their wars of the 1660s, a Makassar poet mockingly called them "maize-worshippers" and "yam-worshippers" (Amin 1670: 104–05).

The three major types of rice cultivation were all widely practised already in Southeast Asia in the sixteenth century: shifting cultivation on low slopes; broadcasting seed on a floodplain; and transplanting seedlings into a ploughed and bunded field. As has been pointed out by Boserup (1965) and others, the decision among these three systems was not determined by technical knowledge, since all three techniques were widely understood and frequently practiced by the same people. The argument of Boserup that a transition from land-extensive shifting cultivation to more intensive wet-rice agriculture was forced by population pressure is only part of the answer. The low man-land ratios in the Southeast Asia of this period would have made it theoretically possible for all to subsist on shifting cultivation, yet we know that irrigation of permanent fields was carried out in the Kyaukse area of Burma and in eastern Java from at least the eighth century (Setten van der Meer 1979; Luce 1940). In fact, the type of cultivation was determined primarily by the physical conditions of each area and only secondarily by population pressure.

Shifting cultivation, whereby a different patch of forest was cleared and burned each year in rotation, was suitable for most sloping areas of adequate drainage. As it was described in Maluku (Galvão 1544: 132–33), "The fields . . . are so poor that, when they sow them one year, they have to allow them a two years' rest if they want another harvest. . . . They make clearings, which they burn off; and with pointed sticks they make holes in them, in which they put two or three grains, covering them with the foot or hands." There are similar descriptions of swidden cultivation of this type from Luzon and the Visayas (Sande 1576: 67; Alcina 1668 III: 89–90), and it must have been the prevalent system in all the sloping or upland areas of Southeast Asia, including most of those today famous for their terraces of wet rice. A 1613 Tagalog dictionary listed twenty-two variants of dry rice (Scott 1982: 525). Swidden has been shown to be the least demanding means to produce a single rice crop in terms of labour input, and to be capable of producing a substantial surplus over the annual requirements of the farming family (Hanks 1972: 56–62). Hill rice of this sort was being exported from northern Vietnam to China in the eighteenth century (Horta 1766: 234), and probably also from the Deli area of northeastern Sumatra to Aceh in the seventeenth (Ito 1984: 361–63). The disadvantage of shifting cultivation is that the nutrients added to the soil by the initial burning off are washed away by rains within one or two seasons, so that new fields must constantly be created. The shifting cycle, together with the relatively low yields per acre, impose an upper limit to population density of about twenty to thirty persons per square kilometre. Despite the possibility of large surpluses per family, therefore, the system makes it difficult to collect such a surplus for export or urban growth.

Even more productive in relation to labour input was the system of broadcasting seed on a flood plain just prior to its inundation. Hanks

(1972: 64) has calculated that this method can produce enough rice to feed the farmer for thirty-eight times the number of days he has put into cultivation (as against nine times for shifting cultivation). The river brought its own nutrients with it in each annual flooding, so that large yields could be obtained from those rice varieties which were adjusted to grow quickly in water, with a minimal labour input. A Persian in the Chao Phraya floodplain of central Siam observed (Ibrahim 1688: 153–54):

> This is the way they grow the rice. When the time is right for planting, they plough the land in a very careless manner and scatter seed all over the surface of the soil. Then they depart and wait for nature to provide them with results. The monsoon arrives just after their ploughing and the fields become saturated with water. Every day the water mounts up until it finally covers all the land. Under water the seeds turn into green plants and raise their heads up through the earth. They actually spring to the height of 5 or 6 cubits. When the plants reach maturity, the farmers return in their boats and gather the harvest.

The same fortunate natural circumstances provided rich rice harvests from the Tonle Sap floodplain of Cambodia (Couto, cited Groslier 1958: 73–74; Ishii 1971: 170), the lower Pegu and Salween rivers of Burma (Barbosa 1518 II: 153; Lieberman 1984: 18), and numerous smaller rivers of Arakan, the eastern Malayan Peninsula, and Vietnam.

Most of central Siam was still forested in the seventeenth century, and the primary export of that region was not rice but deerskins. Nevertheless, the high yields made possible by the annual inundation produced a large rice surplus for the city of Ayutthaya (which probably contained more than 10 percent of the central Siam population) and for export when required. Around 1500 Siam was reportedly sending thirty rice junks to Melaka every year (Pires 1515: 107). Since we know that rice junks averaged 400–500 metric tonnes' burden in the sixteenth century (Manguin 1980: 268; Bouchon 1979: 143), we can estimate the total Siamese export at over 10,000 tonnes. Pegu ports sent at least forty rice-laden vessels (with perhaps 14,000 tonnes of rice) to Pasai, Pedir, and Melaka (Pires 1515: 98; Bouchon 1979: 139) at the beginning of the century. After the Burmese conquest of Pegu, on the other hand, much of the surplus production of the annually flooded delta area went up the Irrawaddy to the Burmese capital. In the eighteenth century "several thousand" river boats were employed in this internal trade (Symes 1827 II: 64–65). Cambodia could export about 7,000 tonnes a year around 1600 (Mandelslo 1662: 106), which usually supplied Patani, Pahang, and Brunei. Songkhla (Singora) and

Nakhon Sithammarat (Ligor) also exported 800 tonnes a year to Patani and Pahang around 1620 (van Hasell 1620: 647).

The largest rice exporter of all, however, was Java, and its characteristic method was the third—transplanting of seedlings into a bunded, ploughed field, in which the water level was carefully controlled. This wet-rice method of planting was described as follows in Luzon:

> They put a basketful of it [seed] into the river to soak. After a few days they take it from the water; what is bad and has not sprouted is thrown away. The rest is put on a bamboo mat and covered with earth, and placed where it is kept moist by the water. After the sprouting grains have germinated sufficiently, they are transplanted one by one, as lettuce is cultivated in Spain. In this way they have abundance of rice in a short time (Sande 1576: 67; cf. Scott 1982: 526).

The point of such transplanting was of course to maximize the use of the valuable bunded field, carefully crafted with a comparatively high labour input to ensure that water (whether from reliable rains or from irrigation channels) remained in the field throughout the growing period. This method gave the highest yields per hectare of land, though not the highest return for labour input. It required and made possible a much greater density of agricultural population than either of the other two methods, and this in turn made collection and exportation of the surplus much easier.

Moreover, the wet-rice technique made possible a second crop of rice in the year wherever there was an adequate supply of water—preferably nutrient-filled river water brought through irrigation channels. Such channels were probably quite widespread in the more densely settled areas of Southeast Asia by the sixteenth century, and there is definite evidence for them in Java, South Sulawesi, Luzon, Panay (Visayas), Upper Burma, and Siam. As early as 1400 it was reported of northeastern Java and northern Sumatra that "the rice ripens twice in one year" (Ma Huan 1433: 91, 117), while the Burmese chronicles assert that one irrigated area in Kyaukse was so fertile that it produced three crops a year in the twelfth century (*Glass Palace Chronicle*: 127). The Kyaukse irrigation system was perhaps the largest in Southern Asia, covering nearly fifty thousand hectares by the late eighteenth century (Lieberman 1984: 19). Although some favoured areas undoubtedly did produce two wet-rice crops a year, a more common pattern was probably that described for the Cagayan valley in Luzon (see fig. 1): "Two crops of rice are gathered, one being irrigated, and the other allowed to grow by itself" (Dasmarinas 1592: 251).

Fig. 1 Filipinos at work in the fields in the early eighteenth century, as represented on the 1734 map of the Philippines by Murillo Velarde. The woman under the house is husking rice.

Java had both the population and the rich soils for intensive cultivation of this type. Lush wet-rice fields were reported along much of its northern littoral, in the Mataram (Yogyakarta) area, and in East Java around Surabaya-Majapahit and on the plateau of Malang (van Goens 1646: 52, 205, 208; Valentijn 1726 III: 282–86). Central Java, exporting through the port of Japara, was the biggest supplier of Melaka, where it was sending fifty to sixty rice junks (about 15,000 tonnes of rice) a year in the early sixteenth century (Araujo 1510: 28).

Japara was also a major food supplier for Banjarmasin, Maluku, and the big port cities of West Java (Banten and Jakatra-Batavia). In 1615 the Dutch estimated that they could buy 2,000 tonnes of rice a year in Japara (van den Broecke 1634 I: 58), while in 1648 they in fact imported 8,000 tonnes to Batavia (van Goens 1656: 181). East Java, which exported primarily to the Moluccas and the Lesser Sunda Islands, was able to deliver 2,000 to 4,000 tonnes in Surabaya each year around 1700 (Valentijn 1726 III: 300–01).

Rice was undoubtedly the largest bulk item of Southeast Asian trade, making nonsense of Van Leur's premise (1934: 90) that its basis was in luxurious "splendid and trifling" goods. If rice exports were not larger still, this was because of limits on storage and distribution, rather than on production itself. Whenever there was a major urban market for rice, sources of supply were quick to develop—as evidenced by the three hundred tonnes a year which Deli in northeast Sumatra (never a rice-surplus area in modern times) was able to provide for the city of Aceh at its height in the 1640s (Ito 1984: 363). When the capacity to import rice was reduced by Dutch blockade or by impoverishment, local rice fields quickly developed, as in the environs of Aceh in the 1650s and of Banten in the 1630s. "It is almost incredible what watercourses they have cut, and what a goodly compass of ground they [Bantenese] have these two years past manured for these purposes" (Hoare 1630: 89).

We have a little more detail on one case where a rice surplus was deliberately developed for export, in the Maros plain just north of Makassar in Sulawesi. This area was conquered by Makassar about 1590, and subsequently the land was "shared out in villages and allotments among the Makassarese nobility, who have each developed their plantations here insofar as they have men available each year" (Speelman 1670 II: 11). The effective ruler of Makassar in the two decades which followed, Karaeng Matoaya of Tallo', saw the opportunity to develop a reliable rice surplus which could be sold in the Moluccas against return cargoes of valuable spices. It was reported in 1606:

> Throughout the whole country in every town and marketplace he has erected fine barns full of rice, which is not allowed to be sold until the new crop is in, so as to suffer no shortage in any unseasonable year. He is very diligent in drawing trade to his country, to which end he expressly keeps an agent in Banda whom he provides every year with rice, cloth, and everything which is required there in order to get as much mace in his country as possible, and so to draw some merchants to him (van der Hagen 1607: 82).

This astute ruler was among the main sellers of rice to European traders setting out for the Moluccas (West 1617: 63). His protégé, the king of Gowa, was also in the rice market, and "here are other kings which I hope will furnish us" (Throgmorton 1617: 226). Several of the Makassar aristocracy, in other words, were using their irrigated lands in the Maros area to produce a surplus for export. The English in one month took 190 *koyang* (450 tonnes) of this rice (Staverton 1618: 19). At its peak, therefore, the total exported was probably in excess of 1,000 tonnes per year, though this declined rapidly with the growth of urban population (*Dagh-Register* 1625: 179; Speelman 1670 III: 67).

Land Tenure

Despite these pockets of intensive rice cultivation, Southeast Asia was still endowed everywhere with abundant uncultivated land in hill and forest, which was available to anyone who wished to clear it.

> Many and very extensive lands remain lacking anyone to cultivate them. Although it is true that each village or populated area has its own boundaries . . . anyone who comes to settle among them, even though he was never seen nor heard of, is given an option to select voluntarily all and as much land as he might wish without asking him for a cent for it nor any agreement whatever. . . . He who worked or cultivated it is master of it and especially if he planted coconut or fruit trees. These are always his without there being in this regard disputes or lawsuits (Alcina 1668 III: 81).

The permanent utilization of land, either through the planting of fruit-bearing trees or palms or through the creation of bunded, irrigated fields for annual planting, was the closest that Southeast Asian societies came to full personal property rights in land, though the community did not surrender residual rights to grazing even on such land, or to reallocating it if the land fell into disuse (van Vollenhoven 1918: 95–105, 179–98, 278). Although such wet-rice land was individually controlled and inherited, areas of shifting cultivation were regarded as the common property of the community, as explained by Plasencia (1589: 174–75) in the case of Luzon: "The lands which they inhabited were divided among the whole village (*barangay*), especially the irrigated portion, and thus each one knew his own. No one belonging to another village would cultivate them unless after purchase or inheritance. The lands on the *tingues*, or mountain-ridges, are not divided, but owned in common by the village." Even in heavily populated Java as late as the nineteenth century there was much forested land which could be cleared by anyone for shifting or for permanent cultivation (Crawfurd 1820 I: 277, 296–99, 366).

The effect of this open land frontier was not, as one might have expected, to produce an egalitarian society, with each family controlling the amount of land it could work. Households were typically large, and dependants were numerous. Even though land was not in itself a valued scarce resource, there were many other means by which the rich attracted or coerced the poor into serving them—control of better-favoured irrigated plots near a river, ownership of animals and equipment for ploughing, protection and patronage, and the bride-price, which was the prerequisite for a man to set up an independent household. Many areas appear to have been opened up for cultivation at the behest of a ruler, who sent dependants into the forest under the control of one of his retainers or kinsmen, who might well become the local chief or lord. The revival of Nakhon Sithammarat in the fifteenth century is described by its chronicler as a succession of commands by its ruler: "A was ordered to take people and turn the forest to rice fields in district X" (*Crystal Sands*; 112–14); a similar pattern seems to have obtained in Java (Pigeaud 1962: 87, 470–74).

The shortage of manpower relative to land tended rather to produce a patriarchal social pattern in which men rather than land became the object of competition among the strong. The majority of the population in rural areas should probably be categorized as dependants or bondsmen. The open frontier did mean, however, that a desperate dependant could leave a cruel master either to find another patron or to inhabit the forest fringe, perhaps living as a hunter or outlaw until able to establish a farm plot of his own. This option of choosing a dangerous freedom over a more secure bondage must certainly have acted as a check on the abuse of dependants by their masters.

Tools

The tools of agriculture were remarkably simple and uniform, and all showed sparing use of iron, which was scarce. For wet-rice agriculture the key items were a metal-tipped wooden plough and a wooden rake, both towed behind a buffalo or cow (fig. 2). The plough may not have spread as widely as wet-rice techniques, however, as Scott (1982: 523) suggests that Filipinos had no word for it before the seventeenth century. Shifting cultivation required some form of iron machete for forest clearing, a hoe or mattock, and a dibble or planting-stick. Harvesting in most areas was done by women using a small finger-knife which cut one stalk at a time. The sickle appears also to have been

Fig. 2 Early nineteenth-century pencil sketch of a Javanese ploughman.

introduced quite early, perhaps from China, but came into general use only in the Mainland's wet-rice growing plains—notably in northern Vietnam, central Thailand, and Burma. The reason may be the predominance of the broadcast, flooded-field system in these river valleys, which gave farmers a large area of long-stalked rice and therefore required the quickest possible harvesting method.

Throughout the islands, the Malay Peninsula (among southern Thais as well as Malays), and many areas of the Mainland, the finger-knife remained popular despite knowledge of the sickle. Even southern Vietnamese, who today have forgotten its use, employed the finger-knife as late as the nineteenth century (Brown 1861: 210–11). Nineteenth-century ethnographers, puzzled at what appeared the inefficiency of this method, were usually told that it was more respectful to the goddess or female spirit of the rice (Skeat 1900: 58; McNair 1878: 160; Raffles 1817 I: 114). It also had very practical advantages, however, particularly for hill rice. Individual stalks could be cut as they ripened, thus spreading the labour load over a longer period and making weeding of hillside plots unnecessary. Even in permanent fields the finger-knife made it possible for a second crop of sugar, cotton, or tobacco to be planted before the rice harvest and not to be damaged by the rice harvesters (Miles 1979).

Throughout Southeast Asia it was the slow but reliable water buffalo which was the essential draft animal, used preeminently for ploughing but also occasionally for carting produce. Only in those populous areas most influenced by India—Burma, Siam, Cambodia, Java, and Bali—were there also white Brahmin cattle. Introduced primarily for their meat and for cartage, they were also occasionally used in the fields (La Loubère 1691: 18).

Diet and Food Supplies

In the interior there was plenty of rice, fruit, betel, sugar and coconuts. What they did not have was tamarind, onions, garlic, spices, salt and shrimp-paste.—Hikayat Banjar: 415

Rice was overwhelmingly dominant as a source of calories. Two other food items regarded as so indispensable that they were traded on a considerable scale were salt and fish. It was noted of the Visayan Islands: "The inhabitants of the mountains cannot live without the fish, salt, and other articles of food . . . of other districts; nor, on the other hand, can those of the coast live without the rice and cotton of the mountaineers" (Loarca 1582: 121).

Most coastal people appear to have had methods for making salt. The Moluccans did it by throwing seawater on beach fires and then boiling the ash in more salt water (Galvão 1544: 137). Some coastal areas with a pronounced dry season were able to make a business of salt making for export by letting the sun dry salt water in bunded salt pans adjacent to the coast (often used for fish breeding in the wet season). There were salt pans all along the north coast of eastern Java, providing one of the major exports of the ports between Juana and Surabaya. Merchants took this East Java salt to Sulawesi and the Moluccas and traded it either directly or through Banten to Sumatra: "From Jaratan, Gresik, Pati, Juana and the nearby places they bring good coarse salt. One usually buys 800 *gantang* for 150,000 *cash* and sells it at Banten for 3 *gantang* for a thousand. They take it also to Sumatra [to ports such] as Baros, Pariaman, Tulang Bawang, Inderagiri, Jambi" (Lodewycksz 1598: 100; cf. ibid.: 102, 104; Davis 1600: 187; Willemsz 1642: 512). Similarly, the coastal salt pans around Phetburi at the head of the Gulf of Siam supplied salt for much of Siam and the Malay Peninsula (Pires 1515: 107; Nieuhoff 1662: 219; van Neck

1604: 229–30; Pallegoix 1854 I: 98, 117). According to a southern Thai chronicle (*Crystal Sands*: 102), the first Thai state on the gulf arose at Phetburi on the basis of working these salt pans for the benefit of established Thai kingdoms further inland, beginning perhaps in the twelfth century.

Though the majority of Southeast Asians lived close to fishing grounds in ocean or river, they were not prepared to accept the limitations the seasonal vagaries of the catch imposed on the consumption of fresh fish. The daily fare of fish was chiefly in a dried or pickled form, so that it was always on hand and could, moreover, form "a great article of internal commerce" (Crawfurd 1820 I: 197). Banjarmasin, for example, supplied dried fish to the cities of Java (Lodewycksz 1598: 119). A meal of rice was not complete without at least some fish, and it was especially the protein-rich spicy paste of pickled fish (Malay *belacan*, Thai *kapi*, Burmese *nga-pee*, Vietnamese *nuoc mam*) which was the favourite of Southeast Asians everywhere.

> Although it be true, that they [Cochin-Chinese] like better of fish than of flesh, yet the chief cause why they are so much given to fishing is, the desire they have to provide a sauce which they call *Balaciam* (belacan), that is made of a salted fish mollified and dissolved in water; whereof they make a biting liquor, not unlike unto mustard . . . for sauce only to quicken their appetite in eating of their rice, which they suppose would otherwise be unsavoury (Borri 1633 III: C; cf. La Loubère 1691: 35).

The variety and abundance of the fish harvests of Southeast Asia were a marvel to foreign visitors; Marco Polo (1298: 227) was not alone in declaring, "The fish here are the best in the world" (cf. Borri 1633 III: C; Rhodes 1653: 207). Although the Cheng Ho expeditions of the fifteenth century complained about the scarcity or expense of rice, meat, or vegetables at some Southeast Asian ports, the cheapness and abundance of fish was everywhere noted. In Melaka and Champa fishing was reported as the chief male occupation, well ahead of agriculture (Ma Huan 1433: 82, 110, 114, 123).

Taken overall, fishing was certainly the second industry of Southeast Asia. Crawfurd (1820 I: 195) thought, "There is no art which they have indeed carried to such perfection." The two most efficient methods in use were surrounding shoals of fish with seine nets dragged by a number of boats working cooperatively, and trapping fish in permanent enclosures of bamboo and cane, sometimes supplemented by nets (Dampier 1699: 91; Morga 1609: 258; Brunei expedition 1579: 208; Scott 1982: 527). These methods required the cooperation of several fishermen, but in addition almost every coastal family did some occasional fishing with a line or small net.

Foreign sources report less about vegetables than about the profusion of spices and fruits. The Chinese expeditions of Cheng Ho, accustomed to a wide variety of vegetables in their own cooking, were critical of the range offered in most Southeast Asian ports: cucumbers, onions, ginger, and various gourds and melons were the most widespread (Ma Huan 1433: 82, 107, 112). Only in Java did they find all they wanted, in addition to various tropical rarities. "They have all the gourds and vegetables; the only things wanting are peaches, plums, and leaks" (ibid.: 92). Mung beans (*Phaseolus aureus*) and cucumber (*Cucumis sativus*) were common throughout Southeast Asia by 1500, and soybeans were probably also being introduced in all those places frequented by Chinese (Navarrete 1676 II: 196).

Spices were of much greater interest to Europeans, since these were the valuable rarities for which they had journeyed across the world. In the markets of Southeast Asia they found not only the better-known cloves, nutmeg, and mace of Maluku, and the pepper grown widely throughout the Archipelago, but a profusion of unfamiliar plants often reputed to have medicinal value as well as flavour. Tamarind, turmeric, ginger, cubeb, calamus, and numerous other spices were used in flavouring food as well as in medicines (Lodewycksz 1598: 140–52; Dampier 1699: 88). Despite the plethora of spices, neither Chinese nor European visitors remarked upon the spiciness of local meals, perhaps because these meat eaters, needing to disguise the taste of their own aging meat, were at that time as accustomed to spiciness as Southeast Asians. For those "below the winds," fish-paste and turmeric appear to have been the most widespread "hot" ingredients until the introduction of the chili-pepper from South America in the late sixteenth century. This spread very quickly, however, so that the Dutch could report in 1596 that it grew in parts of Java and "the Governor of Banten uses it in place of pepper, though it is not widespread" (Lodewycksz 1598: 146). Black pepper, though sold to the world, was not prominent in the diet of Southeast Asians (Marsden 1783: 62).

The relative paucity of vegetables was compensated for by an abundance of fruits. Europeans and Chinese were both impressed by their variety, and overindulgence in these unaccustomed delights was blamed by Bontius and others for much sickness of Europeans in the East (Bontius 1629: 26, 38; Brunei expedition 1579: 235). Coconut and banana were major food sources, while durian, mango, mangosteen, jackfruit, rambutan, and numerous other fruits provided seasonal delicacies. Mango was used also as a pickled garnish for rice (Dampier 1697: 266). In addition, Southeast Asia offered a wider range of citrus fruits than other parts of the world, with the lime and the giant pomelo probably the most important sources of vitamins (Burkhill 1935 I: 561–76; Morga 1609: 254). The papaya and the pineapple were introduced from the Americas in the late sixteenth century and spread rapidly, especially in the Archipelago. Southeast Asians quickly discovered the medicinal properties of papaya, which became a part of the indigenous pharmacopoeia.

The region was exceptionally well endowed with sources of sugar. Sugar cane was probably native to Southeast Asia; it grew wild and was also cultivated in most well-watered areas. It was sold in markets mainly as confectionery to be chewed. Cane sugar first became a major item of export to China and Japan during the seventeenth century, with the introduction of Chinese methods of refining. Cultivators in West Java shifted from pepper to cane sugar around 1630, since the sugar "yields greater benefit" (Hoare 1630: 98; Willoughby 1635: 113). Another major export industry in cane sugar developed in the Quangnam area of south-central Vietnam, reportedly sending forty thousand barrels to China alone by the early eighteenth century (Nguyen 1970: 53–54). Cane sugar was also the most important Siamese cargo taken to Japan by Ayutthaya-based Chinese traders in the late seventeenth century (Ishii 1971: 169–70).

As a sweetening for desserts and cakes, Southeast Asians themselves made greater use of brown sugar derived from boiling the sap of the *arenga*, or sugar palm, also native to the region and a prolific source of liquid sugar. Honey was less important than in Europe at the time; regarded primarily as a medicine, it was gathered from wild bees (Symes 1827 II: 87). Nevertheless, the Dutch found it cheap and abundant in the market of Banten, which drew its supplies of honey from as far afield as Palembang and Timor and its palm sugar from Japara and Jakatra along the north coast of Java (Lodewycksz 1598: 119).

In the constant traffic of foodstuffs around the waters of Southeast Asia, Central and East Java was the largest net exporter. In 1511 the Portuguese captured two Javanese junks which had been carrying to Melaka salted fish, rice, *arak*, palm wine, coconuts, and palm fabrics (Empoli 1514: 134). The Banjarmasin chronicle has one of its fourteenth- or fifteenth-century heroes bringing back to Borneo (from his time away in Surabaya) "a thousand cakes of sugar, a hundred coconuts, four Shanghai jars of coconut oil, two jars of tamarind, a hundred baskets of garlic, a hundred baskets of onions, ten sacks of rice" (*Hikayat Banjar*: 362–63). During two months of 1642 twelve Javanese junks reached Aceh, and their main cargo was foodstuffs: "salt, sugar, peas, beans, and other goods" (Willemsz 1642: 512, 524).

Meat Eating as Ritual

The thick forest cover of Southeast Asia ruled out the pastoral tradition which made Europeans and Central and Western Asians such great meat eaters. Many areas, including most of Borneo and Mindanao, were sparsely enough peopled to make possible a hunter-gatherer style of life, but even for the tiny minority of such foragers the forest offered more readily available vegetable than animal resources. The low level of meat eating by Southeast Asians was attested by numerous European witnesses:

There are so few [goats in the Philippines], that wherever 15 or 20 Spaniards arrive, no goats will be seen for the next two or three years (Artieda 1573: 202).

Their [Siamese] diet is but mean, as rice, fish and herbs (Schouten 1636: 146).

They say that if there were two thousand Christians in their country [Aceh], it would quickly be exhausted of beef and chickens (Beaulieu 1666: 100).

The Siamese . . . do rarely eat of any flesh, though it be given to them (La Loubère 1691: 37).

The eating of meat always had a ritual character because of its close association with the sacrifice of an animal life. Meat was only eaten fresh, immediately after killing. The slaughter, distribution, and consumption of an animal therefore constituted a feast of which many people would partake. The distinctly "heating" quality of the most important sacrificial animals—buffalo and chicken (pig is more ambiguous)—in the humoral system of Southeast Asia was no doubt linked to the frenzied merrymaking which accompanied the bigger feasts (Dasmariñas 1590A: 429; Hart 1969: 80, 88). This sacrificial character was most overt where animism had given least ground to the new world religions, so that the spirits of the dead could be publicly invited to partake of the feast. Yet even at the Muslim court centres the meat eating which accompanied the most important ritual events, particularly funerals and weddings, retained some of the associations of a life being offered to the ancestors.

All the important rites of passage—teeth filing or circumcision at puberty; marriage; death—as well as the construction of a new building or boat, the purification of a village from evil or disease, or the celebration of the great annual feasts of Islam or of the state, called for the killing of animals and sharing of meat among the community. The rich would kill buffaloes, goats, or pigs, while the poor would endeavour to provide at least a chicken. At royal courts the occasions for feasting were numerous and included the sumptuous reception of foreign and local dignitaries—part of the ongoing theatre whereby rulers established their legitimacy. King Narai of Siam served up 150 different dishes to a French embassy in 1685 (Tachard 1686: 178). When the remnants of Magellan's expedition reached Brunei in 1521, they were fêted with an array of meat the like of which they had never seen: "Each tray [of nine] contained ten or twelve porcelain dishes full of veal, capons, chickens, peacocks and other animals, and fish. We supped on the ground upon a palm mat from thirty or thirty-two different kinds of meat, besides the fish and other things" (Pigafetta 1524: 189).

This provision of what seemed an excessive amount of meat was not only a demonstration of royal greatness but also a means of distributing a limited supply of meat around the community, as Van Goens (1656: 234–35) noted in Java:

> Food is set out very lavishly on mats, provided with banana leaves about two feet long by one foot broad in place of table cloths. Their fare is like ours, salted, roasted, stuffed, fried, etc., but using only oil in place of butter. Their feasting is often very coarse, consisting of whole roasted sheep, goats, or quarters of oxen or buffaloes, of which they make a great feast. They also have very hot spiced soup. . . . The rice . . . stands before them in mounds so high that it is as high as their shoulders (if they are sitting on their shanks). The roasted chickens and other birds, and various dry viands, are piled up so lavishly everywhere that it appears to be a scandalous waste, which it is not, however; for as soon as the king and the gentry have eaten, all these foods with the said mats are wholly removed and given to the servants of these men, from which there is seldom a surplus; or if anything remains they take it home, to share with their children a present at the king's expense.

The most generally available meats were chicken, pig, and water buffalo. Cattle of the Indian type had been introduced in limited numbers to the areas most influenced by India but were completely absent from eastern Indonesia and the Philippines. The wild cattle (*banteng*, or *Bos sondaicus*) native to Java, Bali, Borneo, and Indochina were hunted for meat in all those places. Only in Bali, where the population density had resulted in a taming of the forest such as occurred nowhere else, had these Southeast Asian cattle been domesticated to become excellent tropical beef cattle—though at least in the nineteenth century the Hindu Balinese themselves declined to eat them (Zollinger 1847: 344). The tougher domestic water buffalo was available everywhere, but its slow reproductive rate (one offspring only every three or more years) made farmers reluctant to slaughter these essential ploughing animals. In many areas, particularly Luzon, the buffalo was also hunted as a wild animal.

Pigs of various types had been at home in the forests of Southeast Asia for thousands of years and were domesticated by at least 3000 B.C. (Bellwood 1978: 75). The most efficient converter of grains into meat and capable of subsisting on a variety of refuse, the pig was the major source of meat in every place where Islam had not penetrated. Europeans believed Southeast Asian pork healthier than pork in Europe (La Loubère 1691: 38; Pallegoix 1854 I: 213; Morga 1609: 254). Muslims encouraged the breeding of goats as a replacement for the pig, though goats were already present (before Islam) as far east as Sulawesi but not in the Philippines (Ma Huan 1433: 92, 101, 107; Pelras 1981: 157). Wild deer were hunted for meat and hides throughout Southeast Asia, while the domesticated horse (also eaten in many parts of Indonesia) had spread as far as the Lesser Sunda Islands and Sulawesi, but not to the Philippines.

Even though meat consumption was relatively low, commercial cattle farming had already developed for urban markets, and there was some shipment of livestock from port to port. "Along the highways people lead cattle to trade, ride horses to sell," reads Ram Kamheng's account (1293: 26) of his utopian order in Sukhothai. Bali and Madura were already exporting livestock to Java in the fourteenth century, as they continued to do for centuries, since "pigs, sheep, buffaloes, cattle, fowls and dogs" were among the "tribute" they sent to Majapahit (*Nagara-kertagama* 1365: 31). Outside the city of Aceh "the Country people live either on breeding Heads of Cattle . . . or Fowls, especially they who live near the city, which they send weekly thither to sell," while the "savannahs" of grass higher up the hills "swarm with buffaloes" (Dampier 1699: 91, 89). In Makassar in 1609 the Dutch were able to purchase fifty to sixty buffaloes from a single owner (Pelras 1981: 157). In general, Europeans secured adequate meat at what they thought to be very reasonable prices. One Spanish rial (two guilders) could buy thirty to sixty chickens in the Javanese heartland in the 1640s, though only three in Manila in the 1580s. A good buffalo cost four rials in Manila, seven to nine rials in Banten in 1596, four to five rials in Japara, but only two rials in the interior of Java (van Goens 1656: 181; *Verhael* 1597: 25; Mendoza 1583: 150).

There is reason to believe that the consumption of meat by Southeast Asians gradually declined in both variety and quantity as the influence of the world religions became more established. Ma Huan (1433: 93), himself a Muslim, was appalled at the diet of non-

Muslim Javanese: "very dirty and bad—things like snakes, ants, and all kinds of insects and worms." The *Nagara-kertagama* (1365: 106) listed the meats served at the court of Majapahit as "mutton, buffalo, poultry, wild boar, bees, fish and ducks," but added another list of meats not served to the pious because of Hindu prohibition, though much enjoyed by the ordinary population: "Frogs, worms, tortoises, mice, dogs; how many there are who like these (meats)! They are flooded with them, so they appear to be well pleased." Hinduism, it seems, had little practical effect in restricting sources of protein.

Islam was more egalitarian and therefore more effective in its taboos. Despite the popularity of pork, the fervour with which Muslims avoided it appears to have convinced even many non-Islamic peoples that there must be something inauspicious about it. Abstention from pork became the first and most striking sign of adherence to Islam. When Magellan's men visited Tidore, in other respects not notably devout after a half-century of Islam, the king "asked us, in order to show our love for him, to kill all the swine that we had in the ships, in return for which he would give us an equal number of goats and fowls. We killed them in order to show him a pleasure, and hung them under the deck. When those people happen to see any swine they cover their faces in order that they might not look upon them or catch their odour" (Pigafetta 1524: 208–09). The Makassarese of Sulawesi were reputed in the sixteenth century to be resisting Islam because pork was their major meat source (Dias 1559: 306). According to the local chronicle of Bulo-bulo in the Sindjai region, when this district was invited to accept Islam in the seventeenth century by the ruler of Makassar under the veiled threat of war if it refused, one prominent chief defiantly declared that he would not bow to Islam even if the rivers flowed with blood, as long as there were pigs to eat in the forests of Bulo-bulo. Miraculously, the story goes, all the pigs disappeared that very night; so the chief and all his men were obliged to convert (Matthes 1864: 257–58).

Dogs were also eaten in some places. In sharp contrast to the cat, which was never eaten and was often regarded as semisacred because it protected the rice against predatory rodents, the dog was "an unowned vagrant" in Southeast Asian villages (Crawfurd 1856: 382), not a special friend of man. Islam regarded the dog as ritually unclean, like pigs, frogs, snakes, and reptiles, and converts seldom ate it.

The banning of such meat sources, particularly the pig, may very well have led to an overall reduction in the consumption of animal protein. It has been demonstrated for twentieth-century Borneo that Ngaju Dayaks who become Muslim consume less meat than their animist cousins, even though they are typically more wealthy (Miles 1976: 29–50). Since Islam also reduced (though it did not remove) the necessity for ritual sacrifices to honour the ancestors, it probably did contribute to the low share of animal protein in the diet of modern Southeast Asians.

In the Buddhist countries of the Mainland there were no prohibitions on food, so that Burmese and Siamese were still eating lizards, frogs, bats, silkworms, rats, and boa constrictors as late as the nineteenth century (Ibrahim 1688: 157; Symes 1827 II: 61; Pallegoix 1854 I: 213). Killing, on the other hand, incurred serious demerit for a Theravada Buddhist. Cattle could be eaten if they died naturally, but their blood should not be spilled. Unlike Muslim states in the South which often banned pigs altogether, the Buddhist state did not attempt to decide on behalf of its subjects how they should resolve this dilemma. If Muslims, Chinese, hill peoples, or even poor Buddhists did not mind incurring the demerit of killing a beast, that was their own affair, and all could enjoy the meat (Shway Yoe 1882 I: 83). There was therefore much variety of approach in the seventeenth century. "Some [monks] eat Meat, provided it is given them slain, others never eat any. Some do kill animals, other kill none at all; and others do kill very rarely, and for some sacrifice" (La Loubère 1691: 119; also Choisy 1686: 242).

Later Burmese kings, such as Shembuan (d. 1776), issued proclamations forbidding the killing of animals, which at the least made public slaughter difficult (Symes 1827 II: 108–09). If Burmese and Thais ate progressively less meat in the seventeenth to nineteenth centuries, however, it was because ritual occasions such as funerals and weddings became increasingly the business of Buddhist monks. Even though rural and northern Thais in the nineteenth century still did not regard such a feast as satisfactory without the sacrifice of an animal (Graham 1912: 126–27), those who were under stronger influence from the Buddhist *sangha* celebrated in other ways.

Water and Wine

> *Within this city of Sukhotai there is a gushing rock-spring of water as clear in colour and as good to drink of as is the water of the Khong in the dry season.*
>
> *—Ram Kamheng 1293: 27*

Water was the everyday drink of Southeast Asians, much to the surprise of both tea-drinking Chinese (Ma Huan 1433: 93) and alcohol-addicted Dutch and English. In hilly districts clear water was often available from mountain streams, whence it could be conducted to the house through split bamboo pipes (Marsden 1783: 61). Even the houses of Brunei, erected over an arm of the sea but close to water sources in the adjacent hills, were able to enjoy mountain water "with great cleanliness and at small cost running inside their houses in the manner of a trough all day and night" (Dasmariñas 1590B: 3). Inhabitants of the major coastal and riverine settlements were less fortunate; they had to take their water from the river. Canal digging to bring fresh river water closer to urban settlements was one of the more important public works undertaken by rulers in Patani and Makassar (*Hikayat Patani*: 105–06; Reid 1983A: 146–48). A clear-water stream was diverted in 1613 to flow right through the palace of Aceh (Copland 1614: 213). Wells were especially important in smaller islands (see, for example, Galvão 1544: 39), and also in settlements remote from river and stream (Sangermano 1818: 213). The availability of good water from natural springs and shallow wells was a definite factor in the siting of many towns and royal centres.

Visiting Europeans who followed the Southeast Asian example by drawing water from the river near major cities suffered appallingly from waterborne diseases. The water of Banten they soon learned to avoid because "it first waxeth white, and afterward crawleth full of maggots" (*True Report* 1599: 33; also *Verhael* 1597: 29; *LREIC* I: 289). In nearby Jakatra-Batavia, nevertheless, the great Dutch physician Bontius (1629: 130) continued to recommend the river water "if drawn a little above the town." How did Southeast Asians in these cities avoid the same terrible mortality from drinking river water? Chinese did so by boiling the water for tea, but we know that the habit of tea drinking had by the seventeenth century spread only to the Vietnamese and to a small number of the urban elite elsewhere in Southeast Asia (Borri 1633: V; Dampier 1697: 277, 279). La Loubère (1691: 21) pointed out that among the better-class Siamese of the capital it had become "a necessary civility to present tea to all that visit them," whereas "the use of tea is unknown in all the other places of the Kingdom."

One of the Southeast Asian methods was to let the river water stand for long enough to clear, as La Loubère (21) again explained:

> Pure water is their ordinary Drink; they love only to drink it perfum'd. . . . As the Siamese go not to draw it at the Springs, which are doubtless too remote, it is wholesome only when it has been settled more or fewer days, according as the Inundation is higher or lower. . . . For when the Waters retire . . . they are more corrosive, do cause Disenteries and Lasks [diar-

rhoea], and cannot be drunk without danger, till they have let them stand in great Jars or Pitchers, the space of three Weeks or a Month.

The practice of adding lemon, cinnamon, nutmeg, and other flavourings to the water was also popular elsewhere (Gervaise 1701: 75; Bontius 1629: 131–32; Raffles 1817 I: 100), but it cannot have done much to counteract the bacteria. Allowing it to stand in large earthenware jars, an even more widespread practice, would have improved the clarity and taste of the water but would not have rendered it wholesome.

There is evidence that at least some Southeast Asians had begun to boil badly polluted river water, perhaps following the example of the Chinese, who according to Rhodes (1653: 31) never drank water cold. "They laugh at us when we tell them we drink water fresh, and they say this causes us many diseases." Ibn Muhammad Ibrahim (1688: 157) mentioned that the Siamese drank boiled water with their meals, and in the early nineteenth century Raffles (1817 I: 100) reported that among the better-class Javanese, water "is invariably boiled first, and generally drunk warm." In the 1680s a Dutch resident of Batavia, Ten Rhijne, had noticed that "most Hindustanners and other natives of this place" never drank water unless it had been boiled, because there were "little invisible creatures" in the water which were thereby killed (cited de Haan 1922 II: 329). Although Ten Rhijne apparently did not choose to apply this important lesson to his own drinking habits, there were other seventeenth-century Dutchmen who did let their water stand and then boil it—notably at Banjarmasin, where the river water was particularly filthy.

Even though more than two centuries would pass before the theory behind the boiling of water was understood, it seems likely that Europeans first learned its practical advantages in Southeast Asia, probably by following the local or Chinese example. Boiling water was costly of time and fuel, however, and it did not spread to the majority of rural Southeast Asians, as it still has not today.

Other beverages were known in the cities, though for a limited clientele. "The Moors of Siam drink coffee, which comes to them from Arabia, and the Portuguese do drink Chocolate, when it comes to them from Manilla" (La Loubère 1691: 23; cf. Gervaise 1688: 75). These drinks became popular locally only in the eighteenth century, after coffee had been planted by the Dutch in Java in the 1690s.

Water was the everyday staple, but no feast was complete without alcohol. The numerous sources of sugar made possible an equally varied supply of liquor, as indicated by the menu for a Majapahit feast (*Nagara-kertagama* 1365: 106): "*tuak* [palm wine] of the coconut palm, *tuak* of the *lontar* palm, *arak* (distilled liquor) from the sugar palm, *kilang* (fermented cooked molasses), *brem* (fermented rice), and *tampo* (double-fermented rice).[1] The same text makes clear that the quantity of liquor consumed was an index of the success of the feast. That pre-Muslim Javanese had a particular reputation for heavy drinking is also borne out by the Malay epic of Hang Tuah (*Hikayat Hang Tuah*: 251–52), in which the Malay hero escapes from a plot to kill him at a Majapahit feast because "the vizir Gajah Mada and all the [Javanese] nobles were completely drunk."

In eastern Indonesia and the Philippines the most popular form of alcohol was a tuak (Tagalog *tuba*) derived from one of the palms—lontar, coconut, or sugar (arenga). This palm wine was drunk everywhere in Southeast Asia except Vietnam, but in the westerly areas, including the cities of Borneo and Java, the stronger distilled liquor, arak, was apparently more popular (La Loubère 1691: 22; Pigafetta 1524: 185–86).

Alcohol was as much a part of feasting as was the killing and eating of animals, and perhaps for similar reasons. At funerals, the central and most boisterous feasts, the noise and licentiousness of the proceedings marked a liminal condition which somehow regenerated life at the point of death. Alcohol, like the other widespread narcotic, betel, was closely associated with the ancestors, perhaps because it induced a condition similar to the trance through which shamans communicated with the dead. In the Philippines one of the names for such a feast was *paganito*, the propitiation of the *anito*, or spirit.

> They start their anito, drinking and eating and ringing bells and other instruments, with the women and young people dancing. Thus, in the twenty or thirty days during which the feasts last, they do not stop dancing and singing until some get tired and others take their place: while the chiefs and brave Indians [Filipinos] eat and drink until they fall drunk, and are brought by their slaves and women elsewhere to sleep. When they wake up they return to the feast and get drunk anew. (Dasmarinas 1590A: 395; cf. Morga 1609: 251; Chirino 1604: 331–32).

Even if the Spanish were inclined to exaggerate the licentiousness of these feasts, their unanimous evidence about the heavy drinking on

1. But note that Jacobs (1971: 376) identifies the "*tampois* of Borneo, which is a ladies' drink, sweet and exciting" (Galvão 1544: 146) with a liquor made from the fruit of the *tampoi* tree.

ritual occasions is confirmed by the practice of many Borneo and Sulawesi peoples in modern times. Huntingdon and Metcalf (1979: 56–57) have suggested concerning the secondary burial practice of such peoples that there was a (subconscious) association between the emergence of a spirit from a putrefying corpse and the making of alcohol by fermentation of rice, sometimes in the same jars that were used for the dead.

Islam and Buddhism both censured the drinking of alcohol, "the mother of all uncleanness," as ar-Raniri called it (Wilkinson 1903 I: 44). In contrast to the immediate rejection of pork by Muslims, however, this disapproval took effect very slowly. Arab writers regarded Melaka as a degenerate place where "the Muslim eats dogs for meat for there are no food laws. They drink wine in the markets" (Ibn Majid 1462: 206). The Malay writer of the *Sejarah Melayu* (1612: 153) gave his own answer to such charges in an engaging anecdote in which the inebriated Sri Rama got the better of a puritanical ulama from "above the winds" who tried to reprove him. Even in such strong Muslim centres as Brunei, Mindanao, and Aceh, arak was regularly provided at court entertainments (Dasmariñas 1590B: 10; Pigafetta 1524: 186; Dampier 1697: 251). Of feasts in Muslim Ternate, Galvão (1544: 144) wrote: "They never drink water; they consider it a discourtesy to do so, and an act of civility to rise drunk or, as they call it, *koteto*. They pay no attention to the precept of Mohammed, but, while drinking like Flemings they rather joke about it, soliciting each other that all may take part in it together . . . . In these islands there is so much [liquor] and it is used in such large quantities that the report of it would not seem to be true."

In Siam and Burma the king and court usually avoided drinking in public, "all strong drink being prohibited by the clergy and laws, and esteemed scandalous" (Schouten 1636: 127). Nevertheless, King Prasat Thong (1630–56) was a notoriously heavy drinker whose example was said to have encouraged a greater use of arak among all classes (van Vliet 1636: 83). Here too the copious consumption of arak by the ordinary populace was associated with feasting, especially the great annual feasts, when ordinary conventions were waived (Schouten 1636: 146; La Loubère 1691: 22; Brugière 1829: 202).

Alcohol was too well established an accompaniment of important rituals to disappear quickly in the face of the new religions. Never, however, have Southeast Asians drunk individually, with the desperation of the urban poor of eighteenth- and nineteenth-century Europe. The closest European analogy to their feasting is the ritualized merrymaking of a mediaeval May Day.

Eating and Feasting

Feasting was sharply differentiated from the ordinary daily meal. Not only was the fare of the twice-daily family meal much simpler, lacking meat and alcohol, but the meal itself was to be eaten as swiftly and silently as possible. Relaxed conversation might occur after the meal, when the betel was brought out; to interrupt somebody with conversation while he was eating was deemed a grave discourtesy. Pallegoix (1854 I: 218) considered the fifteen minutes it took a Thai to consume his major meal as a "sacred" time, when even a master would not interrupt a servant. Errington (1979) has analysed a similar attitude in South Sulawesi in terms of the danger of eating, as a time when the sanctuary of the body is vulnerable because it is being penetrated by the intake of food.

Nevertheless, in most of Southeast Asia the family unit ate together, the women with the men (Raffles 1817 I: 100; Crawfurd 1820 I: 73). They would eat on the floor, using banana leaves or shallow wooden bowls as plates. Hands and mouths were cleaned with water before and after the meal, and the right hand was used for eating: "They use no spoons to eat their rice, but every Man takes a handful out of the Platter, and by wetting his hand in Water, that it may not stick to his hand, squeezes it into a lump, as hard as possibly he can make it, and then crams it into his mouth. They all strive to make these lumps as big as their mouth can receive them . . . so that sometimes they almost choak themselves" (Dampier 1697: 225).There was no drinking during the meal, but always a draft of water after it.

Among the upper classes the master of the house would eat first, served by women, as a mark of his status. Royal courts and noble houses were marked by the elegance of the bowls in which the side dishes were served. Special table manners did not distinguish the man of quality from the peasant, as the increasingly elaborate eating styles of Renaissance Europe did (Braudel 1967: 136–41; Farb and Armelagos 1980: 244–49). The essentials of propriety—washing before and after, and eating exclusively with the right hand—were shared by the whole society. As late as the nineteenth century it could still be said that in this matter "the princes and the king only differ from their subjects by the richness of their table service and the variety of their dishes" (Pallegoix 1854 I: 218).

Everyday hospitality consisted in the sharing of betel, not food. Moreover, there were no public eating places except where Chinese and Europeans introduced them. "There are no Inns at Siam. . . . A Frenchman . . . resolved to keep an Inn there, and some Europeans only did sometimes go thither. And although amongst the Siamese . . . it be an established practice to entertain one another, yet it is rarely in this country, and with much ceremony, and especially no open Table is there kept" (La Loubère 1691: 30). La Loubère guessed that this had something to do with men protecting their wives from view, as the celibate monks were more hospitable; but since women regularly bought and sold in the market this is unconvincing. The explanation lies rather in the essentially silent, rapid, and private nature of everyday eating. There was no middle ground between the simple domestic meal and the feast, which was always prolonged, with after-dinner drinking, dancing, and entertainment continuing long into the night (fig. 3): "These [Moluccan] people are fond of banquets at all their feasts, wars and amusements; for whatever they have to do, first they must eat and drink. . . . They eat from mid-day on and stay at table until midnight, or sometimes until daybreak. They rise to see to their needs and then start eating again. And from halfway on they sing and play instruments and make jokes, riddles, and pleasantries" (Galvão 1544: 141–45).

Betel and Tobacco

Whereas alcohol was associated with feasting, the daily social lubricant throughout Southeast Asia was betel. This mildly narcotic relaxant required the interaction of three essential ingredients—the nut of the areca palm (*Areca catechu*), the leaf (or in eastern Indonesia the pod or catkin) of the betel vine (*Piper betle*), and lime. That the first two grow naturally in Southeast Asia is borne out by the extraordinary diversity of indigenous words for them. The third, lime, which was readily obtained from crushed shells, reacted chemically with compounds in the areca nut to produce the alkaloids (arecadaine, arecoline, guvacine) that relaxed the brain and central nervous system (Reid 1985: 532–33). The three ingredients together also produced the copious red saliva which chewers spat out.

Although betel chewing was also widespread in South India and South China by the fifteenth century, it appears to have originated in Southeast Asia. In that region it occupied a central place in the ritual as well as the social life of every people of whom we have knowledge. Chinese sources from as early as the T'ang period mention the role of betel in marriage ritual, and the word used for it, *pin-lang*, appears to be a very early Chinese borrowing from Malay (Wheatley 1961: 56, 78–79; Chau Ju-kua c. 1250: 155). Ma Huan (1433: 92–93) said of the Javanese: "Men and women take areca-nut and betel-leaf, and mix

Fig. 3 A feast in Banda (South Maluku) in 1599, based on descriptions of Dutch travellers, pictured standing at right

them with lime, made from clam-shells; their mouths are never without this mixture. . . . When they receive passing guests, they entertain them, not with tea, but only with areca-nut." To visitors it seemed as though Southeast Asians were never without their chew of betel. "They use it so continuously that they never take it from their mouths; therefore these peoples can be said to go around always ruminating" (Galvão 1544: 57). Pigafetta (1524: 32) thought the reason all the islanders he met used it was that "it was very cooling to the heart, and if they ceased to use it they would die." Similarly in Cochin-China, Borri (1633: C) reported that "there is in every house some or other appointed to no other office, but only to infold these morsels of areca in the Betle. . . . These morsels thus prepared are put into boxes, and they usually go chewing on them all day long, not only within doors, but even when they go up and down the streets, or spaek with any, in all places and at all times."

For travellers a bag of betel ingredients was more essential than food, as it helped them withstand the pangs of hunger and exhaustion. Warriors, too, needed it to revive their strength and courage (*Hikayat Pocut Muhamat*: 223–25). In social intercourse it took the place occupied today by coffee, tea, alcohol, and cigarettes. When making a visit or even pausing to chat in the street, men and women would exchange betel and chew it together. A bronze betel set was one of the few essential metal items in any substantial household (fig. 4). Rulers and aristocrats always had betel carriers in their retinue, usually favoured young women, or, in the case of Ternate, female dwarfs deliberately crippled in youth to add to thc cxotic charisma of the court (Galvão 1544: 115).

Because the offering of betel was the essence of courtesy and hospitality, the ancestral spirits had also to be given it on every significant ritual occasion. The chewing of betel, or the offering of areca nut and betel leaves together or apart, was an integral part of every ritual of birth, death, or healing. It was especially central to the rituals of courtship and marriage. Because it sweetened the breath and relaxed the mind, it was seen as a natural prerequisite to lovemaking (Penzer 1952: 197, 222; Pires 1515: 516). Placing the nut, the lime, and other ingredients in a delicately rolled betel leaf was one of the intimate services a woman could perform for a man, and was therefore symbolic of marriage or betrothal in some cultures, and of an invitation to love in others. The complementarity of the two central ingredients was seen as symbolic of sexual union, with the "heat" of the areca nut balancing the "cool" of the betel leaves. In eastern Indonesia the sexual symbolism became more explicit, since the long slender pod of a local genus of betel vine, used instead of the leaves, had a maleness to match the feminine roundness of the areca nut (Forth 1981: 360).

Tobacco, introduced to Southeast Asia by Europeans, gradually came to fill a similar combination of relaxant, social, and medicinal roles. The tobacco plant appears to have reached the Philippines from Mexico in the 1570s, and it spread from there to Java in 1601—that, at least, was the year when the practice of smoking was recorded at the Mataram court (*Babad ing Sangkala* 1738: 29). In 1603 the ruler of Aceh (Sumatra) was using tobacco (Warwijck 1604: 15), and in 1604 the Bantenese elite were fond of smoking it (Scott 1606: 173). The practice of the Javanese court, at least when entertaining Europeans, was to smoke a long reed pipe in the Dutch style (van Goens 1656: 257; Stavorinus 1798 I: 245). Apparently this remained an affectation of elite males, who emulated some European traders. The form in which tobacco use became popular was the smoking of cheroots, known in the seventeenth century by the Malay term *bungkus* (bundle). These were made of homegrown shredded tobacco, often mixed with other aromatics or flavourings, wrapped in a strong leaf such as maize or nipah palm, broadened at the outer end. The term is first found in Java in 1658, and the cheroot seems to have reached there via the Moluccas from the Philippines (de Haan 1922 II: 25, 135). Tobacco

Fig. 4 Betel being offered to Ki Amad, hero of the Islamic romance Amad-Muhammad, as represented in a coastal Javanese illustrated manuscript dated 1828

smoking in this form had begun to be popular among men and women and quite young children by the end of the seventeenth century. "The women, even the most considerable, are entirely addicted thereunto" (La Loubère 1691: 50). Tobacco appears at this stage to have been regarded as a stronger and more expensive alternative to betel. It became still more popular a century later when it was made one of the ingredients of the chewed betel quid (Reid 1985: 535–38).

A Healthy People?

The first generation of Europeans in Asia suffered very high mortality, but those who survived insisted that it was not the climate that was at fault, but dangerous "excesses" of diet. "The danger of mortality is not due to climate, but to distempers of the body. . . . The climate is indeed a paradise compared to our muddy climate in Europe, and to the temperate is very healthy" (Hawley 1626: 154; cf. Sande 1576: 66; Bontius 1629: 129; Schouten 1641: 128; Hamilton 1727: 33). They noticed that the inhabitants were not afflicted by the same mortality but seemed remarkably healthy by European standards. The Visayans, for example, "are healthy people, for the climate of that land is good. Among them are found no crippled, maimed, deaf or dumb persons. . . . Therefore they reach an advanced age in perfect health" (Loarca 1582: 116–17). In Aceh, it seemed to a visiting Persian, "illness other than the burden of old age is very rare" (Ibrahim 1688: 179). A long-term resident of Cochin-China concluded that its climate was "so benign, that they never have any pestilence, neither do the people know what kind of thing it is, or what it meaneth" (Borri 1633: I; cf. van Goens 1656: 180; Rhodes 1653: 31). Up to the end of the eighteenth century European visitors continued to be surprised at the sound physical condition of Southeast Asians, virtually none of whom were "either crump-shouldered or lame, rickety or deaf" (Gervaise 1701: 63; cf. Gervaise 1688: 122; Marsden 1783: 44; La Bissachère 1812: 63). "Perhaps a single province in France contains as many blind and lame as the whole of Siam" (Brugière 1829: 191).

Such comments are of course as revealing of the miserable conditions in Europe as of the health of Southeast Asians. They are also inherently subjective. The only indices we have of nutritional and health status which can to some extent escape such subjectivity are stature and age at death. However meagre the data on these variables is, it must be treasured as the best available means of comparing physical well-being across different times and places.

Social historians have recently come to recognize in physical height and growth patterns a precious index of comparative nutritional levels. Genetic influences on height have been shown to be much less important than nutrition, so that in most premodern populations there is a very marked difference in stature between the rich and the poor (Fogel et al. 1982; Tanner 1979). Fortunately, some of the pioneering savants of the early nineteenth century also believed, though for different reasons, that physical stature was an important comparative measure and left some valuable measurements of sample groups.

With the exception of Stamford Raffles' claim (1818: 350) to have encountered a people "in general about six feet high" in the highlands of South Sumatra, there is a remarkable consistency about the estimates of Southeast Asian heights. Differences between rich and poor appear to have been less than in eighteenth- and nineteenth-century Europe, or in twentieth-century Asia, with adult male heights ranging from about 147 to 167 cm (4′10″ to 5′6″). "A considerable number" of adult males were measured during the British mission to Siam and Cochin China in 1821, and the average came to 160 cm (5′3″) for Thais and Malays and a centimetre less for Vietnamese (Finlayson 1826: 75, 227, 376). Cameron (1865: 131) agreed with this measure for Malays, while Crawfurd reckoned Malays and Austronesians in general to average 5′2″ (157 cm) for men and 4′11″ (150 cm) for women. Siamese were about an inch taller (Crawfurd 1820 I: 19; 1830, 297; cf. Earl 1837: 166). There may have been a slight decline in the height of Siamese during the nineteenth century, if Graham (1912: 142) is correct in his end-of-century estimate of 5′1″ (155 cm) for men and 4′11″ for women. Broader surveys of the Indonesian population in the twentieth century (Nyèssen 1929: 80; Coolie Budget Commission 1941: 26–30) average at 157 cm for men and 150 cm for women, suggesting that no significant change occurred there between 1800 and 1940. Vietnamese at the end of the nineteenth century were reckoned still to be just under 160 cm for men and 153 cm for women, while Cambodians were slightly taller (Bouinais and Paulus 1885 I: 226, 502). Lao were reckoned a little taller than lowland Thai (Graham 1912: 159), perhaps because of their larger meat consumption.

Southeast Asian height in the early nineteenth century appears then to have averaged 157 cm (5′2″), or a little above, for adult men. This was observed to be about two inches less than the average height of Chinese and four inches less than that of Europeans (Crawfurd 1820 I: 19; 1856: 173). European male heights, though differing widely between social classes, have indeed been shown to have averaged about 167 cm (5′6″) in the early nineteenth century, increasing by another ten centimetres by the mid-twentieth (Tanner 1979). If we go back to the eighteenth century, however, the discrepancy between Europeans and Southeast Asians disappears altogether. Barrow (1806: 223) reported that Javanese in 1793 were "about the middle size of Europeans," while Marsden (1783: 44) and Stavorinus (1798 II: 183) gave similar testimony for Sumatrans and Bugis.

Reports of the sixteenth and seventeenth centuries are almost unanimous that the peoples of Southeast Asia were "of medium stature"—meaning about the same height as the Europeans who described them (Morga 1609: 247; Pyrard 1619 II: 156; Colin 1663: 60; Dampier 1699: 33, 90). The Moluccans and Javanese were sometimes seen as "short" (Galvão 1544: 71; Craen 1606: 180, 199), but on the other hand people from Brunei, Makassar, Pegu, and Siam were reported to be "tall" (Fitch 1591: 154; van Noort 1601: 202–03; van der Hagen 1607: 82). While such comparative estimates are suggestive, more concrete data will only emerge from analysis of skeletal remains in those sites which can be dated by the trade ceramics buried with the dead. In one large cemetery of the period 1350–1500, at Catalagan (Batangas) in the southwest corner of Luzon, more than five hundred grave sites were excavated in the 1950s, yielding 117 adult skeletons sufficiently intact to be measured accurately. Their heights ranged from 144 to 180 cm, with an average of 160 cm (5′3″). Male and female skeletons could not be distinguished, though both were buried at the site (Fox 1959: 354). As an average of men and women, this is 5 cm (2″) more than the heights recorded in the nineteenth and early twentieth centuries.

The best conclusion I can draw from this scattered evidence is that on average Southeast Asians of the seventeenth century were as tall as Europeans, but that a discrepancy appeared as European nutritional levels began to improve about 1800. European data itself is not good for heights before the late eighteenth century, though we know that British marines averaged only 5′4″ and sixteen-year-old poor London naval recruits less than 5′ in the 1770s (Sokoloff and Villaflor 1982: 457; Floud and Wachter 1982). Southeast Asians did not gain in height (and therefore nutritional level) between the seventeenth and twentieth centuries; the evidence is stronger for a slight decline.

Life expectancy is a more dangerous index to trust to the casual observation of visitors, since they may have been unaware of levels of infant mortality—usually the most critical variable. European observers of the sixteenth and seventeenth centuries came from societies where the average life expectancy at birth was about thirty-two, although those who had survived the first ten years of life could expect to reach their mid-forties (Stone 1979: 55; Laslett 1965: 96–98). When Europeans comment on the age of Southeast Asians, it is to say that they are "long-lived according to present standards" (Galvão 1544: 71), or that they "grow very old, the men as well as the women" (van Goens 1656: 180; cf. Loarca 1582: 117; "Tweede Boeck" 1601: 90; Mandelslo 1662: 128, 130; Valentijn, 1726 III: ii, 255). At the beginning of the nineteenth century, when European expectations of life were beginning to rise, Vietnamese and Thais were still thought to live unusually long (La Bissachère 1812 I: 68; Sternstein 1984: 60), while for Indonesians it was claimed only that longevity was similar to that in Europe (Raffles 1817 I: 77; Crawfurd 1820 I: 30).

Systematic analysis of Southeast Asian birth and death data has reached no further back than the early nineteenth century. A careful study drawn from parish registers of one district in Luzon, for example, reveals a relatively high life expectancy, averaging 42.0 for men and women together in the earliest period investigated (1805–20) and a subsequent steady deterioration to only 17.5 years at the grim nadir around 1900 (Ng 1979: 56–57).

For the seventeenth century there is only fragmentary evidence, but it is nevertheless suggestive. The Makassar court diary (*Lontara'-bilang Gowa*) is one source which does register births and deaths, if only for a tiny elite. The diary records events as they occur each day, beginning about 1624. From then until 1660 (when conflicts with the Dutch began the rapid decline of Makassar) it includes the birth dates of twenty-one men and ten women whose death dates also appear later in the diary (which runs to 1750).[2] These cases show ages at death ranging from 15 to 86 for the ten women, with an average of 51.5. The twenty-one men were aged between 17 and 85 at the time of their death, with an average of 45.5. If the five men who died in battle (at 59, 31, 25, 17, and 17) are excluded, the men who died naturally averaged 50.44 years.

Because of the absence of recorded child deaths in the only available version of the diary, these figures should be regarded as reflecting longevity among those who had already reached some age held to mark definitive arrival. It seems likely that the diarist refrained from recording a birth until the child had survived at least the 40- or 100-day anniversary regarded as especially critical; he could not have delayed indefinitely without endangering both his accuracy and his format.

That child deaths did occur on a scale almost as high as Europe's is indicated by the Catalagan cemetery site in Luzon, where 110 of the 433 skeletons excavated (25 percent) were estimated to be of children up to ten years old (Fox 1959: 349). It is probably safe to conclude only that the Makassar aristocrats who reached their teens could expect to live to fifty.

Twentieth-century figures for the major countries of Southeast Asia show life expectancy at birth to be only a little over forty, with the usual heavy mortality in the first year—about 14 percent of live births in Java in the 1960s (Hull and Rohde 1980: 9–10). The above data suggest that the situation three hundred years earlier had been

2. The diary also provides the ages at death of a number of other people for whom there is no birth entry. One such woman, Karaeng Panaikang, was alleged to be 105 at her death. As well as being less reliable, such cases have a bias in favour of those who survived long enough to be thought important at death, and to include them would raise the averages by a couple of years. By excluding them, we are left with a sample of people selected by their significance at birth.

no worse than that indicated by these modern figures, and substantially better than it appeared to be at the beginning of the twentieth century before modern medicine and hygiene had begun to take effect.

If Southeast Asians also lived longer than Renaissance Europeans, as seems likely, one important reason may have been a lower child mortality. In contrast to the indifference and even deliberate neglect the European poor reportedly showed for their children (Stone 1979: 55–59), Southeast Asians appear to have had fewer children, spaced farther apart, and to have given both boys and girls a relatively high degree of love and attention (La Loubère 1691: 50; Crawfurd 1820 I: 83; Raffles 1817 I: 70; Ng 1979: 150–56).

The relatively good health of Southeast Asians in the age of commerce should not surprise us if we compare their diet, medicine, and hygiene with those of contemporary Europeans. For the great majority of Southeast Asians serious hunger or malnutrition was never a danger. The basic daily adult requirement of one *kati* (625 grams) of rice a day was not difficult to produce in the country or to buy in the city, and it contained in itself enough calories and protein for healthy development. The relative lack of animal proteins was probably on balance an advantage, as it spared Southeast Asians from diseases spread through maggoty meat. Large-scale famine appears to have occurred only as a result of warfare. Since people could obtain their daily needs for a couple of farthings, La Loubère observed (1691: 35), "it is no wonder if the Siamese are not in any great care about their Subsistence, and if in the evening there is heard nothing but singing in their houses."

Hygiene

The abundance of water is one of the characteristics of the lands below the winds, and prodigality with its use was habitual among the inhabitants. Having no need to heat water for washing as in colder climates, they were among the most assiduous washers to be found anywhere, and therefore a source of amazement to Europeans, who distrusted water.

> From the day they are born these [Philippine] Islanders are raised in the water, and so from childhood both men and women swim like fish. . . . They bathe at all hours, indiscriminately, for pleasure and cleanliness, and not even women who have just delivered avoid bathing, or fail to immerse a newly born infant in the river itself or in the cold springs. . . . They bathe crouching almost sitting down, out of modesty, with the water up to their neck and with extreme care not to expose them-

selves. . . . The most usual hour for the bath is at sunset, for since they cease their work then they take to the river for a restful and cooling bath, taking back for their daily needs a vessel of water. . . . At the door of every house they keep a jar of water and whosoever comes in, whether a stranger or one of the household, draws some water from it to wash his feet before entering . . . the water pouring down through the floor of the house, which is all made of bamboo slats (Chirino 1604: 258; cf. Morga 1609: 249).

They are here [Aceh], as at Mindanao, very superstitious in washing and cleansing themselves from defilements, and for that reason they delight to live near the rivers or streams. . . . The river of Achin near the city is always full of people of both sexes and all ages. . . . Even the sick are brought to the river to wash (Dampier 1699: 95–96).

Whereas the conventional wisdom in Europe was that bathing was voluptuous or dangerous, Asians associated it with purification and "cooling," without which the body could not be healthy. Moreover, the care of the body, the washing and perfuming of the hair, a pleasant odour of the breath and the body, and neatness and elegance in dress were all matters of great importance for Southeast Asians, in contrast to house and furniture, which earned very little attention. Thais reputedly bathed three or four times a day (La Loubère 1691: 28–29; Pallegoix 1854 I: 223), and everybody bathed at least once. Where there was no river, people bathed by pouring a bucket of well water over their heads. In either case the water tended to carry the germs of the lower body away from the head, a safer practice than that of the confined bath shared by many family members, common in cold climates. Burmese appear to have distinguished between wells for drinking water and those for washing (Brown 1926: 47). At rivers the place for drawing water was usually upstream from the men's and women's bathing places. In the more congested conditions of cities, particularly after the population explosion of the nineteenth century, the faith of Southeast Asians in the cleansing efficacy of running river water could become an obstacle to better health. Such attitudes were still a safeguard for most in the seventeenth century, however, by contrast with the dangerous antipathy to washing on the part of contemporary Europeans.

Even in their biggest cities Southeast Asians lived in a dispersed pattern of single-story, elevated, wooden houses surrounded by trees. The disposal of household refuse was for the most part left to pigs, chickens, or dogs which foraged beneath the house, and to the seasonal floods which carried everything away once a year. The open and elevated style of house at least kept it free of the worst accumulations of decaying debris, in a way which was impossible in the congested cities of Europe, the Middle East, or China before the era of rubbish collection and sewage.

They always wash after meals [in Mindanao], or if they touch anything that is unclean; for which reason they spend abundance of water in their houses. This water, with the washing of their dishes, and what other filth they make, they pour down near their fire-place; for their chambers are not boarded, but floored with split bamboos, like lathe, so that the water presently falls underneath their dwelling rooms, where it breeds maggots, and makes a prodigious stink. Besides this filthiness, the sick people ease themselves and make water in their chambers; there being a small hole made purposely in the floor, to let it drop through. But healthy sound people commonly ease themselves, and make water, in the river (Dampier 1697: 226).

Once again, this habit of defecating in the river (or at the seashore) was based on the assumption that running water was cleansing. It had merits when compared with contemporary European and Indian use of urban streets and stagnant drains for lack of alternatives (Smith 1979: 197–98; Das Gupta 1979: 33).

Medicine

They are not accustomed here to give syrups, nor purgatives, and still less to practice bloodletting, their only medicine being commonly known herbs and their juices. When they are in a fever they immerse themselves in cold water up to the neck. . . . They do not sew up cuts but heal them with banana buds roasted, and when still hot, soaked in oil.

—Galvão 1544: 177

In examining the medical practice of Southeast Asians, we should not be too long delayed by the question of theoretical schools. Indian Ayurvedic theory had its students, especially in Burma, Siam, and Java; and Chinese medical theory was influential in Vietnam and to a lesser extent in Siam. Greek and Arabian ideas, mediated through Islam, introduced the doctrine that four elements—water, earth, fire, and air—governed the functioning of the body, while the Chinese system stressed the need for balance between two opposed principles, the "hot" *yang* and the "cool" *yin*. The most important practical effect of both schools was to strengthen what may have been an indigenous Southeast Asian belief that illness arose from excessive heat (fevers, pregnancy), from dangerous loss of heat (childbirth), or from the entry of excessive dry or moist air (chest complaints). The emphasis on cooling rituals and medicines seems to belong as much to

Southeast Asian as to Chinese practice (Hart 1969; Gimlette 1915: 8–42; Manderson 1981: 509–10).

Medical texts deriving from the Indian tradition were translated and rewritten in Java, Bali, Burma, Siam, and Cambodia, but they played a greater part in the realm of religion and the sacred than in expanding experimental knowledge.[3] Such texts would be consulted by courtiers and scholars when epidemics showed the kingdom to be badly out of joint or when the king was ill. One thirteenth-century king of Angkor appears to have endowed a hundred hospices dedicated to applying the scholarly tradition of medicine, presumably in the belief that large-scale disease would be attributed to royal impropriety (Frédéric 1981: 269–70). At least in the seventeenth century, however, the great majority of healing was done by local practitioners relying on local folk remedies and herbs. La Loubère (1691: 62) was speaking of them when he commented that "medicine cannot merit the name of a Science amongst the Siamese. . . . They trouble not to have any principle of Medicine, but only a number of Receipts, which they have learnt from their ancestors, and in which they never alter anything. They have no regard to the particular symptoms of a disease: and yet they fail not to cure a great many" (cf. Crawfurd 1820 I: 328).

The experimentally based "science" to which La Loubère referred was primarily that of anatomy and surgery, which had begun to make marked progress in Europe. European surgeons were unique in their readiness to cut, lance, hack, and bleed the body. When Beeckman (1718: 103–04) had himself bled in Banjarmasin, his Banjar friends at first thought he had gone mad to let out willingly his "very soul and life." When he explained that the English needed periodic bleeding because they consumed so much meat and wine, which thickened the blood, he was told they were "still greater fools, in putting yourselves to such great charges on purpose to receive pain for it."

In the long run, European curiosity about the practical mechanics of the body would bring outstanding breakthroughs. In the sixteenth and seventeenth centuries Europeans were already in demand in Asian cities as surgeons, specializing in amputation, the setting of serious fractures, the removal of growths, and even bleeding (Beaulieu 1666: 61; Fryke 1692: 133; La Loubère 1691: 62; Sangermano 1818: 173). On balance, however, this interventionist style of early European "scientific" medicine probably killed more patients than it cured. Europeans in the East initially had more to learn than to teach, and they found from experience that for most complaints it was safer to trust an Asian

3. Javanese and Balinese medical texts are discussed in Pigeaud 1967: 265–68 and in Lovric 1987. The much rarer Malay writings on the subject are listed in Juynboll 1899: 305–06.

than a European practitioner (Stavorinus 1798 I: 247; Dampier 1699: 336–37; 1697: 103; Brugière 1829: 199). The reason for this was nicely put by Borri (1633: G): "Their medicines do not alter nature, but assist her in her ordinary functions, drying up the peccant humours, without any trouble to the sick person at all." Two centuries later both Crawfurd (1820 I: 329) and Pallegoix (1854 I: 342) gratefully recognized that Indonesian and Thai medicine at least did no harm.

Herbal concoctions, bathing, and massage were the stock remedies of Southeast Asian medicine. Skilled masseurs were capable not only of providing "incredible" relief for rheumatism and soreness (Shway Yoe 1882: 417), but also of setting minor fractures and either easing childbirth or preventing it by abortion (Borri 1633: G; La Loubère 1691: 63; Stavorinus 1798 I: 247). Europeans were equally impressed by the fact that the major Southeast Asian centres "abound with medicinal drugs and herbs" (Dampier 1699: 88). The first Dutch fleet recorded fifty-five kinds of spices and herbs in the relevant section of the Banten market, "with many others which we have now forgotten." The medicinal uses of many of them were carefully recorded (Lodewycksz 1598: 112, 150–57; cf. Schoute 1929: 106–08).

That many of these herbs were effective against various digestive and intestinal disorders and also against infection, there is no doubt. Of all the herbs consumed, particular attention should be paid to betel leaves, since these were constantly chewed by Southeast Asians of all ages. According to local tradition, betel chewing prevented tooth decay, aided digestion, and prevented dysentery. The juice of the betel leaf has been used against eye infections, infections in wounds and sores, and various menstrual and other ailments (Reid 1985: 533–35). Modern research on this subject, though still in its infancy, has confirmed many of these claims. Betel chewers are markedly less prone to dental decay (Schamschula et al. 1977; Möller et al. 1977). Areca compounds have been shown to curb intestinal parasites, notably roundworms and tapeworms (Hsia 1937; Chung and Ko 1976; Chopra et al. 1956: 23). An extract of betel leaves has been found to be effective against a range of specific bacteria, including some of the shigella type responsible for dysentery and the salmonella types responsible for typhoid (Nguyen Duc Minh: 68–69). It seems likely that the betel-chewing habit alone may have protected Southeast Asians from many waterborne diseases, as well as contributing to the remarkable freedom from infection noted by several observers (Beaulieu 1666: 102; Sangermano 1818: 173; Crawfurd 1820 I: 31).

Like popular practitioners throughout the world, Southeast Asian healers ministered to the soul as much as to the body. Endicott (1970: 26) puts this point strongly by claiming that "Malay 'medicine' is almost entirely magical; even when procedures of real medical value are used, the reasons given are magical." Health was related to the status of the life-force within men, known as *semangat* in most of the Indonesian world and as *khon* or *khwan* to Thai speakers (Endicott 1970; Cuisinier 1951; Terwiel 1980: 53–60; Errington 1983). Some ritual acts designed to strengthen this life-force or to protect it against the malign or mischievous interference of powerful external spirits accompanied virtually every healing act, even those involving simple fractures. In cases of psychological disturbance and of epidemic illness, the whole cure became a ritual one. Psychological disorders had typically to be cured by a female or transvestite shaman, able to communicate by means of trance with the spirits tormenting the patient.

When sick they use many kinds of rites, some with more paraphernalia and others less, depending on the quality of each. . . . There are those who light a sheaf of grass and throw it out of the window, saying that by doing so the bad anitos [spirits] responsible for the malady would be scared into leaving. Others cast lots by tying a string to their hand, a piece of wood, or the tooth of a crocodile, and manipulating it themselves, saying that the cause of the malady of one is so-and-so. . . . Some who are not so well-to-do offer a little cooked rice and a bit of fish and wine, requesting of the anito for health; others offer a moderate drinking feast in which assists a priestess or a priest of the sick, whom they call *catalonan*, who administers what is needed and then says that the cause of the illness is that the soul has left the body and until it returns the sick would not recover. . . . Later the catalonan goes to a corner alone talking to himself and after a while returns to the sick and tells the latter to be happy because his soul is already back in the body and he would get well; with this they hold a drinking feast. (Dasmariñas 1590A: 430–31; cf. Alcina 1668 III: 227–41; Galvão 1544: 181; Colin 1663: 75–76; Sangermano 1818: 172.)

Most Southeast Asian communities also had an annual ritual devoted to cleansing the village or keeping evil spirits from it. In Islamized areas this survived as *mandi Safar*, a ritualized group bathing on the last Wednesday of the Muslim month *Safar* (Pijper 1977: 146–57; Snouck Hurgronje 1893 I: 206–07; Kiefer 1972: 123–24), while in Buddhist countries the modern descendant appears to be the ritual cleansing of images followed by a merry, generalized water throwing (fig. 5) at the New Year festival in April (Symes 1827, II: 210–12; Shway Yoe 1882: 345–51).[4] One animistic progenitor of such modern purification rituals, in which water always played a large role,

4. The habit of throwing water at New Year is not mentioned in seventeenth-century accounts of Siam, though it was common in Burma (Cox 1821: 195; and see fig. 5). Strong rulers may have found it indecorous in the royal capital, but it seems likely to have had very old roots in rural purification rituals.

Fig. 5 New Year water-throwing celebrations in Pegu, as rendered in Holland on the basis of seventeenth-century descriptions

was described by Alcina (1668, III: 232–35) as it occurred in the Visayas. Food was placed on rafts once a year and floated down the river as an offering to the protective spirits to ensure health, fertility, and security. "In time of pestilence they performed this with more solemnity because they made a large raft out of canes and on it they placed a seat. They went to the bank of the river and, after having eaten and drunk as much as they wished, they called to the pestilence, saying . . . 'go away on this seat and on this raft.' Then they threw it into the water and with it, so they believed, the pestilence or contagious illness." Almost exactly the same rituals have been observed within the past century in Sumatra and Malaya, both annually and after epidemic outbreaks (Snouck Hurgronje 1893: 417–18; Skeat 1900: 433–36; Evans 1923: 279–80). Muslim Chams of the ancient Champa homeland sent a paper monkey and offerings of food downriver on a model boat at the climax of their greatest annual ritual (Aymonier 1891: 88–91).

Mental and sometimes even physical illness was also frequently attributed to sorcery or malign magic. Such magic was especially favoured by unsuccessful lovers, so that adolescent infatuation or hysteria was routinely ascribed to the magical wiles of some suitor. Magic could also kill, it was believed. Every society had its famed practitioners for both applying and counteracting such magic (Lieban 1967: 1–2; Hamilton 1727: 45–48). The growing hold of the world religions in the cosmopolitan cities, however, tended to create an association between magic and the "old religion" of the interior. When a pretender to the Aceh throne, for example, wanted to get rid of the incumbent in the 1580s, he reportedly recruited two animist Batak *datu* (magical healers) to cast spells which made the sultan fall ill (*Hikayat Aceh* 1630: 91–93).

Seventeenth-century Southeast Asia, like other parts of the world, had an abstract scholarly tradition of medicine (not experimentally based), an empirical folk medicine, and magic. Everybody had access to the last two, while only a narrow elite of literati were acquainted with the first. Then as now, patients were highly opportunistic, choosing the practitioner who had the best reputation for getting results, and every successful practitioner mixed elements of magic with medicine. Educated Europeans were apt to believe that magic had a larger place and "science" a smaller one in Southeast Asia than in Europe. This was truer of rural than of urban areas, however, which lends force to Christopher Hill's comment that "there is less magic in twentieth- than in sixteenth-century England because there is more industry. Magic is agrarian" (cited Thomas 1971: 794–95). Agrarian communities in the Philippines aroused the derision of observers (Spanish friars) because of their credulity toward magic; but in large cosmopolitan cities such as Banten, Aceh, and Makassar, Europeans more commonly reported on the range and efficacy of indigenous treatments. If it seems, from the vantage point of the twentieth century, that both magic and folk remedies have survived better in Southeast Asia than in Europe, this probably results from the stunting of urban civilization in Southeast Asia at the end of the seventeenth century.

Epidemic and Endemic Illness

Some seventeenth-century European observers believed that Southeast Asia was altogether free from the epidemics which then ravaged Europe (above; also Bontius 1629: 104; Crawfurd 1820 I: 31–32). The reality may have been a relatively mild epidemic cycle. The openness of most of Southeast Asia to the world's commercial traffic must already have created immunities to most of the serious killer diseases before the European advent, in sharp contrast to the situation in the New World, Australia, and the Pacific Islands. In addition, the habit of washing and the relatively dispersed village-type dwelling pattern even in the largest cities may have limited the spread of the worst urban infections of Europe and India, such as plague and typhoid.

Little information is available on the prevalence of disease in Southeast Asia before the sixteenth century. The only references in the indigenous literature come from a later date, and these suggest that smallpox and other disfiguring diseases—leprosy and yaws or syphilis—were the most feared. A seventeenth-century story about the fourteenth-century founding of Ayutthaya mentions a promise that the city would be freed from the curse of smallpox but also relates that epidemics killed everybody who tried to live there until the surrounding marsh was filled in (suggesting malaria) (van Vliet 1640: 57–58). The Malay law code (*Undang-undang Melaka*, 102–03, 138–39) gave severe skin disease as a legitimate cause for invalidating marriage or repudiating the purchase of a slave. Syphilis is suggested by a number of stories of rulers who either contracted or were cured of their disease by sleeping with a particular woman—venereal disease being popularly believed to be cured by further intercourse with a healthy woman. The Malay term for syphilis is "royal disease" (*sakit raja singa*), perhaps because kings alone could be promiscuous on a grand scale. Sultan Iskandar Muda of Aceh reportedly nearly died from the dose he contracted from a princess of Perak (Beaulieu 1666: 103; Snouck Hurgronje 1893 I: 133). The most famous royal syphilitic was the fifteenth-century ruler of Majapahit, Brawijaya, whom the chronicles describe as having been cured by sleeping with a slave girl from Wandan (*Babad Tanah Jawa*: 24).[5] Although this is not definite proof that the syphilis spirochete was in Southeast Asia before Europeans brought it from the New World, the reasons for resisting such a claim are no longer as impressive as they once seemed to be (McNeill 1976: 202–03).

In the sixteenth and seventeenth centuries, for which more satisfactory evidence exists, it is clear that smallpox was the most feared epidemic disease in most parts of Southeast Asia:

> There are some contagious diseases, but the real plague of this country [Siam] is the small pox: it oftentimes makes dreadful ravage, and then they inter the bodies without burning them: but because their piety always makes them desire to render them this last respect, they do afterwards dig them up again: and . . . they dare not do it till three years after, or longer,

5. Jordaan and de Josselin de Jong (1985) have analysed a number of such royal sicknesses as myths referring to impediments in the relation between ruler and ruled.

by reason, as they say, that they have experimented, that this contagion breaks out afresh, if they dig them up sooner (La Loubère 1691: 39; cf. Crawfurd 1820 I: 33).

Portuguese and Spanish accounts (Jacobs 1974: 242, 449; Chirino 1604: 254) specify smallpox epidemics as killing many in the Moluccas and Philippines—Ternate in 1558, Amboina in 1564, and Balayan about 1592. In seventeenth-century Pegu (Lower Burma) smallpox was also the most feared. As soon as it struck a village, the healthy villagers would leave the afflicted behind and begin to build on a new site a few miles away (Hamilton 1727: 33). In the major centres of population and trade smallpox had probably become endemic by the sixteenth century, so that its victims were primarily children without immunity, revisited every seven to ten years. Galvão (1544: 179) reported for "the Indies," for example, that an epidemic was said to recur every seven years. In more isolated populations, such as many in Borneo and the Philippines, on the other hand, smallpox remained a less frequent but dreaded visitor, wiping out a large portion of any population not previously exposed to it. The smallpox spirit played a major part in folk mythology, especially in Borneo (Scharer 1946: 20; St. John 1862 I: 61–62; Snouck Hurgronje 1893 II: 416; Gimlette 1915: 38–39). The Kadazans of Tuaran, for example, believed early in this century that their periodic suffering from smallpox was the result of a pact between the creator god and the smallpox spirit, who would visit the people once every forty years to carry off his quota of half the living population (Evans 1923: 48–49).

Whether the more intense commercial interaction between Southeast Asia and the rest of Eurasia from the fourteenth century onward brought new diseases to the region may never be known. Maritime contacts with India and the Middle East, the most important of the early "civilized disease pools" (McNeill 1976: 78–140), had been close for a millennium, so that most of the important modern killers had probably already made their appearance and stimulated a degree of resistance. There are local traditions about terrible epidemics in a vague past, several centuries before the time of recording. Thus the Balinese Calon Arang story situates a severe epidemic in the Java of Erlangga in the eleventh century (Covarrubias 1937: 328–29); a Lombok legend links epidemics with the acceptance of Islam there in the seventeenth century (Bosch 1951: 155); while Banjarese prophecies link diseases with the adoption of alien Malay, Makassarese, Dutch, or other habits, perhaps in the seventeenth century (*Hikayat Banjar*: 264, 328). Since the written record goes no further back than the age of commerce, it would be unwise to put much faith in such evidence for a worsening disease pattern at that time. On the other hand, the sudden coming of Spaniards to the Philippines by way of the Americas may have brought some novel diseases to at least the more isolated communities there. This might explain what appears to be a slight decline in Philippine population between the two earliest estimates of 1591 and 1637, as well as the particularly severe "famine and pestilence" which hit Panay in 1568–70, just after the Spanish arrival, reportedly carrying off half its population ("Relation" 1572: 170). The advent of other Europeans along a route already well travelled for centuries seems not to have had a significant effect on the disease pattern.

For similar reasons, few diseases were unique to Southeast Asia. The major novelty for Europeans was beri-beri, the name of which appears to derive (despite claims for Sinhalese) from the Malay word for sheep, presumably because it weakened the limbs so that men tottered like new lambs (Bontius 1629: 1–5). The first references to the disease occur in Portuguese letters from Maluku in the mid-sixteenth century (Jacobs 1974: 254–55, 550–52), and that region continued its reputation for this scourge in the seventeenth. Since we now know that beri-beri results from a deficiency of thiamine (Vitamin B1), which is contained in the outer skin of rice and other grains, it is easy to see why the disease occurred in the non-rice-growing corners of the region where the main staple was not rice but sago.

Reasonably good information exists about the occurrence of epidemics in the seventeenth century, although it remains very difficult to isolate the diseases. The major outbreaks appear as follows in the sources:

Date	*Location*	*Description*	*Source*
1614	Kedah (Malaya)	"plague," killing ⅔ of population	Beaulieu 1666: 246
1618	Banda (Maluku)	"pestilential fever"	Reael 1618: 82
1621–22, 1622–23	Siam	"outbreak of pustules" in which many died	Terwiel 1987: 147, citing chronicles
1625–26	Java	"great epidemics"	*Babad ing Sangkala:* 35
		"chest illness," from which people died within an hour, killing ⅓ population in Banten and ⅔ in some regions of Central Java	de Graaf 1958: 131
1628	Luzon	"epidemic pest"	Velarde 1749: 47–49

Date	*Location*	*Description*	*Source*
1633	Banda	"pestilential sickness," killing many	Brouwer 1633: 397
1636	Makassar	"an epidemic raged"	*Lontara'-bilang Gowa:* 12
		"plague," 60,000 died in 40 days	Presidency Bantam 1636: 73
1643–44	Mataram (Java)	"epidemic—hundreds died each day"	*Babad ing Sangkala:* 42–45
1657	Maluku	"epidemic of mad and violent fevers"	Rumphius 1690: 98
1659	Siam	smallpox killed "a third of the population" in six months	Smith 1974: 271, citing Dutch reports
1665	Sumatra, Java, Bali, Makassar	"an epidemic raged"	*Lontara'-bilang Gowa:* 27
		"pestilence . . . very much lessened" population of Makassar	Gervaise 1701: 60
		"plague"	Turner 1665
		"many deaths" in Mataram	*Dagh-Register* 1665: 80, 149
1682	Siam	famine and smallpox kill large numbers	Japanese trade report, in Ishii 1971: 69
1685–86	Central Luzon	smallpox widespread in Asia, depopulating parts of Luzon cordillera, killing especially infants	Diaz 1718: 234; Salazar 1742: 75

There seems little doubt that the epidemics in Siam were smallpox. Pneumonic plague may possibly have been the cause of the terrible Java epidemic of 1625–26. The fierce and widespread epidemic of 1665 was specifically likened in an English report to the plague that was raging at the same time in Holland (Turner 1665); and this identification is somewhat strengthened by the fact that it was most severe in the larger cities, such as Banten, Mataram, and Makassar. Cholera of the severe *asiatica* or *morbus* form is usually regarded as not having reached Southeast Asia before the terrible pandemic of 1820–22 (Semmelink 1885; Boomgaard 1987; Terwiel 1987). The reasons for this view, as for similar opinions about bubonic plague before 1911, are not persuasive; they need to be read against the careful descriptions of what appear to be both phenomena given by Bontius (1629: 26–29).

3

Material Culture

[In] the food, beds, and houses of the Burmese, they are as parsimonious as they are splendid and extravagant in their dress. They have always in their mouths that their dress is seen by everybody; but no one comes into their houses to observe what they eat and how they are lodged.

—*Sangermano 1818: 159*

Light Houses, Noble Temples

The peoples of monsoon Asia devoted very little of their time and resources to their housing. No doubt the mild climate and the availability of fast-growing trees, palms, and bamboos as building materials were the fundamental reasons for this low priority. Because houses were so cheap to build, they were regarded as impermanent and inappropriate as the place to sink capital. Although the building materials were easy to acquire and use, they were also perishable. The thatch roof, matting walls, and split bamboo flooring would all have to be replaced within ten years, if the house had not been abandoned earlier because of fire, war, shifting cultivation, or some ill-omened death or illness (Nguyen 1934: 188). The poles of the house were not sunk into the ground but rested upon it, to ensure that the house could be bodily moved if required. La Loubère (1691, 29) saw three Siamese houses carried away "in less than an hour" to clear a view from the royal palace, while twenty houses were carried off by their occupants when a site was required in Makassar to build the English factory in 1613 (Jourdain 1617: 293).

Rebuilding a simple house was not much more onerous than removing it. Crawfurd (1820 I: 162) estimated that a house of ordinary type would never require more than sixty man-days of labour; fifty Burmese labourers built a comfortable four-roomed dwelling for

Symes (1827 I: 283) in four hours. Europeans were amazed at the speed of rebuilding the great cities after they had been devastated by fire. La Loubère (1691: 29) saw three hundred houses at Ayutthaya rebuilt in two days, and Lodewycksz (1598: 108) saw the whole coastal section of Banten rebuilt in three or four.

Although there were some specialist builders and carpenters, the basic skills of house building were widespread—"every man almost is a carpenter" (Dampier 1697: 227). Kin and neighbours exchanged labour to help erect a house. The impermanence of houses and the relative ease of building and rebuilding them are important factors in the social structure of Southeast Asia.

Despite the great variety of house-building styles among different peoples and social classes in Southeast Asia, certain common features stood out. A steep roof was made necessary by the heavy monsoonal rains, and elevation on strong wooden poles was necessitated in the first place as a protection against flooding (see fig. 6). Nothing is more characteristic of the region than this elevation, with a ladder or staircase giving access to the house. The Malay word for household is *rumah-tangga* ("house-ladder").

The extent of the elevation varied greatly, though the commonest floor heights were between one and three metres—generally higher in the islands and Siam than in Burma and Indochina. Rulers and nobles sought to be higher than their subjects, however, so that imposing royal palaces were reported as high as six metres in Mindanao and twelve metres in northern Sumatra (Dampier 1697: 225; Ma Huan 1433: 123; cf. La Loubère 1691: 165; Symes 1827 I: 218; Davis 1600: 147; Carletti 1606: 86). In the sixteenth and seventeenth centuries only the inhabitants of northern Vietnam, Java, and Bali had begun to build houses on the ground, though in earlier periods they too had used the basic pole houses (Nguyen 1934: 186; Pigeaud 1962: 509). Among southern Vietnamese and Moluccans, the other peoples who have built on the ground in modern times, the pole house was then still the rule. "Their [Cochin-Chinese] houses are so constructed that they can be opened up below to let the water pass through, and for this reason they are always perched on huge stilts" (Rhodes 1653: 44; cf. Borri 1633: D; Galvão 1544: 105). It is easy to understand why people in the most densely settled areas, where large timbers first became scarce, were the first to lower their houses to ground level.

The supporting poles also formed the central structure of the house, with a frame first lashed to them and then flooring, walls, and roofing material bound on (fig. 7). Boards were used very sparingly, to keep the building light and open. "The floors, even though they belong

Fig. 6a A simple Thai house in the wet season

Fig. 6b Village scene from an early nineteenth-century fresco in the Thonburi (Siam) temple, Wat Suwannaram

Fig. 7 A simple Visayan house, with treehouses probably used as granaries or refuges

to the *Principales* [Filipino elite] are never made of boards. This for them would be less cleanly. . . . Even though water is spilled and other filth, since [the floor] is a kind of grill work, although thick, and often one can put one's outstretched hand through it, everything falls through below" (Alcina 1668 IV: 38). Moreover, without a saw the making of planks was a laborious business of splitting logs with an axe and planing them with an adze, though "the goodness of the plank thus hewed, which hath its grain preserved entire, makes amends for their cost and pains" (Dampier 1697: 227).

Other common features of Southeast Asian houses were a cooking hearth recessed into the floor, usually at the back or women's area, and a public verandah or other room to receive visitors at the front. These two areas were often at a lower level than the central sleeping area, so that there was no single floor level for the whole house (Alcina 1668 IV: 38; La Loubère 1691: 32). The central row of poles which supported the roof ridge was of special importance ritually as well as structurally, and sacrifices or offerings were often made at one of these poles (Nguyen 1934: xii–xiv, 179; Turton 1978: 116–17).

Even some of the earliest observers were aware that the house structure had a religious as well as a practical rationale, though modern ethnography has made this much clearer. Europeans, puzzled that the single-storey, elevated pattern was seldom varied, were given explanations in terms of the sacred importance of height. Burmese explained to Sangermano (1818: 162) that it was "an indignity to lie under other people, especially under women," while Thais told La Loubère (1691: 30) that the king must not be lower than his subjects when he rode past on his elephant (though in reality he was, the Frenchman wryly observed). This ordering by height made of each house a miniature cosmos, in which the lowest level, beneath the floor, was primarily for animals and refuse (though often used also for household tasks such as weaving). The central level was for human habitation and was itself differentiated between the lower public or working areas and the higher ceremonial or sleeping ones. The most honoured place of all was in the rafters, the abode of the sacred store of rice and the place where offerings were often made to ancestors (Nguyen 1934: 471; Errington 1979: 13). The house was usually aligned along an east-west axis, with one side of it especially associated with the female and the other with the male domain (Wessing 1978: 53–59; Turton 1978: 120; Hilton 1956).

Very rarely did domestic building depart from the pattern of the wooden elevated house. The houses of nobles and rulers were built higher, larger, and more magnificent, but of similar materials. The Sultan of Aceh's palace in 1599 was "built as the rest are, but much higher" (Davis 1600: 148). The palace of the Sultan of Tidore was impressively raised on forty-six wooden pillars (van der Hagen 1607: 38), while Arung Palakka of Bone had ninety-one, Sultan Mansur of Melaka probably ninety, and the audience hall of the eighteenth-century Burmese capital seventy-seven (Valentijn 1726 III: 122; *Sejarah Melayu* 1612: 86–87; Symes 1827 I: 106). In seventeenth-century Mindanao the Sultan's house stood "on about 180 great posts or trees, a great deal higher up than the common building, with great broad stairs made to go up" (Dampier 1697: 225). The staircase was also a feature of the palace, erected on great wooden pillars in 1636 within the fortress of Sombaopu at Makassar. It was like "a long, wide bridge . . . so beautifully made that people could go up on horse as well as on foot" (1638 map cited Reid 1983B: 145; cf. *Lontara'-bilang Gowa:* 92).

If domestic architecture was light and impermanent, religious buildings were built to last. As we know from the magnificent ruins of Angkor, Pagan, and Borobodur, Southeast Asians were no strangers to the techniques of building in stone and brick, at least when their religiopolitical systems demanded the erection of timeless monuments to the glory of a king and the god with which he identified. Islam in the south and Theravada Buddhism in the north had new priorities, while the growing role of international commerce subverted that extraordinary autocracy which had directed surplus resources to royal religious monuments. So greatly did building styles change that by the seventeenth century "the old Siamese histories testify that [Angkor] was so exquisite and ingenious that no human being could have built it. Therefore, they say that angels from heaven came to help in building this magnificent city in Cambodia" (van Vliet 1640: 60).

Temples and tombs continued to be built from brick and stone, though on a much more modest scale. The gilt-covered stupas containing relics of the Buddha were the most ambitious Southeast Asian buildings of our period, while Ayutthaya (fig. 8), Pegu, and other Buddhist capitals were decorated with numerous public temples constructed of bricks and mortar, with decorative tiles on the roof (Frederici 1581: 249; Schouten 1636: 125; La Loubère 1691: 31–32). Mosques were typically constructed of wood and thatch, but in the great mosques of Melaka and Aceh at least the foundations and outer walls were made of stone and mortar (Albuquerque 1557 III: 136; Dampier 1699: 90). In the mosques and holy tombs of Java, roofs continued to be tiled, and brickwork in styles reminiscent of Majapahit to be used for gateways, minarets, and outer walls (van Neck 1599: 87), as can still be seen in Cirebon, Demak, Kudus, Ampel, and Sendangduwur (and see figs. 10a and 10b).

Despite these and other obvious continuities with a Hindu-Javanese past, the Southeast Asian mosque of the sixteenth and seventeenth centuries had its own distinctive form, essentially similar from Aceh in the west to Maluku and Mindanao in the east. The main building was square, often with a veranda (*serambi*) added on the east side, light walls, and (usually four) massive wooden pillars supporting a multitiered thatch roof (figs. 9a and 9b). A strong masonry wall usually surrounded the whole complex. The origins of this pattern have been much debated, in particular as to whether the multitiered roof was a continuation of Hindu-Javanese representations of Mount Meru, such as can still be seen in Bali (Guillot 1985: 8–11; Candrasasmita 1985: 204–06), or whether it owed more to the Muslim

Fig. 8 Ordination hall of Wat Na Phra Men, at Ayutthaya, one of the best-preserved monastic buildings of the Ayutthayan period

Chinese builders who were thought to be particularly influential in fifteenth-century Demak and Japara (Slametmuljana 1976: 244–47; de Graaf and Pigeaud 1984: 28–29, 179–80). Chinese builders may well have assisted with several major mosques, but a similar mosque style would not have been accepted throughout the Archipelago in the sixteenth century unless it had successfully incorporated older religious and architectural patterns.

Nevertheless, the presence of large numbers of Chinese, Western Asians, and Europeans in Southeast Asian ports after 1500 certainly extended the use of brick. The major mosque of Patani was built by Chinese labour at the end of the sixteenth century (van Neck 1604: 22), and it was exceptional: "a stately edifice of brickwork, gilt very richly within, and adorned with pillars, curiously wrought with figures" (Nieuhoff 1662: 218). Siamese rulers of the seventeenth century had numerous palace buildings built of brick, probably on foreign

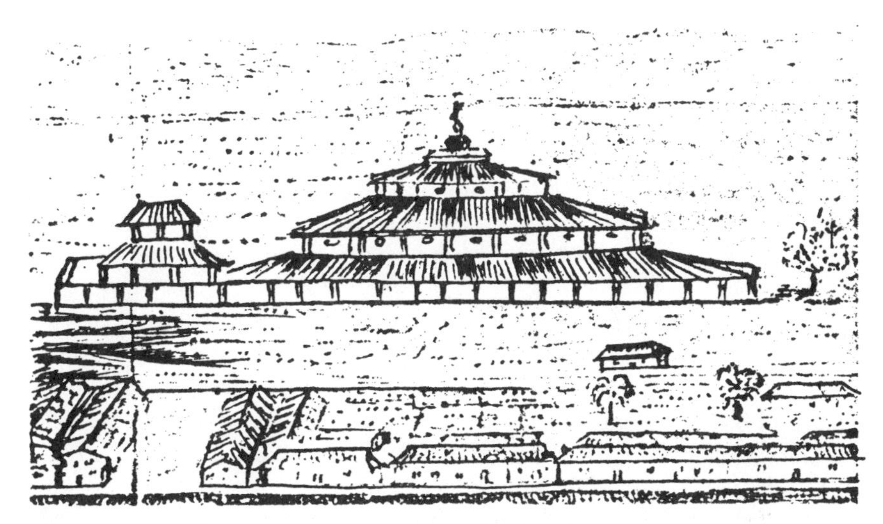

Fig. 9a View of the great mosque of Aceh, sketched about 1650. Fig. 24 is a contemporary rendering of the same mosque.

Fig. 9b A traditional Acehnese mosque (Sumatra), photographed in the late nineteenth century

suggestion, even though this cannot have been as comfortable as their accustomed wood (La Loubère 1691: 31). In the middle of the seventeenth century the ruler and leading nobles of both Banten and Aceh also appear to have built themselves solid brick edifices (Fryke 1692: 60; de Graaff 1701: 12–13). Stone and mortar found further uses in the ingenious representations of mountain and sea in the pleasure gardens where Southeast Asian kings went for spiritual and physical refreshment (Brakel 1975: 60–61; Lombard 1974; Dumarcay 1982; Eredia 1613: 24–25).

Roof tiles were used more widely than bricks. In Angkor the wealthy elite were already using them in the thirteenth century (Chou Ta-kuan 1297: 12–13), and the practice was continued in Cambodian, Thai, and Burmese palaces. The roof of the *mahligai* palace of Melaka was decorated with gleaming copper and tin (*Sejarah Melayu* 1612: 138).

If in life even kings preferred the comfort and coolness of wood, in death they sought abiding monuments. In Melaka the Portuguese were able to find stone enough to build their great fortress A Famosa by tearing down "some ancient sepulchres of bygone kings" and the walls and foundations of the mosques (Albuquerque 1557: 136). Van Neck (1599: 87) found the stone royal sepulchre adjacent to the mosque "certainly the strongest and noblest building that I have seen in Banten."

The virtually universal use of impermanent wood, thatch, and palm for domestic building appears to have sprung in the first place from a natural preference for a cool, open airiness. Numerous outsiders reported, however, that the habit resulted from a ban placed on buildings of stone or brick by various Southeast Asian kings. Most of the stronger courts probably reserved certain styles for royalty. The first Islamic ruler of Melaka prohibited any but royal buildings from having enclosed verandas (*Sejarah Melayu* 1612: 54), while in Ayutthaya only royal or religious buildings could be gilded or painted (van Vliet 1636: 83). The rule followed in eighteenth-century Burma that each rank of society must build according to prescribed forms, with tiled roofs reserved for the higher ranks (Sangermano 1818: 161; Symes 1827 I: 282), appears to have existed five centuries earlier in Cambodia (Chou Ta-kuan 1297: 12–13). But it was probably the challenge of Europeans which gave rise to a complete prohibition of all building in permanent materials by anyone but the king.

Before 1600 observers are unanimous in stating that although domestic buildings were all of the impermanent type, merchants in the cities built warehouses of brick to preserve their trade goods from

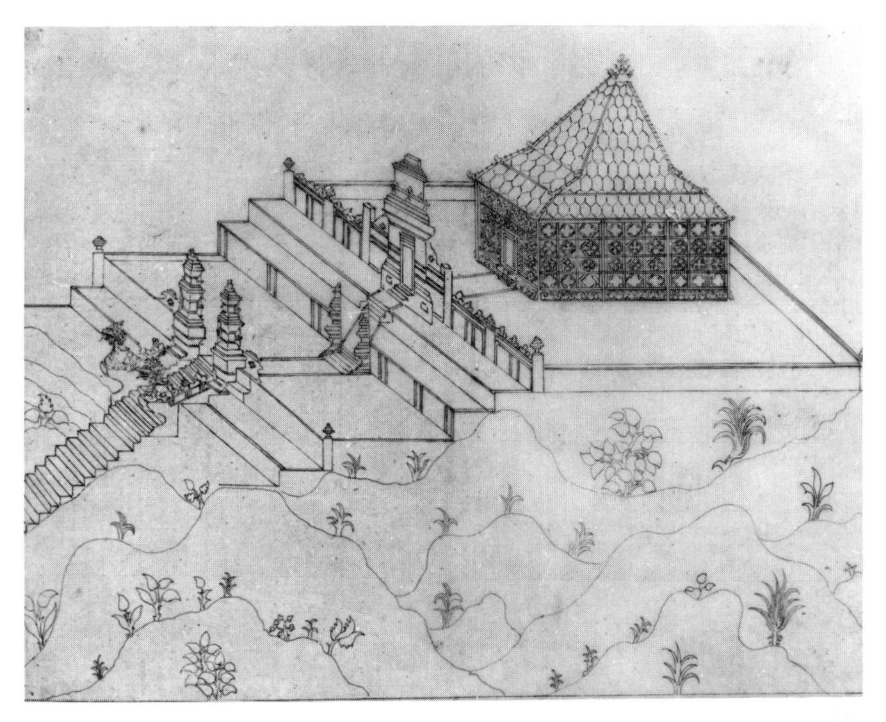

Fig. 10a Sixteenth-century grave of Sunan Giri, on sacred hill near Gresik, Java; pencil sketch from 1840s

Fig. 10b Surakarta mosque, from a pencil sketch of 1847

fire. Ma Huan (1433: 87) noted of Java: "Every family has a store-room built of bricks in the ground. It is three or four *ch'ih* (93–124 cm) in height; (in this) they store the private belongings of the family; upon this they live, sit and sleep." This was a reference to the half-submerged storehouses called in Malay gudang, from which comes the English word *godown*. The Portuguese observed them in Melaka and the ports of Burma in the early sixteenth century—"*gudôes*, subterranean buildings in which the merchants stored the cloths from Coromandel to ensure against fire" (Eredia 1613: 32; cf. Barros 1563 II: ii, 55; Albuquerque 1557: 127; Frederici 1581: 244–45; Bouchon 1979: 141). In Banten around 1600 all substantial merchants still used such gudang for their merchandise, while the Chinese quarter of the city was built predominantly of brick (Scott 1606: 169–70; Lodewycksz 1598: 108).

European traders, however, were constantly trying to expand these small, windowless warehouses into redoubts which could withstand not only fire but also armed attack. The rulers of Aceh and Banten at first allowed the English and Dutch, as they had the Portuguese, to buy or build gudang of a relatively generous type. Dutch attempts to build a larger one in 1604, "appropriate for turning into a fort on an opportunity," aroused great suspicion in Banten (Warwijck 1604: 53; cf. l'Hermite 1612: 384). The Dutch were more successful in neighbouring Jakatra (Batavia), where they obtained permission to build a two-storey stone building in 1615 and fortified it without permission in 1618 (Masselman 1963: 321–22, 360–85). Sultan Agung, much the strongest ruler in Java, presciently remarked, "Jacatra hath a thorne in her foote, which [I] must take the pains to pluck out, for fear the whole body should be endangered. This thorn is, the castle of the Hollanders, who have now so fortified themselves (through bribery) that they regard not the king nor his country, but set him at defiance" (cited Pring 1619). In the event the Dutch proved impossible even for Sultan Agung to dislodge or control. No ruler would make the same mistake again. The English in Banten complained later that the sultan was "fearful to let us build a new house, in remembrance of the first entrance of the Dutch in Jacatra, unless we will build one side of brick and the other of timber" (Willoughby 1636). In Makassar, similarly, the Portuguese and English were forbidden "to place one stone upon another" (cited Boxer 1967: 30) or even to use tiles on their roofs (Macassar factory 1659). In Perak the Dutch attempt to construct a stone building in 1651 provoked such hostility that twenty-seven Dutchmen there were murdered (B. Andaya 1979: 46).

Once this lesson was learned by Southeast Asian rulers, it seems to have been applied to subjects as well as foreigners. Indeed, the more a trading family or enterprise made itself a part of the local scene, the less it would be trusted to build a defensible stronghold. In eighteenth-century Burma foreign merchants were sometimes permitted to build in brick but Burmese notables never were, to ensure that "if treason or other capital crimes be detected, the criminals may have no place to shelter" (Hamilton 1727: 26; also Symes 1827 II: 11–21, 100; Sangermano 1818: 162). If we can believe Beaulieu, who recorded the events thirty years after they occurred, the ban on permanent buildings in Aceh arose from a particular royal coup against the powerful merchant-aristocrats who had dominated that city-state until 1589. These *orangkaya*, who had allegedly made the sultan their plaything, had had "beautiful, large, well-secured houses, with cannons at their doors." A new ruler, Ala'ud-din Riayat Shah al-Mukammil (1589–1604), massacred most of these men by a stratagem. Then "he had all the houses of the executed *orangkaya* demolished, took their cannon, arms, and most of their furniture into the castle; forbade anyone to build in stone, to have cannon at their houses, or to make defensive trenches within or without. . . . He provided an example of how future houses should be built, which was of only one storey, with matting walls, as they are today" (Beaulieu 1666: 110–12). In reality the change cannot have been quite so sudden and dramatic, since most houses had always been of the simple, impermanent type. Beaulieu's account nevertheless reinforces the impression that the use made by belligerent Europeans (and perhaps also Turks, Gujeratis, Japanese, and others) of defensible buildings hardened Southeast Asian opinion against them. One of the consequences of this trend was to widen the gulf between the ruler in his walled palace compound and the mass of his subjects living in comfortable but insubstantial houses.

Furniture and Lighting

Houses were furnished as simply as they were built. Since eating was done on the floor, chairs and tables were unknown until introduced to the elite by Chinese and Europeans. Chou Ta-kuan (1297: 31) noted that low tables had been "recently introduced" to Cambodia, and the Dutch were entertained on a few chairs in the Moluccas in 1599 ("Tweede Boeck" 1601: 67). The words for these novelties were borrowed from Chinese or Portuguese. Beds were more common, in the form of elevated benches or platforms in wealthier homes—though many preferred simply to unroll a mat on the floor.

Cutlery was similarly unnecessary, and banana leaves usually served as plates. The chief utensils required in the ordinary house were earthenware rice cookers, bamboo and ceramic containers, and brass betel sets, kettles, and trays.

Distinctions of wealth and status became apparent in the display of textiles and gold dishes. On important occasions or when entertaining guests, wealthy houses were hung with sumptuous cloths (Pigafetta 1524: 57; Albuquerque 1557: 107; Davis 1600: 148). "The rich," the Dutch noted in Banten (*Verhael* 1597: 23), "have their rooms all partitioned with curtains of silk or of cotton cloth." The house provided for French envoys in Ayutthaya had its walls "hung with painted cloth, with ceilings of white Muslin" (La Loubère 1691: 30). A whole street in the Vietnamese capital was ornamented with silk cloth on the occasion of an important reception (Nguyen 1970: 93). The floors of the wealthy were similarly covered with rich carpets, cushions, and mats. The reduction in status of Prince Muzaffer of Bintan around 1520 was noted in the Malay chronicle by the removal of the cushion, sitting mat, and rug on which he had been accustomed to sit. "He was left with nothing to sit upon except a mat such as ordinary people use" (*Sejarah Melayu* 1612: 171). Royal courts vied with one another in the opulence of their textiles, and still more in the size and number of the gold dishes on which they could serve a feast (Pigafetta 1524: 29, 58; Lancaster 1603: 131; *Sejarah Melayu* 1612: 187).

In a region where evening was the pleasantest time of day and feasts and entertainments frequently ended at dawn, efficient means of lighting were essential. Wax candles appear to have been less used than oil-burning lamps. The forests produced a variety of inflammable oils and resins, obtained from the nut of the *kemiri* tree in eastern Indonesia (Gervaise 1701: 20), and from *damar* (the resin of various dipterocarps) in Burma and the western Archipelago. During special feasts whole towns would be ablaze with lights, and burning lamps in coconut shells would be left to float down the river or out to sea (La Loubère 1691: 48; Shway Yoe 1882: 225–26; Galvão 1544: 87).

Southeast Asia possessed two ancient sites where petroleum flowed close enough to the surface to be trapped in wells (see map 4). Each would in time become the foundation of a great modern oil enterprise, though in the age of commerce the petroleum was used chiefly in lighting. The wells of Yenangyaung in Central Burma were producing several hundred tons a day in the eighteenth century, which was transported up and down the Irrawaddy to provide lighting for "the whole empire [of Burma] and many parts of India" (Symes 1827 I:

301–02; also Cox 1821: 33–45). Similarly, much of northern Sumatra drew its lighting oil from natural flows at Perlak, which enriched the kingdom of Pasai and later Aceh (Eredia 1600: 238; Barros 1563 II: ii, 34; III: ii, 277). This oil was regarded as such a natural wonder that Acehnese chroniclers saw it as a sign of God's special blessing on their country (*Hikayat Aceh* 1630: 164), while an early Dutch scientist thought it a remarkable remedy for beri-beri, too good to burn (Bontius 1629: 4–5).

The Body Beautiful

> *His body was yellow as polished gold and his hair curly as a headdress of flowers. His hands arched backward in a sharp angle, his shoulders were broad and straight as those of a* wayang *puppet, his waist was so narrow that you could span it between thumb and forefinger, and his thighs were like those of a molecricket sitting astride a grasshopper. He strode like a strutting peacock.*
>
> —*Hikayat Banjar: 365*

The body itself was the first and most important medium of art. To decorate it distinguished the adult, conscious human from the animal or the child. If it was important for all to keep the body clean, sweet smelling, and attractive, entry into adulthood entailed decoration and artifice, often of a painful kind.

The filing and blackening of teeth was the most universal Southeast Asian device of this type. The Burmese, noted Fitch (1591: 309), "say a dog hath his teeth white, and so they will blacken theirs"; the Vietnamese took exactly the same view (Dampier 1699: 34). Not only savage and despised animals had long white teeth, but also the demons of the spirit world. Thus a part of the rationale for the filing and blackening of teeth in ceremonies at the time of puberty was to ensure that one would not be mistaken at death for an evil spirit (Covarrubias 1937: 135; Forth 1981: 164; Gervaise 1688: 113). Throughout Indonesia and the Philippines teeth were filed at puberty, though methods ranged from modestly trimming the front teeth in Bali to drastically shortening all of them in parts of Sumatra. Tooth filing was not practised in Mainland Southeast Asia, but the blackening of the teeth with various vegetable dyes was as popular in Burma, Siam, and Vietnam as in the islands. The constant chewing of betel helped to keep the teeth the admired dark colour, but younger people conscious of their appearance always sought the jet black produced by additional dyes (Marsden 1783: 52–53; La Loubère 1691: 29).

The boring and distending of the earlobes was another embellishment practised by both men and women, especially by those of the upper class who could afford to fill the enormous hole that was eventually created with elaborate gold ornaments. Cambodian statuary of the classical Angkor period suggests that "the further distended the lobes, the more elevated the man in the social hierarchy" (Frédéric 1981: 250). A Burmese king's ears were described as hanging down "half a palm" because of the weight of jewels in them (Varthema 1510: 220). The practice of stretching the earlobes until they nearly touched the shoulder was shared with ancient India. We should not assume that it was introduced from India, however, since the least Indianized Southeast Asians, in the interior of Borneo and the central Philippines, were among the most committed to it. Alcina (1668A: 20) described as follows the way the ears were distended in the Visayas, and similar methods applied elsewhere in the Archipelago, as opposed to the puberty ritual more characteristic of the Mainland:

> Even newborn male and female babies or those of one or two years have holes pierced in their ears usually with a needle or wire. . . . A twist of rather thick cotton thread is left in the tiny hole until the wound is healed. Then with bamboo or another wood that will keep dry, they make little rammers which they thrust into the hole. These they take care to change from time to time, each time with a gradually bigger one until it is possible to thrust the little finger into the hole. Then they get the leaf of a tree . . . let the leaf dry somewhat then they cut a piece about three fingers long. . . . The rolled leaf they then put into the hole in the ear. . . . The leaf unrolls from its unnatural state with a force so moderate it is not felt at all. . . . The hole is made progressively larger until . . . the hole is big enough for any of the earrings. . . . These earrings they keep changing and gradually enlarging until the hole in the ear is so big that the skin hangs lower than the chin.

As with many other bodily adornments in Southeast Asia, such ear ornaments were equally popular with men and women up to at least the fourteenth century. Extensive intercourse with Muslims and Europeans seems subsequently to have discouraged the practice, particularly for men. Lowland Thai and Javanese men, as well as Malays and others who became Muslim, had abandoned the practice by the seventeenth century. Burmese men and women all wore rolls of thin gold plate in their ears in the eighteenth century (Sangermano 1818: 158; Cox 1821: 3), but the men were abandoning them a century later. The first ear boring continued to be the major coming-of-age ritual for Burmese women (Shway Yoe 1882: 48–51) and a matter of pride for Balinese girls (Covarrubias 1937: 115–16), but only in the more isolated areas, such as Borneo and the Batak area of Sumatra, did men also demonstrate their adult status and their wealth by wearing large ornaments in their earlobes.

Tattooing is another of the bodily art forms characteristic of Southeast Asia, and of course of those Austronesian peoples who left it to people the South Pacific. Probably most Southeast Asian peoples used tattoos extensively at some time in their history. The influence of Confucianism, Islam, and Christianity eliminated the practice from many lowland areas in the age of commerce, however. The Vietnamese state prohibited tattooing as barbarous in the fourteenth century, while Catholic friars drove it from the Visayas and Bikol, where it had been much practised until the seventeenth century (Colin 1663: 63–64). Islam was even more opposed to such magical representations. The Muslim Acehnese had to extirpate tattooing among the North Sumatrans they converted. One of their codes of the seventeenth century, the *Sirat al-Mustakim*, declared, "It is obligatory to abandon . . . the marking of the skin by tattooing with a needle to the point of drawing blood and putting into it indigo or something similar" (cited Veltman 1919: 21). There is no evidence of tattooing among Muslim Malays or Javanese. It may be that the unique Javanese form of cloth dyeing known as *batik*, which began as a process of dotting a wax resist on the cloth, was a replacement for tattooing as a talisman and status marker. "Batik" is the most common word for tattooing in East Indonesian and Philippine languages, and both in its motifs and its ritual functions the Javanese batik evoked the tattooing of other peoples (Wurm and Wilson 1983: 214; Jasper and Pirngadie 1916: 7–8).

The primary function of tattooing in Southeast Asia appears to have been talismanic. The Javanese and Malay fascination with *rajah*, or magically powerful designs (Pigeaud 1967: 268–73), may also be connected with earlier uses of tattoos. Powerful beasts, esoteric patterns, and religious formulae conferred on the body special powers, such as invulnerability (Sangermano 1818: 148; Fitch 1591: 308–09; Shway Yoe 1882: 41–47; Terwiel 1980: 64; Forth 1981: 165). Tattooing was also frequently a mark of bravery and therefore a rite of passage for the young male. In the Philippines (fig. 11), "no tattooing was begun until some brave deed had been performed; and after that, for each one of the parts of the body which was tattooed, some new deed had to be performed" (Colin 1663: 64; cf. Ellis 1981: 249). Similarly in Borneo, particular tattoos appear to have been reserved for the successful headhunter (Rutter 1929: 117–19).

While some of the major lowland states deplored tattooing as a savage custom, others adopted it as a convenient marker of status.

Fig. 11 Tattooing in the Visayas, about 1590

Both in sixteenth-century Burma (Fitch 1591: 309) and in seventeenth-century Siam (La Loubère 1691: 27–28) the characteristic "trouser" covering of hips and legs with tattoo (fig. 12) appeared to be reserved for the upper classes. Distinctive tattoos were also legally required for slaves and state bondsmen in both countries (Lieberman 1984: 41, 105; Terwiel 1983: 124). As a means of ensuring that each man stayed in his allotted place, tattooing was even more reliable than sumptuary laws on clothes.

Fig. 12 Northern Thai dress and tattooing of the male legs, from a mural of nineteenth-century Wat Phra Sing, Chiengmai. Female hairstyles were closer to those of Burma than of Central Thailand.

Hair

Two themes stand out as central in the way Southeast Asians regarded that most variable part of the body—their hair. There was little distinction between men and women in hairstyles (fig. 13), and for both, hair was a crucial symbol and emanation of the self. Carrying

Fig. 13 An eighteenth-century sketch of a Burmese peasant and his wife

some of the power of the person concerned, hair was much used in magic. The hair clippings of rulers were treasured because they contained a little of the inherent power of sovereignty. Enormous care was given to the care of the hair, to ensure that it was always black, lustrous, abundant, and sweet smelling. Rhodes (1653: 157) remarked perceptively that Vietnamese loved their hair "as much as their heads," and it may well be that hair shared some of the sacred primacy of the head in Southeast Asian belief. In Thai the word for hair (*phom*) has become the commonest first-person pronoun.

For this reason the pattern up to the age of commerce appears to have been for both sexes to encourage the hair to grow as long and abundantly as possible. In Burma (Shway Yoe 1882: 72), the Philippines (Alcina 1668A: 18), and no doubt elsewhere it was common to add hairpieces to increase the luxuriant effect. "Both men and women, universally, consider that the hair should be very black and well cared for. For that purpose they use lotions made of certain tree-barks and oils" (Colin 1663: 60; cf. Raffles 1817: 89–90; Valentijn 1726 III: 308).

The cutting off of the hair, therefore, was not so much a sign of repressed sexuality or castration, as has been argued (Berg 1951; Leach 1958), as it was a sacrifice of the self. Alcina (1668A: 18) said of Philippine women, "The greatest pain they can experience is to have their hair taken away or cut. Thus their greatest demonstration of sorrow consists in cutting off their hair . . . a sign that they are mourning the loss of well-loved parents or husband . . . for some religious motive or for bidding the world goodbye." The ceremonial cutting of Arung Palakka's long hair in 1672 after his triumph over Makassar (Andaya 1981: 148; Matthes 1875: 67), and of Susuhunan Pakubuwana I's in 1715 (Ricklefs 1978: 195), can probably be explained in terms of vows to make such a sacrifice in return for divine favour. The cutting or shaving of the hair of subjects, especially court women at the death of the monarch, as was reported of seventeenth-century Aceh, Patani, Siam, and Johor (Mundy 1667: 131; *Hikayat Patani*: 106; Bowrey 1680: 311; Groeneveldt 1880: 135; Ibrahim 1688: 129), may have represented symbolically the sacrifice which in pre-Islamic days would have been made in human lives.

Prior to the acceptance of Islam and Christianity, the differences between male and female hairstyles appear to have been so minor as not to have emphasized sexual distinctiveness. Age status was more sharply distinguished. In parts of island Southeast Asia where the hair of adults remained long until modern times, it was important that children's hair be cut very short—the first time being accompanied by a solemn ritual (Forth 1981: 157–59; Covarrubias 1937: 129–30; Skeat 1900: 44). In Cambodia and Siam, on the other hand, when adults adopted a new short style, unmarried women were distinguished by hair which fell to their shoulders (La Loubère 1691: 28; Aymonier 1900: 30).

For the social historian, the most important and intriguing development is the move in the sixteenth and seventeenth centuries from long to short hair—for men in the island world influenced by Islam and Christianity and for both sexes in Cambodia and Siam. Given the prior association of long hair with adulthood and spiritual potency, this shift can probably be seen as symptomatic of a changed attitude to sexuality, placing greater importance on the ideal of sexual restraint and on the exaggerated distinction (among Muslims and Christians) between men and women (cf. Leach 1958: 153; Firth 1973: 262–67).

Certainly the cutting of men's hair became an important symbol of adherence to Islam. The earliest Javanese Islamic exhortation extant, which dates from the sixteenth century, anathematized any Muslim neophyte who refused the advice of the learned to shave his head and wear a turban "in the manner of the Messenger of God" ("Javanese Code": 34–35). When an Islamic envoy from Mecca presented a sixteenth-century Balinese prince with scissors and shaving gear, the prince realized that this was an invitation to convert and responded by smashing the gift to pieces (Drewes 1978: 66). Urban Malays, whose ethnic identity by the sixteenth century was inseparable from Islam, adopted short male hair with a head cloth as their national style, and those who embraced Islam anywhere in urban Southeast Asia accepted this style as an inherent part of conversion. The Chinese Muslims of Banten, for example, were known as "shorn Chinese" because they had abandoned the long Ming style. "And if once they cut their haire, they may never returne to their countrie againe" (Scott 1606: 176).

The mass conversion of Java and South Sulawesi on a top-down basis did not have the same effect. Long hair was still the norm for Javanese, Bugis, and most Makassarese until the nineteenth century, and even in Islamic Aceh many people continued to believe that it represented a special potency (*Hikayat Pocut Muhamat*: 233). Everywhere, however, those who wished to demonstrate a stricter adherence to Islam, such as religious students or crusading warriors, made a point of cutting their hair. The nineteenth-century Javanese rebel against the Dutch, Diponegoro, made his followers distinguish themselves in this way from the "apostate" Javanese on the Dutch side (Carey 1981: 254; cf. Lennon 1796: 296).

Despite the long-haired male fashion which returned to Europe in the seventeenth century, Christian missionaries gradually imposed a similar short-haired conformity on male Filipinos and Chinese who converted (Alcina 1668A: 18–19; Chirino 1606: 307, 324). The change which affected both sexes in Siam and Cambodia is more mysterious. The characteristic "brush" effect still in vogue in both countries in the nineteenth century, achieved by cutting the top hair about three centimetres long and close-shaving the sides, has been blamed on Khmer influence in Siam and on Siamese influence in Cambodia (Terwiel 1980: 40; Aymonier 1900: 30). It is certain that styles did change in both countries more than once, yet at no point was there a significant difference between male and female. In the Angkor period and in the Thai kingdoms prior to Ayutthaya the dominant mode for the aristocracy appears to have been to roll the hair into a bun, ornamented in various ways according to rank (Chou Ta-kuan 1297: 13; Frédéric

1981: 247–48; Terwiel 1980: 39–41). At the end of the sixteenth century Cambodians were still described as having long hair, "but not as long as the Chinese" (San Antonio 1604: 8), while by 1647 they appear to have adopted the brushlike short style of the next few centuries (Pelliot 1951: 158). Most seventeenth-century observers of Ayutthaya (van Vliet 1636: 84; La Loubère 1691: 28; Kaempfer 1727: 69) describe the short bristly cut for both sexes, while the Chiengmai Chronicle (115) places in the fifteenth century (perhaps anachronistically) a tale of a Chiengmai spy who had to cut his hair very short in order to be unobtrusive in Ayutthaya. Ibrahim (1688: 56) claims, however, that only the poor in Ayutthaya had "no hair at all," while the wealthy aristocrats competed for the most elaborate hairstyles.

It seems reasonable to conclude that the close-cropped brush look (see figs. 14a and 14b) was initially imposed on Cambodians (probably first) and Thais as a mark of inferior status, perhaps associated with the vast number of Cambodian captives, including some Thais previously captured by Cambodia, who helped repopulate Siam in the 1590s. Subsequent kings may then have adopted it as the "national style." The association of short hair with slave status appeared still to apply in Burma around 1700 (Hamilton 1727: 28). Whatever the real reason, later Muslim and Christian writers found it necessary to look for fanciful explanations for the very short hair of Thai women, which they found "unnatural." One Malay *hikayat* attributed the style to a king of Siam enraged at having found a long hair in his rice (Ricklefs and Voorhoeve 1977: 100), while another story alleged that it had been adopted to trick Burmese attackers into believing that the women left behind in a besieged city were male warriors (Smith 1946: 80).

Islam and Christianity were the main, but not the only, factors in the gradual abandonment of long hair, tattooing, and elongated earlobes during the sixteenth and seventeenth centuries. The very long fingernails affected by the nonlabouring classes, which were strongly disapproved by Islam and Christianity, also began to wane during the same period (Drewes 1978: 66; Borri 1633: F). Although these changes were often made in the name of the universal religions, they may be considered part of a process of secularization commonly associated with rapid urbanization. The body began to be seen less as a source of magical potency to be sharply differentiated from the natural world of animals, and more as a neutral and natural vehicle for a transcendent soul. As in many other fields, this transition to modern attitudes began in the age of commerce but was subsequently frozen or retarded by the decay of Southeast Asian city life.

Fig. 14a Thai male hair style in the mid-nineteenth century, as worn by a high official

Fig. 14b Thai female hair style worn by King Mongkut's queen. Women shaved the sides of the head less closely than men, but trimmed a circle very short around the tuft. A woman's hair was sometimes likened to an open lotus.

Clothing

> *After his meal he would don his sarong and he would undo it twelve or thirteen times until he had got it to his liking. Then would come the jacket and the head-cloth, and the process with the sarong would be repeated with them until they too were to his liking. With the scarf also the same thing would happen . . . he would get as far as the door of his house when he would go back to his wife and ask her if there was anything amiss with his clothes.*
>
> —*Sejarah Melayu 1612: 127*

The great care lavished on personal appearance extended to clothing and especially jewellery. Wealth was most extravagantly displayed on these two items, and even the poor made great efforts to appear elegantly dressed on important occasions (Sangermano 1818: 159; Finlayson 1826: 373). Europeans were frequently astonished at the way seemingly ordinary Southeast Asians presented themselves with hundreds of dollars' worth of gold on their persons (Alcina 1668A: 21–22; MacMicking 1851: 134). Rulers made a bigger impact, like the Sultan of Ternate who met Drake in sumptuous gold-thread clothes, gold jewellery, and a massive necklace "of perfect gold" (Drake 1580: 70), or like the Sultan of Johor in 1606: "Round his neck hung three golden chains studded with jewels, round his left arm were two thick golden bracelets and one round his right arm. In addition he wore six exquisite rings on his fingers, and he also wore a dagger at his side, made in a peculiar way and called *kris*. Its hilt and sheath were made of pure hammered gold studded with many diamonds, rubies and sapphires, which led the Dutch to estimate this dagger at some 50,000 guilders" (Verken 1606, cited Kratz 1981: 70).

Despite such extravagance, the difference in dress between rich and poor, servant and master, king and commoner, was less marked than in preindustrial Europe, where each man's station and even vocation could be read in the prescribed style of dress (Sennet 1977). "In Pegu," wrote Frederici (1581: 268), "the fashion of their apparel is all one as well the noble man as the simple: the only difference is in the fineness of the cloth." Sumptuary laws frequently reserved certain colours or patterns for various grades of the nobility, as well as dictating the extent to which gold jewellery could be worn. The Malay prohibition on the use of yellow by commoners is attributed to the first Islamic ruler of Melaka in the early fifteenth century (*Sejarah Melayu* 1612: 54; Pires 1515: 265), though it undoubtedly continued older Southeast Asian associations of gold with kingship (Symes 1827 I: 300; Brugière 1829: 192).The items of clothing themselves were the same for all, however, to the surprise of Western observers ("Relation" 1572: 1666; Mandelslo 1662: 115; Ibrahim 1688: 56).

To all visitors to Southeast Asia, whether from Europe, China, or Western Asia, the "nakedness" of the inhabitants came as something of a shock. By this they meant that Southeast Asians almost invariably had bare feet, bare heads (except Muslims and some nobles), and frequently were also naked above the waist (figs. 15a and 15b). To the Spanish it seemed peculiarly galling that "a wretched, little, naked, barefooted Moro"—the sultan of Aceh—should be giving the Portuguese a hard time on the battlefield (Sande 1576: 65). Whether they were ogling the Cambodian girls' "breasts of milky whiteness," like Chou Ta-kuan (1297: 15), or attempting to cover them up, like the Spanish friars in the Philippines, outsiders tended to see such a display of flesh as something primitive and wanton. More careful observers noticed that in fact Southeast Asians were exceedingly modest—"the most scrupulous in the world"—about their genitals. French sailors had to be provided with sarongs before the Siamese would let them swim in the river (La Loubère 1691: 26).

Sewn garments with sleeves or legs appear to have made a late entry into Southeast Asia, with the exception of Vietnam. When the Portuguese arrived, tunics were being worn only by Muslims or those in close contact with them (notably the Tagalogs), by upper-class Burmese, and otherwise only as a rarity here and there by those who could afford to buy them. Two reasons for this may have been the mild climate and the limited dispersion of the techniques of needlework. The acceptance of sewn tunics was also slowed, however, by the survival of the sense that the body itself was a work of art. Long after the advent of sewn garments and even machine-made shirts, Javanese, Balinese, and Thais left as much as possible of the upper body bare for formal occasions, oiling the skin with perfumed and coloured cosmetics. Crawfurd (1820 I: 29) could still say of the Javanese that "when in full dress, they are almost naked." Similarly, at nineteenth-century South Sulawesi weddings the groom still wore no jacket, while the bride and other unmarried women wore a *baju* (tunic) so transparent that it concealed nothing (Valentijn 1723 III: 118; Brooke 1848: 81). On festive occasions even the *kebaya*, the loose upper garment which Malay women appear to have picked up from the Portuguese (Winstedt 1935: 98), was usually of transparent material.

Children were left naked for their first six to nine years, save for a medallion or *cache-sexe* hung in front of their genitals. Thereafter the basic garment for both men and women was an unsewn strip of cloth wound one or more times around the body. Women sometimes (es-

Fig. 15a Dress of an ordinary Javanese man and woman (left) going to market in Banten, and of a wealthier Javanese merchant with his servant (right), as represented by a Dutch engraver on the basis of the description in Lodewycksz 1598

Fig. 15b Dress of an ordinary Thai woman and child

pecially after Islam) hoisted it up under the armpits to cover the breasts; elsewhere they tucked it around the waist like men. Thai and Burmese men (in a later period also Thai women) brought the end of the cloth between the legs and tucked it in at the waist in the manner of the Indian *dhoti*. Burmese women wrapped their cloth only once around the body, so that it opened when walking to show the leg up to the thigh (fig. 13). Numerous early European observers made much of the indecency of this practice, and ascribed it to an early queen anxious to divert Burmese men away from homosexual proclivities (Frederici 1581: 269; Sangermano 1818: 157–58). Like many such tales, this tells us more about European attitudes than Burmese.

In Java up to the advent of Islam, in Siam until the eighteenth century, and in Cambodia, Bali, and Lombok till even more recently, the standard addition to the wraparound *sarung* for women was a loose scarf, generally draped over the breasts with the two ends slung over the shoulders (Pigeaud 1962: 158; La Loubère 1691: 26; Zollinger 1847: 334). With the coming of Islam the women of Java appear to have made greater use of another garment also found in ancient India—a narrow strip of cloth wrapped tightly around the chest, depressing the breasts (*Verhael* 1597: 29; Crawfurd 1820 I: 210; and see fig. 15a).

This basic pattern of Southeast Asian dress was being transformed in diverse ways between the fifteenth and seventeenth centuries. The appetite for innovation, in dress as in every other sphere, was characteristic of the period of trade and urban growth. A Pegu chronicle relates of the reign of Queen Shinsawbu (1453–72) that foreign merchants arrived in great numbers and "unusual wearing apparel became abundant and the people had fine clothes" (cited Lieberman 1984: 26). The Malay annals claim a more active role for Sultan Mahmud of Melaka (1488–1511) in sending a mission to South India to obtain forty varieties of rare cloths (*Sejarah Melayu* 1612: 140–41). European traders (like the Indians and Chinese before them) were pressed by the court elite for further novelties: "It is strange to see the earnest emulation of these [Banten] Princes to procure rarities that others have not, to impress conceit of greatness in the vulgar. . . . No price shall stumble them for ornaments if liked, rings, jewels, antique pieces of plate" (Hawley 1627: 374). European cloth could not rival Indian or Chinese in appeal, but some of the elaborately made upper garments did find a market. Three hundred Spanish dollars' worth of "waistcoats sold at Banten" were recorded for 1633 by the English (*SP 1630–34*: 449).

A frequent innovation was to sport a jacket of European or West Asian design over an expensive cloth used as a traditional sarong. The effect seemed incongruous to observers like Navarrete (1676 I: 116), who met the rulers of Makassar wearing "European cloth coats over their bare skins, their arms naked . . . and their bellies uncovered after their fashion." More comfortable local variations of these sewn garments were soon devised. It is not too much to say that most of the national styles of dress of modern times owe their origins to the experimentation of the fifteenth to seventeenth centuries.

One interesting indication of this experimentation is found in the seventeenth-century Banjarmasin court chronicle, which sought to impose on an unruly people a conservative social order based on what it conceived to be a pure Javanese model. The chronicle put into the mouth of the founding raja (anachronistically) the following counsel:

> Do not any of you dress according to the style of the Dutch, or of the Chinese, or of the Siamese, or of the Acehnese, or of the Makassarese, or of the Bugis. Do not imitate any of them. You should not even follow the old custom of dress from the time when we still lived in Keling [South India?], for that is no longer our country. We have now set up a country of our own, following the ways and manners of Majapahit. We should therefore all dress like the Javanese. According to the tales of the old men of long ago, whenever the people of a country followed the dress of other countries, misery inevitably fell upon the country (*Hikayat Banjar*: 264).

For most of the new states, the process of redefining a national style was closely involved with religious change. Entry into Islam or Christianity was almost invariably marked by some change in dress, as in hairstyle and body ornamentation. For many peoples (though not the Javanese) the Malay cultural compromise became the accepted dress of Islam. A tunic (*baju* or *kebaya*) was added to the basic sarong for women and a similar loose jacket and head cloth for men. The woman's scarf (*selendang*) survived to serve other purposes. An unusually rapid transition occurred in seventeenth-century Makassar, perhaps because at the time of its conversion it was already a cosmopolitan city socially "overdue" for change in a bourgeois direction. A Dutch description of the city in 1607, two years after its leaders had accepted Islam, noted that the use of penis balls (see next chapter) and the cropping of female hair were already declining as a result of the change and Malay hairstyles were coming in. The slaves and poorer women in the back streets, on the other hand, still had "their upper body with the breasts completely naked" (van der Hagen 1607: 82). Just forty years later another visitor to the city noted that "the women are entirely covered from head to foot, in such fashion that not even their faces can be seen" (Rhodes 1653: 206–07).

In the Philippines there was the same assumption that a change of religious identity required a change of clothes. The Spanish regarded the Visayan style of tattooed men and scantily dressed women as especially reprehensible, but even the Muslim-influenced Tagalog dress showed too much of the belly to please the Spanish. Within a century Colin (1663: 63) could report with some satisfaction: "Now they have begun to wear the Spanish clothes and ornaments, namely chains, necklaces, skirts, shoes and mantillas, or black veils. The men wear hats, short jackets, breeches and shoes. Consequently, the present dress of the Indios in these regions is now almost Spanish."

Vietnamese appear to have gone much further much earlier along the path of replacing the ornamented body by a profusion of clothes. Borri hailed their women as "the most modest in all India," with their several layers of clothing allowing no part of the body to be seen (1633: F). It is nevertheless possible to regard the Vietnamese dress of both sexes as an elaboration of a basic sarong pattern, prior to the imposition by Emperor Vo Vuong in 1774 of a Chinese-style tunic and trousers (Huard and Durand 1954: 177–78; Woodside 1971: 134).

Textile Production and Trade

Situated between the world's two major sources of fine cloth—India for cottons and China for silks—Southeast Asia became internationally known as a consumer rather than a producer of textiles. Without the constant demand for Indian cottons in particular, it would not have been possible for first Indian and then European traders to gain their foothold in Southeast Asia. The woven cloths of Gujerat, the Coromandel Coast, and Bengal largely paid for the spices and pepper which the Indonesian islands sent to the west.

This pattern was made possible by the extravagance of Southeast Asians on clothing and ornamentation, above all other items of expenditure, not by any lack of textile production below the winds. Cloth was Southeast Asia's leading item of manufacture, and cotton its leading agricultural product after foodstuffs. Strips of local cotton cloth were even used as currency in parts of Sulawesi and Buton, while in Java, Makassar, and Luzon the first European colonial demands for tribute were made in terms of local cloth (Coté 1979: 56; Rouffaer 1904: 12–13; Riquel 1573: 241; Stavorinus 1798 II: 261). Indian and Chinese cloths were bought by the wealthier elite because of their brilliant colour, their fine patterns, and their status as rarities, but the bulk of the population always wore local or regional cloths.

Crawfurd (1820 I: 176–78) may be right, for the Archipelago at least, in concluding that weaving was first developed for a cloth made of tree fibre, since the vocabulary of weaving is Austronesian while the terms for cotton and silk production are Sanskritic. The reference, however, is to a very distant past. By the sixteenth and seventeenth centuries cotton was cultivated widely in Southeast Asia and worn by most of its people. Vestiges of what may have been an older system remained in those regions which did not have a distinct enough dry season to grow cotton successfully and which could not afford to import it. Most of Malaya (except Kelantan) was in the former category, but it imported cloth from India, Java, and Sulawesi (Eredia 1613: 39). In the less-favoured regions of South Sumatra, Borneo, Sulawesi, and the Moluccas a nonlasting cloth akin to Polynesian tapa was made by soaking the inner bark of certain trees and then beating it until it became flat and soft. In the rain, however, it had to be taken off lest it fall apart (Pigafetta 1524: 72; Navarrete 1676: 110; Marsden 1783: 49).

Finer cloth could be made by those who had access to abaca, the fibre from the stem of the *Musa textilis*. This bananalike tree was native to the Philippines; and the peoples of Cebu, Negros, Samar-Leyte, and Mindanao, as well as northern Sulawesi, clothed themselves primarily from it. In drier Luzon and Panay cotton could be grown and was much preferred (Alcina 1668 III: 99; Loarca 1582: 43–73; Dampier 1697: 217; Jasper and Pirngadie 1912: 55).

Cotton had been cultivated in Southeast Asia and exported to China for a very long time. Chinese records suggest that the plant may have been introduced to South China from Vietnam in the seventh century (Nguyen 1970: 52). From the thirteenth to the seventeenth century Chinese traders bought cotton yarn and cloth at various Southeast Asian ports, especially in Vietnam, Luzon, and Java (Chau Ju-kua 1250: 46–48, 78, 160–61; Morga 1609: 263; Wheatley 1961: 77–83). At least by the eighteenth century, when the first detailed accounts appear, central Burma was producing large quantities of cotton, which were taken up the Irrawaddy to a central market at Sagaing. There it was cleaned and turned into yarn for sale to merchants who took it into Yunnan and other parts of China (Symes 1827 II: 187; Cox 1821: 46).

Other major cotton-growing areas, which exported to closer markets within the islands, were East Java, Bali (fig. 16), Sumbawa, Buton, and the southeastern corner of South Sulawesi. Cotton was among the exports of Cambodia around 1600, reaching markets as far south as Patani (Groslier 1958: 152; van Neck 1604: 229). Perhaps this cotton was grown in the same area on the west bank of the Mekong above Phnom Penh, which in the nineteenth century produced sufficient quantities "to supply all of Cochin-China" (Mouhot 1864 II: 22; cf. Bouinais and Paulus 1885 I: 333, 533, 569). Siam and Sumatra also

Fig. 16 A Balinese painting of the 1940s depicting the traditional harvesting of cotton

produced cotton for local consumption. One of the main Sumatran production areas was the coastal strip between Padang and Indrapura on the west coast, which supplied all of Minangkabau until the Dutch suppressed the cultivation in favour of pepper in the late seventeenth century (Oki 1979: 147–48).

Silk was much less popular, even though both mulberry trees and silk worms may have been indigenous to Southeast Asia. Both occur naturally in parts of Indonesia, where the worms are of the presumably earlier polyvoltine type able to reproduce at any time of year. To Chinese, who had developed the grafting of trees and breeding of worms to a high and labour-intensive art, Indonesian methods as observed in northern Sumatra seemed crude and haphazard, producing a rough yellow silk (Ma Huan 1433: 119; Groeneveldt 1880: 93). Ludovico di Varthema (1510: 234) reported that the worms there grew naturally on trees in the forest, as well as in gardens. Two Malay chronicles record a legend that the founder of the first important Muslim port-state below the winds, at Pasai in northern Sumatra, had the miraculous ability to turn worms into gold and silver (*Hikayat Raja-Raja Pasai*: 51; *Sejarah Melayu* 1612: 40–41). This probably reflects the importance of domesticating silkworms in the early development of Pasai. The silk of that region was an important source of supply for Sumatra and even India up to the first quarter of the seventeenth century (Barros 1563 III: i, 508; Beaulieu 1666: 99; Nicholls 1617: 73). Albuquerque learned about the silk of Pasai when he was on the way to the conquest of Melaka in 1511. He sent his Genoese troubleshooter, Giovanni da Empoli, back there from India to negotiate for the supply of all the silk Pasai could produce. Empoli was told by the Raja that this would cost the Portuguese one hundred thousand ducats, "the same price for which it was previously sold to the Gujeratis" (Empoli 1514: 148). Even if that was a great exaggeration, the output of silk in northern Sumatra (conquered by Aceh in the 1520s) declined rapidly in the ensuing century, as Chinese silk became more readily available and little was done to replace the mulberry trees encroached upon by rice and pepper cultivation.

The other important source of silk of this yellow native type was South Sulawesi, where cultivation continued in the Bugis state of Wajo into modern times. This silk cultivation, which provided the colourful Bugis dress sarong, was noted by Couto (1645 V: ii, 86) on the basis of reports from the 1540s.

In the countries of the Mainland the techniques of silk production appear to have been influenced by the much more painstaking methods of China. A tradition in Burma ascribed the introduction of silkworms from China to the eleventh-century reign of the great King Anawhrata (Shway Yoe 1882: 268). Thais, who had perhaps brought silk making with them from China during the preceding millennium, were introducing it to Cambodia during the visit there of Chou Ta-kuan (1297: 30)—though in the central Thai lowlands mulberries proved impossible to establish (La Loubère 1691: 13). Only in Vietnam did silk production take precedence over cotton. "All the inhabitants clothe themselves in silk" (San Antonio 1604: 24). Vietnamese techniques for processing and dyeing the silk appear to have been as advanced and meticulous as those of China and Japan in the seventeenth century, and the product was in demand by foreign traders. The largest bulk exports were, however, in the form of raw silk, taken by Japanese traders on a considerable scale until this trade was stopped by the Tokugawa in 1617 (Nguyen 1970: 52, 93–94, 190).

Spinning the thread, whether by a simple wheel or a spindle and distaff, dyeing it with indigo, saffron, cotton husks (red), and various root extracts, and weaving the cloth on a narrow backstrap loom were all the work of women. The basic pattern was common to many preindustrial societies in which each household aimed to be self-sufficient in cloth. "In every [Javanese] cottage there is a spinning-wheel and loom" (Raffles 1817 I: 86; cf. Symes 1827 I: 229; Gervaise 1701: 74). Yet even where there was intense regional specialization on production of cloth for export, the business remained in the hands of women, unlike the pattern in India and China. Crawfurd (1820 I: 178) regarded this as indicative of the low state of Southeast Asian development in textiles. It should probably rather be seen as part of a dualistic view of the world which saw most tasks as explicitly male or female.

The technology of textile production was surprisingly uniform. The spinning wheel appeared not to have reached the Philippines by 1600 (Scott 1982: 528), but it was found as far east as South Sulawesi and Maluku. The backstrap loom which, in Cambodia, Chou Ta-kuan (1297: 30) thought so small it was hardly a loom at all, was used by women throughout the region. Production was slow. It was calculated for eighteenth-century Java that it took a woman a month to spin a pound of cotton thread and another month to weave a cloth ten yards long (Hooijman 1780: 423–25; cf. Crawfurd 1820 I: 178–79). The main problem was the narrowness imposed on the cloth by the backstrap system, so that only "short, narrow and smallish fabrics" were produced (Galvão 1544: 123). Two widths had to be sewn together to make a sarong of the length required by the new Malayo-Muslim style.

In the use of colours and designs, on the other hand, there was a high degree of specialization. In the sixteenth century it appeared that East Java, Bali, and Sumbawa were the major exporters of cloth, capitalizing on the large-scale cotton growing in the drier areas of these islands. Javanese cloth was already reaching northern Sumatra early in the fifteenth century (Groeneveldt 1880: 88), and at the end of the sixteenth the striped *lurik* of Panarukan and Pasuruan was still popular in Melaka (Lodewycksz 1598: 100–01). For the important Moluccan market, however, even Javenese traders stopped at Gresik for Madurese cloth, or better, at Bali or Sumbawa to take on colourful cottons woven by the *ikat* method for which those islands were already renowned (Heemskerk 1600: 448, 452; Lodewycksz 1598: 119–20). Javanese weavers were handicapped by their inability to weave a pattern into the cloth with differently coloured threads, while the batik method of dyeing a design onto the cloth by waxing the remainder was not yet economically competitive because of its enormous labour input.

In the course of the seventeenth century South Sulawesi emerged as the leading cloth exporter of the Archipelago. The process was certainly assisted by Makassar's success in becoming the main staging point for non-Dutch spice traders heading towards Maluku and by its conquest of such established export centres as Sumbawa (1617) and

Selayar. The Moluccas provided an important market in the first stage of this export expansion. Some credit should also go to that spirit of innovation for which Makassarese were renowned in the seventeenth century and Bugis in the eighteenth, since their cloth achieved a unique reputation for fine, consistent weave and clear colours—mainly in the checked pattern favoured by Muslims (Rouffaer 1904: 4; Forrest 1792: 79). Cotton growing and weaving were concentrated in the island of Selayar and the nearby South Sulawesi mainland districts of Bulukumba and Bira. Both were strategically situated on the route towards Maluku, but were too dry and barren for rice growing. The men of these regions therefore devoted themselves to shipbuilding and the women to weaving. By the 1660s Selayar cloth was being traded through Makassar to Borneo ports, the Lesser Sundas, and Manila (Speelman 1670A: 103–07, 112–13). With the fall of Makassar to the Dutch in 1669, Bugis merchants began to dominate the trade in Makassarese cottons, taking them to all the islands of the Malay world (Lennon 1796: 271–72, 326; Marsden 1783: 52; Donselaar 1857: 302).

Local cloths were never valued as highly, however, as the fine Gujerati cloths the brilliant colours of which could not be matched below the winds. When seeking to emphasize the magnificence of a royal gift, a Thai chronicle explained it was woven entirely of imported silk "without any admixture of Thai thread" (*Traibhumikatha* 1345: 176). One clove-rich king in Maluku gave another as a wedding gift five hundred of the most prized cloths, the colourfully ornamented silk *patola* of Gujerat, though each one was reputedly valued there at half a tonne of cloves (Pigafetta 1524: 76; cf. Barbosa 1518: 198–99).

Because exotic cloth was the largest item of luxury expenditure, the level of imports is a good indicator of the level of prosperity. In periods of uninhibited export of spices and other local products, massive imports of Indian cloth probably filled most of the needs of the urban populations and reached also those of the rural elite. The cloth imports to Melaka about 1510 accounted for most of the cargoes of fifteen large ships a year from Gujerat, Coromandel, and Bengal, estimated by Pires (1515: 92, 269–72; cf. Meilink-Roelofsz 1962: 87–88) to be worth over half a million cruzados. About half this number of ships were carrying Indian cloth to Aceh in the first half of the seventeenth century (Verhoeff 1611: 242; Mundy 1667: 329–30, 338; Clark 1643: 282), when an English factor there believed he could sell a total of 4,500 corges (90,000 pieces) of Indian cloth per year as well as 100 *bahar* (17 tonnes) of raw cotton (Nicholls 1617: 71). Ayutthaya is estimated to have been importing about 75,00 guilders' (30,000 rials') worth of Indian cloth per year in the seventeenth century (Smith 1974:

259). Makassar far outweighed this amount in the 1630s with an estimated consumption (partly for reexport) of 120,000 rials at Indian prices, or double that at Makassar prices (Coulson and Ivy 1636: 294). When trade was curtailed, on the other hand, as it was in Banten during Dutch military actions, the local looms became busy and there was a rapid reversion to self-sufficiency in cloth (Coen 1617: 293; Meilink-Roelofsz 1962: 244, 258).

Gold and Silver Working

> *Paduka Sri Sultan . . . sole King of Sumatra . . . whose presence is as the finest gold; King of Priaman and of the mountain of gold . . . king of two umbrellas of beaten gold, having for his seats mats of gold . . . all his seals half gold, half silver, his vessels for bathing of pure gold, his sepulchre of gold . . . his services complete in gold and silver.*
>
> *—Sultan Iskandar Muda's letter in Copland 1614: 211–12*

Personal adornments were the principal items of luxury expenditure after cloth. Gold jewellery in particular was in constant demand as at once a means of saving, an indication of wealth and status, and an ornament. For this purpose Southeast Asians used a very pure and soft gold that could readily be reworked, cut, and sold in whole or in part in response to any commercial need. Though only the powerful would presume to display their wealth in the extravagant manner of the Johor ruler just described, even otherwise naked children of some status would be decorated with gold and silver bangles and pendants (La Loubère 1691: 27; Goudswaard 1860: 347).

With some exceptions Southeast Asian states did not mint gold or silver coins as currency. The cost of a purchase was instead weighed out very carefully in gold or silver. Merchants therefore had to know how to weigh gold (in the islands) or silver (in the Mainland) in order to conduct their business. Chirino (1604: 363) claimed that every Filipino carried a small scale for this purpose, and Tagalogs surprised the early Spaniards by taking out their touchstones and checking the quality of the gold offered for even a small purchase of food (Sande 1577: 100).

The importance placed on gold in the lands below the winds was doubtless a consequence of its widespread occurrence there—particularly in Sumatra, the Malay Peninsula, Luzon, Champa, and northern Sulawesi (see map 3).

Until the early seventeenth century the mines of the Minangkabau area of central Sumatra were the region's most prolific, respon-

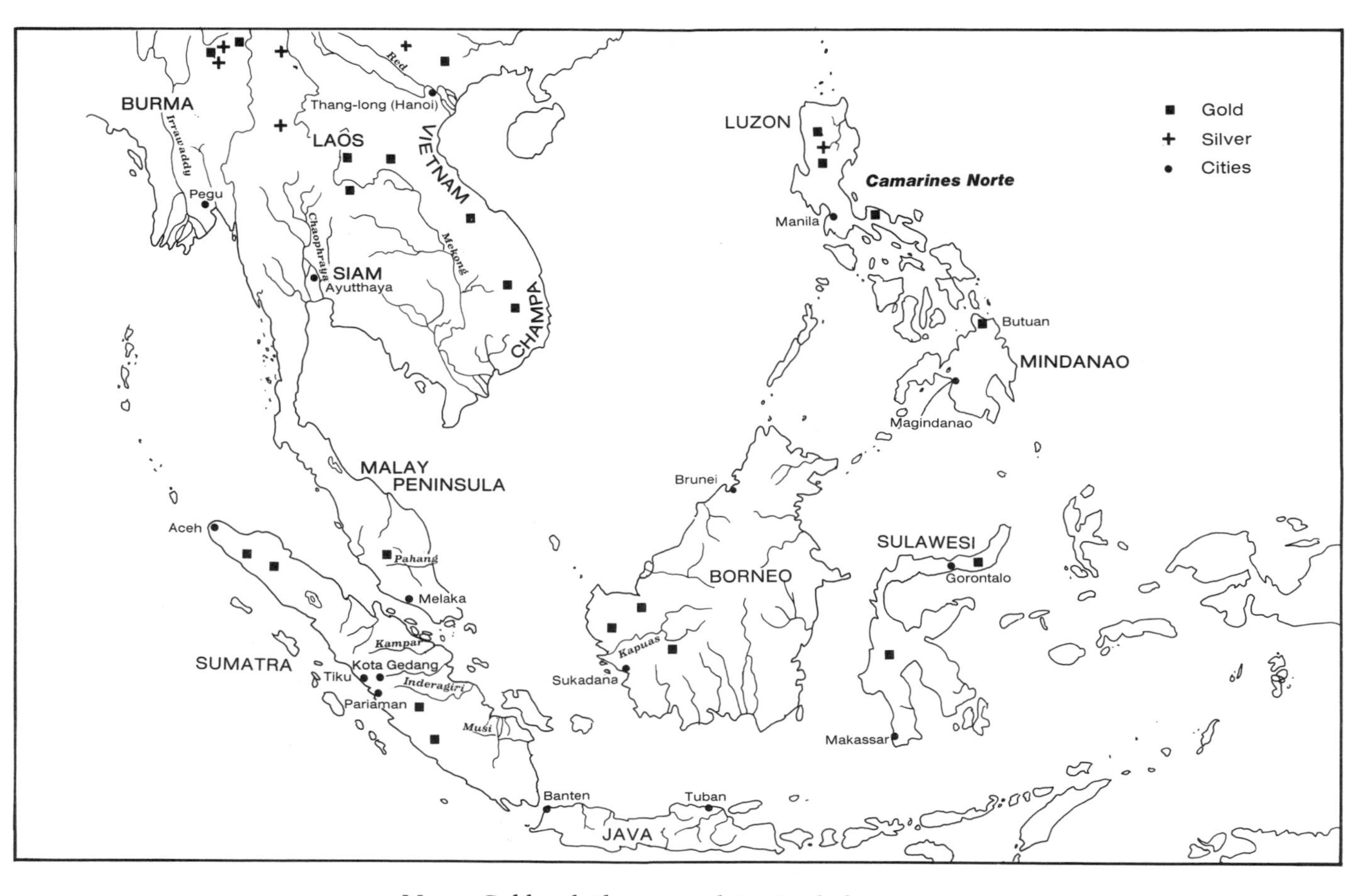

Map 3 Gold and silver in exploitation before 1700

sible for the legendary wealth in gold of the early kingdom of Sri Vijaya. Gold was sieved from the sand of the eastern rivers and mined in the Minangkabau hills. There were said at one time to be 1,200 different mines there (Marsden 1783: 168; cf. Eredia 1600: 238–39). A Portuguese captive in Melaka learned that nine to ten bahar[1] of gold were imported to that city each year, brought partly from Minangkabau and partly from Pahang in eastern Malaya (Araujo 1510: 28). After the Portuguese capture of Melaka and the expansion of Aceh down the west coast of Sumatra, most of this Minangkabau gold was directed to Aceh through the ports of Tiku and Pariaman. It contributed to the fantastic wealth of the strongest of Aceh's kings, Iskandar Muda (1607–36), who was reputed at one time to possess one hundred bahar of gold (Beaulieu 1666: 55, 44; cf. Dobbin 1983: 23–26). Though Aceh's access to these Minangkabau mines was lost in the 1660s, new mines had been developed in the more northerly stretch of the gold-bearing Bukit Barisan range within Aceh territory. As in Minangkabau, the miners' work was back-breaking, dangerous, and scourged by disease, but the profits for their financial backers in the capital were enormous, giving the Aceh of the late seventeenth century the reputation of being the most affluent city in the region (Dampier 1699: 93–94; Ibrahim 1688: 174–75; *Hikayat Pocut Muhamat*: 114–15; Veltman 1919: 72–76).

Much of the gold trade in the Philippines was controlled by the Igorots of the Luzon cordillera: "They do not refine the gold completely, nor bring it to perfection, they take it down to certain places in Ilocos, where they trade it for rice, pigs, carabaos, blankets and other things which they lack. The people of Ilocos complete the refining and preparation, and through them it is distributed throughout the land" (Morga 1609: 261).

Gold was also mined and panned in the mountainous north of mainland Southeast Asia, in the regions adjacent to gold-rich Yunnan. Of the mainland states, however, only Champa and Nguyen-ruled southern Vietnam were net exporters. After the fifteenth-century Vietnamese expansion into the formerly Cham province of Quangnam, the Nguyen rulers were able to mine and export its high-grade gold to Melaka (Pires 1515: 115; Nguyen 1970: 90–91; Whitmore 1983: 376). Siam and Burma obtained their gold from Lao and Shan

1. Most authorities, including such contemporary European observers as Barbosa (1518 II: 175), assume the bahar of gold to be the same as the bahar of pepper, i.e., about 180 kg. *Klinkert's Nieuw Maleisch-Nederlandsch Woordenboek*, however, insists that when weighing gold a bahar was only 7.25 kg, which would make Melaka's imports an unsurprising 70 kg a year.

sources in the north and used all they obtained for personal adornment or to gild the religious monuments which dotted the landscape. Burma was probably a net importer of gold, notably from Yunnan. Java certainly was, since it alone of the major population centres was devoid of its own sources of gold in this period. Van Goens (1656: 182–83) was puzzled at how gold was nevertheless still cheap in Java in relation to silver. He could only explain it by the constant plundering of pre-Islamic graves in which so much gold had been buried that it must previously have been either mined or imported on a considerable scale.

Silver was both less valued and less available in Southeast Asia, though it did occur in many places where gold was mined—Sumatra and the hills of what are today northern Burma, Laos, and Vietnam. The biggest source was the Bawdwin mine in the Shan area on one of the Irrawaddy tributaries, which is calculated to have produced an average of about three thousand kilograms of silver a year from the fifteenth to the eighteenth century, when it was worked primarily by Chinese (Deyell 1983: 222–23).

Taken overall, Southeast Asia was relatively rich in gold and poor in silver. There was a net outflow of gold: from Sumatra and Malaya to pay for Indian cloth (Beaulieu 1666: 57–58); from the Philippines to Mexico as "tribute" levied by the Spanish conquerors (Schurz 1939: 32); and from southern Vietnam to pay for sulphur and other imports. Silver, of minor interest prior to the sixteenth century except in Burma and Laos, began to pour into the region thereafter. For the Japanese during their brief foray into Asian trade in the sixteenth and early seventeenth centuries, and for the Portuguese, the Spanish, and the Dutch with abundant supplies of New World silver, the grey metal was the great key to unlock the riches of Southeast Asia. During the seventeenth century silver coinage gradually came to dominate all local markets. It consequently became ever more widely available for reworking in the form of utensils.

The functions of gold and silver as ornaments and status markers as well as investments ensured that wherever there was wealth there were goldsmiths. The same craftsmen handled both metals, and silver was frequently blended with gold in a ratio of one to two (Veltman 1904: 346). All the royal capitals were particularly well provided with goldsmiths to fill the needs of the ruler and the wealthy merchant-aristocrats. Sultan Iskandar Muda alone was said to have three hundred in his service at Aceh, and he managed to lure another French one away from Admiral Beaulieu (Beaulieu 1666: 90, 100). Many of the wealthy royal centres, such as Surakarta, Jogjakarta, Tuban, and

Sidayu in Java, established a tradition of gold working which survived the collapse of the royal court, subsequently sending itinerant smiths out to sell or do commission work on a temporary basis in newer centres. Sidayu in 1868 still had 125 goldsmiths with 197 apprentices (de Haan 1912 III: 217; Rouffaer 1904: 91–95). Kota Gedang, one of the long-term gold-working villages of Minangkabau (Sumatra), still had 347 goldsmiths working around 1890 ("Inlandsche" 1894: 315).

The weaving of gold and silver thread into ornate silk cloths became another highly developed art. The Islamic capitals which were near sources of gold, notably Aceh, Siak, and Kota Gedang in Sumatra, were renowned for their rich sarongs, scarves, and head cloths. Envoys to the Aceh court were presented with such cloths "richly wrought with gold, of very cunning work" (Lancaster 1603: 112). Despite its own wealth in gold, Aceh imported gold thread on occasion from Gresik in eastern Java (Vlamingh 1644: 609). Presumably Javanese craftsmen were able to make a profit simply by processing imported gold into thread and reexporting it.

The ingenuity and delicacy of Southeast Asian gold and silver work were universally admired. Even the normally sardonic Crawfurd (1820 I: 183) conceded that here "they far surpass their efforts in the other mechanic arts." Goldsmithing accounted for almost half the vocabulary of metalworking in the Tagalog Dictionary of 1613 (Scott 1982: 533). Even though the twenty-two items of an Acehnese goldsmith's equipment seemed very simple to nineteenth-century Europeans, they provided a range of techniques and a sophistication of delicate filigree work which was not matched in other crafts (Veltman 1904: 343–45; cf. Marsden 1783: 178–80). The French missionary, Vachet, having presented one of the seventeenth-century Nguyen princes of Cochin-China with a chiming clock with a silver face, was surprised at the ability of one of the royal goldsmiths to fix one of its defective wheels. Still more astonished was he when "at the end of twenty-three or twenty-four days, he put two clocks in my hand which were so alike that the eye could not distinguish the old from the new, which would have seemed to me unbelievable or a dream if I had not experienced it myself: the two clocks were equally accurate" (cited Nguyen 1970: 98).

Craft Specialization

The intensity of maritime and riverine commerce encouraged specialization of production for virtually all ceramic and metal ware. Villages entirely devoted to pottery, stoneware, lime extraction, or metal smelting might be located close to the source of the crucial raw material. Cloth-making, leather-working, or boat-building centres were often in areas ill-suited for profitable rice growing, like the dry areas in southeastern Sulawesi or eastern Java.

It was, however, the large cities of the age of commerce which attracted the major concentrations of manufacturing. Here were the wealthiest consumers of fine craftsmanship, including the royal courts; here also were the intersecting trade routes both local and international, along which local specialities could be transported and exchanged. It was therefore natural that numerous specialist quarters of craftsmen sprang up in the suburbs of each city. In the capital of Aceh there were "Gold-smithes, Gun-founders, Ship-wrights, Taylors, Wevers, Hatters, Pot-makers and Aquavitae stillers . . . Cutlers, and Smiths" (Davis 1600: 151). Similarly, Schouten (1636: 147) observed that "the Siammers who live in Towns and populous places are either Courtiers, Officers, Merchants, Watermen, Fishermen, Tradesmen or Artificers, each one containing himself in his vocation." Thang-long (Hanoi) had the same variety of crafts, but also papermakers and lacquer and silk workers (Dampier 1699: 46).

As a British envoy sailed up the Irrawaddy in 1795, he noticed that the villages became more frequent as he appoached the Burmese capital of Amarapura, eventually merging into each other. "Each . . . was for the most part inhabited with one particular class of people, professing some separate trade, or following some peculiar occupation" (Symes 1827 II: 10). Many of the thirty-six *phuong* (administrative quarters) of Thang-long were named after the craft practised there. Each such quarter controlled a particular street of shops devoted to their type of product (Nguyen 1970: 116). The cities which had been great production centres continued to exhibit this pattern into the nineteenth century. The city of Brunei, for example, included one *kampung* each of *kris* makers, brass workers, and oil makers, two of blacksmiths, and three of makers of matting walls and roofs of *nipah* palms (St John 1862 II: 254–56). Similarly, in nineteenth-century Surabaya craftsmen continued to live in their specialist kampung—leather workers in Tukangan, copper workers in Kranggan, ivory and wood carvers in Bubutan, furniture makers in Tambak-gringsing, *songket* weavers in Ampel (Jasper 1904: 1; Hageman 1859: 141).

Despite their highly developed skills, specialist craftsmen did not develop into large-scale producers with their own substantial capital. The essential unit of production throughout Southeast Asia was the household, with a few dependent relatives or apprentices working for the craftsman. Rather than working consistently to accumulate a large stock, such units tended to produce only when commissioned. Dampier (1697: 227) noted in the capital of Magindanao (southern Philippines) that goldsmiths and silversmiths would "make anything that you desire, but they have no shop furnished with ware readymade for sale." Likewise, the numerous lacquerware, silk, and ceramic workers in the northern Vietnamese capital would only be set to work when trading vessels arrived and advanced the money to have these export goods produced (Dampier 1699: 49). Craftsmen seemed loath to take the risk of using expensive metal on a job without a prior paid order. Even two centuries later, in Surabaya in the 1850s, Javanese craftsmen were characterized as working only when they had received an advance for a particular job which established a temporary bond of patronage and protection with the buyer. When the job was finished, this bond was broken and the craftsman ceased to produce (Hageman 1859: 142). The source of this pattern may have been in part the separation of function between trader and craftsman, but the major factor was a lack of security for the capital of the independent worker. Without a patron to protect or guarantee the fruit of his labours, the craftsman could not risk stockpiling goods which might attract the greed of powerful men.

Often craftsmen were described by outsiders as slaves or bondsmen, and indeed the line is difficult to draw between bought slaves encouraged to earn their own upkeep on the side and craftsmen obligated by standing contracts to a particular patron. "Yet there is nothing of rigour used by the Master to his Slave, except it be the very meanest, such as do all sorts of servile work: but those who can turn their hands to anything besides drudgery live well enough by their industry. Nay, they are encouraged by their Masters who often lend them Money to begin some trade or business withall" (Dampier 1699: 98, referring to Aceh). In Banten in 1596, female slaves frequently spun and wove cloth as a marketable item for their master (Lodewycksz 1598: 129). Melaka before the Portuguese conquest in 1511 was largely populated with Javanese who were slaves or dependants of the great Javanese merchants who supplied Melaka with foodstuffs and took much of its trade. The wealthiest merchant, who bore the title Utama Diraja, was alleged to control eight thousand such "slaves" (Empoli 1514: 139–40; Barros 1563 II: ii, 52). These Javanese were the leading craftsmen of the great emporium: "They are very clever at cabinet-making. Other trades which they follow are the making of arquebusses and all other kinds of firearms" (Barbosa 1518 II: 193). Albuquerque was so impressed with their skills that he shipped sixty Javanese carpenters from the Melaka dockyard to India after he had conquered the city, believing these "very handy workmen" would make it possible to repair Portuguese ships on the Indian coast. The carpenters never reached India; they mutinied and took their Portuguese vessel to Pasai, where they were extremely welcome (Albuquerque 1557: 168).

In the royal capitals, the main concentrations of manufacture, the court itself provided a large share of the demand. Craftsmen were frequently well treated and even honoured by their powerful patrons, but their labour was regarded as a tribute to the king or merchant-official. They were not so much paid for services as maintained with patronage. Under the arbitrary conditions which prevailed in some of these capitals, this system interfered considerably with production for the market. In 1643–44, for example, "gamelan-makers and smiths" were suddenly pressed into service by Sultan Agung of Mataram to try to make a giant cannon (*Babad ing Sangkala* 1738: 44–45). In Siam Europeans saw the corvée system as the major impediment to the development of craftsmanship: "There is no person in this country that dares to distinguish himself in any art for fear of being forced to work gratis all his life for the service of this prince" (La Loubère 1691: 69; cf. Poivre 1747: 57–60; Crawfurd 1828: 322).

Where we do find concentrations of craftsmen actively selling their products through a far-flung marketing system, these tend to be in former capitals where the royal patron had declined or moved away. Such north-coast Javanese manufacturing centres of the nineteenth century as Gresik and Surabaya (bronze), Tuban and Sidayu (gold), and Japara (furniture) are cases in point. The Sudanese copper workers of Cianjur and Sumedang, the Minangkabau arms, gold, and metalwork manufacturers, and metalworkers of other highland peoples throughout Southeast Asia were saved by their isolation from direct bondage, but at least somewhere in their past we can usually trace a tributary relationship to some court. The most active nineteenth-century production centre in Indonesia for small arms and bronze ware was Negara, far up a tributary of the Barito River in South Borneo. Although we hear little of its metalworkers prior to the nineteenth century, they almost certainly go back to the sixteenth century, when Negara was the pre-Islamic royal capital of the area. Once the Sultanate of Banjarmasin was established near the mouth of the Barito, the craftsmen of Negara were freer to produce for the market—and grew so numerous that they were obliged to do so. Though the Sultan no longer maintained them, he still required them to produce arms for him at no cost as their form of tribute (Marschall 1968: 137–39; Lombard 1979: 240–41; Ras 1968: 626).

Ceramics

Earthenware pottery, which had been made in most areas of Southeast Asia for thousands of years, had spread to its remotest parts by the age of commerce. The potter's wheel had been widely but not so universally adapted. In the eastern Archipelago and the Philippines, household ware was still made exclusively with the "paddle-and-anvil" technique (Scott 1982: 531; Ellen and Glover 1974: 359). Essential ceramic products included water containers and carriers, the spouted *kendi* as a drinking vessel, lamps and incense burners, oil containers and mixing bowls. Such vessels were fired at relatively low heat, and they were not glazed but waterproofed with a coating of damar after firing.

Every stage of the pottery production process was the preserve of women, at least in the island world. Today it is taboo for a man in Maluku even to visit the site from which the clay is dug (Ellen and Glover 1974: 356). Where there was suitable clay, specialist villages developed where women would produce the earthenware for a surrounding area up to one hundred kilometres in extent. Some potting villages near trade centres shipped their finest produce much further afield—from north Java to ports around Maluku and Borneo, for example (ibid.: 354–55; Fox 1959: 373–74; Jacobs 1894 II: 137–38).

High-quality Chinese glazed ceramics were a major trade item over longer distances. Beautifully decorated and fired at much higher temperatures than was possible in local kilns, these plates and bowls became items of great value and status. In the Philippines, Sulawesi, and the Moluccas they were placed around the corpse at burial to accompany the dead on the journey to another world. In Java, Bali, and South Sulawesi they were inlaid as a decoration in the walls of mosques, tombs, and palaces. For the wealthiest Southeast Asians they replaced earthenware as drinking vessels, finger bowls, and dishes. Recent excavations at Kota China and Muara Jambi in Sumatra, at Brunei and the Sarawak river delta in Borneo, at Manila and Batangas in Luzon, at Banten and Tuban in Java, and at several underwater wreck sites in the Gulf of Thailand enable us to date the immense flow of imported ceramic material which began slowly around the tenth century and reached a peak between the late thirteenth and early sixteenth centuries (Locsin 1967; Milner, McKinnon, and Sinar 1978: 25–30; Hutterer 1977: 178–79; Parker 1979; Intakosai 1984).

This peak period of demand in the islands of Southeast Asia was not met from China alone. At the end of the thirteenth century an increasing proportion of imported porcelain began to come from new Southeast Asian high-temperature kilns in the northern Mainland areas. Thai traditions assert that it was the arrival of some expert Chinese potters at the kilns just outside Sukhothai during the reign of the great Ram Kamheng (1292–99) which enabled the established local potters to produce finer glazes for export (Spinks 1965: 14–17). The hundreds of kilns dating back to the tenth century that have recently been discovered in the area of Si Satchanalai, north of Sukhothai, make clear that Thai production was vigorous long before this Chinese influence, however (Hein 1985). In the fourteenth and fifteenth centuries fine celadons were exported from Si Satchanalai and Sukhothai which rivalled those of the famous kilns of Longquan in China's Zhejiang Province. Nevertheless, Thai monochromed *kendis*, cover bowls, and other wares for the Southeast Asian market were distinctive in both design and colour.

Vietnamese ceramic production appears to have been as technically advanced as Chinese at least from the time of the Han Dynasty's occupation of the country. Not until the fourteenth century, however, do we see Vietnam suddenly entering the export trade to Japan and the islands of Southeast Asia. The most innovative period for the Vietnamese kilns in the Hanoi and Thanh-hoi areas was the fourteenth and fifteenth centuries, when both an iron-black colour and the more familiar cobalt-derived blue were used to create characteristic underglazed designs of a spidery, calligraphy-like type. During the later fifteenth century a more intense effort to supply Southeast Asian markets already accustomed to Chinese wares produced greater conformity to Chinese designs (Guy 1986).

From the fifteenth century to the seventeenth, Thai and Vietnamese ceramics occupied a major place in Southeast Asian trade, supplying a substantial proportion of the market in better-quality imported ware. Some idea of the scale of this trade, even near its end, is conveyed by Dampier's remark in the late seventeenth century that one English trader bought "the best part of 100,000" cheap bowls in Thang-long (Hanoi), selling most of them at an enormous profit in West Sumatra (Dampier 1699: 48). Recent excavations of fifteenth- and sixteenth-century burial sites in the Philippines and eastern Indonesia have yielded significant proportions of Thai and Vietnamese items, with Thai ware especially prominent in the southernmost sites. Of more than fourteen thousand finds classified by the South Sulawesi Antiquities Service in the period 1973–77, 21 percent were of Thai and 6 percent of Vietnamese origin, as against 26 percent classified as Ming, 28 percent "Swatow," and less than 1 percent Yuan

(Hadimuljono and Macknight 1983: 77). In the fifteenth-century Catalagan site in southern Luzon about 17 percent of the imported ceramic ware unearthed was Thai and 2 percent Vietnamese (Fox 1959: 361).

Metalwork: The Key to Power

This [iron] is occupied by Raja Jegedong
Able to forge iron to make it last
Extremely tough and very sharp
It is occupied by Raja Panggai
Originator of letters and reader of the compass.
—*Iban knife-sharpening chant, in Harrisson and O'Connor 1969: 80*

The working of metals was the creation of power, since metal implements were required first for war and second for agriculture. Metals, especially iron, were seen as conveying strength and integrity. Those rituals that were intended to confer invulnerability or wholeness typically included a metal object whose essence entered and fused with the warrior to make him strong (Endicott 1970: 133–34; Forth 1981: 125–27; Hickey 1982: 132–35). Even though metalworkers shared the relatively low status of manual workers everywhere, there was also an aura of the sacred about them. The most powerful household *nat* of Upper Burma was the spirit of a powerful blacksmith killed by a jealous king (Nash 1965: 169). Blacksmiths were always male, with skills handed down in particular families and villages. The term for master metalworker—*pande* in Javanese and Balinese, *pandai* in Malay, *panre* in Bugis—came to designate high competence in any art or science.

Metalworking frequently played a role in the formation of states. In Javanese tradition the division of the island between the kingdoms of Majapahit in the east and Pajajaran in the west was attributed to a magically powerful royal blacksmith, Siyung Wanara, who killed his father and fought with his brother (*Babad Tanah Jawa*: 14–17; Raffles 1817 II: 97–103). The second king of Bone, the leading Bugis state of Sulawesi, bore the title *Petta Panre Bessi,* or "Our Lord the Blacksmith" (Sulaiman 1979: 54). In the Visayas, where kingship was in process of developing in the sixteenth century, "the most important notables were and are blacksmiths" (Alcina 1668 III: 104). Wherever states developed, metalworkers were brought to the capital to ensure the control of this powerful resource. Specialist metalworking villages and suburbs under royal patronage were a feature of the major states.

Iron, copper, tin, nickel, and lead are all relatively abundant in

Southeast Asia (map 4), though least accessible in the main centres of population—Java, Bali, the floodplains of the Chao Phraya and Mekong. The technology of mining, prospecting, refining, and smelting was substantially less developed than in China or Europe, however. The labour-intensive methods whereby relatively low-grade surface ores were smelted to a workable state ensured that Southeast Asian metals remained highly priced and precious in comparison to imports from China, Japan, or Europe. Southeast Asia was therefore a net importer of all industrial metals except tin, the most easily processed of them, which was mined in the Malay Peninsula and exported at least as far as India.

Metalworkers who could refashion copper or iron into useful implements were widespread, and raw materials to supply them were always in demand. When the Dutch burned one of their ships at Bawean, northeast of Java, in 1597, vessels appeared from all sides to salvage the iron from it (Lodewycksz 1598: 178). When the Spanish had to burn one of their ships at Mindanao in 1606, they first removed as many of the bolts and nails as they could to prevent them from falling into the hands of their Muslim enemies (Morga 1609: 233). Successive European traders found that iron, lead, copper, and the products made from them were among the very few European items that were saleable.

Iron

Southeast Asian houses and boats used virtually no iron, a sign of its preciousness. Blacksmiths were in demand primarily to make the critical items of agriculture and war—plough tips, harvesting knives, mattocks, fishhooks, machetes, swords, spear tips, and the famous kris of the Malay world. Most large markets had a section selling such wares, the essentials of ordinary households. In interior or mountain villages where communications were difficult and local warfare frequent, every large village would have its blacksmith to produce items such as these. In the more settled conditions of the river valleys and maritime cities, production was centralized in certain villages or urban quarters which might sell their produce to markets hundreds of kilometres away.

Burma, Siam, Cambodia, northern Vietnam, and the central part of Sumatra appear to have been roughly self-sufficient in iron, though cheap imports from China and northern Europe were often welcome. Siam even exported some iron to the Philippines in the 1670s (White 1678: 424). The art of smelting appears to have been restricted to those

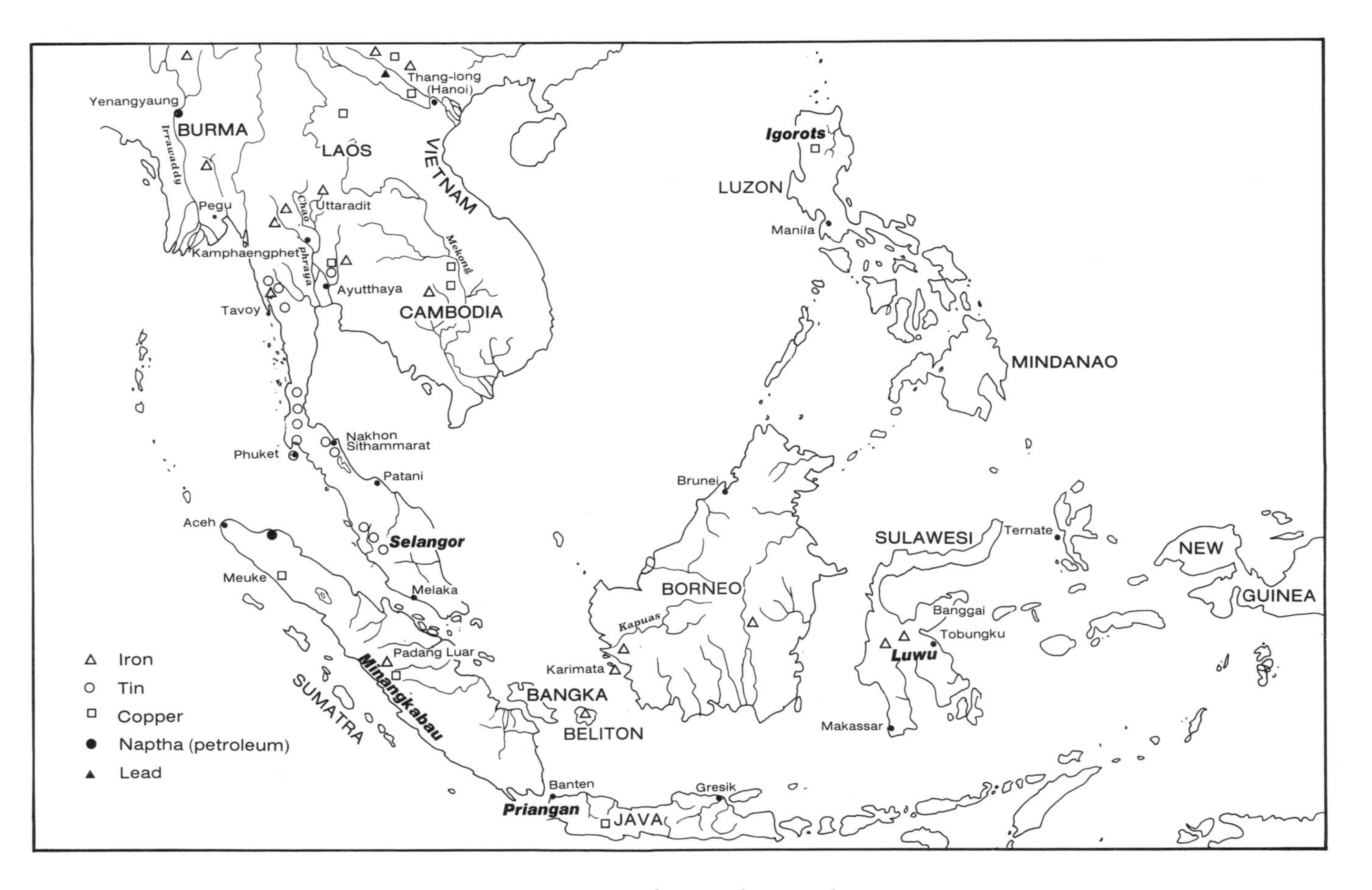

Map 4 Sources of minerals around 1600

peoples living near workable ore deposits—frequently hill peoples who had not developed an elaborate written culture. The iron of Angkor and Cambodia, for example, was probably produced by the Kui minority inhabiting the iron-rich hills bordering Laos in the north (Frédéric 1981: 161). Burma and Siam drew their iron primarily from the mountain ranges near their common border and processed it in specialist villages near Prome and Tavoy in Burma and near Kampongphet and Sukhothai in Siam (Sangermano 1818: 205; Cox 1821: 29; La Loubère 1691: 14; Suchitta 1983: 18). Iron was also mined in the Lopburi region not far north of the Thai capital of Ayutthaya, while some of the prize sword-making iron, naturally strengthened with manganese, came from mines in the Uttaradit area, north of Sukhothai (Suchitta 1983: 16–18).

In Sumatra it appears that the Iron Mountain (*Gunung Besi*) of the Minangkabau district had been mined for several centuries before the iron industry based on it was described by Marsden in the late eighteenth century. By then the exhaustion of the available wood for charcoal had forced the smelting operation to move a day's journey northward, to Salimpaung (Dobbin 1974: 330–33). Marsden (1783: 347) was convinced that Minangkabau craftsmen had "from the earliest times, manufactured arms for their own use and to supply the northern inhabitants of the island." Further south, Beliton and Bangka both exported iron and iron implements, partly through their overlord in Palembang (Pires 1515: 156–57; Speelman 1670A: 113; cf. Crawfurd 1820 III: 489; Court 1821: 136, 160).

The islands to the east provide more intriguing problems, in that extensive maritime trade in iron and ironwork had to fill the needs of many areas which were naturally deficient. Seventeenth-century accounts of the Philippines insist that blacksmiths in both Luzon and the Visayas had to rely on imported Chinese iron (Alcina 1668 III: 104; Scott 1982: 532; Sande 1576: 74), although slag remains in Cebu and elsewhere suggest that local lateritic ores had been smelted in a somewhat earlier period (Hutterer 1973: 37; Harrisson and O'Connor 1969: 315). The technology of smelting such ores by roasting with charcoal seems to have been sufficiently widespread to suggest that only the relative cheapness and good quality of Chinese iron could have driven it out. In more isolated parts of the Luzon Cordillera, iron smelting was reported by one traveller to have survived into the nineteenth century (Meyer 1890: 63).

Java was renowned for its beautiful ironwork, and its krisses and swords were exported as far as India (Pires 1515: 93, 179). Although the legendary associations of the pre-1500 West Java kingdom of Pajajaran with ironworkers might suggest that the titaniferous ores of the mountains of southwest Java had once been exploited, there is no evidence that the kris industry of Majapahit or any subsequent Javanese ironwork obtained its raw material locally. Borneo and Sulawesi almost certainly provided Java with most of its iron.

The likeliest source for the nickel-rich iron used in making the laminated krisses of Majapahit was central Sulawesi. Lateritic ores containing up to 50 percent iron and substantial nickel traces were found very close to the surface, notably around Lake Matano and in the upper reaches of the Kalaena River (Kruijt 1901: 149–50). Sulawesi iron could be exported through the Gulf of Bone, which was controlled by the kingdom of Luwu, or through the east coast of Sulawesi, dominated in the sixteenth century and earlier by the kingdom of Banggai (Mascarenhas 1564: 433–34). Both Banggai and Luwu are mentioned in the *Nagara-kertagama* (1365: 17) as tributaries of Majapahit, which suggests that their iron exports may already have been important then. In the sixteenth century the spice-exporting kingdoms of the Moluccas drew their iron and weapons from the same source. "A great deal of iron comes from outside, from the islands of Banggai, iron axes, choppers, swords, knives" (Pires 1515: 215–16; cf. Barbosa 1518 II: 205). By the end of that century the key ports of eastern Sulawesi were politically controlled by Ternate. Banggai had become but one of these, and its former tributary, Tobungku, the direct outlet for the Lake Matano iron, was now the more important. Tobungku exported its famous swords and lances not only as tribute to Ternate but also to Makassar and throughout eastern Indonesia (Speelman 1670A: 103–04; Stapel 1922: 5–6; Tobias 1857: 24).

Luwu may well owe its role as the crucible of Bugis kingship (around the fourteenth century) to the iron it was able to channel from the hill peoples who mined it to Javanese and other traders. In the middle of the seventeenth century "Luwu iron" was still one of the major exports from Makassar to eastern Java (Speelman 1670A: 111). Cheaper iron was by then available from Chinese and European sources, but the kris makers of Java still seem to have preferred the nickel-rich Sulawesi iron in order to create the essential contoured-wave design (*pamor*) on their blades. Even around 1800 this central Sulawesi iron was still being sought by kris makers of South Borneo, who needed to mix it with cheaper imported "true iron" so that the nickel traces would bring out the pamor pattern (Marschall 1968: 138).

Even less is known about the iron exports of Borneo, the most abundant potential source of low-grade surface ores in the Archipelago. The quantity of slag left behind in iron workings of the tenth to fourteenth centuries in the Sarawak River delta of northwest Borneo—estimated by Harrisson and O'Connor (1969: 385) at forty thousand tonnes!—makes it almost certain that a major centre of iron export was located there in that period. This centre may well have supplied iron to the blacksmiths of the eastern part of the Malay Peninsula, southern Sumatra and western Java. Around 1600, however, the major Borneo export centre was the island of Karimata, under the control of the small kingdom of Sukadana in southwest Borneo. Malays of the Melaka region wore krisses "of Karimata steel" (Eredia 1600: 232). Banten, then the greatest port in Java, imported "iron in quantity from Karimata" (Lodewycksz 1598: 119). The Dutch soon sought its axes and *parangs* (machetes) as "well designed to suit the ordinary man" (Verhoeven 1609: 105). The Javanese fleet that seized Sukadana in 1622, Mataram's only venture outside Java, must have been intended to secure this source of iron as well as diamonds. The grip of Mataram soon loosened, and Karimata again exported its iron implements throughout the Archipelago. The Dutch bought up almost ten thousand Karimata axes and parangs in 1631 (*Dagh-Register* 1631–34: 28, 47) and eight thousand in 1637, finding them indispensable in the local Indonesian trade, even as far away as Timor (van Diemen 1637: 629). Despite the local sources of supply in Sulawesi, ships from Makassar were sailing regularly to Sukadana two decades later to collect "Karimata axes and parangs." The same two or three vessels a year would sometimes take on ironware from the island of Beliton, further west, which produced "more parangs but fewer axes" than Karimata (Speelman 1670A: 113).

The Beliton iron was probably quarried from Mount Selumar, a wall-like outcrop of magnetitic iron ore with traces of tin, copper, and lead (van Bemmelin 1949 II: 212). Similarly, Karimata production appears to have been based on brown iron ores available on Karimata Island itself (Marschall 1968: 249; *ENI* III: 196). There were innumerable other sites in Borneo where veins of ore broke the surface, however, and many of them must have been mined for relatively local use. In the nineteenth century it was the more isolated upland peoples of Borneo who retained a knowledge of smelting—the Kayans, Kenyahs, and related Dayak peoples in the upper reaches of the Barito, Katingan, Kutai, Kayan, Rejang, and Baram rivers (Harrisson and O'Connor 1969: 342–49). The fullest description is that of Schwaner (1853 I: 109–15), who found in 1847 that there were about ten smelting ovens on the Mantalat River, a small tributary of the Barito, from which iron was distributed throughout southeastern Borneo. The ore used was clayish sferosiderite exposed by the banks of the rivers.

Because of the relative cheapness and variety of Chinese metals and metal goods, the mining and smelting of Southeast Asian ores steadily retreated inland as communications improved. Already in Sung times iron and ironware were "among the commonest commodities shipped from China to the South Seas" (Wheatley 1959: 117) and had penetrated the major trade centres, such as Sri Vijaya. In Melaka around 1510 the imports from China included "copper, iron . . . vases of copper and *fuseleira,* cast iron kettles, bowls, basins, quantities of these things, boxes, fans, plenty of needles of a hundred different kinds, some of them very fine and well made . . . and things of very poor quality like those which come to Portugal from Flanders, countless copper bracelets" (Pires 1515: 125). Similarly, the Chinese brought to Patani, which a century later played a redistributive role like Melaka's, "much porcelain, iron, copper, and various cheap goods that people need here." Traders from Borneo took back quantities of Chinese metal from Patani (van Neck 1604: 229–30). In Sumatra, Indian iron was more prominent, providing over 250 bahar (45 tonnes) of imports per annum to Aceh and Tiku until replaced by European iron in the seventeenth century (Ito 1984: 439). Even though Borneo and Sulawesi provided most of the needs of Java and the Lesser Sunda Islands at the beginning of the seventeenth century, they had ceased to do so by its end. The iron miners and smelters of Karimata, who had to compete directly with Chinese and European iron in the markets of the Archipelago, finally ceased business in 1808 (*ENI* IV: 790). Nineteenth-century ethnographers found that the tradition of smelting local ores persisted only in the relatively inaccessible upland areas of central Sumatra, central Borneo, and central Sulawesi (see figs. 17a and 17b).

The techniques of smelting and working iron (and other metals) were broadly similar in all the Southeast Asian centres described in the nineteenth century, and appear to have changed little in the preceding three centuries. Miners extracted the ore close to the surface, often using fire to widen fissures in the seam and detach large lumps. Then they roasted the ore in the open, which required a vast quantity of wood. Finally they smelted the ore in a pit sunk into the ground and lined with dried clay, using large quantities of charcoal beneath the iron ore to effect the deoxidation. The most distinctively Southeast Asian feature of the operation was the vertical piston system sometimes described as the "Malay bellows."

Two bamboos, of about four inches diameter and five feet in length, stand perpendicularly near the fire; open at the upper end, and stopt below. About an inch or two from the bottom a small joint of bamboo is

Fig. 17a Smelting of iron by Dayaks of Dusun Ulu, high up Barito River in central Borneo, in the nineteenth century

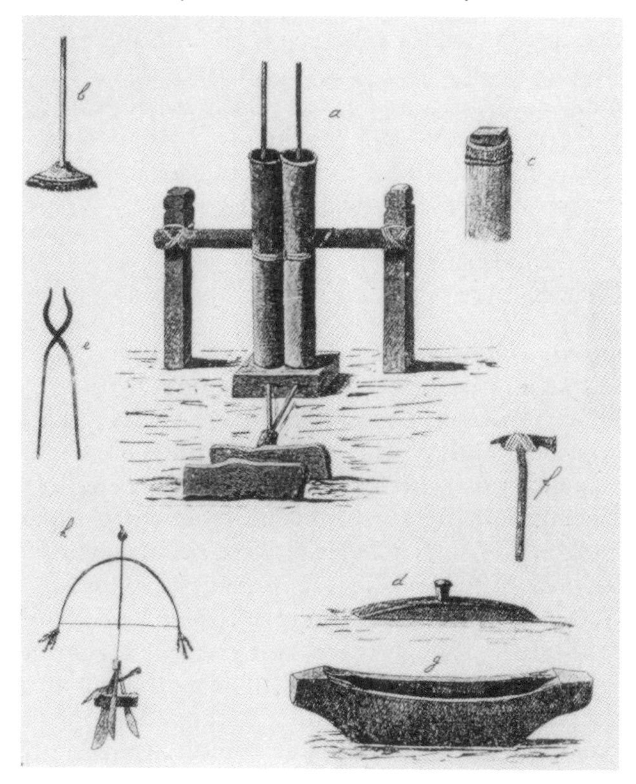

Fig. 17b Iron-working equipment of Central Sulawesi, c. 1900: *a*, bellows and oven; *b*, piston for bellows; *c*, large anvil; *d*, small anvil; *e*, tongs; *f*, small hammer; *g*, water trough; *h*, ritual object (*tamoa*) hung in the forge

inserted into each which serve as nozzels, pointing to, and meeting at, the fire.

> To produce a stream of air, bunches of feathers, or other soft substance, being fastened to long handles, are worked up and down in the upright tubes, like the piston of a pump. These, when pushed downwards, force the air through the small horizontal tubes; and by raising and sinking each alternately, a continual current or blast is kept up, for which purpose a boy is usually placed on a high seat or stand (Marsden 1783: 181).

This description of blacksmith's bellows in Sumatra could be repeated almost exactly throughout the islands of Indonesia and the Philippines, in Burma, Siam, and even Saigon (Meyer 1890: 62–63; Raffles 1817 I: 173; Dampier 1697: 227; Kruijt 1901: 152; Sangermano 1818: 187; Suchitta 1983: 38, 40; White 1824: 278). The cylinders were more often made from tree trunks than bamboo, and frequently the small bambo nozzles were joined in a clay pipe before entering the fire. Although two cylinders were normal for a blacksmith's forge, as many as twelve might be used to fire the furnace used in smelting (Schwaner 1853 I: 111; Harrisson and O'Connor 1969: 345). The antiquity of this system in Southeast Asia is suggested by its occurrence also in Madagascar, to which Indonesians migrated at least a thousand years ago. Its efficiency in directing a strong and continuous current of air is evidenced by its retention by Sulawesi and Borneo blacksmiths even today, when modern bellows are available.

Copper, Tin, and Lead

Since 1960 archaeologists working in northeast Thailand and in Vietnam have been pushing back the origins of bronze working in mainland Southeast Asia as far as 2000 B.C. and earlier, dates which would precede any authenticated metallurgy in South Asia. Claims have been made, though not without opposition, that Southeast Asians may have discovered metalworking independently, earlier than most of their neighbours, in part because of the occurrence of tin and copper in close proximity (Solheim 1968; Bayard 1980; Loofs-Wissowa 1983). In fact, Southeast Asian bronzes frequently had more lead than tin in the mixture, though the copper content seldom fell below 70 percent (van Heekeren 1958: 5, 33, 35). The methods used for mining and smelting these metals were similar to those described for iron, though the roasting required to extract the molten metal from ore was less demanding.

At least from the period of active Ming state trading in the early fifteenth century, Chinese copper cash was extensively imported into Southeast Asia for use as currency (Whitmore 1983: 363–69). In the eighteenth century Dutch copper coinage was in great demand (Dobbin 1983: 70–71). Since copper coins, already alloyed with some tin and lead, were so cheaply and widely available, they may well have become the major source for the manufacture of bronze articles in the age of commerce. Nevertheless, all these minerals continued to be mined at certain sites in Southeast Asia and traded over greater or lesser distances.

A very large share of the world's tin lies in the north-south line that descends from the hills of eastern Burma through the Malay Peninsula to the islands of Bangka and Beliton. The rich reserves of these last two islands remained unknown until 1709, but the central part of the peninsula, between Tavoy and Selangor, was supplying a large part of Asia's needs for tin from at least the tenth century. Tin was the only one of the many exports of fifteenth-century Melaka which originated within its own domain, and its currency consisted of small ingots of tin (Ma Huan 1433: 111; Pires 1515: 270–71, 275). Most of the tin mined around Tavoy appears to have supplied Burma, while that on the east coast of the Peninsula supplied Thailand. It was the mines further south on the west coast of the Peninsula which produced primarily for export, and consequently we know more about them. Perak, and to a lesser extent Selangor, were the main suppliers of tin as tribute to Melaka, a large proportion of which was exported to India. Junkceylon (modern Phuket Island), a tributary of Siam, first begins to be mentioned as a major source of tin exports in the sixteenth century, though the produce of that area must have contributed to the wealth of Tambralinga long before (Gerini 1905: 136–41; Wheatley 1964: 115). In 1596 the tin available in the entrepôt of Banten came from both Perak (then effectively independent) and Junkceylon (Lodewycksz 1598: 119). Perak was too weak to defend its valuable resource, however, and in 1620 it fell to Aceh. For the following forty years the Indian and European traders who sought tin for Indian and other markets had to deal either with Aceh or with the southern dependencies of Siam. Since the Dutch reported profits of 84 percent in selling such tin in India (Maetsuyker 1671: 743), they went to great lengths to obtain it.

The Malay and Thai methods of sluicing and smelting were described by Eredia (1600: 235) in the case of Perak: "The earth is dug out of the mountains and placed on certain tables where the earth is dispersed by water in such a way that only the tin in the form of grains remains on the tables. It is then melted in certain clay moulds and by a process of casting is converted into . . . slabs." Further north there were places where women simply collected pieces of tin-bearing ore exposed on hillsides after heavy rain (Gerini 1905: 159–60). Nevertheless, large quantities were extracted by both of these methods. Eredia (1600: 234) estimated that Perak produced 300 bahar (50 tonnes) each year, and more southerly ports almost as much. In the 1640s the annual shipments of tin from Perak to Aceh were variously estimated at 800 or 2000 bahar (130–330 tonnes) (van der Lijn 1648: 430; Ito 1984: 140). In 1657 one Dutch ship brought a cargo of 100 bahar from Junkceylon; another brought 451 bahar from Nakhon Sithammarat (Maetsuyker 1657: 126). Forrest claimed that Junkceylon was producing 500 tonnes a year in the 1780s and had produced far more at an earlier period, before its tin became a monopoly of Chinese smelters (cited Gerini 1905: 175).

The only significant Southeast Asian sources of lead appear to have been in northern Vietnam and Siam. Siamese lead was exported to Melaka, to Burma, to Cochin-China, and through Tenasserim to Aceh and probably Banten (Pires 1515: 108; Sangermano 1818: 205; White 1678: 425; Compostel 1636: 1216; Lodewycksz 1598: 119). No details were given about how or where this lead was mined until Crawfurd (1828: 419) claimed that in his day the mines were worked by "the barbarous tribe of Lawa," near Pak-Prek, and that they produced about 2000 *pikul* (110 tonnes) a year.

The richest sources of copper in Southeast Asia were probably in the northern hills of North Vietnam, where much of the famous "Dong-son" bronze work of the pre-Christian era had its origin. Production figures of 280 and 220 tonnes of copper per annum for only two mines in the Tu-long region are reported for the eighteenth century, and the output must already have been very substantial in the preceding centuries (Nguyen 1970: 89). While some of this northern copper appears to have been mined by Chinese workers, other mines in the extreme north and extreme south of present-day Laos, in the northern hills of Cambodia, and in the hills between Siam and Burma were worked by tribal hill peoples. They smelted the metal and exchanged it with lowland urban craftsmen who worked it into statues, utensils, and musical instruments (Frédéric 1981: 160; Pallegoix 1854 I: 119).

The skills displayed by illiterate hill peoples in prospecting, mining, and smelting copper can be seen among the Igorots of the Luzon cordillera, whose techniques were described in the nineteenth century. A Spanish engineer who inspected one of their mines in 1850 concluded from the extensive remains that it must have been exploited for at least two centuries (Scott 1974: 246). The Igorots first cleared deposits of ore by sluicing, then cracked off pieces of ore by building fires against it. This ore was "roasted with fuel piled up around it, then melted in crude furnaces under forced draft, then roasted a second time before a real refining in clay crucibles also under forced draft" (ibid.). The attempts of Spanish mining engineers and Chinese labourers to work these copper deposits after 1856 were notably unprofitable, leading one government commission to conclude in 1864:

On contemplating the astonishing labours which the Igorots had made before this company was constituted we do not know which to admire more, the constancy of such hard labour . . . or such intelligence in selecting the richest ore; also astonishing is the method in which they have shored up the excavations they have made, with the waste left inside, which also serves to hide the work done; if we make a comparison . . . we see with sorrow great errors which immediately strike the eye, committed by fraudulent engineers who, in intelligence and mining knowledge, lag far behind those we unduly classify as savages (cited Scott 1974: 247).

This was but one of many instances where modern mechanized mining on a large scale proved unable profitably to exploit ores which had been worked for centuries by upland Southeast Asians. It recalls Sir Frank Swettenham's grudging admission that the Malay *pawang* (magicians) specializing in locating tin ores had "the same nose for tin that a truffle dog has for truffles" (cited B. Andaya 1979: 399). The absence of viable copper mining in certain areas in more recent times, when imported copper was cheaply available, should not lead us to conclude that it cannot have been mined in earlier times.

Sumatra and Java provide a case in point. Although Davis (1600: 147) mentions copper mines in Aceh, the earliest specific information on copper in either island is Marsden's reference (1783: 172) to a rich mine worked by Acehnese on the west coast of Sumatra at Meuke. Copper in the form of malachite was still being collected by the population there in 1916 (van Bemmelin 1949 II: 148). Similarly, Minangkabau gold prospectors frequently found copper ores of value around Lake Singkarak as late as the nineteenth century (ibid.: 151). It seems almost certain that the flourishing coppersmiths of Aceh city and Sungei Puar in Minangkabau once drew much of their copper from local sources. Since Sumatran copper often occurred together with gold, this also helps to explain the great Acehnese love of *suasa* (or *tembaga suasa*), an alloy of gold and copper (Beaulieu 1666: 100; Lancaster 1603: 93; Copland 1616: 210, 213; Jasper and Pirngadie 1930: 7–8: Wilkinson 1903: 1125). Neither Sumatra nor Java is listed among the importers of Japanese and Chinese copper by Tome Pires, whereas Aceh, as well as Java, exported copper vessels (Pires 1515: 180; Compostel 1636: 1200). That the Thai used the Malay word "tembaga" for the gold-copper mixture which they also admired (La Loubère 1691: 14) suggests that this may originally have been imported from Sumatra or Borneo.

Despite van Bemmelen's doubt (1949 II: 155) "whether a self-supporting winning of copper ore will ever be possible" in Java, it is also likely that copper had been mined there prior to the seventeenth century. In 1603 the bronze gongs exported from Java were reported to be half the price of gongs made in Patani by Chinese, presumably with Chinese raw materials (Rouffaer 1904: 99). Moreover, some of the oldest Javanese copper-working centres were situated far inland at places only explicable in terms of proximity to a source of copper. Thus the Priangan area of West Java, where Java's main copper deposits are located, was especially famous for its coppersmiths (*sayang*). A village survey of the region in 1686 listed copper working as the only occupation for thiry-three villages in the Sumedang area east of modern Bandung, while there were two *Kampung Sayang* located near the old Priangan capital of Cianjur (de Haan 1912 III: 216–18). These locations are not far from known occurrences of low-grade copper in Gunung Parang and Gunung Sawal (van Bemmelen 1949 II: 157–58). The most prominent copper workers of the Mataram kingdom were also located at the extreme west of that kingdom's domains, near Ceribon and Krawang, which is also inexplicable unless they had access to Priangan copper (de Haan 1912 III: 218, 347–48). The only significant sources of copper in the eastern or central parts of Java were near Tegalombo, only seventy-five kilometres southeast of Surakarta (van Bemmelen 1949 II: 159), which may perhaps have played a role in the development of Surakarta as a major bronze-working centre.

There is no doubt, however, that a massive influx of Japanese, Chinese, and European copper, especially in the seventeenth century, made most of these local and small-scale mines redundant. Japan, the leading supplier of the late seventeenth century, exported an average of more than three thousand tonnes a year in the period 1670–1715 (Innes 1980: 528–29). The bronze workers who flourished in every royal capital and a number of other centres drew increasing proportions of their raw materials from cheaper imports. Bronze in various alloys continued to be the most important metal to be worked into small cannon as well as household utensils—kettles, lamps, trays, betel sets, and the like. In the Buddhist countries of the north the most ambitious bronze work was for religious purposes, including the forging of colossal statues of the Buddha (Pallegoix 1854 I: 35). Great skill also went into the making of musical instruments of the correct timbre and pitch. The gongs of Java, for the most part manufactured in Gresik near Surabaya, were a crucial export item taken by Javanese traders to Maluku, Borneo, Bali, and the Lesser Sundas, where they became a mark of royal status (Galvão 1544: 105, 141; Barbosa 1518 II: 198, 202–03; Hageman 1860: 43). Similarly, the gongs of Cambodia and Tonkin found their way into the remotest highlands of the Indo-China cordillera, where they were played at every important ritual (Hickey 1982: 186–87, 449).

4

Social Organization

The inhabitants of these islands are not subjected to any law, king or lord. . . . He who owns most slaves, and the strongest, can obtain anything he pleases. . . . They recognize neither lord nor rule; and even their slaves are not under great subjection to their masters and lords, serving them only under certain conditions.

—*Legazpi 1569: 54*

Legazpi confronted in the central Philippines a more strikingly kingless society than most, and his bewilderment is perhaps extreme. Yet throughout Southeast Asia there was a combination of sharply stratified hierarchy with seeming looseness of political structure which would baffle European travellers, empire builders, and ethnographers for centuries. Kings of great power did arise within this framework, but they imposed their will on wide areas only by the force of remarkable personalities and the wealth of flourishing ports. The underlying pattern appears to have been one of descent groups constantly competing for power in the form of dependants. In this part of the world where land was abundant, buildings impermanent, and property insecure, it was in followers that power and wealth were primarily expressed.

Within these groups, descent was (usually) reckoned bilaterally in terms of the status of both father and mother, which provided one element of uncertainty about succession. Another was the sense that he who attracted followers must by definition be destined to rule. Although the ideology of a sacred line of succession from the ancestors was very strong, the flexibility of marriage, the frequency of adoption, and the reality of competition among potential successors made lineage in a genealogical sense not the most crucial part of the system.

What was crucial was the vertical bond of obligation between two individuals. The master provided protection and patronage and at times livelihood. The bondsman's obligations varied with his status, but they would typically include assisting at feasts and other demonstrations of power, serving on voyages and military ventures, and labouring in the construction of boats, houses, and other buildings. Some bondsmen and bondswomen were acquired by inheritance, some as perquisites of office, some as gifts in marriage, while others were captured in battle or sought protection from an enemy. The most characteristic source of obligation to a master, however, was debt. At one extreme an inability to pay substantial debts or judicial fines could lead to sale as a slave. But even ordinary business relationships in which capital was advanced by one party imposed obligations on the other which went beyond the business in question. Similarly, a family which could not afford the expenses of the major ritual occasions that society believed essential—particularly marriage and death—had to acquire a patron or master to provide them. In many societies the difficulty of finding the bride-wealth a man needed to get married became a source of bondage, either to the father-in-law (bride-service) or to the payer of the bride-wealth.

In this way were built up large households or compounds in which everybody had some form of obligation to the head. It was not individual houses nor whole cities which typically surrounded themselves with a protective wall separating the loyal from the hostile, but the compounds of important people. Such lords, to use that term loosely, also had dependants scattered about the city and country. Their own strongholds, however, included close family, dependent relatives, slaves who might also act as concubines and bear children to the lord, and a variety of male and female followers. Within such establishments might be found people of such different statuses that we could call one a slave, another a debt-bondsman, a third a poor relative or adoptee; yet in the eyes of the society itself such distinctions were less important than that all belonged to a certain man or compound.

The best word to describe such a system might be "patriarchal," were it not that women could also be heads of such descent groups and occupied important places within them. The master was in a sense the "father" of all, while slaves and subordinates were often imaged as children. If slaves could be sold, used as collateral for a loan, or confiscated by a ruler as a result of the death or defection of the master, so could children.

Warfare

Attempts to delineate "traditional" models of behaviour must always be treated with caution, and nowhere more than in dealing with warfare. Military technology is the first to be borrowed, since the penalty for failing to do so is immediate and fatal. The age of commerce was one of particularly rapid changes, as the firearms which were transforming warfare and power relations in Europe began to do the same in Asia. Yet some social and environmental factors continued to influence Southeast Asian warfare over a very long term, even as the technology changed.

The perception of forest land as infinitely available and manpower as scarce ensured that competition was fundamentally over control of people. It was often status questions which gave rise to conflict, but the physical objective of the combatants was to seize people rather than territory. Both the constant small-scale raiding of the Philippines, eastern Indonesia, and upland regions everywhere, and the cumbrous encounters of great armies in the mainland states and Java were essentially aimed at increasing the human resources at the disposal of a chief or king. La Loubère (1691: 90) believed this was the reason Siamese armies were not very effective: "They busie themselves only in making slaves. If the Peguans, for example, do on one side invade the lands of Siam, the Siamese will at another place enter on the lands of Pegu, and both parties will carry away whole villages into captivity."

The typical defensive response of the weaker party was therefore to escape capture by fading away into the forest and waiting for the invading force to tire of plunder and to depart. The lightness and impermanence of most urban structures and the portability of wealth kept in precious metals and cloth did not encourage a strategy of defending cities with stone walls, moats, and desperate last stands. Acehnese envoys to Turkey in the sixteenth century reportedly explained the absence of fortifications in their capital by stressing the bravery of Aceh's warriors and the abundance of its elephants (*Hikayat Aceh* 1630: 165–66); the Siamese explained the same phenomenon to Europeans by their fear that if they built forts they might lose them and not be able to retake them (La Loubère 1691: 91). In reality, temporary flight made good sense in the conditions of Southeast Asia, though less so as urban populations grew and European patterns of warfare began to change the rules.

Even when great cities were attacked and seized, the defence was not stubborn and desperate except in the unusual case that a surrounding army cut off all means of retreat. The Dutch general Coen (1615: 119) was told that "the Pangeran of Banten fears no Portuguese, Spanish, Hollanders, or Englishmen, but only the [King of] Mataram. From the latter, he says, no one can flee, but for the others the whole mountains are sufficient for us; they cannot follow us there with their ships." The river ports of eastern Sumatra, Malaya, or Borneo often shifted far inland in response to a seaborne attack. When an English party went to buy pepper at the once flourishing town of Inderagiri in Sumatra, they spent two days looking in vain for some trace of where it had been and then learned that the whole population had moved three days' journey up the river in response to an Acehnese invasion six years earlier (Ivye 1634). The most momentous single Southeast Asian setback, when the Portuguese captured the great port of Melaka in 1511, was initially seen by the defending Malays in the same light: "The king of Melaka . . . drew himself off from the city, a day's journey, taking with him some of the Malay merchants and his captains and governors of the land . . . being of the opinion that Afonso Dalboquerque simply meant to rob the city and then leave it and sail away with the spoil" (Albuquerque 1557: 129).

It was the object of warfare to increase the available manpower, not to waste it in bloody pitched battles. Hence attention was paid primarily to mobilizing large and intimidating forces, catching the enemy off balance, and demonstrating by some initial success that the supernatural forces which decided such things were on one's side. "In all the countries of Below the Winds the peasantry and the army are one and the same and if the army suffers the country itself falls into ruin. Consequently, when the natives of this region wage war, they are extremely careful and the struggle is wholly confined to trickery and deception. They have no intention of killing each other or inflicting any great slaughter because if a general gained a real conquest, he would be shedding his own blood, so to speak" (Ibrahim 1688: 90).

Armies were raised by obliging the nobles and notables of the realm to bring their own men at their own expense, and these commanders were particularly reluctant to risk losing on the battlefield the manpower which was the key to their own position. When a Dutch admiral complained to his Malay ally, the ruler of Johor, about the latter's reluctance to commit troops to battle, the sultan replied that "for him it was not like the Admiral who gave his men upkeep and wages so that they had to do whatever he said. But here each orangkaya or Nobleman had to bring a certain number of people, and each feared to lose his slaves, which are their only wealth" (Matelief 1608: 17). Exactly the same point was made of Banten by Scott (1606: 142). Europeans, Turks, and Persians, accustomed to a much higher rate of casualties in Western warfare, were consistently struck by this reluctance to press on with a battle after the first men had fallen (Artieda 1573: 197; La Loubère 1691: 90). The Abbé de Choisy (1687:

241) thought that the Siamese, Burmese, and Laos made war "like angels," firing into the air or the ground to scare their enemy rather than kill him, and attempting to round up populations and lead them off to their own territory rather than injuring them. Large numbers of people did die as a result of the famine, disease, and disruption brought about by war, but few on the battlefield. The greater ruthlessness to which warfare in the West had accustomed Europeans was undoubtedly a major reason why small numbers of them were able to obtain some crucial victories over superior Southeast Asian forces.

Southeast Asians, and in particular Indonesians from Aceh to the Moluccas, had a considerable reputation for individual bravery if not for military discipline. The indifference to death of the heroes of the wayang appears to have been a model for Javanese not only in combat but even in the bloody tournaments described by Ma Huan and others. These tournaments formed part of a careful ritual and physical preparation designed to produce the individual champion who could turn a battle by his demonstration of martial and spiritual skills. Because of the belief that warfare was a kind of trial by ordeal, in which cosmic forces determined which side was destined to prevail, the fall of a leader or champion usually brought a battle to an abrupt end (*Sejarah Melayu* 1612: 97, 123; Wales 1952: 103). According to the *Hikayat Banjar* (432–37), the Islamization of Banjarmasin was effectively determined when opposing claimants to the throne decided on single combat to avoid a civil war. Two famous Siamese kings, Ram Kamheng and Naresuen, are especially remembered for gaining glorious victories through single combat on elephants with the enemy leader.

When the contestants were roughly evenly matched, war became a series of skirmishes and manoeuvres punctuated by individual combat. The two sides might erect temporary stockades within hailing distance of each other and engage in challenges and small skirmishes over an extended period. "There is a great deal of bravado but not much fighting" (Anderson 1826: 275). Dampier (1697: 231; 1699: 100) witnessed two wars of this type—a civil war in Aceh in which thousands were mobilized on each side but no one evidently killed, and an ongoing series of skirmishes in Mindanao between the Sultan and the "Alfurs" of the mountains. In the Moluccas this ceaseless skirmishing made it appear that "they are always waging war, they enjoy it; they live and support themselves by it" (Galvão 1544: 169). On the Mainland, wars were usually larger-scale affairs involving the mobilization of thousands. Nevertheless, a Thai historian has calculated that Ayutthaya fought at least seventy documented wars during the 417 years of the dynasty (cited Battye 1974: 1).

For the Malay world the key element of attack was the amok. Used most frequently in the Malay chronicles as a verb (*mengamok*), it could mean simply to attack, but preeminently with a kris or sword in a furious charge designed to kill or scatter a number of the enemy even if one's own life was forfeited in the process. If such a charge succeeded in wounding the opposing leader, it might be enough in itself to decide the battle. The amok of Java were especially renowned, according to Tomé Pires (1515: 266, cf. 176): "The *amocos* are knights among them, men who resolve to die, and who go ahead with this resolution and die." Even in the systematic formations of Balinese armies (see fig. 18), the attack would usually be commenced by amok specialists dressed in white as a symbol of their self-sacrifice (*ENI* II: 317). Opium or cannabis was often used to inspire such a warrior to defy death (Pires 1515: 176; Fryke 1692: 48; Raffles 1817 I: 298), but probably this was only part of a lengthy ritual and spiritual preparation designed to induce a trancelike state of assumed invulnerability.

Southeast Asian chronicles and inscriptions were concerned to magnify the grandeur and charisma of rulers, and they therefore tended to attribute victory to supernatural rather than technical factors. Patani's defeat of Palembang, for example, was attributed to the *daulat* (sacred kingship) of Sultan Manzur Shah (*Hikayat Patani*: 89). Since power was seen as deriving from spiritual sources, it was generally believed that rulers and warriors achieved their success through ascetic and ritual preparation, meditation, magical charms, and their own god-given sanctity, as much as through the strength of their armies.

The *Sejarah Melayu* (1612: 71) explained one of the Malay victories over the Siamese in the fifteenth century by the demonstration of Malay powers of invulnerability before the Thai court, which immediately lost all courage for a fight. That story may be apocryphal, but we know that the Malays and especially the Makassarese enjoyed a similar reputation in Siam in the seventeenth century. A Persian envoy reported, "In general the science of mantras, spells and incantations is practised to a great extent in Siam, but no-one surpasses these Makassars who put a special spell on their daggers" (Ibrahim 1688: 136).

Invulnerability to blades and bullets was considered the mark of a great warrior. In contests such as the great Acehnese civil war of the early eighteenth century both sides were considered to possess experts in this art who had become invulnerable (*kebal*) through the recitation of sacred formulas or the carrying on their person of an especially potent talisman, usually of metal. "The invulnerable Pang Peureuba

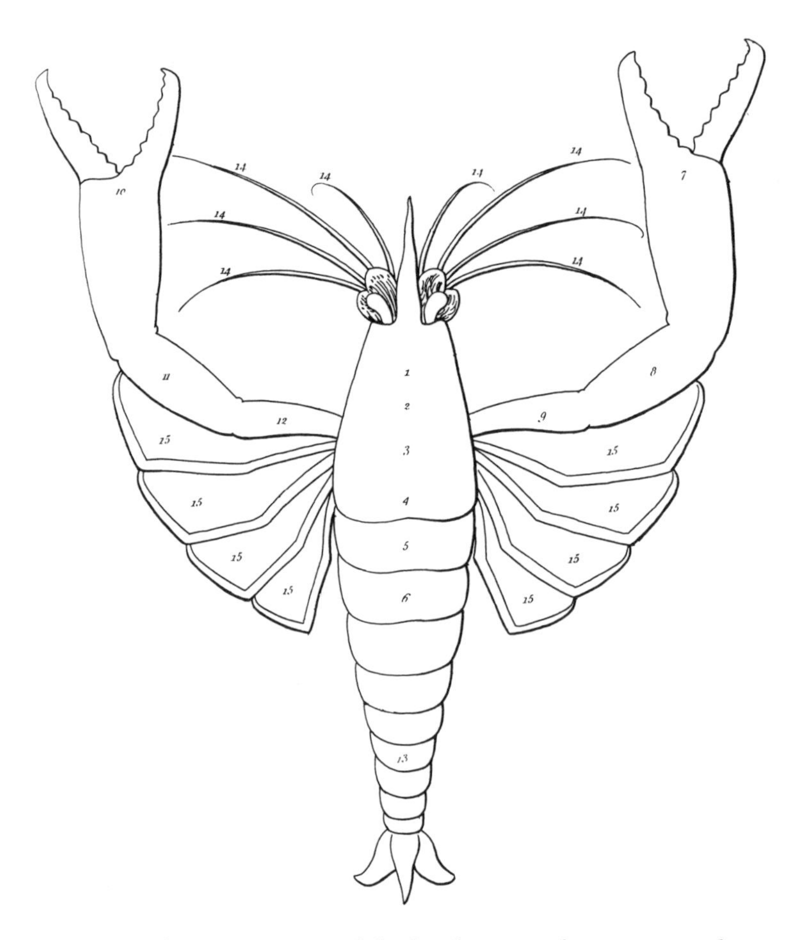

Fig. 18 Javanese literary notions of the battle array of Mataram in the seventeenth century. The feelers (*14*) represent special troops of the commander (*senapati*), perhaps analogous to *amok* fighters. The sovereign (*4*) is in the body of the crayfish, preceded by his sons and relatives (*3*), the commander (*2*), and the ministers (*1*). Other numbers represent the troops of different nobles and officials.

was hit. His skin was as slippery as oil, so that one saw the bullets slide off" (*Hikayat Pocut Muhamat*: 229, cf. 249; Siegel 1979: 113, 137–38, 149; Wales 1952: 95, 133–34). The Portuguese who encountered such a warrior on their way to Melaka in 1511 were not too far from the Malay mental world to relate how this Malay captain did not bleed from all the wounds they inflicted on him until they removed the bone

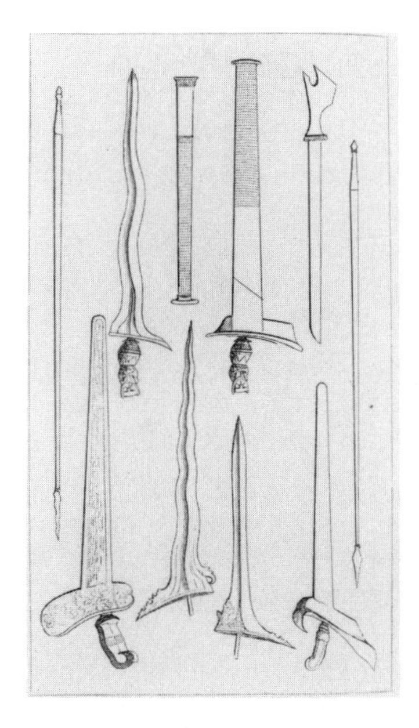

Fig. 19 Krisses and spears of Java

amulet on his arm, "and when they took this off all his blood flowed away and he expired" (Albuquerque 1557: 61).

This belief in individual invulnerability, still alive today, should not be taken to mean that the technical skills of war were neglected in favour of the magical. No one forebore to equip himself with the best available weapons, including those of Chinese, Turkish, or European make, whenever these proved their efficacy.

The most important weapons of Southeast Asian warfare, the sword, dagger, and spear, were in the hands of everybody. No Javanese, Malay, or Makassarese was fully dressed without his kris (fig. 19). Rather than having a paid professional army, most kings relied upon the ability of courtiers to mobilize their followers for war whenever required. The physical basis of the power of monarchs was therefore fragile. Only by vigilance, charisma, good fortune, and usually ruthlessness could a great king maintain his hold on the aristocracy and thereby on the mass of their followers. Success in war created its own momentum for a king, since the captives and booty so acquired buttressed his power just as victory enhanced his charisma. For similar reasons, failure in war could see great states dissolve with remarkable speed.

Until the sixteenth century the technological advantages of rulers over their subjects appear not to have been great. The king controlled elephants (in the Mainland and Sumatra), though these had greater psychological value than military effectiveness against a determined foe. His other great weapons were the war galleys which most major rulers kept near the palace under their own control, even if particular noblemen and villages were detailed to man each one.

Two further elements were introduced during the age of commerce which had profound results on the effectiveness of states against both foreigners and their own subjects. Cannon appear to have been introduced by Chinese, Gujeratis, and Turks in the fifteenth century in the form of small bronze culverins, often highly ornate in workmanship but (like elephants) less likely to injure the enemy than to intimidate him through the suggestion of supernatural power. As more manoeuverable cannon and muskets were introduced by Europeans and later manufactured in Southeast Asia, this factor tended to give rise to a small number of powerful kings able to monopolize the new technology in their domains.

The second factor was the growth of specialized mercenary forces, usually foreigners specially trained in the use of firearms. Southeast Asian states had always expected all to participate in warfare, including any foreign vessels temporarily in port. Foreign Gujerati, Malay, or Chinese vessels often played a significant part in deciding the outcome of some naval attack on a port. European trading companies exacted a higher price for such support, however. The most successful rulers of the period learned that the best way to utilize the professionalism of the European (and Japanese) soldiers in their midst was to pay adventurers and renegades as full-time mercenaries, much more dedicated to the business of killing than any earlier Southeast Asian forces.

The initial impact of these new factors must have been exaggerated by the importance of individual prowess and supernatural portents in Southeast Asian warfare. The advantage of surprise very quickly faded as the new methods were absorbed. Galvão (1544: 171) put the point nicely in relation to Maluku:

> Formerly, upon seeing a man with a helmet, they said "There comes an iron head" and all of them ran away presuming that we were invincible and not subject to death. But at present they know that under that helmet there is a head that can be cut off, and a body that is not immortal. And seeing us fire muskets, they imagined that our mouths breathed out a deadly fire; and at hearing bombards shooting and the Portuguese being mentioned, pregnant women had a miscarriage because among them artillery was unknown nor had they any inkling of it. But for a long time now, they make war with us and do not hold us in much esteem; and all of them would have eaten us at one table if God had not assisted us miraculously.

To acquire the new weapons by purchase and eventually by manufacture was not difficult. More complex was the process of social and political change which new methods of warfare (and trade and production) set in train. This process transformed Southeast Asia rapidly, giving rise to states of unprecedented power. It transformed Europe even more rapidly, however, with results which would ultimately be fateful for Southeast Asia as for the rest of the world.

Labour Mobilization: Slavery and Obligation

> *At Achim [Aceh] every one is for selling himself. Some of the chief lords have not less than a thousand slaves, all principal merchants, who have a great number of slaves themselves. . . .*
>
> *This is the true and rational origin of that mild law of slavery which obtains in some countries: and mild it ought to be, as founded on the free choice a man makes of a master, for his own benefit; which forms a mutual convention between the two parties*
>
> *(Montesquieu 1748: 239).*

The importance of vertical bonding in Southeast Asia was influenced by three vital factors. First, control over manpower was seen as the vital index of power and status, since labour rather than land was identified as a scarce resource. As Scott (1606: 142) wrote of the Banten elite, "Their wealth lyeth altogether in Slaves, so that if their Slaves be kild, they are beggared." Second, human transactions were generally expressed in monetary terms. Maritime commerce had for so many centuries penetrated their region that Southeast Asians appeared accustomed to thinking even of themselves as assets having a cash value. Third, there was a relatively low level of legal and financial security available from the state, so that both patrons and clients needed each other's protection and support. One Chinese reported that the people of Melaka "say that it is better to have slaves than to have land, because slaves are a protection to their masters" (Hwang Chung 1537: 128). These three conditions gave rise to a system of bonding based largely on debt, where loyalties were strong and intimate, yet at the same time transferable and even salable.

To early European traders attempting to hire labour in Southeast Asian ports the wage costs seemed unnaturally high. Table 3 shows prices traders reported paying for a day's labour in various cities, expressed in terms of the cost of a day's supply of rice in the same cities. The only figure which could be described as a subsistence wage is the lowest category appearing in Manguin's list of Portuguese labour in Melaka, representing provisions for the slaves of the Portuguese

Table 3 Labour Costs in Terms of Rice

Location	*Source*	*Daily Wage*	*Rice Equivalent of Wage in* Gantang[a]	*Wage as Multiple of a Daily Rice Requirement*
Martaban 1512	Bouchon 1979: 142–43	1.00 *vis* (caulker)	130.0	650.0
		0.05 *vis* (labourer)	6.5	32.5
Melaka 1519	Manguin 1983: 212–13	paid in rice		
		(craftsman)	4.0	20.0
		(slave labourer)	0.54	2.7
Banten 1596	Lodewycksz 1598: 129	1000 *cash* (slaves)	3.0	15.0
Manila 1590	Salazar 1590: 229	1 *real* (Chinese)	12.0	60.0
Jambi 1615	EIC Merchants 1615: 201	12 pence + food (Chinese)	3.4	17.0
Aceh 1642	Willemsz 1642: 508–20	1.5 *mas* (Chinese carpenter)	4.5	22.5
		0.75 *mas* (slave labourer)	2.2	11.0
		1 *mas* (Acehnese thatcher)	3.0	15.0
Ayutthaya 1655	Smith 1974: 316	1 *fuang* (Thai labourer)	8.0	40.0

[a]One *gantang* (1.75 litres) of rice weighs about 3.1 kg, or five times the daily consumption of an adult worker.

themselves. All other workers received at least ten times a subsistence wage and frequently far more.

The explanation of these rates is that there was no free wage labour to be had, except occasionally among either Chinese ("hard workers and very greedy for money"—Salazar 1590: 229) or other foreigners temporarily in port. Indigenous labour could only be rented from the owners, who evidently charged heavily for it. "It is their custom to rent slaves. They pay the slave a sum of money, which he gives to his master, and then they use the slave that day for whatever work they wish" (Ibrahim 1688: 177–78; cf. Dampier 1699: 94; Terwiel 1983: 124–25). The *Undang-undang Melaka* (88–93, 162–23) contains many provisions for what happens when people "hire" (*mengupah*) or "borrow" (*meminjam*) slaves, but none for wage contracts. Even the offer of high wages did not attract "freemen" to do the job because manual labour was associated with servitude. "You will not find a native Malay, however poor he be, who will lift on his own back his own things or those of another, however much he be paid for it. All their work is done by slaves" (Barros 1563 II, ii: 24; cf. Dampier 1699: 94; Scott 1606: 170–71).

Southeast Asian law codes acknowledged a number of paths by which a person could enter a state of bondage. These could be systematized as:

1. Inheriting the bondage of one's parents
2. Sale into bondage by parents, husband, or oneself
3. Capture in war
4. Judicial punishment (or inability to pay fines)
5. Failure to meet debts.

Debts were by far the most common source of bondage, whether acquired through trading, inability to pay the bride-price in marriage, crop failure or other calamity, or gambling. Bondage can also be seen as the concept underlying all the other categories if the war captive is understood to owe his life in exchange for death on the battlefield. Even in modern times there has been a close association between debt and labour obligation in Southeast Asia, and a tendency on the part of employers to use advances rather than adequate wages to secure their labour force. In the precolonial economies the obligations attached to debt were legally and strictly enforced: "They never deny their debts. . . . Whoever does not avow his debt and is caught is punished by death" (Galvão 1544: 126).

Montesquieu's description (at the beginning of this section) of a congenial slavery into which people voluntarily sold themselves was based on Dampier but might equally have been drawn from La Loubère (1691: 77) and a number of other European observers. It should serve as a warning against using the English word "slavery" without qualification. Most of the Southeast Asian terms which early European travellers translated as slave could in other circumstances be rendered as debtor, dependant, or subject. Although the salability of the bondsman's debts and obligations makes slave the closest European equivalent, slavery was never developed into an abstract legal category in contradistinction to the freedoms guaranteed by the state, as happened in Greece and Rome. There were Southeast Asian societies, especially in upland areas, which operated what I have called a "closed" system of slavery designed to retain a fixed pool of slave labour by emphasizing its ritual and legal subordination (Reid 1983: 161–63). For most groups, however, the boundary between slavery and other forms of bondage was porous and indistinct. The important question was to whom a man was bonded rather than the precise quality of that bondage. For general purposes, therefore, I use the broader term "bondsman," reserving "slave" for those who were newly sold, captured, and transferred to private possession or for those within the closed systems.

Strong kings always sought to expand the numbers of subjects under their direct control and to limit the number of private bondsmen, who were exempt from corvée obligations to the crown. Especially in Siam and Burma, the two strongest monarchies, all the population except nobles, their slaves, monks, and temple slaves were obliged to labour for the king for up to half of their time. To sell oneself to a wealthy aristocrat could therefore be quite advantageous, and the denunciation of this practice by successive kings indicates that many were taking advantage of it. The extent of private slavery was an index of the fluctuating degree of pluralism within the body politic (Lieberman 1984: 107–09, 163; Rabibhadana 1969: 110).

In the absence of free wage labour, bondage was the primary source of labour mobility. Typically it was the stronger and wealthier societies of the cities and the rice-growing lowlands which absorbed servile labour from among the stateless swidden cultivators or hunter-gatherers. Sometimes hill peoples sold the victims of their own internal warring; more often they were simply raided for slaves. The Cambodian capital at its height appears to have obtained its entire labour force by this means. "As slaves, one buys savages who perform this service. Those who have many slaves possess more than a hundred . . . only the poor have none at all. The savages are the people of the mountainous wastelands. They constitute a race apart" (Chou Ta-kuan 1297, 19). Similarly, the Malay population of the coastal low-lands of Malaya, Sumatra, and Borneo gradually absorbed animist hill peoples during the five centuries before 1900, by a mixture of raiding, tribute, and purchase, especially of children (Endicott 1983: 216–24; Anderson 1826: 297–99; Keppel 1846: 338–39).

In the maritime cities most of the servile labour came in through trade or conquest. Aceh brought thousands of captives back to its capital as a result of the conquests of Sultan Iskandar Muda in Malaya, just as the Thai and Burmese kings did by land. Melaka and Patani had a predominately Javanese labour force, most of which had come in as part of the following of wealthy Javanese traders. Slaves also came to these and other cities as one of the major items of trade. Since slave export was almost invariably linked with internal disunity, the state-less societies and microstates of eastern Indonesia, New Guinea, Bali, and Nias were consistently among the exporters. South Sulawesi ex-ported many slaves both in the sixteenth century and the eighteenth, but not during the period (1600–68) when the whole peninsula was dominated by the strong state of Makassar. Around 1500 Java was the largest single exporter of slaves, perhaps as a result of the divisive wars of Islamization. Through the still Hindu ports of Sunda Kelapa and Balambangan, Java supplied much of the urban working class of the Malay cities. Islamization created a major change in the nature of slave trading, since the *shari'a* law forbade the sale or enslavement of fellow Muslims. Once Islam completed its conquest of Java in the sixteenth century, that island ceased to export its people. The major Muslim cities were thenceforth supplied with slaves from beyond the frontier of Islam. Aceh obtained its servile labour from Nias, southern India, and Arakan; Banten and Makassar from the Moluccas and Lesser Sunda Islands; Patani from Cambodia, Champa, and Borneo. Certain small sultanates, notably Sulu, Buton, and Tidore, began to make a profitable business of raiding for slaves in eastern Indonesia or the Philippines and marketing the human victims to the wealthy cities—or to the expanding seventeenth-century pepper estates of southern Borneo (Reid 1983: 31–32, 170).

Chou Ta-kuan's description of the savage slaves of Angkor as a despised race, with whom no nonslave would cohabit, certainly re-ferred to an exceptional and temporary situation in the cities. The first generation of imported or captured slaves must have occupied the bottom rung of the social ladder, but they appear to have been assim-ilated gradually into the dominant population as newer arrivals took their place at the bottom. Intermarriage seems to have been relatively common, for there are numerous regulations about the status of the children of unions between slave and nonslave, even when the latter was the woman (*Undang-undang Melaka*: 92–93; Morga 1609: 273; *Adatrechtbundels* XXXI: 183). Some slaves were formally freed in return for services or at the death of their masters. A Makassar law code provided for disputes which arose over deathbed testaments promising manumission (*Adatrechtbundels* XVII: 169–70). It was probably more common, however, for the slavery of captured or bought newcomers gradually to transform itself into a looser sort of dependency with the passage of generations and the process of assimilation into the dominant culture.

Although indigenous conceptions of bondage did not include a sharp antithesis between the categories of slave and free, the conditions of the age of commerce may have encouraged movement in that direction. This period was marked by an expanding urban culture, similar to that which gave rise to such an antithesis in the Greek city-states (Anderson 1978: 22). Merchants from diverse backgrounds needed legal safeguards for their slaves as property, in a way that was unnecessary in either the closed slave systems relying on shared cultural assumptions or in the agrarian autocracies. The constant influx of new captives and imports created a market situation which needed to be regulated. Moreover, many members of the slave-owning merchant class had strong roots in the Islamic world, which had a clear body of law on slaves as property.

The legal codes drawn up in Southeast Asian cities therefore paid considerable attention to slaves. Malay codes of law typically devoted about a quarter of their total attention to questions of slavery (Matheson and Hooker 1983: 205). Slaves were given a precise legal value, usually amounting to half that of a freeman, in terms of the compensation which had to be paid by or to the owner. If the analogy with the Greek city-states is to hold, there should also have been some progress towards an abstract idea of freedom as the antithesis of slavery. In the larger Malay-speaking cities and in South Sulawesi we do indeed see the word "merdeka" beginning to express not only "freeman" but also something close to abstract freedom for a nation and perhaps an individual (Reid 1983: 21–22). This kind of antithesis, however, remained centred in the cosmopolitan pluralist cities and was marginal to the region as a whole.

If labour was performed on the basis of obligation, should the system be labelled a "slave mode of production"? This would be appropriate only if slavery made possible centralized control of a large body of workers who would produce on a scale different from the household-oriented economy. There is some evidence that a dozen or more bonded women sometimes wove for a single master, producing a salable cloth surplus, and that new agricultural land was opened up by bondsmen who had no choice in the matter (ibid.: 22–23, 171). Miners, sailors, and construction workers were frequently referred to as slaves. The evidence on the way these men were maintained, however, shows that they worked certain days for their master and certain days for themselves, or else remitted a specified amount of their product to their lord. The Southeast Asian bondage system made possible considerable mobility of labour at the behest of the elite, but in other respects it did not involve methods of production substantially different from feudalism or a household system.

Large-scale mobilization occurred on behalf of rulers, who claimed a right to the labour of all their subjects. To aid in war, in tours by the king, and in great royal feasts or construction projects a large section of available manpower could be called upon. The most extreme demands were those of seventeenth-century Siam for corvée of six months in the year by ordinary *phrai luang*—a burden similar to that placed on royal slaves elsewhere. In practice, however, manpower could be mobilized only through nobles and officials to whom these subjects were attached as clients. The farther they were from the royal court, the less likely it was that any substantial part of their time would be spent on the direct purposes of the king. In peaceful, stable periods the capacity of the court to mobilize more than its most direct bondsmen was gradually attenuated by the claims of more immediate patrons.

For construction of their forts and palaces rulers tended to use the lowest category of bondsmen—war captives. In Aceh "the king uses them to cut wood, dig stone from the quarries, make mortar and build" (Beaulieu 1666: 108). The same was true of Melaka, but in both cases the king spared himself the burden of feeding this labour force by leaving them free for half their time to earn their own livelihood (Albuquerque 1557: 135).

The mobilization of the artisan class was of particular importance in the production system, as rulers well knew. Since craftsmen were needed to forge the weapons of war, their mobilization by the court could be justified initially in military terms. Quaritch Wales (1934: 141) argues that Ayutthaya followed the four-part division of ancient Indian armies but replaced the fourth category, chariots, with artisans. The Hierarchy Laws formalized ten different sections (*krom*) of artisans within that half of the population mobilized for war. Each krom had its own official responsible for coordinating its service—one each for painters, carvers, sculptors, turners, founders, potters, moulders, gilders, coppersmiths, and plasterers (ibid.: 151). By the relatively peaceful seventeenth century these krom had drifted into the civil domain, but they remained tied to the court or to powerful nobles. "It is accordingly a matter of difficulty for a private individual, or a stranger, to obtain the services even of the most homely mechanic" (Crawfurd 1828: 322).

The rapidly growing city of Makassar offers interesting evidence on the way such craftsmen were mobilized by a state which had begun from almost nothing in 1500. The Goa (Makassar) chronicle records the advent of new manufacturing capability with each new king. Under King Tunipalangga (1548–66), bricks, gunpowder, cannon, and various other items were first manufactured in Makassar. The same king is recorded as creating a number of officials called *tumakkajannangngang* (from the Makassarese root *jannang*, "supervisor"—cf. Malay *jenang*) to supervise each of a number of crafts: "blacksmiths, goldsmiths, house builders, boat builders, blowpipe makers, copper workers, grinders, turners, rope makers" (*Sejarah Goa*: 25). Tumakkajannangngang has been glossed as "guild master" (Wolhoff and Abdurrahim: 86), but this should not lead us to suppose any contractual autonomy within the city on the part of the group of craftsmen. These were officials analogous to the Siamese heads of krom, whose duties were to regulate the obligations of craftsmen to the court (Ligtvoet 1880: 98–99; Cense 1979: 175). It is probably significant that the chronicle also credits Tunipalangga with being the first king to impose heavy corvée obligations on his people (*Sejarah Goa*: 30). His successor Tunijallo (1566–90) added arrow makers to the list of crafts with their own supervisor and also created a new official as head of all the craft supervisors (ibid.: 50). This was always a high official and relative of the king, whose function was to mobilize all the categories of craftsmen on behalf of the court.

It would be wrong to characterize the social and economic system of Southeast Asia as either feudalism or slavery. At the heart of both those systems in Europe was a legal bond recognized by state and church alike. Within the cities of feudal Europe and ancient Rome there were legally acknowledged conditions of freedom which would play an important role in the accumulation of capital that eventually gave rise to capitalism. By comparison, the Southeast Asian system was both more personal and more monetary. Loyalty was more important than law, and everybody had a master. Money was necessary to buy men's loyalty through debt, not to buy their labour on a temporary wage basis. It was dangerous if not impossible to accumulate capital unless one also accumulated bondsmen to protect and use that capital.

Justice and Law

> *A prince is like a dalang [puppeteer], his subjects like wayang [puppets], and the law is as the wick of the lamp used in these entertainments: for a prince can do with his subjects what he pleases . . . the prince having the law, and the dalang the lamp, to prevent them from going out of the right way . . . so should a prince, a prime minister, and chief officers of the court, direct the administration of the country with such propriety, that the people may attach themselves to them; they must see that the guilty are punished, that the innocent be not persecuted, and that all persons falsely accused be immediately released, and remunerated for the sufferings they may have endured*
> *(Javanese code Niti Praja, trans. Raffles 1817 I: 276–77).*

The sources of law in Southeast Asia appear to be diverse. On the one hand, the ancient Indian *Dharmasastra* was frequently copied and translated in royal courts, except in Vietnam where T'ang dynasty codes played a similar role. In the sixteenth and seventeenth centuries Islamic law books were becoming influential. On the other hand, local oral tradition continued to be interpreted by the village elders. The strongest rulers held seemingly monolithic legal powers, while in many areas each village and ethnic community maintained its own judicial system.

As in other fields, however, some characteristic Southeast Asian features animated almost all of these seemingly diverse systems. Justice was swift and direct. Plaintiffs and defendants pleaded their respective causes in person and were subjected to elaborate oaths to encourage them to tell the truth. In the absence of adequate evidence the two parties were subjected to an ordeal as a divinely sanctioned test of guilt. Capital punishment was common, especially for crimes or insults against the ruling class, but virtually every other punishment was in money terms. Offences against property, and especially denial of debts, were taken very seriously.

The Indian law books, especially the Code of Manu (*Manava-Dharmasastra*), were greatly honoured in Burma, Siam, Cambodia, and Java-Bali as the defining documents of the natural order, which kings were obliged to uphold. They were copied, translated, and incorporated into local law codes, with stricter adherence to the original text in Burma and Siam and a stronger tendency to adapt to local needs in Java (Hoadley and Hooker 1981: 1–29). It was regarded as important that rulers and judges should have these sacred books in their possession; yet they appear seldom to have consulted the texts in specific cases (Pallegoix 1854 I: 357; Sangermano 1818: 87; Lingat 1952: 111–12; Pigeaud 1967 I: 306–07). The *sastras* did not lend themselves readily to the specifics of sentencing. In practice, as is evident from the descriptions of outside observers in various parts of Southeast Asia, cases were decided in terms of the decrees of the ruler in power and of local traditions. Even the laws decreed by Malay sultans (*Undang-undang Melaka*: 88) acknowledged that sentencing should be determined by "the law of the city or the villages" (*negeri atau dusun*). When the Dutch acquired influence in Java's northern ports, they tried repeatedly to oblige local rulers to administer justice in accordance with "the old law books," believing that the situation they witnessed represented a backsliding from some more orderly past (Hazeu 1905: 119–21). Not until the twentieth century did they recognize that oral tradition was more important than written in the conduct of justice in Java.

Justice was administered by the ruler and indeed, as the quotation at the beginning of this section indicates, was seen as a vital aspect of his kingship. The ideal king heard suits personally and gave judgement in his audience hall or under the banyan tree of the town square. This was still practicable in the Philippines, where the whole village assembled to hear the datu pronounce his judgement (Plasencia 1589: 179). Even in the large states the most important cases were heard before the king personally, as Frederici (1581: 250) noted of Pegu. Most cases, of course, were settled by the village head, or by the local governor empowered to administer justice on the king's behalf on all cases not requiring the death penalty. The governor, like the king himself, would be assisted and advised by legal specialists, but in principle he himself gave the judgement. As was said of eighteenth-century Burma, "every man of high rank" was a magistrate and therefore had a hall of justice adjacent to his house to show that the king's justice was accessible to all (Symes 1827 II: 19; cf. Sangermano 1818: 83).

The most highly developed legal system was probably that of Burma, where suits had to be submitted to the courts in writing and advocates could represent the plaintiff and defendant in the case. Yet even here "lawsuits are terminated much more expeditiously than is generally the case in our part of the world," being generally concluded in one day, "provided always that the litigants are not rich" (Sangermano 1818: 86). In Siam petitions had also to be in writing and had to go through several initial hearings before the governor made his decision. But the principal parties pleaded their own case, women reportedly doing so more effectively than men because of their greater vivacity and fluency (Gervaise 1688: 88). Here too, "every suit ought to end in three days," though some did last for years (La Loubère 1691:

86). In Brunei "there is no lawsuit that takes two days" (Dasmariñas 1590B: 7), while in Banten cases generally began and ended the same evening (Lodewycksz 1598: 127).

In the island world the judicial process appears to have been wholly oral. "They have no [written] laws; they judge from reason. . . . Unknown to them are attorneys, clerks, replications and rejoinders, and other ways to lengthen and protract things," wrote Galvão (1544: 127), enviously, of the Moluccans. His surprise was similar to that of Hwang Chung (1537: 127) about the merchants of Melaka: "Though they make bargains for thousands they make no written contract, but bind themselves by pointing to heaven, and this engagement they dare not break."

Throughout Southeast Asia, however, the means to decide innocence or guilt was the same. It was assumed that the divine order itself would punish the offender if he spoke falsely. The two parties to the dispute would therefore be obliged to swear elaborate oaths inviting supernatural retribution. The Burmese oath was a masterpiece of bloodcurdling horrors which fills three pages of Sangermano (1818: 87–90): "May all such as do not speak the truth die of inflammatory diseases, pains of the stomach, and bloody vomit. . . . May their bodies be broken in pieces, may they lose all their goods, may they suffer putrid and ulcerous diseases . . . may their bodies be covered with pustules and buboes. . . . May they be killed with swords, lances and every sort of weapon; and as soon as dead, may they be precipitated into the eight great hells and 120 smaller ones . . . and after they shall have suffered in these hells every species of torment, may they be changed into animals, swine, dogs, etc." According to Crawfurd (1820 III: 88–89) the Javanese involved in a lawsuit swore more simply, "If I swear falsely, may I meet with misfortune; but if I speak the truth, may I receive the blessings of the Prophet of God, of all the saints of Java, and of my Lord and King."

If after such oaths the two principals to a case maintained their contrary versions and there were no reliable witnesses, then the matter was put to divine judgement through a system of ordeal. The most widespread forms of ordeal were total immersion in water, with the first person having to come up for air being declared the guilty one, and plunging a hand in boiling water or molten tin. The same two methods were the principal alternatives in Burma (Fitch 1591: 309; Sangermano 1818: 90), in Siam (van Vliet 1636: 71; Gervaise 1688: 89), in Cambodia (Chou Ta-kuan 1297: 23), in the Philippines (Colin 1663: 85), in Maluku (Galvão 1544: 131), and throughout the Malay world

(*Undang-undang Melaka*: 88–89; Dasmarinãs 1590B: 7; Hoare 1620: fol. 172; Hsieh 1820: 17–18). Similar ordeals were still in use in Borneo within the last century (St. John 1862 I: 77; Rutter 1929: 175).

The Siamese practice was described by a Persian visitor as follows:

> When the two parties of a lawsuit cannot settle their case . . . they have recourse to the oath of water. They carry out this test in the big river which flows through Siam, at a spot where the water is only a few hand spans deep. Both the plaintiff and the defendent are required to dunk their heads under the water at the same time. . . . The man who has been truthful in his testimony is calm and remains under water as long as he can, but the liar becomes upset and cannot control the head of his lawsuit. The falsehood of his testimony rises up through the water like a hollow bubble and bursts. His case is lost.
>
> This test is really more effective than it sounds because the Siamese claim that whenever they put their heads under water they see all sorts of frightening things (Ibrahim 1688: 127).

The sceptical La Loubère (1691: 87) was less impressed with the system's effectiveness, giving an example from his time in Ayutthaya: "A Frenchman, from whom a Siamese had stole some tin, was persuaded, for lack of proof, to put his hand into the melted tin; and he drew it out almost consumed. The Siamese being more cunning extricated himself, I know not how, without burning; and was sent away absolved; and yet six months after, in another suit . . . he was convicted of the robbery. . . . But a thousand such like events persuade not the Siamese to change their form."

A variety of other alternatives were available to test the veracity of the parties. In the Archipelago it was often possible to elect to fight with particular weapons to decide the issue. In Siam the two parties sometimes walked on hot coals. The choice of ordeal appears to have been in the hands of the defendant. "It is not at the will of the judge but at that of the defendant; and if by chance the plaintiff wants not to pass through the proof that the defendant chooses, he [defendant] is given as free" (Dasmariñas 1590B: 7).

Execution was the prescribed punishment for a wide range of offences, particularly those which touched royal sovereignty. Treason was everywhere a capital offence, and usually also murder, but so were highway robbery and arson in Burma (Sangermano 1818: 84–85), the use of insulting words to a chief in the Philippines (Morga 1606: 277), stealing from or profaning a monastery in Siam (van Vliet 1636: 72), the counterfeiting of money or theft of royal property in the Malay world (Dasmariñas 1590B: 7; Scott 1606: 110). In Aceh four royal concubines were brutally killed in 1636 for stealing silver plates from the palace, and a man was executed in 1642 for stealing a horse (Ito 1984: 172–73). Adultery with the wife of an upper-class Malay was also punished by death. In the Malay world and Java the honourable form of execution was to be stabbed with a kris to the heart. According to Ma Huan (1433: 88) not a day passed in Java without such an execution, and it was also common in Melaka (Pires 1515: 266) and Brunei (Dasmariñas 1590B: 7–8). For those traitors and others of whom a ghastly example was to be made, however, there were many more horrible deaths—decapitation, impaling on a stake, dismembering, burning alive, exposure in some excruciating position, trampling by elephants, or devouring by tigers.

Except in Vietnam, which once again followed an East Asian pattern of physical punishments (and beheading—Dampier 1699: 58–59), there was little use of lesser forms of corporal punishment. It seemed strange to Chinese visitors that floggings were in most places "unheard of" (Chou Ta-kuan 1297: 22; cf. Ma Huan 1433: 88). The reason for the rarity of such punishment was perhaps that given by Crawfurd (1820 III: 105), that a blow on the body was regarded as a mortal insult. In Siam and Burma there was nevertheless a system of beating criminals who were paraded through the streets, to ensure that they cried out their crimes sufficiently loudly (van Vliet 1636: 72; Shway Yoe 1882: 516–17).

The great majority of crimes were punished by fines or by stiffer penalties which were commuted to fines. Beaulieu (1666: 101) witnessed what he was assured was a normal procedure in one of the courts of Aceh in 1621. A man was condemned to thirty strokes of the rattan because his neighbour complained that he had been seen watching the neighbour's wife while she bathed: "The executioner, being ready to begin, withdrew him three or four steps from the *balai* [court] and lifted his arm high; the condemned man then began to negotiate, and made an offer of six mas [gold coins]; the executioner demanded forty, but as the culprit was slow in agreeing to this sum he suffered such a rough blow that the deal was quickly concluded at twenty mas, which he paid in cash, and on that consideration it was necessary only to give twenty-nine blows of the rattan on his clothes. . . . This deal was struck in the presence of all, and in full view of the judge."

In cases of theft or injury, the condemned person typically had not only to make restitution to his victim but also to pay a similar amount to the king or his judicial representative (Pires 1515: 267; La Loubère 1691: 87; *Sulu Code* 1878: 91). In Maluku, on the other hand, the judge received only one tenth of the damages (Galvão 1544: 126). Where there was no victim, or in Banten sometimes even in cases of murder (Scott 1606: 171), a single fine went to the crown. The law codes of the period are filled with different fines according to the offence and the category of offender and victim. The formula *dandaku danda* ("I fine with fines") appears frequently on early inscriptions in Java and Sumatra, as part of the essential royal prerogative (Hall 1976: 80). In microstates not much involved with trade such fines must have been one of the major sources of a chief's revenue.

The condemned person unable to pay the fine became a slave, not a prisoner. If it was a question of a theft, injury, or unpaid debt to another party, the culprit would become his slave until the amount due was paid. When the unpaid fine was due to the crown, the condemned man could be either sold to pay for it or retained for royal service. The frequency with which slavery resulted from relatively minor crimes, especially against property, led outsiders to view the law as very strict in this respect, in comparison with the relaxed attitude to crimes against the person (Morga 1606: 277; Plasencia 1589: 179). It should be remembered, however, that slavery was less feared in Southeast Asia than it would have been in Europe.

As for Islamic law, the extent to which it was imposed varied greatly with time and place. In many important respects the shari'a differs from the Southeast Asian pattern described so far, especially in the frequency of such punishments as maiming and whipping, the absence of any concept of ordeal, and the punishments for moral lapses such as gambling, drinking, and sexual misconduct. Like other trading minorities, Muslim merchants must often have been permitted their own separate judicial system in non-Muslim ports. Even in nominally Muslim Javanese states it was common to grant the stricter Muslims of the *kauman* surrounding the urban mosque the right to be judged by the shari'a as interpreted by a learned Muslim (Hazeu 1905: 56, 151). When the state itself became Muslim, there was some incorporation of Islamic law into that of the state. This process never displaced the indigenous law completely, though it went furthest in seventeenth-century Aceh. All the Muslim states were inclined to borrow from the locally dominant Shafi law books in matters of commercial and personal law. The Malay law codes of the sixteenth and later centuries copied Arabic models closely on questions of sale, investment, and bankruptcy, presumably because there were no indigenous models to offer the polyglot merchant community who needed such laws. To a considerable extent Muslim marriage, divorce, and inheritance law was also incorporated into Malay law codes, if not generally into Malay practice. In matters of sexual morality the *Un-*

dang-undang Melaka tends to give a milder local alternative as well as the Islamic penalty (Liaw 1976: 31–40). In criminal matters and especially in royal prerogatives, on the other hand, Islam had relatively little long-term influence on Southeast Asian practice.

The imposition of strict Islamic law against gambling and alcohol, and of its prescribed penalties against theft, required a strong ruler prepared to side with the urban ulama against local tradition. The strongest of Acehnese kings, Iskandar Muda (1607–36), was described by an admiring chronicler as "the ruler who enforced the Islamic religion and required his people to pray five times a day, and to fast during Ramadhan and the optional extra fast, and forbade them all to drink *arak* or to gamble" (Raniri 1644: 36). We know that this ruler had at least two drunken Acehnese executed by pouring molten lead down their throats (even though he drank a good deal of liquor himself at royal feasts), while his daughter and successor had the hands of two English employees cut off in 1642 for having tried to distill arak (Ito 1984: 170–71). In general, however, embargoes against alcohol and the gambling always associated with cock fighting did not last for long in any state, so deep-rooted were these practices in society.

The Islamic penalty for theft, the loss by amputation of the right hand, left leg, left hand, and so on, for successive thefts of property worth at least a gram of gold, was applied in a number of Southeast Asian sultanates at the height of Islamic influence—in Banten between 1651 and 1680 under Sultan Ageng (Dampier 1699: 97), in Brunei in the sixteenth century (Dasmariñas 1590B: 7), and in some Malay states and Magindanao at a later period (Skeat 1953: 55, 124; *Luwaran*: 68). Aceh had an Islamic court which sentenced thieves to amputation throughout the seventeenth century, and a succession of visitors reported seeing such amputees in the streets (see fig. 20), even though repeated offenders were banished to the offshore island of Sabang (Warwijck 1604: 14; Bowrey 1680: 314; Dampier 1699: 96). Under Sultan Iskandar Muda the practice of maiming went far beyond Islamic prescriptions, extending to the removal of noses, lips, ears, and genitals from subjects who displeased him (Beaulieu 1660: 102; Mundy 1667: 135).

Whereas many Muslim states added some tokens of Islamic jurisprudence to their legal system, Aceh in this period began also to adopt its spirit. The notion of ordeal, with its assumption that the supernatural order would reveal the guilty one without the need for complex laws of evidence, was foreign to Islamic law. Most Muslim states continued to use a system of ordeal, the Malays giving it an Islamic overlay by having the two parties reach into boiling water or oil or

Fig. 20 An Acehnese criminal after having his hands and feet amputated

molten tin to retrieve a potsherd on which a verse of the Koran was written (*Undang-undang Melaka*: 88–89). In Aceh, however, Sultan Iskandar Thani (1637–41) is recorded as forbidding the use of traditional systems of ordeal in the name of Islam (Raniri 1644: 45). This marks one of the high points in the movement away from magic and towards a legally based urban mentality in Southeast Asia. Yet it appears to have been short-lived, for ordeal was again in use in Aceh towards the end of the century (Ito 1984: 178–79).

The effectiveness of these systems of law was extremely varied.

Where a strong and humane ruler had a relatively homogeneous population to deal with, visitors were often impressed by the low rate of crime. In Ternate Galvão (1544: 129) believed that "murder hardly ever occurs," so that it was treated very seriously when it did. At a later period, in nineteenth-century Bangkok, Pallegoix (1854 I: 367) remarked, "It is astonishing that in a city of four hundred thousand souls there are so few troubles and disorders, although the commissioners of police do not make their rounds; one does not see patrols of soldiers prowling in all directions as in European towns." One of the reasons for this effectiveness was undoubtedly the principle of collective responsibility, whereby family members or neighbours were held responsible for any crime committed in their community. This applied not only in Siam and Maluku but also in the Malay world as a whole (*Sulu Code* 1878: 95; Wilkinson 1908: 5). If a thief or murderer could not be identified, the appropriate fine would be imposed on the community where the body or other evidence was found. "In that way they often come to know the truth because he who has to pay detects the crime" (Galvão 1544: 129).

On the other hand, some of the pluralistic trading cities appeared to be almost lawless, with the authorities unable or unwilling to control the quarrelling foreign seamen in the port. Melaka in 1500 seems to have been such a city, so that foreign merchants slept on their ships for safety (Varthema 1510: 226). Banten a century later was another, and Edmund Scott's experience there (1606: 105) allowed him "to speake of little else but murther, theft, warres, fire and treason." Sultan Iskandar Muda justified his own tyrannical regime in Aceh by pointing out that it too had previously been "a haven for murderers and brigands, where the stronger trampled on the weak, and the great oppressed the small; where one had to defend oneself against armed robbers in broad daylight, and to barricade one's house at night" (Beaulieu 1666: 62).

Although it was the general pattern to allow ethnic minorities a measure of judicial autonomy, some rulers carried this principle to the borders of anarchy. The Raja of Jambi, in southern Sumatra, warned the English against his own people, who were "given much to theft; so that we are like to find no justice against them unless we take them in the action; then we may do with them as we please" (Westby 1615: 167–68). The Europeans contributed to this lawless situation by taking advantage wherever possible of their superior arms. The first English commander in the East, James Lancaster, successfully demanded permission from the child-king of Banten to kill anyone he found in the vicinity of the English residence in that city. "After four or five were thus slain, we lived in reasonable peace and quiet" (Lancaster 1603: 115).

Sexual Relations

Relations between the sexes represented one aspect of the social system in which a distinctive Southeast Asian pattern was especially evident. Even the gradual strengthening of the influence of Islam, Christianity, Buddhism, and Confucianism in their respective spheres over the last four centuries has by no means eliminated a common pattern of relatively high female autonomy and economic importance. In the sixteenth and seventeenth centuries the region probably represented one extreme of human experience on these issues. It would be wrong to say that women were *equal* to men—indeed, there were very few areas in which they competed directly. Women had different functions from men, but these included transplanting and harvesting rice, weaving, and marketing. Their reproductive role gave them magical and ritual powers which it was difficult for men to match. These factors may explain why the value of daughters was never questioned in Southeast Asia as it was in China, India, and the Middle East; on the contrary, "the more daughters a man has, the richer he is" (Galvão 1544: 89; cf. Legazpi 1569: 61).

Throughout Southeast Asia wealth passed from the male to the female side in marriage—the reverse of European dowry. Vietnam in modern times has been the exception to this pattern as to many others, because of the progressive imposition of the sternly patriarchal Confucian system beginning in the fifteenth century. Yet in southern Vietnam as late as the seventeenth century men continued what must have been an older Southeast Asian pattern, giving bride-wealth at marriage and even residing with the families of their brides (Yu 1978: 92–96).

To some early Christian missionaries the practice of paying bride-wealth was disapproved as a form of buying a wife (Chirino 1604: 262; Polanco 1556; 209). Although the terminology of the market was occasionally used in this as in other transactions, the practice of bride-wealth in fact demonstrated the high economic value of women and contributed to their autonomy. In contrast to the other major area of bride-price, Africa, where the wealth went to the bride's father and was eventually inherited through the male line, Southeast Asian women benefited directly from the system (Boserup 1970: 48–49; Goody 1976: 8). Tomé Pires (1515: 267) put it strongly for the Malays he knew: "The man must give the woman ten *tahil* and six *mas* of gold as dowry which must always be actually in her power." In other cases bride-wealth was paid to the bride's parents, who transferred some property to their daughter.

In sharp contrast to the Chinese pattern, the married couple more frequently resided in the wife's than in the husband's village. In Thailand, Burma, and Malaya that was the rule (La Loubère 1691: 51; Pallegoix 1854 I: 230; Shway Yoe 1882: 59; Wilkinson 1908A: 37). Southeast Asian legal codes differed markedly from their supposed Indian or Chinese (in Vietnam) models in their common insistence that property be held jointly by the married couple and administered together (Lingat 1952: 38–39, 135–41, 153, 166). In inheritance all children had an equal claim regardless of sex, though favoured children or those caring for the aged might obtain a larger share (La Loubère 1691: 52; Reynolds 1979: 935; Plasencia 1589: 181). Islamic law, which required that sons receive double the inheritance of daughters, was never effectively implemented (Saleeby 1905: 66; Geertz 1963: 47, 81). The stern Chinese legal principle that wives had no say in the disposal of family property found its way into some nineteenth-century Vietnamese law codes, but never into Vietnamese practice (Lingat 1952: 30–36, 92–96).

The relative autonomy enjoyed by women extended to sexual relations. Southeast Asian literature of the period leaves us in little doubt that women took a very active part in courtship and lovemaking, and demanded as much as they gave by way of sexual and emotional gratification. The literature describes the physical attractiveness of male heroes and their appeal to women as enthusiastically as it does the reverse. One of the themes of classical Malay and Javanese literature is the physical attraction of such heroes as Panji and Hang Tuah: "If Hang Tuah passed, married women tore themselves from the embraces of their husbands so that they could go out and see him" (*Sejarah Melayu* 1612: 78; cf. *Wangbang Wideya*: 113; Rassers 1922: 29). Romantic tales of love were as prominent as in any other of the world's literatures. The Panji stories of the prince's quest for his beloved are a good case in point because they became enormously popular in Java between the fifteenth and seventeenth centuries, spreading from there to the Malay world and in the eighteenth century to Thailand, Burma, and Cambodia, where they inspired the Inao cycle (Rassers 1922; Pigeaud 1967: 206–09; Dhaninivat 1956).

Even more characteristic of an essentially Southeast Asian genius were (and are) the earthy rhyming quatrains known as *pantun* in Malay and *lam* in many of the Tai languages. They did not always deal with matters of love, but their most characteristic spontaneous expression was as a dialogue between man and woman or the two parties to a marriage negotiation, taking the form of a battle of the sexes in which each tried to outdo the other in wit and suggestive allusion (Compton 1979). A very similar form of spontaneous contest in poetry and music was enormously popular in the central Philippines up to early Spanish times:

> It [*balak*] is always between a man and a woman and most commonly concerns affairs of love. They use it in two ways, either answering or replying to each other vocally on amatory matters, all evil . . . with remarkable sharpness and quickness, or else on two instruments. . . . On these they talk and reply to each other (Alcina 1668 III: 34–35).
>
> They gather and join together to look each other over, they make love to one another and court each other [on these instruments] with much more feeling or sensuality . . . than by word of mouth (ibid.: 68–69).

As usual, Chou Ta-kuan (1297: 17) had a colourful way of describing the expectations the Cambodian women of his day had of their men. "If the husband is called away for more than ten days, the wife is apt to say, 'I am not a spirit; how am I supposed to sleep alone?' " The ideal of the ever faithful wife left behind during her husband's travels was upheld in the pages of Indian-derived epics, but not in everyday life. At Javanese marriages, according to Raffles (1815 I: 318), the groom was solemnly warned, "If you should happen to be absent from her for the space of seven months on shore, or one year at sea, without giving her any subsistence . . . your marriage shall be dissolved, if your wife desires it, without any further form or process." Vietnamese law as promulgated in the fifteenth century (once again diverging sharply from Chinese practice) set a similar period of five months' absence, or twelve months if the marriage had produced children (Lingat 1952: 89n).

The most graphic demonstration of the strong position women enjoyed in sexual matters was the painful surgery men endured on their penis to increase the erotic pleasure of women. Once again, this is a phenomenon whose dispersion throughout Southeast Asia is very striking, though it appears to be absent in other parts of the world. Although it is the Indian *Kama Sutra* which makes the earliest reference to such surgery, this probably refers to Southeast Asian practice. A careful recent survey of the ethnographic evidence (Brown, Edwards, and Moore) suggests that the phenomenon may best be understood as a symptom of the power and autonomy enjoyed by Southeast Asian women. The authors show (citing Tausug evidence, though female circumcision is today widely practised in Indonesia and was reported in seventeenth-century Makassar—Gervaise 1701: 139) that some women also undergo a clitoral circumcision kept secret from men and purported to enhance female sexual pleasure. The early Southeast Asian pattern appears to be the opposite of that in parts of Africa, where surgery was designed either to enhance sexual gratification in men or to decrease it in women.

The most draconian surgery was the insertion of a metal pin, complemented by a variety of wheels, spurs, or studs, in the central and southern Philippines and parts of Borneo. Pigafetta (1524: 43) was the first of the astonished Europeans to describe the practice:

> The males, large and small, have their penis pierced from one side to the other near the head with a gold or tin bolt as large as a goose quill. In both ends of the same bolt some have what resembles a spur, with points upon the ends; others are like the head of a cart nail. I very often asked many, both old and young, to see their penis, because I could not credit it. In the middle of the bolt is a hole, through which they urinate. . . . They say their women wish it so, and that if they did otherwise they would not have communication with them. When the men wish to have communication with their women, the latter themselves take the penis not in the regular way and commence very gently to introduce it, with the spur on top first, and then the other part. When it is inside it takes its regular position; and thus the penis always stays inside until it gets soft, for otherwise they could not pull it out.

The same phenomenon is described by many others, in different Visayan islands and in Mindanao (Loarca 1582: 116; Pretty 1588: 242; Dasmariñas 1590A: 417–18; Carletti 1606: 83–84; Morga 1609: 278), who agree that its purpose was always explained as enhancing sexual pleasure, especially for the women. Some peoples of northwest Borneo, notably the Iban and the Kayan, continued this practice until modern times, and their oral tradition attributes its origins to a legendary woman who found sexual intercourse without such an aid less satisfying than masturbation (Harrison 1964: 165–66).

The same result was obtained in other parts of Southeast Asia by the less painful but probably more delicate operation of inserting small balls or bells under the loose skin of the penis. The earliest report is from the Chinese Muslim Ma Huan (1433: 104). He reported that in Siam,

> when a man has attained his twentieth year, they take the skin which surrounds the *membrum virile*, and with a fine knife . . . they open it up and insert a dozen tin beads inside the skin; they close it up and protect it

with medicinal herbs. . . . The beads look like a cluster of grapes. . . . If it is the king . . . or a great chief or a wealthy man, they use gold to make hollow beads, inside which a grain of sand is placed. . . . They make a tinkling sound, and this is regarded as beautiful.

Numerous European writers note the same phenomenon in Pegu during the fifteenth and sixteenth centuries, and Tomé Pires (1515: 102–03) described it as a special feature of the Pegu men among all the varied traders visiting Melaka. "The Pegu lords wear as many as nine gold ones, with beautiful trebble, contralto and tenor tones, the size of the Alvares plums in our country; and those who are too poor . . . have them in lead." Pires adds, perhaps with tongue in cheek, "Our Malay women rejoice greatly when the Pegu men come to their country, and they are very fond of them. The reason for this must be their sweet harmony." The primary purpose seems again the pleasure of the female. When the Dutch admiral Jacob van Neck asked in some astonishment what purpose was served by the sweet-sounding little golden bells the wealthy Thais of Patani carried in their penises, they replied that "the women obtain inexpressible pleasure from it" (van Neck 1604: 226; cf. Fitch 1591: 308).

Penis balls extended as far as Makassar, where "the men carry usually one, two, or more balls in their penis, of the same size as those of Siam, but not hollow or clinking, rather of ivory or solid fishbone" (van der Hagen 1607: 82). Islam quickly suppressed the practice, but some non-Islamic Torajans of the interior of Sulawesi still wore such balls at the end of the nineteenth century (Adriani and Kruyt 1912–14 II: 392). At least in one part of central Luzon men used small balls "the size of chick-peas" (Dasmariñas 1590A: 444). Although a Siamese style of bell is attested for Java by only one secondhand source (Pigafetta 1524: 95), something of the kind must have existed there prior to Islamization because the lingas of the two fifteenth-century temples of Sukuh and Cetu, near Surakarta, are embellished with three or four small balls (Stutterheim 1930: 31; and see fig. 21). Both Islam and Christianity did all they could to get rid of this custom. The Muslim circumcision ritual at puberty provided an alternative initiation to manhood.[1] Spanish officials gave a beating to any Visayan they found wearing a penis pin (Dasmariñas 1590A: 418). By the mid-seventeenth century we hear no more of erotic surgery in the coastal, accessible areas of Southeast Asia.

1. Some may have confused the two rituals, however. The non-Muslim Huaulu named their subincision of boys' penises (*pasunate*) after the Arabic circumcision (Valeri 1985).

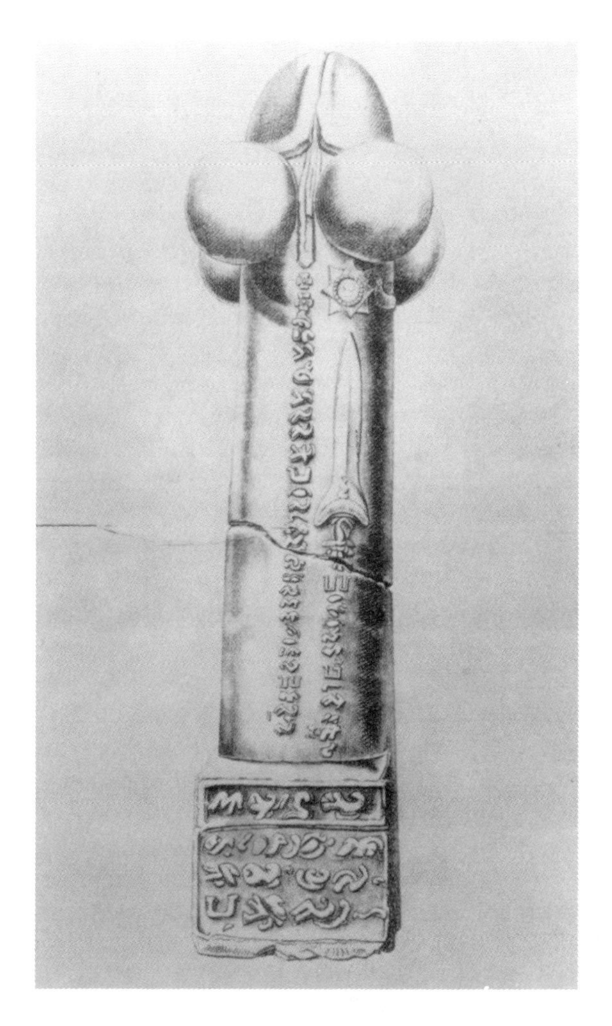

Fig. 21 Penis balls represented in a linga of the fifteenth-century Hindu temple Candi Sukuh, in central Java

Marriage

The dominant marriage pattern was one of monogamy, with divorce relatively easy for both sides. Chirino (1604: 319) said that he "was in the Philippines almost ten years without knowing of a man married to several women." Among rulers there were spectacular exceptions to this rule of monogamy; for them an abundance of wives was both an indication of status and a diplomatic weapon. Subordinate lineages presented their daughters as wives to a king "as a form of tribute, an act of homage, and an oath of fealty" (Geertz 1980: 35). A more widespread pattern among the rich was one of casual sexual relations with slave members of the household. Such relations, which were sharply distinguished from marriage by the absence of ritual and the low claim on inheritance of any progeny resulting, are best regarded as an aspect of the bondage system.

Among the overwhelming majority of ordinary people, the pattern of monogamy was reinforced by the ease of divorce, the preferred means of ending an unsatisfactory union. In the Philippines, "marriages last only so long as harmony prevails, for at the slightest cause in the world they divorce one another" (Chirino 1604: 321; cf. Morga 1609: 275). In Siam, similarly, "Husband and Wife may part again at pleasure, dealing their goods and children without further circumstance, and may re-marry if they think good, without fear of shame or punishment" (Schouten 1636: 146; cf. La Loubère 1691: 53; van Vliet 1636: 86). It was noted at a later date of both the Chams of southern Vietnam (Aymonier 1891: 30–31) and the Javanese that women were particularly inclined to initiate divorce. "A woman may at any time, when dissatisfied with her husband, demand a dissolution of the marriage contract, by paying him a sum established by custom" (Raffles, 1817 I: 320). Throughout the island world the rule appeared to be that the wife (or her parents) kept the bride-wealth if the husband took the initiative to end the marriage, but had to repay it if she was primarily responsible (Plasencia 1589:813; Dasmariñas 1590A: 410–11; Pires 1515: 267; Beaulieu 1666: 100; Polanco 1556: 209). At least in the Philippines (Chirino 1614: 321) and Siam (La Loubère 1691: 53; van Vliet 1636: 86) the children of a marriage were divided at divorce, the first going to the mother, the second to the father, and so on.

The court diary of seventeenth-century Makassar provides a glimpse of the pattern of frequent divorce as it operated at the top of society, where political and property calculations cannot have been absent. Even here, where it might have been expected, divorce is not described as a decision by a powerful male, X, to exchange his marriage partner, but rather as "X and Y separated from each other" (*sikattoi*, from root *katto*, "cut off"). A not untypical female career in this elite group is that of Karaeng Balla-Jawaya, who was born in 1634 to one of the highest Makassar lineages. At the age of thirteen she married Karaeng Bonto-marannu, later to be one of the great Makassar war leaders. At twenty-five she separated from him and soon after married his rival, Karaeng Karunrung, the effective prime minister. At thirty-one (in 1666) she separated from him, perhaps because he was in exile, and two years later married Arung Palakka, who was in the process of conquering her country with Dutch help. At thirty-six she separated from him, and eventually died at the age of eighty-six (*Lontara'-bilang Gowa*: 95–199). Another highborn lady, Karaeng Tangngalla, was betrothed as a child to the future sultan, Mohammad Said, separated from him, and then at the age of seventeen married him. Later, aged twenty-eight, she separated from him again. She next appears in the court diary in 1649, marrying Karaeng Leengkese, the brother of Karaeng Balla-Jawaya. Six years later she separated from him; but in 1657, at the age of forty-three, she returned to him and stayed until her death in 1661 (*Lontara'-bilang Gowa*: 87–119; cf. *Sejarah Gowa*: 66).

That the majority Muslim population of Indonesia and Malaysia had divorce rates in excess of 50 percent as late as the 1960s is sometimes attributed to the influence of Islam in sanctioning easy divorce for men. Much more important, however, was the pan-Southeast-Asian pattern of female autonomy, which meant that divorce did not markedly reduce a woman's livelihood, status, or network of kin support (van Vollenhoven 1918: 79; Nash 1965: 253; Djamour 1959: 139). In noting the acceptance the Javanese gave to women of twenty-two or twenty-three living with their fourth or fifth husband, Earl (1837: 59) attributed this attitude entirely to the freedom and economic independence enjoyed by women (cf. Crawfurd 1820 I: 78–79; St. John 1862 I: 165–67).

Christian Europe was until the eighteenth century a very "chaste" society in comparative terms, with an exceptionally late average age of marriage (in the twenties), with high proportions never marrying and with a low rate of extramarital conceptions by later standards. (In England this rate rose from only 12 percent of births in 1680 to 50 percent by 1800—Stone 1984: 46; Wrigley and Schofield 1981: 254–60.) Southeast Asia was in many respects the complete antithesis of that chaste pattern, and it seemed to European observers of the time that its inhabitants were preoccupied with sex. The Portuguese liked to say that the Malays were "fond of music and given to love" (Barbosa 1518 II: 176; cf. Barros 1563 II, vi: 24; Eredia 1613: 31, 40), while Javanese, like Burmese, Thais, and Filipinos, were characterized as "very lasciviously given, both men and women" (Scott 1606: 173). What this meant was that pre-marital sexual relations were regarded indulgently, and virginity at marriage was not expected of either party. If pregnancy resulted from these pre-marital activities, the couple were expected to marry, and failing that, resort might be had to abortion or (at least in the Philippines) to infanticide (Dasmariñas 1590A: 427).

Within marriage, on the other hand, the fidelity and devotedness of Southeast Asian couples appears to have surprised Europeans. The women of Banjarmasin, for example, were "very constant when married, but very loose when single" (Beeckman 1718: 41; cf. Valentijn 1726 III: 312; Low 1848: 196; Finlayson 1826: 309–10). In pre-Islamic South Sulawesi fornication with an unmarried woman was overlooked, but with a married (upper-class?) woman was punished with death (Schurhammer 1977: 530). Even Spanish chroniclers who took a dim view of the sexual morality of Filipinos sometimes conceded that "the men treat their wives well, and love them according to their habits" (Legazpi 1569: 61). Galvão (1544: 89) marvelled at how Moluccan wives, "although they always go round among the men, and then nearly naked . . . do not fail to be very chaste and good, which seems to be quite impossible among such a debauched people." A nineteenth-century observer (Cameron 1865: 131) was probably correct in positing a connection between the ease of divorce in rural Malaya and the affection which appeared to characterize Malay marriages. The economic autonomy of women and their capacity to escape from unsatisfactory unions obliged husbands as well as wives to make some effort to keep the marriage intact. One example of how such a pattern operated to constrain foreign men accustomed to different patterns is given by Scott (1606: 127), who commented on a Chinese beating his Vietnamese wife in Banten that this could not have happened if the wife had been a local woman, "for the Javans will hardly suffer them to beat their women."

Curiously, when female virginity is mentioned as a major factor in marriage, it is as an impediment rather than an asset. In the pre-Spanish Philippines, according to Morga (1609: 278), there were (ritual?) specialists whose function was to deflower virgins, "it being thought an obstacle and impediment to marriage for a girl to be a virgin." In Pegu and other ports of Burma and Siam, foreign traders were asked to initiate brides (Varthema 1510: 202–04; cf. Lach 1965: 554). In Angkor the priests broke the hymen of young girls in a costly ritual marking the passage to adulthood and to sexual activity (Chou Ta-kuan 1297: 17–18). The Western literature offers more titillation than explanation for such practices, generally suggesting that Southeast Asian men preferred their women experienced. It seems far more likely that the hymenal blood was considered dangerous or polluting to men, as is the case today with menstrual blood in many areas.

The pattern of premarital sexual activity and easy divorce, together with the commercial element potentially involved in the paying of bride-wealth, ensured that temporary marriage or concubinage rather than prostitution became the dominant means of coping with the vast annual influx of foreign traders to the major ports. The system in Patani was described as follows:

> When foreigners come there from other lands to do their business . . . men come and ask them whether they do not desire a woman; these young women and girls themselves also come and present themselves, from whom they may choose the one most agreeable to them, provided they agree what he shall pay for certain months. Once they agree about the money (which does not amount to much for so great a convenience), she comes to his house, and serves him by day as his maidservant and by night as his wedded wife. He is then not able to consort with other women or he will be in grave trouble with his wife, while she is similarly wholly forbidden to converse with other men, but the marriage lasts as long as he keeps his residence there, in good peace and unity. When he wants to depart he gives her whatever is promised, and so they leave each other in friendship, and she may then look for another man as she wishes, in all propriety, without scandal (van Neck 1604: 225).

Exactly the same pattern is described for Javanese traders in Banda for the nutmeg season ("Tweede Boeck" 1601: 77), for Europeans and others in Vietnam, Cambodia, Siam, and Burma (Dampier 1697: 268; Dampier 1699: 40–41; Symes 1827 I: 253; Navarrete 1676: 268). Hamilton (1727: 28) related in affectionate detail how the system worked in Pegu, where a formal marriage ritual was held for these temporary relationships, to which both parties were bound by legal obligation. Like Chou Ta-kuan (1297: 27) in Cambodia, he appreciated the double advantage of such local wives as not only bedmates but commercial partners. "If their Husbands have any goods to sell, they set up a shop and sell them by retail, to a much better account than they could be sold for by wholesale."

The boundary between such temporary marriages and durable ones must often have been uncertain, and interracial unions were a feature of all the commercial cities of Southeast Asia. Outsiders found it strange and reprehensible that religion was also no bar to marriage: in Melaka "the infidel marries Muslim women while the Muslim takes pagans to wife" (Ibn Majid 1462: 206; cf. Pires 1515: 268); in Makassar "Christian Men kept Mahometan women, and Mahometan Men, Christian women" (Navarrete 1676: 122–23). Only when women close to the court sought to marry foreigners did it provoke strong opposition, as in the case of the ill-fated romance of a Dutch factor and a Siamese princess, which probably gave rise to King Prasat Thong's 1657 decree prohibiting Thai women from marrying foreigners (Smith 1974: 285–87).

Although temporary marriage had also been known to Islam at

the time of Muhammad (Bouhdiba 1975: 126–27), the Muslim ports of the Archipelago may have tended to restrict explicitly temporary marriages to slave women, who differed from the free in that they could be sold by one "husband" to another and had few rights over children. In Banten the practice of Chinese traders was described as "to buy women slaves . . . by whom they have manie children. And when they returne to their owne countrey . . . they sell their women, but their children they carrie with them" (Scott 1606: 176). The English in places may have had a similar practice, if we can believe their great enemy, Jan Pieterszoon Coen (1619: 478), who rejoiced that the English factors in Sukadana (West Borneo) were so impoverished that "they had to sell their whores" to pay for their victuals.

Prostitution was much rarer than temporary marriage or concubinage, but it began to appear in the major cities in the late sixteenth century. In every case the prostitutes were slave women belonging to the king or nobles. The Spanish described such slave women as offering themselves in small boats in the water city of Brunei in the 1570s (Dasmariñas 1590B: 14); the Dutch described a similar phenomenon in Patani in 1602, though it was less common and less respectable than temporary marriage (van Neck 1604: 225). In the 1680s a particular Thai official was licensed by the king to run a monopoly of prostitution in the capital, Ayutthaya, using six hundred women bought or enslaved for various offences. This appears to have been the origin of a Thai tradition of drawing significant state revenue from prostitution (La Loubère 1691: 74, 85; Pallegoix 1854 I: 311). Eighteenth-century Rangoon, similarly, had a whole "village of prostitutes," all slaves (Symes 1827 I: 252–53). It seems probable that this type of slave prostitution in the major port cities of the region developed in response to a demand from Europeans and Chinese with different expectations. It may also have been stimulated by a growing sense, at least among Muslims, of the impropriety of temporary marriages with foreigners and unbelievers.

The broad pattern of sexual relations—relative premarital freedom, monogamy and fidelity within marriage (which was easily dissolved by divorce), and a strong female position in the sexual game—conflicted in different ways with the practices of all the world religions which were increasing their hold on Southeast Asia in the age of commerce. The sharpest conflict might have been expected with Islamic law, which made women both legally and economically dependent on their husbands and markedly restricted their rights to initiate divorce. Pre-marital sexual relations (*zina'*) were also punished very severely under Islamic law, and Arab parents until recently tended to marry off their girls soon after puberty to prevent this from occurring (Gibb and Kramers 1961: 564–70, 658–59).

The impact of these Islamic attitudes below the winds was greatest among the wealthy urban mercantile elite, whose children were already subject to greater control because their marriages involved both property and status. Even in Buddhist Siam the elite differed from the populace in guarding their daughters carefully before marriage and in retaining both the wives "they love not, and those they love" (La Loubère 1691: 53, 51). Muslim-influenced law codes show an acute awareness of the conflict between the demands of the shari'a and local realities. The *Sulu Code* (1878: 92–93) deliberately ignored Islamic law and punished each type of adultery by a different fine, while the *Luwaran* of nearby Magindanao (17–72) recorded the full Islamic law on zina', with its capital punishment for those found in extramarital relations. The Melaka legal code (*Undang-undang Melaka*: 158–61) included the latter as a kind of optional addendum. If nothing else, the growing minority of international Muslim traders in Melaka made it impossible to ignore the shari'a altogether. In the main body of the code, however, the laws are set out with typically Southeast Asian flexibility:

> If a man seduces someone's daughter, and the father comes to know, he shall be fined 2¼ *tahil* by the judge. If a marriage is suitable, he shall be made to marry, and be required to pay the full expenses. . . .
>
> If a man seizes a free woman and then rapes her, and the latter informs the judge, he shall be summoned by the judge and ordered to marry her. If he refuses to marry, he shall be fined 3 *tahil*, 1 *paha*, and pay a wedding-gift. . . . But according to the Law of God, if he is *muhsan* (an adult Muslim), he shall be stoned (ibid.: 84–85; cf. Moyer 1975: 185–86).

The Muslim elite of the cities in the seventeenth century took these Islamic penalties very seriously, especially when the zina' offence was between married people. Van Neck (1604: 224) witnessed the outcome of a tragic affair in Patani, in which one Malay nobleman was obliged to strangle his own daughter and another to kris his own son, after the married daughter had been caught receiving love gifts from her admirer. In Aceh and Brunei around 1600 similar death sentences appear to have been common, in at least one case by flogging to death as the Islamic law prescribes (Ito 1984: 168–70; Dasmariñas 1590B: 9). Nevertheless, since such rigorous implementation of the shari'a was extremely rare even in the most Islamic parts of Southeast Asia in the nineteenth century (Snouck Hurgronje 1893 I: 10–14;

Saleeby 1905: 66, 92–93; Hsieh 1820: 20), the stern model imposed by some rulers on the cosmopolitan trading cities cannot have penetrated their hinterlands in any depth.

The *talak* formula of Islamic law, whereby a man could divorce his wife (but not the reverse) by thrice repeating a simple repudiation, was also known in the cosmopolitan ports of the region and took its place as part of God's law in the Melaka Code (*Undang-undang Melaka*: 132–33). Since the economic and social position of the divorced Southeast Asian woman was at least as strong as that of the man, however, this religious prescription had little effect on the practice of divorce. As the great Arab navigator Ibn Majid (1462: 206) complained, Malays "do not treat divorce as a religious act." A Spanish observer in Brunei noted that husbands were entitled to divorce their wives for the most trivial reasons, but that in practice "they usually divorce voluntarily, both together wanting it; and they agree to return half the dowry and to divide the children if they have them" (Dasmariñas 1590B: 9).

Young Brides?

When Europeans commented on the age of marriage in Southeast Asia, it was always to marvel at the youth of the bridal couple. Since Europe was then in a phase of late marriage very exceptional in world history—English brides averaged twenty-six years and grooms twenty-eight in the seventeenth century (Wrigley and Schofield 1981: 225)—this is not remarkable. Yet the extremely young ages of marriage reported can create a false impression. Thus the ruler of Gelgel (Bali) was amazed to learn that the Dutch envoys to his court remained unmarried at twenty-three and twenty-five, and claimed that in Bali men married at twelve years and women were betrothed at nine (Lintgens 1597: 77). In Banten at the same period Europeans reported child brides of five to ten years being carried in procession through the streets, and claimed this was to prevent unmarried children being taken into the palace in bondage if their fathers were to die ("Tweede Boeck" 1601: 149; Mandelslo 1606: 115; Barrow 1806: 226). La Loubère (1691: 51) simply noted that Siamese girls married "young," since they were capable of bearing children at the age of twelve. Morga (1609: 277) reported that while waiting for his wife to be old enough for sex, a Filipino man was allowed to sleep openly with her older sisters.

Marriages at or before puberty are difficult to reconcile with the pattern of female autonomy and relative sexual freedom before marriage. There are strong reasons to believe, however, that such marriages were not the norm. First, the onset of puberty apparently occurred much earlier than in Europe, a consequence of climate as well as relatively good nutrition (Eveleth 1979: 384–87; Laslett 1980). Craen (1606: 180, 199) reported that Indonesian girls of twelve and thirteen were sexually active, which coincides with Jacobs' more careful later finding (1894 I: 209) that Acehnese girls began to menstruate between the twelfth and thirteenth year. A survey in nineteenth-century Cochin-China found that although the first signs of puberty appeared in girls of twelve, the "average age of nubility" was sixteen years four months (Bouinais and Paulus 1885 I: 228).

Second, the spectacularly opulent weddings of the rich and highborn which so impressed contemporary observers were almost certainly atypical. The same anomaly of some very youthful marriages by aristocratic women long misled historians of Europe (Laslett 1965: 84–92). In Southeast Asia, too, the elite were anxious to avoid unacceptable liaisons by their daughters or doubtful parentage for their grandchildren, and therefore sought betrothals with appropriate spouses at an early age. In the wealthy trading cities most firmly committed to Islam—Aceh, Banten, Brunei, and Patani—the habit of arranging marriages for daughters at the age of puberty appears to have spread through a wider sector of society, in reaction to the prevailing premarital sexual permissiveness. Aceh and Banten were notorious for exceptionally early female marriage in the nineteenth century (Jacobs 1894 I: 27), while modern Indonesian census data still shows a markedly lower average bridal age in regions noted for strict Islamic adherence. Muslim Madurese and Sundanese women were marrying on average at a little over fourteen in the 1940s, while Hindu Balinese women waited until they were nearly eighteen (B.P.S. 1980: 38). This relatively late marriage pattern for twentieth-century Balinese, who appear to have undergone no dramatic reversal of religious and ethical values since the seventeenth century, should make us cautious about the early impressions of Europeans. Similarly, recent careful studies of Philippine marriage registers have shown a mean age of first marriage for women of above 20.5, from the time when data becomes reliable in the 1820s (Ng 1979: 138; Owen 1985), even though contemporary Europeans believed that brides there were exceptionally young. Burma too appears, in the seventeenth century, to have had a pattern of marriage relatively late by the standards of most other preindustrial societies (Lieberman 1984: 20).

Third, even the elite may not have married quite as early on average as some illustrious cases suggest. One highborn Makassarese lady has already been mentioned who married for the first time at thirteen. For all the eight aristocratic women whose birth and marriage dates are reliably given in the Makassar court diary (*Lontara'-bilang Gowa*), however, the average age of first marriage is fifteen years nine months.

I am inclined to conclude that marriages at the age of puberty (twelve to fourteen) were an exception, found primarily among just that wealthy nobility which provided the most spectacular wedding ceremonies. In the population at large, women probably married between fifteen and twenty-one, allowing them several years in which to begin the courting games so popular in the region.

Childbirth and Fertility

The low birthrate which characterized Southeast Asia in the seventeenth century and earlier seems to have been caused in the first place by endemic low-level warfare and instability (see chapter 2). Even in conditions of peace, however, there may have been some significant restraints of birth, both deliberate and involuntary.

One relative constant in Southeast Asia over the past five centuries has been a longer interval between children than in Europe. One reason for this, it is now clear, is that prolonged lactation tends to lengthen the period of anovulation in mothers by an average of about nine months. Southeast Asian mothers until very recently suckled their young for at least two years. "Women [in Siam] do not suckle their children for five or six months, as in Europe, but for two and even three years, even while giving them rice and bananas to eat" (Pallegoix 1854 I: 224). A systematic study of births in a nineteenth-century Luzon village has shown an average child spacing of twenty-nine months, which is almost exactly the natural interval if mothers continue breast-feeding (Ng 1979: 152–59). Nevertheless, these Philippine mothers produced on average about six children (ibid.: 166, 169)—far more than appears to have been the case in the earlier period.

A number of firsthand accounts insist that although Southeast Asian women began their childbearing early in comparison with Europe or China, they also ended it early (Beeckman 1718: 42; Chou Ta-kuan 1297: 17; Marsden 1783: 284–85). Some authorities, including the Burmese Census Report for 1891, gave as a reason for early loss of fertility the practice of "roasting" mothers after childbirth (Sangermano 1818: 164; Shway Yoe 1882: 1–2; Graham 1912: 148). The earliest observation of this practice is that of La Loubère (1691: 66–67) for Siamese and Burmese, but its occurrence throughout mainland

Southeast Asia, Malaya, northern Sumatra, parts of Borneo, the Moluccas, and the Visayas in the nineteenth century (Jacobs 1894 I: 141–44; Skeat 1900: 342–43; Manderson 1981: 513–15) suggests that it was already widespread during the age of commerce. Women were purified and heated after the dangerously "cooling" effect of childbirth by being placed above or beside a fire for periods of between three and forty days. The consequence was frequently that women emerged "scorched and blackened," with severe blistering of the skin (Sangermano 1818: 164). This may have made women look prematurely aged, but it is doubtful that it could really have affected fertility.

Another uncertain factor is gonorrhea. Modern studies of relatively isolated, animist peoples in North Borneo in the 1930s (Muruts) and eastern Indonesia in the 1960s (Sumba) have shown an incidence of gonorrhea in 80 and 90 percent, respectively, of the women examined. In the Sumba survey infertility had resulted for 25 percent of the women (Mitchell 1982; Tregonning 1965: 163). In such societies, which were a great deal more typical before the spread of Islam and Christianity, premarital sexual relations were not prohibited. Moreover, there was a widespread belief that the way for a man to free himself from the "female contamination" represented by venereal disease was to couple with a healthy woman and thereby return the "alien" element to her (Mitchell 1982: Jordaan and de Josselin de Jong 1985: 256–57; La Bissachère 1812 I: 67). Although such attitudes could have made gonorrhea endemic, we cannot know whether they did so. There are plenty of references to the prevalence of venereal disease, especially in Java, Bali, and Lombok (Pigafetta 1524: 94; Drake 1580: 73; Crawfurd 1820 I: 33–34; Zollinger 1851: 338). But until the twentieth century there is no reliable way to distinguish gonorrhea from syphilis or to draw any conclusions about fertility.

We are on safer ground in asserting that Southeast Asian women had some control over their own fertility and that deliberate limitation of births was a major factor. In the Malay epic *Sejarah Melayu* (1612: 166) abortion is described as a normal occurrence. Ethnographers in many parts of the region have established that contraceptive herbs and massage to induce abortion were part of female lore (Nash 1963: 252, 265; St. John 1862 II: 261; Snouck Hurgronje 1893 I: 113; Rutter 1929: 73; Forth 1981: 13). The desire to limit births appears to have been particularly strong among animist swidden cultivators, perhaps because the work load of women in such systems did not allow them to spend much time in pregnancy and child rearing (see chapter 2).

A striking example of this was the Visayan Islands of the Philippines, less affected by external Islamic influences than the Manila area at the time of the Spanish arrival. "It is considered a disgrace among them to have many children," noted Loarca (1582: 119), "for they say that when the property is to be divided among all the children, they will all be poor." Another observer noted:

> Women dislike to give birth many times, specially those who inhabit towns near the sea, saying that in having many children they are like pigs. . . . After having one or two, the next time they get pregnant, when they are already three or four months, they kill the creature in the body and abort. There are women for this calling and by massaging the stomach and placing certain herbs . . . the pregnant woman aborts (Dasmariñas 1590A: 413; cf. Pedrosa 1983: 13–20).

One visitor believed that the Visayan penis pin was partly designed to reduce the likelihood of pregnancy as a result of intercourse (Carletti 1606: 84); and reduced fecundity among users of the pin in Borneo has been noted by a modern ethnographer (Appell 1968: 205).

The growing numbers of Buddhists, Christians, and Muslims, particularly in the cities and irrigated rice areas where the female work load was less heavy and insecurity less constant, appear to have chosen to have larger families (Dasmariñas 1590A: 427). Whether the family was large or small, children of both sexes were cherished and indulged. "The union of families is such," wrote La Loubère of Siam (1691: 74), that "no person in this country dreads marriage, nor a number of children." The frequently acerbic Crawfurd (1820 I: 83) conceded that "in the relation between parent and child . . . the character of the Indian Islanders appears most unexceptionable and most amiable."

Female Roles

It is already clear that women had a relatively high degree of economic autonomy in premodern Southeast Asia. Nevertheless, it was taken for granted that the opposition of male and female characteristics was a fundamental part of the cosmic dualism. Perhaps for this very reason it was not thought necessary to create artificial markers of gender through dress, hairstyle, or speech patterns, none of which stressed the male-female distinction. A rash of recent studies on the anthropology of gender in Indonesia has uncovered a variety of expressions of the complementary opposition of male and female. Maleness is typically associated with white (semen), warmth, sky, form, control, and deliberate creativity; the female with red (blood), coolness, earth, substance, spontaneity, and natural creativity. The male feature is often seen (at least by males) as preferred, but both are necessary and the union of the two is a powerful ideal (van der Kroef 1956; Valeri 1985; Duff-Cooper 1985; Keeler 1983).

Such theoretical distinctions help explain the clear boundaries between male and female domains in the house, the fields, and the marketplace. Since everyday activities formed part of this cosmic dualism, especially when they affected plant and animal life, it was not a matter of indifference whether men or women performed them. Male work included all that pertained to metals and animals—ploughing, felling the jungle, hunting, metalworking, woodworking, and house building—as well as statecraft and formal (international) religion. The female domain included transplanting, harvesting, vegetable growing, food preparation, weaving, pottery making (in most areas), and marketing, as well as ancestor cults and mediation with the spirits.

At village level these dichotomies have not changed greatly in the last four centuries. The male domain has expanded enormously, however, through the greater role of statecraft and formal religion, and the ability of larger sections of the population to imitate aristocratic mores which portray women as dependent, decorous, and loyal. In the age of commerce, assumptions of male superiority already affected the courts and the urban elite, who listened to Indian epics of Rama and Sita, studied Chinese Confucian classics (in Vietnam), or were tutored by the theologians of Theravada Buddhism, Islam, or Christianity. In 1399, for example, the Thai queen of Sukhothai prayed that through her merit she might be "reborn as a male," thus moving up the Buddhist hierarchy (Reynolds 1979: 929).

That there was a discrepancy between courtly ideals and everyday reality there is no doubt. What requires examination is the extent to which women in that period were still able to extend their spheres of action into those larger events which are the normal subjects for historians. By examining successively trade, diplomacy, warfare, entertainment, literature, and statecraft we shall see that Southeast Asian women were playing an unusually influential role by comparison with later periods or with other parts of the world.

Since marketing was a female domain par excellence, this is the place to start. Even today Southeast Asian countries top the comparative statistics assembled by Ester Boserup (1970: 87–89) for female participation in trade and marketing. Fifty-six percent of those so listed in Thailand were women, 51 percent in the Philippines, 47 percent in Burma, and 46 percent in Cambodia. Although Indonesia had a lower rate, 31 percent, this still contrasted sharply with other

Muslim countries, particularly in the Middle East (1 to 5 percent). In Bangkok at the time of the 1947 census, three times as many Thai women as men were registered as owners or managers of businesses (Skinner 1957: 301). A famous Minangkabau poem first written down in the 1820s exhorted mothers to teach their daughters "to judge the rise and fall of prices" (cited Dobbin 1983: 50). Southeast Asian women are still expected to show more commercially shrewd and thrifty attitudes than men, and male Chinese and European traders are apt to be derided for having the mean spirit of a woman on such matters (Alexander 1984: 36).

Although the casual visitor to Southeast Asia today might not be aware of the female trading role, which is now restricted to rural and small-scale markets, this has not always been the case. Early European and Chinese traders were constantly surprised to find themselves dealing with women:

In Cambodia it is the women who take charge of trade (Chou 1297: 20).

It is their [Siamese] custom that all affairs are managed by their wives . . . all trading transactions great and small (Ma Huan 1433: 104).

The women of Siam are the only merchants in buying goods, and some of them trade very considerably (Hamilton 1727: 96).

The money-changers are here [Aceh], as at Tonkin, most women (Dampier 1699: 92, also 47).

In Cochin-China every man is a soldier. The commercial operations are performed by women (White 1824: 261; also Chapman, quoted Yu 1978: 102).

Women in the Birman country . . . manage the more important mercantile concerns of their husbands (Symes 1827 I: 255).

It is the women [of Maluku] who negotiate, do business, buy and sell (Galvão 1544: 75).

[In Melaka] women hold a market at night (Hwang Chung 1537: 128; cf. Pires 1515: 274).

It is usual for the husband to entrust his pecuniary affairs entirely to his wife. The women alone attend the markets, and conduct all the business of buying and selling. It is proverbial to say the Javanese men are fools in money concerns (Raffles 1817 I: 353).

The prominence of foreigners and of the ruling circle in the trade of most Southeast Asian cities ensured that most of the large-scale merchants and shipowners were male. A significant number of local women did, however, join this circle. A famous one was Nyai Gede Pinateh, a promoter of Islam and "foster-mother" of Sunan Giri, whose tomb is still honoured at Gresik. She was a foreign-born Muslim whose origins are placed by different traditions in Palembang, China, or Cambodia. Around 1500 she appears to have been acting as *shahbandar* (harbour master) of Gresik and reportedly sent her ships to trade in Bali, Maluku, and Cambodia (Raffles 1817 II: 115–20; Meilink-Roelofsz 1962: 108; Lombard and Salmon 1985: 74). Some royal women used their access to capital to good effect. In the 1660s the wife of Sultan Hasanuddin of Makassar, Lomo' Tombo, owned ships which she sent on very profitable trade missions to Johor (Speelman 1670A: 111). The women who occupied the thrones of Aceh, Jambi, and Inderagiri in the seventeenth century similarly traded and speculated at least as vigorously as their male counterparts (Coolhaas 1964: 21, 93, 257, 775).

Besides these privileged royal women, the Dutch and English dealt with some formidable female traders. In Cochin-China they haggled over pepper prices with "a great woman merchant (*coopvrouw*) of Sinoa [Hue]" who had made the journey to the capital of Cochin-China in order to check the market. She represented a firm comprising two sisters and a brother which could deliver much pepper, and although she travelled with a male companion, "the woman did the talking and the man listened and agreed" (Wonderaer 1602: 80). A woman of Mon descent, Soet Pegu, used her position as sexual and commercial partner of successive Dutch factors in Ayutthaya to virtually monopolize Dutch-Thai trade in the 1640s and thereby also gain great influence at court (Pombejra 1984: 2–3; van Opstall 1985: 109–12). One of the Patani *orangkaya* who had debts with the English was a woman, Datu Newanan (Browne 1616: 108), and the Dutch in Aceh were buying up tin for export from "another Acehnese woman" (Compostel 1636: fol. 1200).

From trade it was not a great step to diplomacy, especially for those who had been both commercial and sexual partners of foreign traders. Such women frequently became fluent in the languages needed in commerce. Thus the first Dutch mission to Cochin-China found that the king dealt with them through a Vietnamese woman who spoke excellent Portuguese and Malay and had long resided in Macao. She, along with another elderly woman who had had two Portuguese husbands as well as one Vietnamese, had been the principal translator for the Cochin-China court for thirty years (Wonderaer 1602: 22, 38). Similarly, the elderly Burmese wife of the shahbandar of Rangoon, who had earlier been married to the French commander of the Burmese royal guard, was an indispensable intermediary between foreigners and that royal court in the eighteenth century (Cox 1821:

319–21). Later the Sultan of Deli, in Sumatra, ordered "a most extraordinary and eccentric old woman" named Che Laut to accompany John Anderson on his embassy to various Sumatran states. She was "a prodigy of learning," spoke Chinese, Thai, Chuliah, Bengali, and Acehnese and knew the politics of all the Sumatran coastal states intimately (Anderson 1826: 44–45).

In some parts of the island world there appears to have been a positive preference for using women as envoys, particularly in the peacemaking process. Unfortunately our most explicit source for this, Mendes Pinto, is not the most reliable; sometimes he was inclined to embellish his narrative for dramatic effect. After describing the embassy of an old woman named Nyai Pombaya from the ruler of Demak to Banten while he was in the latter port in 1540, Pinto explained that the rulers of Java had always been accustomed "to treat of the most important matters of their state by mediation of women, especially when it concerns peace . . . and all the reason they give for it is, 'that God has given more gentleness and inclination to courtesie, yea and more authority to women than men, who are severe, as they say, and by consequent less agreeable to those unto whom they are sent'" (Pinto 1614: 375). While Pinto may not have personally visited all the places he claimed, there is usually a basis of fact in his stories. In this case, confirmation is available from a more careful reporter who lived in Banten for several years half a century later: "If the King . . . send a man [to fetch someone] the parties may refuse to come; but if he once send a woman, he may not refuse nor make excuse. Moreover if any inferior bodie have a suit to a man of authoritie, if they come not themselves, they alwayes send a woman" (Scott 1606: 170). Women frequently appear as negotiators or witnesses on earlier Javanese inscriptions (Casparis 1981: 147). Elsewhere, in Sulawesi, the Torajans sent an old, blind, aristocratic lady to negotiate for peace with the attacking Bugis forces of Arung Palakka in 1683 (Andaya 1981: 260).

Of course men were also used as envoys, and overwhelmingly so as the international norms of Muslim and Christian states took greater effect in the seventeenth century. What the above comments suggest is that the preoccupation of elite males with ordering the political system in terms of hierarchies of status, and the obligation for them to avenge any infraction of that status (especially in Java—Pires 1515: 176; Ma Huan 1433: 88), made them dangerous emissaries for those who really sought peace. Men could not bargain as women were expected to, nor subordinate their sense of honour to the need for a settlement.

This peacemaking role is difficult to reconcile with the tradition of female warriors. Since warfare is normally an exclusively male business, every culture is probably inclined to romanticize and celebrate those exceptional women who emerge to save a desperate situation. Vietnam has no heroes more renowned than the Trung sisters, who rose up against the Chinese in A.D. 43. Thais remember two sisters who led the successful defence of Phuket in 1785: Queen Suriyothai, who was killed defending Ayutthaya in 1564; and Lady Mo, who rescued Khorat in 1826 after leading an escape by several hundred captive women (Gerini 1905: 179–83). Women were also said to have played a spirited part in the defence of Madura against Sultan Agung of Mataram in 1624 (de Graaf 1958: 90). If such militant heroines played a larger role in Southeast Asia than elsewhere, it is probably because status was more prominent than gender, and women were not excluded from taking the lead if the occasion required it.

More specific to the region was the habit which powerful rulers had of surrounding themselves with large numbers of women, of whom some had the role of bodyguards. The king of Angkor was said to have had four to five thousand women in his palace (Chou Ta-kuan 1297: 15–16), Iskandar Muda of Aceh three thousand (see fig. 22), and Sultan Agung of Mataram ten thousand. At least in the two latter cases these palace women included a corps trained in the use of arms, who mounted guard on the palace and took part in royal processions (Beaulieu 1666: 102; van Goens 1656: 256–60). A women's corps (*prajurit estri*) drilling regularly with rifles was still maintained in late-eighteenth-century Java by the first Mangkunegaran ruler (Kumar 1980: 4–6). The Siamese palace similarly had a female guard (*Sanam Dahar*) responsible for the inner or women's quarters (Wales 1934: 146; La Loubère 1691: 100).

This pattern appears to have stemmed from the distrust which autocratic rulers felt towards any men close to them. In the island world at least, men were expected to respond immediately, with the arms they always carried, to any slight to their honour. The history of the period offers many tragic examples of where this could lead (*Sejarah Melayu* 1612: 98; *Sejarah Goa*: 40). An unusually autocratic Aceh ruler, Sultan al Mukammil (1584–1604), even had a woman as commander of his navy, "for he will trust no other" (Davis 1600: 150). There appears to be no evidence that the confidence the rulers placed in these women was ever betrayed by murder, as happened frequently at the hands of males. Nor is it established that the female corps took part in major battles. Their existence therefore tends to confirm the assumption that violence, the use of arms, and the defence of a touchy sense of honour were fundamentally men's business, and that women

Fig. 22 Female guards at court of Aceh, as fancifully portrayed in the seventeenth-century woodcut published with van Warwijck 1604

could be trusted not to use the arms they carried. Nevertheless, such corps probably gave rise to exaggerated travellers' tales of Amazon warriors in Southeast Asia (Ibn Battuta 1354: 279–81).

It is not surprising to find women prominent in entertainment. They were strongly represented in dance, music, and drama groups throughout Southeast Asia. In Cebu, Magellan was entertained by an orchestra of girls, and in Banten a mixed group of jugglers and actors performed for a royal circumcision (Pigafetta 1524: 154–55; Scott 1606: 155). Among the few nonroyal women celebrated in the chronicles are a spectacular singer and dancer at the court of Majapahit, and Dang Sirat, a Malay opera star in Patani, who turned the head of the visiting prince of Johor (*Nagara-kertagama* 1365: 107–08; *Hikayat Patani*: 115–17). In the Javanese *wayang kulit* tradition the female singer was almost as central as the puppeteer, and though the latter is today normally male there was at least one very famous female exception in the seventeenth century (Sutton 1984; Pigeaud 1938: 61). In Brunei as late as the nineteenth century the professional storytellers were women, moving from house to house to recite *hikayat* and *sya'ir* to audiences who were also largely female (St. John 1862 II: 260).

Since most premodern Southeast Asian writers were anonymous, we cannot know what share women had either in composing verses for recitation or in writing them down. In the eighteenth century there were outstanding women poets in Hanoi (Ho Xuan Huong) and Surakarta, while it may have been a Siamese princess of the period who reworked the Indonesian Panji story into Thai (Nguyen and Huu 1973: 170; Kumar 1980; Dhaninivat 1956: 139). The Malay woman who tutored John Anderson about Sumatran politics in the 1820s, Che Laut, was also a poet and historian, while Matthes' most valuable informant about Bugis literature in the 1850s was a princess of Tanette who was "truly well read"—at once historian, court letter writer, and collector of manuscripts (Matthes 1852: 172). There were several poets among the ladies of King Narai's court in Ayutthaya, and the best-known epic romance of that brilliant period, the *Lilit Phra Lo*, describes from a female viewpoint (whether or not from that of a female author) how two court ladies lure the male hero into the palace for their amusement (Diller 1983; Schweisguth 1951: 84–90).

The association of learning with the formal religious systems probably increased literacy for men but reduced it for women. In the seventeenth century Thai and Burmese boys went to the monasteries at about their seventh year and acquired a basic literacy, whereas girls "very seldom learn to write and read" (van Vliet 1636: 88). Islam educated boys less universally than Theravada Buddhism, but ignored girls in a similar fashion. There was, however, an older literate tradition for both sexes, which survived longer in some places than others. In the Philippines the early Spanish friars claimed that literacy in the old indigenous script was almost universal for both sexes, and that the women wrote and read "much more fluently" than the men (Alcina 1668 III: 39; cf. Dasmariñas 1590A: 424). The reason for this high female literacy, also noted in those parts of Sumatra where the old ways survived, appears to be that the old script was used for everyday pragmatic purposes, not for the male spheres of formal religion and government (see chapter 5). This unusual pattern makes it necessary to resist any assumptions about male authorship of the anonymous Southeast Asian classics, except for those which emerged from the monastic religious tradition.

Female monarchy is anathema alike to the Hindu, Buddhist, Islamic, and Chinese traditions of statecraft. Austronesian societies, however, which include Polynesia and Madagascar as well as Indonesia and the Philippines, have been more inclined than any other major population group to place highborn women on the throne. Sulawesi, where birth always took priority over sex in succession, may be an extreme case. Six of the thirty-two rulers of Bone (the largest Bugis state) since its fourteenth-century origins have been women. When James Brooke visited the neighbouring Bugis state of Wajo he found that four of the six great chiefs (*arung*) were female (Brooke 1848 I: 74–75). Where Indian (or, in Vietnam, Chinese) influences had been stronger, especially in the more exalted courts of the mainland, female rule was rare. Siam has never put a woman on the throne, and Vietnam and Burma very seldom did so. In Muslim Southeast Asia the Islamic model of male kingship seemed finally to prevail by about 1700; few women ruled after that.

Between the fifteenth and seventeenth centuries, however, there was a remarkable tendency for those states that participated most fully in the expanding commerce of the region to be governed by women. Many states raised women to the throne only when at the peak of their commercial importance. Pasai, the first major Muslim port below the winds, had two queens in succession between 1405 and 1434, just before it was eclipsed by Melaka as the main Malacca Straits port (Cowan 1938: 209–10). The only woman on a Burmese throne in this period was Shinsawbu (1453–72), who presided over the emergence of Pegu as a major entrepôt in the Bay of Bengal. Japara, on Java's north coast, was a significant naval and commercial power only under its famous queen, Kali-nyamat, in the third quarter of the sixteenth century. Similarly, the woman rulers of the diamond-exporting centre of Sukadana in Southwest Borneo (c. 1608–22), of pepper-rich Jambi in east Sumatra (1630–c. 1655), of Kelantan on the Malayan east coast (1610–71), and of the sandalwood entrepôt of Solor, to the east of Flores (c. 1650–70), were on the throne during the brief period when these states were important commercial centres. Banten never had a female sovereign, but it became the major port of the Java Sea during the long minority of Sultan Abdul Kadir (1596–1618). During five of these years (1600–05) the dominant figure was Nyai Gede Wanagiri, "the old woman that commands the protector and all the rest . . . although she bee not of the kings blood, but only for her wisdom is held in such estimation among them of all sorts that shee ruleth as if shee were solelye queene of that countrey" (Scott 1606: 130; also Djajadiningrat 1913: 153–54).

This pattern is too striking to be put down to the accidents of inheritance, particularly as the periods of female rule in Pasai, Kelantan, and Solor involved two successive queens. In the sultanates of Aceh and Patani a deliberate preference becomes quite clear. In each of these cases four successive women occupied the throne, only the first of whom was especially well qualified by descent. The century of female rule in Patani (1584–1688) embraced the whole of the period when it was a major entrepôt for the China trade. The four queens of Aceh (1641–99) witnessed the military and political decline that followed the conquests of Iskandar Muda (1607–36), but they nevertheless maintained Aceh as the most important independent port in island Southeast Asia.

Female rule was one of the few devices available to a commercially oriented aristocracy to limit the despotic powers of kings and make the state safe for international commerce (Reid 1979: 408–12). Iskandar Muda had been a particularly frightening example of the dangers of absolutism, seeking to monopolize trade with the English and Dutch while killing, terrorizing, and dispossessing his own orangkaya (merchant-aristocrats). Having experimented with the female alternative, these aristocrats of Aceh and Patani sought to perpetuate it. In Patani the first queen "has reigned very peaceably with her councillors . . . so that all the subjects consider her government better than that of the dead king. For all necessities are very cheap here now, whereas in the king's time (so they say) they were dearer by half, because of the great exactions which then occurred" (van Neck 1604: 226). Similarly, Aceh in the time of its first queen was noted by its greatest chronicler to be frequented by international trade because of her just rule. The capital "was extremely prosperous at that time, foodstuffs were very cheap, and everybody lived in peace" (Raniri 1644: 59). In contrast, "the very name of a kinge is long since become nautious to them . . . through the Tyranical Government of theire last kinge" (Bowrey 1680: 296; cf. Ibrahim 1688: 174). Theft was strictly punished under the queens, and property rights were respected. The orangkaya found they could govern collectively with the queen as sovereign and referee, and there was something of the quality of Elizabethan England in the way they vied for her favour but accepted her eventual judgement between them.

This was not simply a case of powerful males making use of a powerless female as a figurehead, for women were also active in both Aceh and Patani as traders and orangkaya. In Patani the level of official tribute was lowered under the fourth queen because she was said to have been independently wealthy from her inheritance and her extensive trade (*Hikayat Patani*: 114). In choosing to put women on the throne the orangkaya were opting not only for mild rule but for businesslike rule. As in other fields, men were expected to defend a high sense of status and honour on the battlefield but to be profligate with their wealth. It was women's business to understand market forces, to drive hard bargains, and to conserve their capital. In general, these expectations of women as rulers were not disappointed. Female rule failed only when Patani and Aceh ran out of credible candidates who still had the charisma of monarchy about them, and when the orangkaya of the port capital began to lose their influence to forces less interested in trade.

5

Festivals and Amusements

What, then, is the right way of living? Life must be lived as play, playing certain games, making sacrifices, singing and dancing, and then a man will be able to propitiate the gods, and defend himself against his enemies, and win in the contest.

—*Plato,* Laws, *quoted Huizinga 1938: 19*

Because their climate was mild and their basic diet of rice, fish, and fruits more dependably available than in most parts of the world, Southeast Asians had natural advantages in escaping from the constant struggle for subsistence. They may have had more time to devote to what would today be classified as leisure than most other peoples of that era. Certainly it appeared to Europeans that the Southeast Asians they encountered had a remarkable amount of spare time and were able to employ their evenings in singing, feasting, gaming, and entertaining one another (La Loubère 1691: 35; *Verhael* 1597: 30; Eredia 1613: 39). It may be, however, that the concept of leisure as free time, opposed to the daily requirement of labour, is a modern product of industrial society. For Southeast Asians of the period, participation in festivals, rituals, and feasts appears to have been a social obligation as important as productive work itself. Both Thais and Malays used the everyday word for work (*ngan* in Thai, *kerja* in Malay) to describe their participation in festive and ritual events.

Local languages did, however, recognize the more universal categories of amusement and play. The chronicles frequently relate how the people enjoyed themselves with theatre, games, and dances; again, the Thai and Malay words for play (*len* and *main*, respectively) cover a wide range of activity, from bullfights and theatre to illicit lovemaking. Much of such amusement was of course private and scarcely accessible to the historian. It became public at the great seasonal festivals and personal rites of passage, in which the whole community participated. These occasions had many features in common with festivals in other parts of the world—a religious core, a sense of community, contests, gambling, theatre, buffoonery, and a lifting of usual taboos. In general, however, the public festivals of Southeast Asia appear to have reinforced rather than challenged hierarchy. Disorder, sexual licence, and social mixing might often occur around the periphery of the festivals, but there is little evidence of the structured role reversals of the Provençal *reynages* (Le Roy Ladurie 1979: 303–04), and still less of the totally autonomous people's anti-ritual which Bakhtin (1940: 220) wanted to find in Renaissance carnivals.

The Theatre State

> *I confess that when the King's Ambassadors entered in the River, the beauty of the show surprized me. The river is of an agreeable breadth . . . the banks whereof are two hedgerows, continually green. This would be the best Theatre in the World for the most sumptuous and magnificent feasts; but no magnificence appears like a great number of men devoted to serve you. There were near three thousand embarkt in seventy or eighty balons, which made the train of the Ambassador. . . . All eyes were taken up with the diversity and number of the balons, and with the pleasantness of the river's channel; and yet the ears were diverted by a barbarous but agreeable noise of songs, acclamations and instruments.*
>
> —*La Loubère 1691: 42*

Much of the exuberant cultural life of the region was orchestrated by the state as a vivid assertion of its own status as an "exemplary centre," to use a phrase of Geertz. The royal chronicles have much to say about this area of social life, not because of an interest in everyday amusements but because contests, theatre, music, and dance were demonstrations of the power and splendour of the ruler. "The state drew its force . . . from its imaginative energies, its semiotic capacity to make inequality enchant" (Geertz 1980: 123). By staging spectacular events in which thousands of people took part, the ruler most fully showed himself as the supernatural fulcrum around which his state revolved.

Royal and religious festivals provided an opportunity for the ruler to display himself before his people in all his majesty, with courtiers, officials, soldiers, followers, and even foreigners all assigned their proper place in the pageant (fig. 23). Royal coronations, marriages, funerals, and puberty rituals, the annual religious festivals, ceremo-

Fig. 23 Royal procession to the mosque in Ternate for weekly Friday prayer, 1599; a contemporary Dutch woodcut based on the description in "Tweede Boeck." *A*, the mosque (intended to represent the multitiered roof); *B*, the procession; *C*, the palace of Ternate, built with Portuguese assistance.

nies to ensure the fertility and well-being of the country, and even the reception of foreign ambassadors were occasions for public processions and entertainments. Certain important Malay, Javanese, and Siamese texts set out in great detail the ceremonies to be followed at royal rituals of this sort, who should be present, and in what order. The *Adat Aceh* (35–37), for example, prescribes the procession to accompany Sultan Iskandar Muda to the mosque at the feast of Id al-Adha. It begins with richly caparisoned horsemen, followed by lancers and the ruler himself on his elephant surounded by his most illustrious warriors; then hundreds of court officials and soldiery, thousands of slaves, pages, and retainers; then the whole army behind its commanders "like the waves of the sea," all the foreign traders, 30 ornamented elephants, 200 troop leaders, 2000 sword-bearing soldiers, 2000 each of three differently armed corps of soldiers. We know that such magnificence was not solely in the minds of court writers, for various foreign accounts of Aceh in this period describe these magnificent processions in which foreigners too were expected to take part (see fig. 24). Though sometimes "very confuzed and on heapes, there being scarce room and time for order," these processions never failed to impress (Mundy 1667: 123; cf. Croft 1613: 168–72; Verhoeff 1611: 240). On the occasion of the funeral of Sultan Iskandar Thani in 1641 an eyewitness recorded a procession involving 260 elephants carrying rich silks, their tusks gilded or covered in silver, as well as some

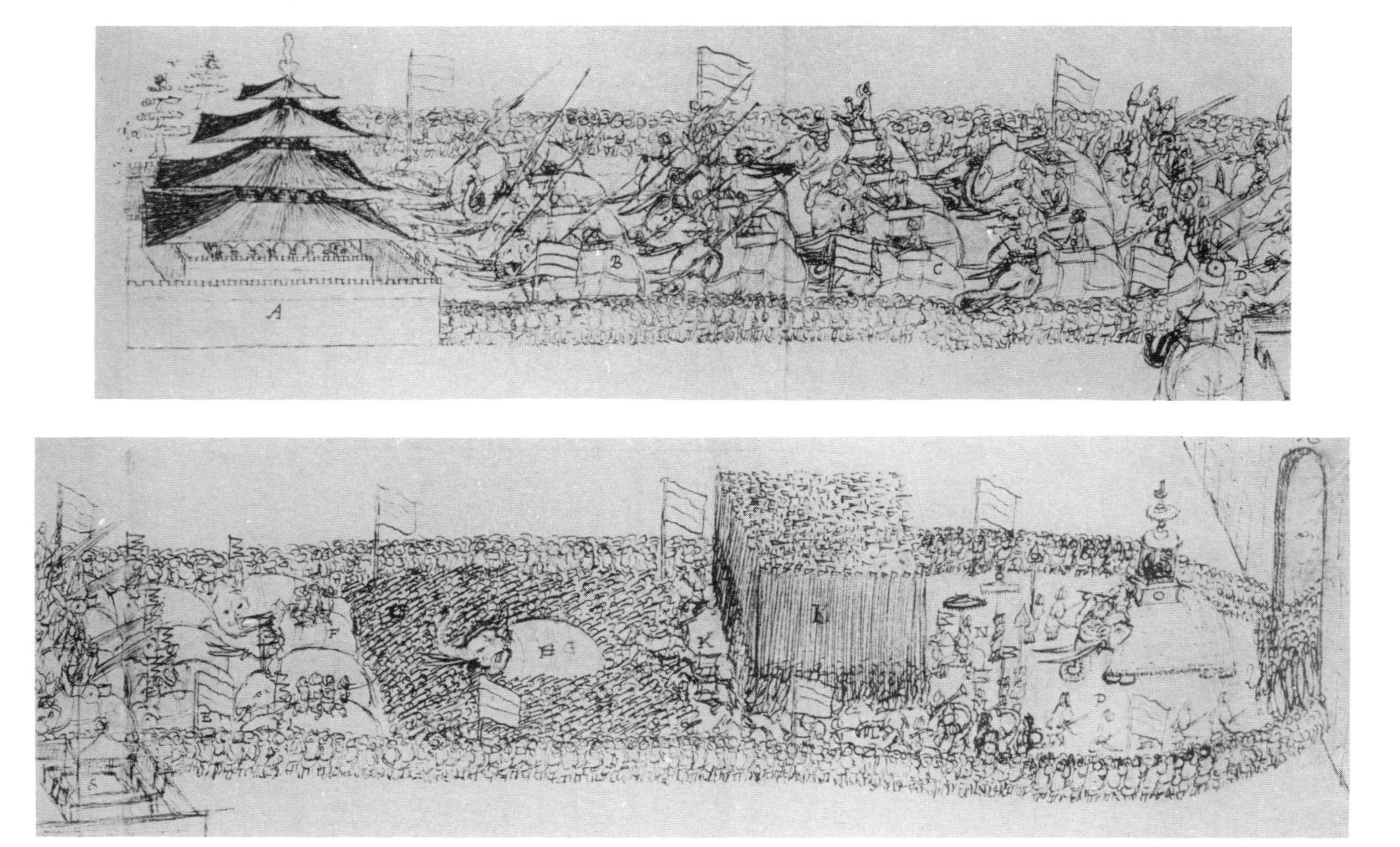

Fig. 24 Royal procession to the mosque for Id al-Adha (feast of sacrifice during the period of pilgrimage), in Aceh, 1637, when five hundred young buffaloes were sacrificed and the meat distributed, sketched by Peter Mundy. Mundy's notation includes, from left: *A*, the Great Mosque; *B–G*, elephants variously arrayed; *S*, raised platform where Sultan alighted and changed elephants; *I*, pikemen; *O*, Sultan on his "stately elephant covered down to the feet."

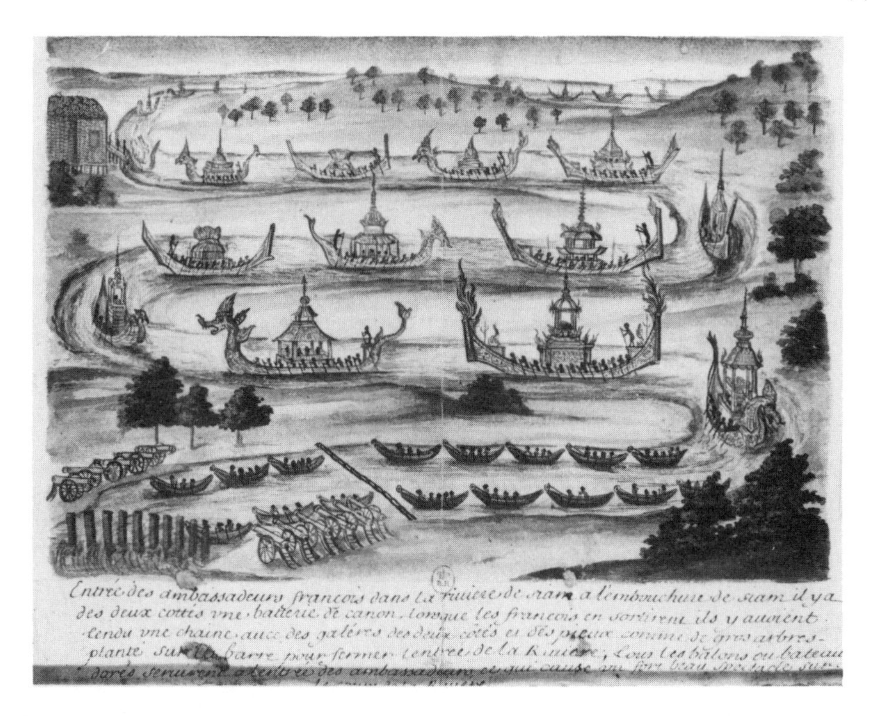

Fig. 25 A contemporary French drawing of the reception of the French Embassy to Siam at the mouth of the Chao Phraya River in 1685. Twelve court officials, each in his own galley, were sent to receive the letter from the king of France and to convey it upriver to the capital.

rhinoceroses, Persian horses, and thousands of followers (de Graaff 1701: 14).

The counterpart of the splendid procession of elephants and soldiery by land was the procession by water (see fig. 25). Almost all rulers had their impressive royal galleys decorated to represent in some sense the Indic *naga* (dragon-serpent). In Maluku, Siam, and the river ports of Borneo these were the favoured vehicles for a royal progress (see figs. 26a and 26b). Like the parades of troops and animals, the sumptuous galleys showed the monarch and his subjects as one, the hundreds of oarsmen moving in exact time, demonstrating the antithesis of that "loosely structured" social organization which characterized Southeast Asia in some other respects.

In the seventeenth century the greatest annual occasions for demonstrating the king's majesty were the sacred days of Islam and Buddhism. Just as the sultan of Aceh used such feasts as Id al-Adha (and also Id al-Fitr and the Prophet's birthday) to demonstrate at once his Indic semidivine magnificence and his patronage of the new universal

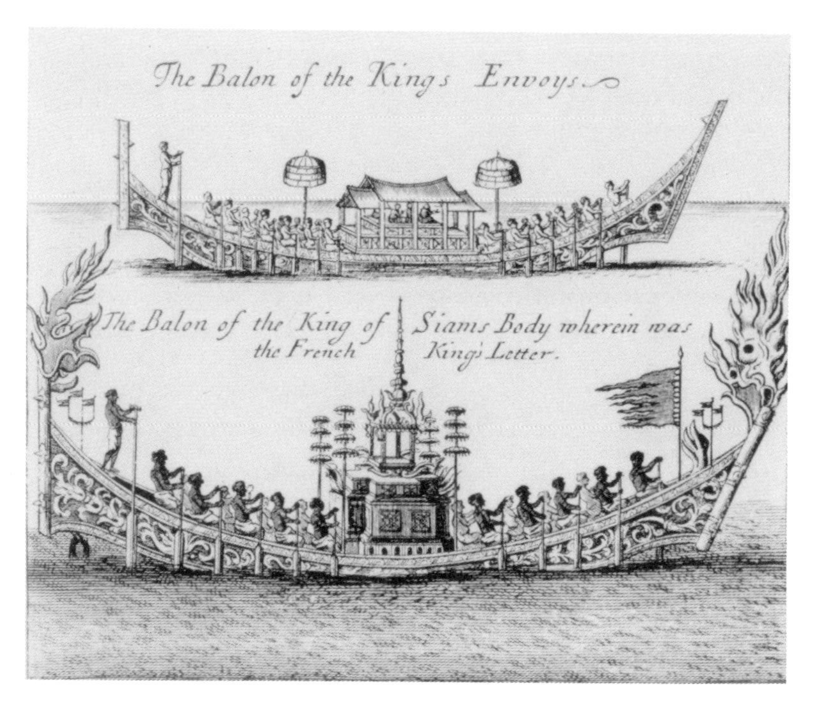

Fig. 26a Siamese royal galleys

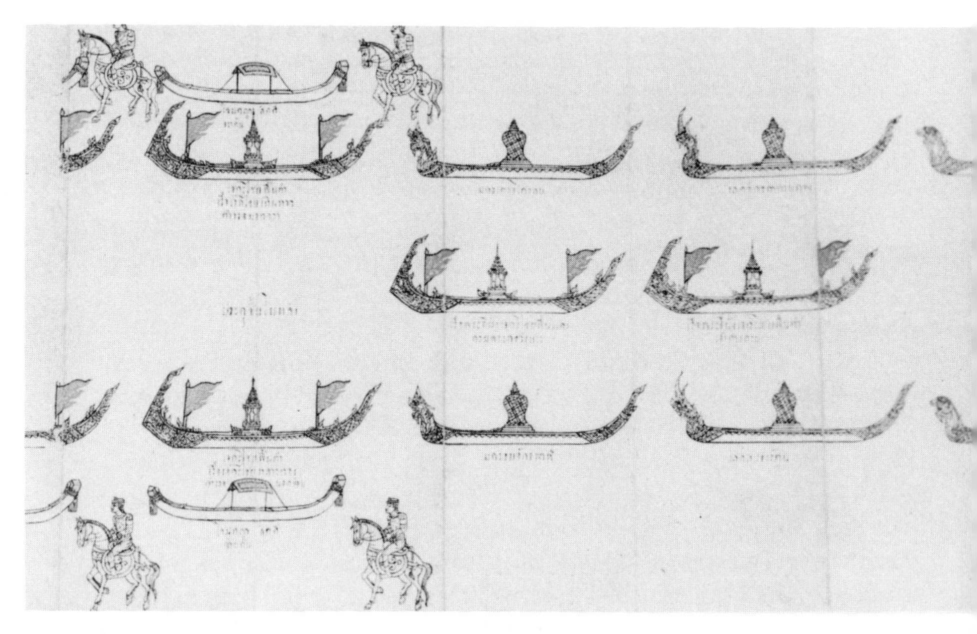

Fig. 26b Arrangement of royal galleys during procession—fragment of a 1916 Thai copy of an Ayutthaya manuscript.

faith, the rulers of Siam increasingly chose to make their rare appearances before their subjects on the great occasions of Buddhism. The most spectacular royal procession of the year appears to have been, for much of the sixteenth and seventeenth centuries, the "sending away of the waters" at the end of the rainy season in late October, when the magical power of the monarch and of the splendid boats embodying the naga-spirits which animated the water ensured the rapid retreat of the floodwaters (Couto 1645 VI, ii: 125–27; Archaimbault 1972; Wales 1931: 225–26). Even though the magical meaning of the event was still potent in Laos and Cambodia in the early twentieth century, the secularizing reign of Narai (1656-88) in Ayutthaya had created a new justification for this magnificent display in the very correct Theravada practice of Kathina, when valuable gifts were given to the chief monasteries and temples under his protection. As a sceptical French Jesuit put it, "this Prince having found by many years experience, that the waters increased sometimes, for all they were ordered to abate, hath left off that ridiculous ceremony, and thought it enough this year by going in triumph to the Pagoda, to show the zeal he has for his religion" (Tachard 1686: 187; cf. La Loubère 1691: 43; Wales 1931: 200–12).

While this is an important indication of the shift to a more urban and rational mentality that marked the seventeenth century, it may be that the thousands of onlookers were unaware of any change. They certainly continued to acknowledge their king as the centre of a splendid theatre at a seasonal turning point which provided its own dramatic backdrop. The increasingly religious emphasis of the ceremony enabled them to identify themselves not only as Siamese and subjects of a mighty king, but also as Buddhist, with some of the cosmopolitan implications that could carry. The annual procession was described by many astonished visitors, including a Dutch resident at the time of King Prasat Thong:

> In front go about 200 mandarins every one with his own beautiful boat and sitting in a small pavilion which is gilded and decorated according to the rank of the owner. These boats are rowed by 30 to 60 rowers. Then follow the boats for the luggage and kitchen necessaries. After these boats come the state boats of the king, wherein nobody else but the rowers are sitting whose number amounts to from 50 to 70 men. Each of these boats carries a little gilded pavilion of pyramidal shape or other decoration. Then come four or five boats with musicians and finally four or five ingeniously shaped, varnished and gilded boats. . . .
>
> In the finest boat the king is seated under a decorated canopy . . . hidden in all kinds of costly things, so that neither his body nor his face can be seen. He is surrounded by nobles and courtiers who pay him

reverence at the foot of his seat with folded hands and with their bodies bent to the floor. . . . Then follows the king's brother with a suite of eight to ten beautifully painted and gilded boats. . . . The king's mother, the queen, his Majesty's children and some concubines have all their own boats and are sitting in gilded pavilions. . . .

The total number of boats amounts to 350 to 400, and 20,000 to 25,000 persons take part in this procession. Along the way which his Majesty passes, the houses, monasteries and temples are closed with mats, and nobody is allowed to stay in them in order that nobody may look at the king from a place higher than his Majesty. Both sides of the river, for a length of two miles . . . are crowded with boats and innumerable persons who bring reverence to the king with folded hands and bent head (van Vliet 1636: 25–26).

A later French witness attempted an estimate of the crowds lining the shore during this procession and concluded that "there could not be less" than 20,000 boats and 200,000 people thronging the banks (Tachard 1686: 190). In Pegu, too, it was "a marvellous thing to see so many people, so many riches, and such good order" during royal processions at the great annual feasts (Frederici 1581: 250).

Malay chronicles are probably not exaggerating when they tell us that the festivities for a seventeenth-century Banjarmasin wedding went on continuously for forty days and forty nights (*Hikayat Banjar*: 315–23), or that those for a wedding in 1765 between a Johor ruler and a Trengganu princess "lasted about three months" (Ali Haji 1866: 143–44). In both cases elaborate details are given of the processions around the town, the variety of dances, theatrical events, and competitions staged, and the music played. Western traders would have been aware of the state spectacles of which Renaissance European rulers were equally enamoured, and they did not share the need of Malay chroniclers to magnify these Asian states. Nevertheless, they confirmed the lavishness with which royal weddings, coronations, and circumcisions were celebrated.

Scott (1606: 152–62) described the circumcision of the boy king of Banten in July 1605 and "the triumphs that were held there every day for the space of a month and more before his going to church [mosque]." On the square or *alun-alun* in front of the palace a great dais was erected on which the boy king was to sit in state. There he was taken each morning on a man's shoulders under numerous umbrellas, with a *gamelan* playing, surrounded by the guard and by a different set of nobles each day. Each of the principal men of the realm by turn had then to bring him presents of rice, money, cloth, and handicrafts. These gifts were carried by women—"sometimes two hundreth and sometimes three hundreth"—and accompanied by all possible show and pageantry. The women were led by men playing gongs and other gamelan instruments, followed by numerous lancers and swordsmen. Each group put on a show before the king, which might include a drama or dance, "significations of historicall matters of former times," juggling and "strange kinds of tumbling tricks," mock battles which even ran to hastily erected "forts" being assaulted and put to the torch, captive animals, and various ingenious representations. Some brought floats in the form of boats under sail and laden with presents; the raja of Jakatra brought a float carrying a garden replete with trees, flowers, and fish pond, and another which carried the figure of a giant thirty feet high. Scott's Englishmen had also to contribute, like all the other foreign communities. Determined at least to outdo their Dutch rivals, they put on a good show with fireworks and pageants. Not having women to carry the presents, however, "we borrowed thirtie of the prettiest boyes we could get."

Although much of the scholarly interest in the ceremonies conducted at the courts of Southeast Asia has been directed towards unravelling their different layers of symbolic, ritual, and religious meaning, it is important not to overlook their social function. For the majority of the population the festivals served three important purposes: participation in the majesty and hierarchy of the state; economic activity, such as marketing and rendering tribute; and entertainment.

State pageantry was the most effective way in which the citizenry was incorporated into the hierarchic state. A sense of royal majesty was most apparent in the capital; but royal progresses, tribute missions to the court, and above all the replication of royal styles by provincial officials and by the popular theatre took it also to remote villages. The arrival of the northern Europeans must have sounded a faint but ominous note for this important hierarchic function. It was important to the states concerned that Europeans played their part like other wealthy citizens in increasing the grandeur of royal occasions, but these northerners tended to flout the rules of the hierarchic game. Because of their military power and utility most monarchs chose to turn a blind eye to their defiance of status rules. In seventeenth-century Siam the Europeans defied the rule that no one should look upon the king as he passed on his elephant or galley. In Java the English and Dutch refused to sit respectfully on their haunches at royal entertainments. While "for other nations, they would beat them if they refused," the Javanese guards generally opted simply to move away from the stubbornly standing Europeans rather than provoke a major fight (Scott 1606: 159).

Markets were part of every great feast. Such massive assemblages of people were in themselves a guarantee of brisk trading in food and other essentials. It is probable that country folk used the great annual festivals to bring their produce to market and stock up on imported luxuries for the year ahead. Their periodic appearances in the city could also be the occasion to present the tribute or harvest share due to their lord. Pigeaud (1962: 274) has pointed out that the week-long Bubat fair and religious festival at the end of the rice harvest in fourteenth-century Hindu Java was the time for the payment of such obligations to the king and nobles, just as its Islamic replacement, the feast of the Prophet's birthday (*Maulud*), became in later centuries.

As for entertainment, every such royal or religious occasion included not only the spectacle of the procession but also a host of musical, theatrical, and sporting events. According to the Thai traditions recorded by Jeremias van Vliet (1640: 69), Rama T'ibodi (1491–1529) was the most loved of all Thai kings, in part because "he was the first who established the large feasts and gamedays." Van Vliet instanced the annual "swinging festival" as one of the popular entertainments that king had introduced from India. Scholars have sought the religious origins of this spectacular event, in which several men swing high over the crowds below. J. G. Frazier found them in a fertility ritual—a feature rather more marked in the swinging of girls by boys at harvest time in Vietnam and Sulawesi (Huard and Durand 1954: 237–38; Kaudern 1929: 79–85); Quaritch Wales (1931: 238–55) in worship of the sun. Yet for the majority of Thais it appears to have been simply entertainment for Siva, who they believed to be the most fun loving of the Hindu gods (ibid.: 239). The Siamese nation, a French observer pointed out, "is a great lover of shows and splendid ceremonies" (Tachard 1686: 215).

The enjoyment which the ordinary people had from these festivities was another indication of the power and cosmic beneficence of a great ruler, and the chronicles themselves make a point of explaining that "men, women and children alike were delighted at the various spectacles they beheld and the music which they heard" (*Hikayat Banjar*: 316). The throngs of people who assembled from all the surrounding villages at the time of such a festival vividly demonstrated the populousness of the realm, and attracting them by whatever means was part of the skill of kingship. The Ram Kamheng inscription (1293: 27) ends its account of the Thai Buddhist Kathina feast of that period with a description of "the sound of timbrels and lutes, the sound of carolling and singing. Whoever likes to sport, sports; whoever likes to laugh, laughs; whoever likes to sing, sings."

Fig. 27 Elephant kraal of Ayutthaya, frequently restored since the seventeenth century, where the royal elephants were trained

Contests and Tournaments

Among the royal entertainments provided on such occasions, a special place was occupied by the contests between animals (and sometimes men). No great feast passed at the courts of Java, Aceh, Siam, and Burma without some spectacular fight between elephants, tigers, buffaloes, or lesser animals. At smaller towns and markets there was at least a cockfight to enliven every feast.

For Burma, Siam, Cambodia, and Aceh the elephant was the regal animal par excellence. Kings collected them in great numbers (fig. 27), rode them in real and mock battles, and identified with them in contests with other animals. The Thai hero and king Naresuan (1590–1605) was said to have excelled all comers with his skill in elephant jousts as a youth at the court of Pegu (van Vliet 1640: 78); and the youth of the Acehnese hero Sultan Iskandar Muda is described by the court chronicle as full of miraculous feats with elephants and horses (*Hikayat Aceh* c. 1630: 126–43). Once on the throne Iskandar Muda may no longer have ridden his elephants in tournaments, but he certainly enjoyed putting them on show (fig. 28). For a Dutch embassy in 1608 he staged an elephant fight in a ring formed by 58 elephants and 1300 soldiers (Verhoeff 1611: 240). Five years later 200 elephants were arrayed at a spectacle to impress an English mission. Six ele-

Fig. 28 Elephant fight in Aceh, 1637. The sultan and "his guard of women" are seated in the pavilion, *A*. *E* and *H* are female elephants; *N* are the people helping to restrain the male elephants, *D*; to right of pavilion at *F* are pikemen ready to goad the elephants when required.

phants first fought each other, then four buffaloes, and finally a dozen rams (Best 1614: 52; cf. Croft 1613: 158–71; Mundy 1667: 126–30). A very similar elephant battle was staged for the French in Ayutthaya. Here, as in Aceh, dozens of men tugged on ropes tied to the elephants' legs to part them when the fight risked getting out of hand (Tachard 1686: 209–10).

Compared with the much more spirited buffaloes, elephants did little damage to each other and their fights seldom impressed foreign spectators. Their role was certainly symbolic, as became clearer when they were pitted against a tiger (fig. 29), the standard embodiment of danger, disorder, wildness, and the enemies of the state. In these contests it was essential for the elephants to prevail, killing the tiger by repeatedly throwing it high into the air with their tusks. Hence the tiger was usually handicapped by being tied to a stake and made to fight several elephants at once. In Siam the elephants were also protected by armour over head and trunk (Tachard 1686: 211–13; cf. Ibrahim 1688: 72–73; Copland 1614: 210–11). As late as 1822 an English mission to southern Vietnam was regaled with a tiger and elephant fight in which the tiger's mouth was sewn up and its claws extracted. Even so, the first elephant sent against it eventually turned

Fig. 29 Contemporary French drawing of the arena at Ayutthaya in which a tiger was pitted against elephants, 1680s.

tail. The trainer was then savagely beaten, no doubt because the humiliation of his elephant involved the humiliation of the ruler in front of powerful foreigners who were identified with the tiger (Crawfurd 1828: 218–19; Finlayson 1826: 321–23).

In parts of the Archipelago it was the wild or domesticated buffalo (banteng or *kerbau*) which took the place of the elephant in fights with the tiger. The Javanese in particular identified strongly with the buffalo; even Crawfurd (1820 I: 115) admitted "that there is no small satisfaction in seeing this peaceful and docile animal destroy his ferocious and savage enemy," which was the result in nineteen out of twenty fights. At the time of Raffles (1817 I: 347) the Javanese identified the tiger in these contests with the European and therefore took special pleasure in the victory of the buffalo. Such contests were already being staged in seventeenth-century Mataram (van Goens 1646: 238) and later became a standard entertainment for Dutch envoys—probably to put them symbolically in their place (Ricklefs 1974: 274–75; Kumar 1980: 37). A Spanish account of sixteenth-century Champa, which had numerous connections with Java and the Malay world, also describes a festival where tigers were "thrown" to

Fig. 30 A tiger fight (*rampogan*) in Central Java in the early nineteenth century, sketched by de Stuers, c. 1825

buffaloes to be killed in a square made for the purpose (Dasmariñas 1590C: 42).[1]

Even more common at the courts of Java in the eighteenth century was the *rampogan* (fig. 30), in which a tiger was released in a large square formed by hundreds of pikemen and frightened into running onto their spears (Kumar 1980: 37; Raffles 1817 I: 347). This event can probably be understood as a similar symbolic demonstration of the power of the disciplined state over the forces of savage disorder. Even though many Javanese texts are devoted to this sport as to other animal fights (Pigeaud 1967: 276), there is no definite evidence of the existence of the rampogan in the seventeenth century or earlier.

There was, nevertheless, an association between animal fights and human fights which may explain the importance of these events at royal occasions. The association was at its clearest in the weekly tournaments which the Javanese courts held on the square (alun-alun)

1. Malay rulers of the Peninsula also occasionally held buffalo and tiger contests, the most recent occasion being the visit of the Duke of Edinburgh to Johor about 1870, when the buffalo was again an easy victor (Wilkinson 1910: 61; McNair 1878: 266). Such contests do not appear to be mentioned in the Malay literature, however.

always placed to the north of their citadels. They were usually held on a Saturday or Monday (*Senen*), giving rise to the name *Senenan* by which they were later known. The Malay epic *Hikayat Hang Tuah* (105) mentioned such jousting on horseback as part of the entertainment at the Javanese court of Majapahit, but the tournaments were first described in detail by the Dutch in Tuban in 1599 and subsequently at many other courts in central and eastern Java. About four in the afternoon the younger braves of the court would converge on the square after parading through the city on their magnificently attired horses. There they would engage in a series of charges and manoeuvres, one generally pursuing the other down the length of the field, with the aim of knocking each other off their horses with blunted spears (figs. 31a and 31b). In reality this happened seldom, and most attention was paid to the horsemanship displayed in the constant wheeling and turning on the square. The king was always present for these occasions and, at least at Mataram, took part in the jousting (van Goens 1656: 229–33; "Tweede Boeck" 1601: 37–40; Valentijn 1726 III: 313; Raffles 1817 I: 345–46). Even though cavalry played a negligible role in Javanese warfare, this was clearly a metaphor of war in which young aristocrats proved and displayed their qualities. Its Mainland analogy may have been the type of polo (*tii khlii* in Thai) played by aristocrats of Cambodia, Siam, and Burma (fig. 32), whereby they also showed their knightly horsemanship (San Antonio 1604: 7; Gerini 1912: 72; Bowring 1857 II: 330).

Jousting was often followed by an animal fight of some sort, and during the eighteenth and nineteenth centuries, as warfare became less frequent and courts more rigidly hierarchical, the animal fight gradually took over the main role from human combat (Kumar 1980: 37). Prior to 1600 it appears that the jousting of the young bloods had itself been more sanguinary. Ma Huan (1433: 94) recorded the provisions for the family of Javanese killed in annual tournaments with long bamboo spears. Tomé Pires (1515: 174–96; cf. Couto 1645 IV, i: 169) was much impressed with the number, the horsemanship, and the great pride of the knights (*cavaleiros*) of Java: "The noblemen are much in the habit of challenging each other to duels, and they kill each other over their quarrels, and this is the custom of the country. Some of them kill themselves on horseback, and some of them on foot, according to what they have decided" (ibid.: 176). One ruler of Aceh, Sultan Zainal 'Abidin (1579–80), was recorded as being "unwilling even to eat unless he saw blood" (Raniri 1644: 33). According to the chronicles he was so eager to stage fights of elephants, buffaloes, oxen,

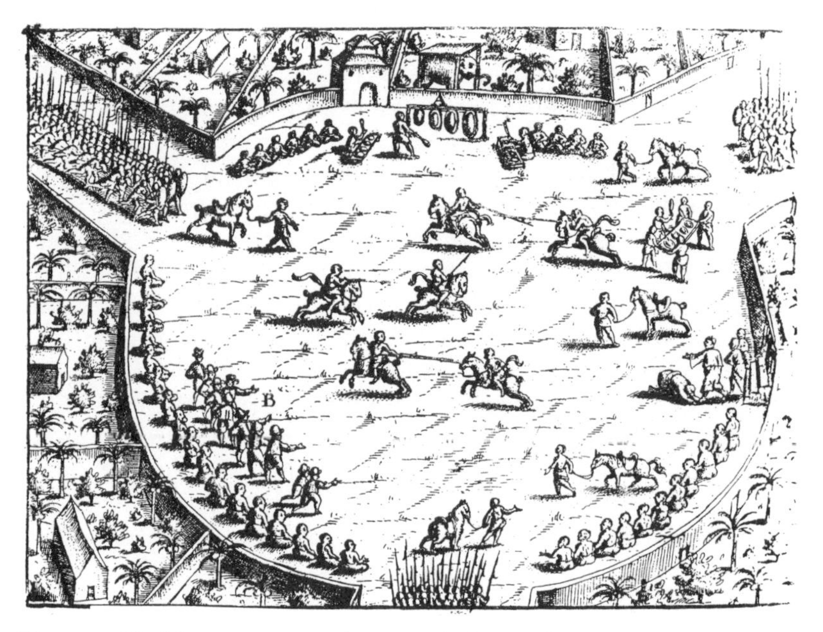

Fig. 31a Weekly tournament (*senenan*) observed by the Dutch in Tuban, Java, in 1599

Fig. 31b *Senenan* in central Java, nineteenth century

Fig. 32 Polo as played at the court of Ava, from a Burmese illustrated manuscript of the mid-nineteenth century

and sheep that men were on several occasions killed by the animals. Moreover, "he ordered Acehnese and Indian swordsmen to cross swords with one another so that several of the swordsmen were killed and several wounded. . . . And he ordered Tiku men and Pariaman men to fight with long krisses so that several of them were wounded" (*Hikayat Aceh* c. 1630: 97). This bloodthirsty king eventually went too far and was deposed by the leading aristocrats. Nevertheless, his coupling of human and animal combat suggests again that the blood of one served to represent the blood of the other.

It seems clear from pre-Muslim inscriptions in Java, and from the continuing practice in Bali, that cockfighting always had a religious significance and formed a necessary part of temple feasts, consecrations, and pilgrimages (fig. 33). The blood of the cocks was seen as sacrificial atonement to the gods, who were always propitiated before the start of a fight (Setten van der Meer 1979: 126–30; Covarrubias 1937: 74, 278). Although in villages cockfights were associated with particular shrines and festivals, at the court centres they were a royal prerogative like the other animal fights (Kumar 1980: 38). One source of the royal preoccupation with staging such events may therefore have been the blood sacrifice necessary for continued fertility, for purification, and for success in war. At remoter times the blood of the

Fig. 33 A cock fight as staged as a scene in a Panji play (*Enaung zat pwe*) at the court of Ava. A royal couple watch the play from the pavilion at right. The play is accompanied by the Burmese orchestra of drums and gongs. From a Burmese illustrated manuscript of the mid-nineteenth century.

fighting animals may have been seen as a substitute for that of humans.

Another idea behind such fights, however, appears to have been that symbolic victory of the king which Hocart (cited Wales 1931: 124–25) believed to be a necessary part of all coronation rituals. We have seen how important it was for the elephant in some countries, and the buffalo in others, to prevail over the tiger. A similar concern was displayed over the sword fights staged at feasts in the Moluccas. "If someone during these games slips and does not fall, people call him . . . 'valiant knight.' If he goes down to the ground, they take it for an omen; and in order to dispel it, they come on the field with a lot of ceremonies, gongs, amulets and exorcisms. . . . They break shields, crush stones, bless herbs, strew earth about, and perform other devilish tricks for more than two hours" (Galvão 1544: 147). The savage reaction of the sultans of Aceh when one of their favorite fighting cocks was defeated may be partly explained by the same sense that the king himself was endangered or humiliated by such a defeat. In 1618 Sultan Iskandar Muda reportedly forced one aristocrat unlucky enough to have defeated the king to watch his wife publicly raped by African slaves, and then had this courtier's genitals cut off "up to the belly" so that he soon expired (van den Broecke 1634: 176; cf. van

Warwijck 1604: 15). Another such defeat in 1621 was punished by cutting off the hand of the cock's owner (Beaulieu 1666: 59).

I am inclined to attribute royal patronage of these contests to the two factors of sacrifice and symbolic victory, both originating in very early religious ideas. The strengthening of Islamic influence in the islands and of Theravada Buddhism in the Mainland affected the contests in different ways. In the Archipelago the trend appears to have been to formalize such combats into state pageants in which the blood of animals rather than humans was shed. Buddhism, however, could not formally countenance the shedding of blood in any form. Under pressure from the monks, King Narai even prohibited cockfights in Ayutthaya (La Loubère 1691: 46–47), though nothing could in practice stop Thais, Cambodians, and Burmese from continuing to enjoy their beloved sport. State-sponsored animal contests in these countries had never been very sanguinary anyway. Instead of animal fights and mock sword fights, the Thai and Burmese courts tended to encourage wrestling and boxing. The Thai style of boxing with much use of the feet (*muay Thai*) was reputedly popularized by the warrior-king Naresuan (1590–1605), because of its military utility. In Burma at least as early as the eighteenth century there were well-regulated bouts of a similar style of boxing and of wrestling on feast days (Symes 1827 I: 200–01).

Another type of contest which continued to enjoy strong royal patronage in Burma and Siam was the boat race. These races were also popular in the islands, notably in Maluku where the long *kora-kora*, each rowed by men from a different village, reached tremendous speeds amid frenzied betting from their partisans (Galvão 1544: 147; cf. Alcina, cited Scott 1985: 20). In Burma and Siam the annual festivities at the time before the river waters began to subside in October provided an opportunity for races to be held after the spectacle of the royal progress to honour the sangha. Once again the need for the king to win a symbolic victory may have lain behind royal patronage of these events (fig. 34). In 1685 the French witnessed how King Narai "would needs be one of the antagonists, but seeing his balon was manned with more rowers, and those all choice men, he quickly got the better on't, and victoriously entered the town" (Tachard 1686: 189–90). For the populace, however, these races were the major occasion for boisterous competition between patronage groups or villages after weeks of training by their champions. Thousands of spectators and partisans lined the banks of the Irrawaddy (fig. 35) or the Chao-Phraya to bet large sums on the outcome, and all decorum was forgotten in the excitment of the race (ibid.: 190; La Loubère 1691: 50; Shway Yoe 1882: 353–62).

Fig. 34 Contemporary French drawing of two Siamese galleys racing before the king (shown ashore) in the 1680s. In foreground is a royal galley.

Fig. 35 A Burmese regatta on the occasion of the water festival in the sixth lunar month (September). In right foreground preparations are under way to stage a drama under the large canopy, with the usual orchestra in attendance. From a Burmese illustrated manuscript of the mid-nineteenth century.

Popular Games

Although most of these large-scale contests were sponsored and to some extent controlled by the rulers, they appear at the same time to have been the most popular entertainments of the people. The passionate involvement of Southeast Asians in competitive games, demonstrated above all by the propensity to gamble on almost any contest, has been remarked by visitors from the sixteenth century onwards (Willemsz 1642: fol. 524; La Loubère 1691: 50; Marsden 1783: 273–74; Lennon 1796: 262; Goudswaard 1860: 351–52; Aymonier 1900: 45). "The Indian islanders . . . are passionately fond of play. . . . On a market day, in every part of the country where open gaming is not absolutely prohibited, men and women, old and young, form themselves into groups in the streets of the market, for the purposes of play. . . . The character of the natives appears for the moment thoroughly changed, for their grave, orderly, and calm manners, are changed into impatience, eagerness, and boisterous noise" (Crawfurd 1820 I: 109–11).

Earlier accounts of states still dominated by powerful monarchies suggest a pattern in which the court itself regulated and presided over much of the large-scale gambling, especially on animal fights. The control of such events by royal courts probably weakened in the eighteenth century, so that later visitors witnessed a more constant and uninhibited pattern of gaming. The cockfights which occupied every afternoon in eighteenth-century central Sulawesi (Woodard 1796: 122) would not have occurred under stronger Javanese, Thai, Burmese, or Acehnese kings.

No adequate study has been made of Southeast Asian gambling, even in more modern periods, which might reveal more adequately the mentality that underlay it. One Javanese text, the *Serat Manising Main*, gives some indication of the ideology which was at work at least among males of the upper class: "He [the gambler] has the spirit of a great nobleman [*priyayi gede*], who gives away money and property without considering the amount. And even if he thereby falls to naked poverty, he remains faithful to this liberality—magnanimous and fully at peace. He surrenders body and soul to the will of God, knowing that everything in this world belongs to the Unseen [God], and that man has only to conform to His will" (quoted Tjan 1941: 7, 9).

Of all such opportunities for gambling, cockfighting was by far the most popular, for reasons which probably have to do with the close identification of the rooster with the male ego. One Spanish friar considered that Filipinos "love their cocks more than their wives and children" (San Agostin 1720: 282; cf. Dasmariñas 1590A: 411), an almost identical judgement to that made of Balinese over a century later by Van Eck (cited Boon 1977: 31). Few aspects of Southeast Asian life were so exclusively male, and male stereotypes were reinforced by the squandering of money in what was essentially a game about status.

Clifford Geertz's brilliant analysis (1973) of what is really at stake in a modern Balinese cockfight, confirmed in essentials for the modern Philippines by Guggenheim (1982: 23), can also explain the importance of this sport throughout the region in a much earlier period. "What the cockfight talks most forcefully about is status relationships, and what it says about them is that they are matters of life and death" (Geertz 1973: 447). The apparently frenzied betting was motivated not so much by hope of big winnings as by identification with the kin group, faction, or village of the cock's owner. The cockfight was therefore a vivid dramatization both of the solidarity of the vertically organized group and of the hostilities generated in its endless status competition with other groups.

In the Malay world cockfights did not always end as peacefully as Geertz's, however, and there are numerous accounts of a desperate loser resorting to violence or being led into slavery for his indebtedness, despite elaborate regulations designed to prevent such misfortunes (Marsden 1783: 274; Newbold 1839 II: 179–83).

For different reasons, each of the Asian religious systems increasing their sway in the region disapproved of cockfighting. Theravada Buddhism could not countenance the shedding of blood. Confucianism, which had a revival in Vietnam in the seventeenth century, looked on cockfighting as barbarous and disorderly, as well as leading people into debt. A Vietnamese edict of 1665 therefore forbade cockfighting as well as other forms of gambling, though not for the first or last time (Yu 1978: 220). If royal attempts to suppress cockfighting on the Mainland were only partially effective, they seem scarcely to have been made in the Archipelago. Although Islam was emphatically opposed to gambling, few rulers in the age of commerce chose to interpret this to cover the cockfight. The pious Sultan Ala'ad-din Perak of Aceh did ban cockfights as well as alcohol in the 1580s (Raniri 1644: 33), but they were sponsored on a grand scale by his successors, including Sultan Iskandar Muda, even though this mighty ruler was imprecisely credited by an admiring Muslim theologian with having banned gambling (ibid.: 36). The law code of Muslim Melaka conceded that cockfighting, like draughts and cardplaying, had to be categorized as gambling, but stopped short of declaring it illegal. Nevertheless, if a gambler got into a brawl after a cockfight and was foolish enough to appeal to the authorities, the disputed bets would be seized by the crown (*Undang-undang Melaka*: 166–67). A later Javanese sultan in 1801 specifically excluded the three most popular Javanese gambling games—cockfights, bird fights, and *kemiri* nut contests—from a decree forbidding gambling (Carey 1981: 117), and in practice some similar compromise appears to have been made by other Muslim rulers.

Just as English children used the chestnut for playing conkers, Southeast Asians exploited their flora for some unique games. Contests over the hardness of kemiri nuts were very popular in the Archipelago wherever the kemiri trees (Candlenut, or *Aleurites moluccana*) grew (Ochse 1931: 260–61; Burkill 1935: 92; Crawfurd 1820 I: 114). A Dutch envoy to Mataram in 1623 noted that "much is won or lost" in contests in which one nut would be placed on top of the other and then both hit with a long flat cane. Sultan Agung of Mataram was a great patron of these contests, but he punished severely some masters of the game who played it with him and used nuts which were not sufficiently highly polished and smooth for his taste (de Haen 1623: 37). In Burma the large flat beans of a giant creeper (*Entada pursaetha*) were stood in a long row like dominoes, and contestants in the game called *gohn-nyin toh pwe* had to knock down either all or a selected number of them with another bean or metal object, much as in modern tenpin bowling. Like so many other children's games this was also a popular form of gambling by adult men (Sangermano 1818: 162–63; Shway Yoe 1882: 369–72).

Rounded seeds and nuts were used as marbles, counters, or balls (Oosterbeek 1905: 56–57). Cowrie shells, used on the Mainland as the lowest form of money, also featured in many games. In Burma cowries were used instead of dice in board games, the number of spaces advanced being determined by throwing six shells and counting the number which landed right side up (Shway Yoe 1882: 374–76). Modern studies have shown that each major Southeast Asian community has dozens of children's games, many of them similar in form to games played in other parts of the world (Anderson 1973; Oosterbeek 1905: 53–57; Skeat 1900: 494–503), but only those played for money by adults can be traced in early sources.

Of the many activities which were both amusements for children and serious business for adult men, kite flying has a special place. During the dry season the air was full of kites constructed with great artistry from paper and bamboo in the image of various birds, beasts, or magical symbols. A sounding split bamboo was typically put at the head of the kite to make a loud humming noise sometimes said to reflect "the voice of the gods" (Oosterbeek 1905: 55). Contests aiming to encumber, bring down, or cut the string of a rival kite attracted intense betting (San Antonio 1604: 7; Skeat 1900: 484–85; Gerini 1912: 72–73).

At least in Siam and Java such contests were patronized by rulers on their ceremonial square before the palace, perhaps because kite flying retained some magical and religious functions in ensuring the change in the monsoons and the retreat of floodwaters (Wales 1931: 221–22). La Loubère (1691: 49) claimed that the king of Siam had his kite in the air continuously for two months during the "winter" (northeast monsoon), "and some Mandarins are nominated to ease one another in holding the string." Kite flying was reported to be the "greatest amusement and pastime" of one Javanese king, Amangkurat I, who had eighteen trees on the square before his palace cut down in 1662 to avoid any interference with it (Ricklefs 1978: 178).

In modern times the spinning of tops has been a popular pastime for boys, though men were also known to bet excitedly on the outcome (Kruyt 1932; Anderson 1973: 279). That tops were in use in Indonesia by the fifteenth century is evident from the variety of indigenous terms and styles employed, even if we have no direct evidence from the period (Kaudern 1929: 147–221). Damar Wulan was already a Javanese culture hero in the seventeenth century, when he was popularly credited with having made the first tops on divine instructions at least three centuries earlier (Kruyt 1932: 573; Pigeaud 1967: 231). In the nineteenth century top spinning retained in many places a close association with the agricultural cycle, and Kruyt (1932: 577–85) may be right in arguing that in earlier times it was believed to be necessary to encourage crops to ripen.

Dice were known in Vedic India and may have been introduced to Southeast Asia in ancient times. Since, however, the words for dice are chiefly of European or Chinese origin (Malay, Javanese, Acehnese, Makassarese *dadu*, from Portuguese *dado*; Thai *taw*, from Tiochiu *táw*), it appears that dice became popular only when borrowed in new forms around the sixteenth century. Even the important episode in the Mahabharata (shown in fig. 36) where the Pendawa king loses his kingdom by gambling with the rival Kurawas is known in Javanese drama as "Pendawa dadu" (Kats 1923: 391). Dice were in use in Maluku in the 1540s (Galvão 1544: 149), and probably were taken up elsewhere as a more convenient way of scoring the many popular board games of the backgammon type.

Fig. 36 A Javanese version of the *Mahabharata* episode in which the Pendawa kingdom is lost through gambling

Playing cards were almost certainly introduced by Chinese and were quickly seized on as a convenient means for gambling (Newbold 1839 II: 183; Goudswaard 1860: 351). As Tjan Tjoe Siem (1941: 3) commented for Java, "betting is as a rule more important than the game itself," and playing simply to pass the time without gambling would have been inconceivable. Cardplaying was evidently important enough in fifteenth-century Melaka to be listed among the disapproved forms of gambling in the *Undang-undang Melaka* (167). Cards were the most common form of gambling among women. As early as 1598 Filipino and mestizo women in Manila reportedly made cardplaying for high stakes "their chief diversion" (Morga 1598: 86–87). Tjan Tjoe Siem (1941) has effectively shown that the sixty-card packs, the games, and most of the vocabulary in the Indonesian Archipelago were of southern Chinese derivation. As some shipwrecked Englishmen found when playing cards with their hosts in eighteenth-century Sulawesi, "their games are unlike ours" (Woodard 1796: 122).

Draughts (or checkers) and chess were both being played for

money in Southeast Asia by the fifteenth century. Although chess was more noticed by Europeans, perhaps because it was primarily a game of aristocrats, draughts was the more widespread (Oosterbeek 1905: 60; *Undang-undang Melaka*: 166).

Diego Lopez was playing chess on the first Portuguese ship to reach Melaka in 1509 when a Javanese of the city came on board. The two men discussed the different types of chess played in their respective countries (Barros 1563 II, iv: 407). Other Iberian sources attest to chess being played in Maluku in the 1540s and at the court of Brunei in 1578 (Galvão 1544: 147; Brunei expedition 1579: 222). The game was popular at the Malay courts, and nowhere more so than in Pasai (northern Sumatra). Each of the two major variants of the Malay Annals mentions chess once, and in both cases it is connected with Pasai. In the reign of Sultan Mansur of Melaka (1459–77) one Tun Bahara from Pasai visited the city and proved too good for all opponents at chess, "without even appearing to concentrate" (*Sejarah Melayu* 1838: 151). On an earlier occasion one of the opulent gifts from a Pasai embassy to the king of Ayutthaya was a golden chessboard with jewelled chessmen (*Sejarah Melayu* 1612: 46). This local expertise may help explain the fact that the Bataks of northern Sumatra, relatively isolated from international commerce for most of the past four centuries, have been the most enthusiastic Southeast Asian chess players in modern times and have produced the best players (Anderson 1826: 50).[2] Whether this tradition originated during the fourteenth-century Pasai sultanate or in an earlier period of Indian influence on Batak society is not clear.

That chess was introduced to Southeast Asia from India there is no doubt—though some Arabic and Persian terms are also used. Southeast Asian languages use some derivation of the Sanskrit word *chaturanga* for their game, which also follows the Indian 8 × 8 square board. *Chaturanga* literally meant "the four elements of an army," meaning elephants, horses, chariots, and foot soldiers. Southeast Asian variants of chess included these same four elements, save that the chariots, never useful in jungle warfare, were sometimes replaced by more appropriate boats. The closeness of Southeast Asian usages to the Sanskrit model can be seen in the following scheme derived from Murray (1913: 28).

2. In 1916, only a decade after the Karo Batak region had been opened to commerce through its first road, a Karo chess master was invited to Java to play against the best Dutch players there. Even though their rules were different from his, he was a match for all but one of the Dutch masters (Harahap 1981).

Sanskrit	*Malay*	*Javanese*	*Burmese*	*Thai*	*English equivalent*
king	king	king	king	*khun* (lord)	king
mantri (minister)	mantri	*patih* (viceroy)	general	seed or knob	queen
elephant	elephant	mantri	elephant	platform	bishop
horse	horse	horse	horse	horse	knight
chariot	chariot	boat	chariot	boat	castle
foot soldier	foot soldier	foot soldier	foot soldier	cowrie shell	pawn

Although most early reports are of chess playing by the court circle, chess does appear to have become a popular pastime at least in some areas, where it was inevitably associated with excited betting (Shway Yoe 1882: 366). While rulers had beautifully carved or bejewelled permanent sets, ordinary folk used simple materials. In Siam shells were used for pawns. In northern Sumatra all the simple pieces were quickly hewn from bamboo—often a new set for each game.

The rules used in the islands and the Malay world differed from modern international ones only in minor respects, such as the king's ability to move two spaces or the knight's move when first checked. The Burmese game had the same number of men and squares but much greater freedom of arrangement, which made it "more like a real battle than any other recognized form" (Shway Yoe 1882: 366). In commencing, the players could place their major pieces anywhere behind the pawns, which were lined up half in the third row of squares and half in the fourth. The general or minister and the elephant had different moves from the queen and bishop, respectively, the elephant moving somewhat like his real-life equivalent—one square either ahead or to any of the four adjacent diagonals.

La Loubère (1691: 50) noted that as well as the indigenous variety of chess (close to the Burmese) Siam had a Chinese form, with the pieces placed on the junctions of lines rather than in the squares. In Vietnam there were also two varieties, one very like the Siamese and the other Chinese (Murray 1913: 108–18).

The one sport which was never a matter of direct competition was the most distinctively Southeast Asian of them all—the type of football which in Malay was known as *sepak raga* ("kick basket"), in Luzon as *sipa*, in Burmese as *chin-lohn*. The Thai term, takraw, has now become accepted as the international name for the sport, today modernized into a competitive volleyball-like sport at the Southeast Asia Games. In the eighteenth century the game was played in Burma, Siam, and southern Vietnam as well as in the Indonesian area. Since each of these countries regarded it as its own rather than borrowed, the sport can probably be assumed to have spread throughout the region much earlier. It was in the Malay world, however, that this game was first described, in exactly the same form it retained until recent times.

It was played with a hollow ball "made of plaited rattan" or basketwork (Galvão 1544: 146–49). An individual, or a group in a circle, would keep the ball in the air by kicking it with the foot or knee, preferably with the inside sole. If northern Sumatrans were renowned for their chess, it was Moluccans who had a special reputation in this sport. The *Sejarah Melayu* (1612: 115) includes a tribute to a chief from Maluku who visited Melaka during the reign of Sultan Ala'ud-din (1477–88):

> He was an expert at sepak raga and the young nobles of Melaka played it with him. . . . When the ball came to him, he would kick it himself a hundred or even 150 times before he passed it to someone else; and he would indicate to whomsoever he proposed to give the ball and then pass it without once making a mistake. Then he would sit down on a chair to rest . . . while the young men went on playing. When the ball came to him, Raja Maluku would kick it himself for as long as it takes to cook pot after pot of rice and the ball would stay up in the air until he wished to pass it to someone else.

Similarly it was in Maluku, at Banda, that the Dutch first encountered takraw; they described and tried to draw (fig. 37) the extraordinary skill of the players, all standing in a ring and passing the ball to one another ("Tweede Boeck" 1601: 84). Although individual masters certainly made a show of their skills, this was not a competitive game. It was designed to promote dexterity and "to exercise the body, to restore elasticity to the back and limbs cramped by sitting, reading, or writing, or even by playing chess" (Shway Yoe 1882: 372; cf. Marsden 1783: 276–77; Sangermano 1818: 163; Gerini 1912: 73; Kaudern 1929: 85–103).

Although takraw was played in Cambodia and southern Vietnam (La Bissachère 1812 II: 91–92), there was also an interesting variation of it in the Mekong delta in the late eighteenth century. The rattan ball was replaced by a kind of shuttlecock made from a leather ball wrapped with string, weighted with Chinese coins and flighted by three long feathers. This object floated down slowly enough to encourage the leaping high kicks beloved of takraw players (Macartney 1798 I: 339). In Sumatra, Java, and Sulawesi feathered shuttlecocks made by sticking chicken feathers in a small bamboo tube were also used; sometimes they were kept in the air by players armed with wooden bats (Kaudern 1929: 105–10). In this form the game was

Fig. 37 Takraw, or *sepak raga*, observed by Dutch travellers (pictured bottom) in Maluku, 1599

analogous with the European predecessor of badminton, battledore and shuttlecock, and may help explain the enthusiastic Southeast Asian response to modern badminton.

Theatre, Dance, and Music

> *The land of Majapahit was extremely populous. There was a constant noise of gongs, drums and dancing to every kind of loud music. There were all kinds of entertainments like* wayang wong *(dance-drama),* wayang kulit *(shadow puppets),* wayang topeng *(masked drama) and dances such as* joget, tandak, bedaya *and* beksan. *These and other pleasures were extremely common by day and night in the land of Majapahit.*
>
> —*Hikayat Raja-raja Pasai: 102*

To European visitors, it seemed that Southeast Asians were always singing, dancing, and performing. Emissaries and important visitors were routinely entertained with dance or theatre at court, and they often had dancers sent to their lodgings to entertain them at night (Dampier 1699: 101). Alcina (1668 III: 64) claimed that "rarely can a

Visayan man or woman be found, unless he is sick, who ceases to sing except when he is asleep. This is the greatest diversion of their feasts and merriment, to sing and dance until they are tired" (cf. Symes 1827 II: 22–23). At a later period Pemberton (1830: 43–44), already unable to stay awake through the constant dramas with which he was entertained on his journey towards Ava, was alarmed to learn that at the capital itself the performances "continued from day to day almost uninterruptedly." Another Englishman (Shway Yoe 1882: 285), presumably unaware of the passions of Javanese and Balinese, insisted that "there is no nation on the face of the earth so fond of theatrical presentations as the Burmese."

Royal courts were the cultural exemplars, setting patterns, authorizing new trends, attracting outstanding performers from the countryside. In this period when the royal capitals were at the same time the dominant economic and political centres and the crucibles for foreign ideas, it is impossible to distinguish between court and popular culture. That would come later, as monarchies began to lose the economic and military battle to foreign elements. In seventeenth-century Siam, Nicolas (1924: 43) has pointed out, the *lakhon nok* (subsequently regarded as popular theatre as opposed to the *lakhon nai* of the court) was the only theatre there was. Rulers of that period could still oblige foreign traders to play their supporting roles in the great royal drama, as when the English and Dutch provided fireworks and pageants for the circumcision of the boy-king of Banten (Scott 1606: 152–62), or when Chinese performed their opera, Europeans their fireworks, Laos their puppet theatre, and Malays and Burmese their music and dance for various feasts in Ayutthaya (Tachard 1686: 184–85). The variety and opulence of the performances was one of the indices of royal grandeur, and except for some dances by secluded court women they were all to be displayed rather than hidden behind the palace walls.

Dramatic and musical forms were spread between city and country by travelling players, moving from village to village and, if successful, ultimately to the court. The great seventeenth-century master of wayang kulit, Andjangmas, travelled to wherever in Java there were patrons needing a performance to enliven a feast. The practice of charging travelling players in Java a tax on the fees they earned in performing is said to have begun in the reign of Amangkurat I between 1646 and 1677 (Pigeaud 1938: 32, 36, 61). The weddings, funerals, and other festivals organized by the court were grander than any others and their performers were brought from a wider area, but like village festivals they were public and popular.

Most people at the time appear to have experienced these performances in the first place as play—albeit play that had the serious implications described by Huizinga (1938: 1–27). Court chroniclers took pride in the large numbers of people enjoying these spectacles. Unless they were entertained, the purposes of the royal or village patron were not served. Chronicles of the period frequently emphasize how the people were entertained by a variety of shows. One Malay text from Banjarmasin described how the old capital had become gloomy, so the king sent to Giri in Java where there were expert dancers, puppeteers, and players (*Hikayat Banjar*: 41). Another text, from Sumbawa, presented the villain attempting to seduce his virtuous captives by proffering "all kinds of entertainments like Indian dances, Siamese theatre, Chinese opera, Javanese puppet theatre and music of the viol, lute, kettledrum, flute, bamboo pipe, flageolet, *kufak* and castanets" (*Hikayat Dewa Mandu*: 257).

It is also clear, however, that theatre and dance (with the music which always accompanied them) provided an essential link between the world of men and the cosmic reality of gods and legendary figures from the past. In the Indianized polities of Burma, Siam, Cambodia, Java, Bali, and to a lesser extent the Malay world, it was especially through these performances that contact was maintained with the Indian religious tradition even after the spread of Islam and Theravada Buddhism. The heroes of the *Ramayana* and the *Mahabharata* were transposed to a legendary past of the Southeast Asian country itself, where they were seen as intensely real progenitors of human society and especially of ordered monarchies. They were not men, however, and were therefore best represented by puppets or masks far removed from realism. Whereas unmasked human actors were used for themes in relatively recent history, it was the puppet and masked drama which were held sacred and usually associated with a divine revelation (Shway Yoe 1882: 293; Crawfurd 1820 I: 126–32).

Theatre without dance and music was inconceivable. The association between dancing and the gods is seen in an Indianized form in the temple reliefs of Angkor and Prambanan, but even where there was no Indian influence dancing was the means to communicate with spirits and gods and to invite their attendance at a feast. Every man and woman could dance and frequently did (figs. 38 and 39). The guests at a wedding often processed around the town with music and dance (Gervaise 1688: 95–96). Normally grave Burmese might break into dance in the excitement of a boat race or a buffalo fight (Shway Yoe 1882: 308, 360). The higher one moved up the social scale the more one's actions when in the public eye were expected to replicate the move-

Fig. 38 Burmese dancers forming part of a procession in honour of the white elephant; from a Burmese illustrated manuscript of the mid-nineteenth century

ments of the gods. As Crawfurd (1820 I: 122–23) pointed out, when Javanese entered or left the royal presence, or when Bugis swore an oath, declared war, or ran amok, they danced. What this meant, perhaps, was that dance was a means of channeling emotion, concentrating energies, and assuming some of the character of the gods or spirits as they were represented in everyday theatre.

Though it can be assumed that dance was extremely ancient, the process by which it was incorporated into more elaborate forms of dance drama and theatre is far from clear. Only in Vietnam is there a definite record of the introduction of the Chinese-inspired dance drama (*hat boi*) in 1285, after the capture of a talented Chinese actor. Although little is known of this early form except that it celebrated episodes of Vietnamese history at the court, the medium was popularized around 1600 by a northern actor who had become a refugee in the southern Nguyen-ruled kingdom. With the addition of exciting battle scenes and mournful songs borrowed from Cham styles, hat boi gradually became the national theatrical tradition (Hauch 1972: 11–13; Huynh 1970: 16–22).

The other Southeast Asian theatres used Indian epic themes probably introduced during the first Christian millennium, especially the universally popular *Ramayana*. The forms of the theatre familiar in modern times, however, are by no means so old. The earliest evidence

Fig. 39 Wedding procession in Java, early nineteenth century, from a contemporary woodcut

of Javanese shadow puppets (wayang kulit) does indeed go back as far as a ninth-century inscription and a more explicit eleventh-century chronicle (Kats 1923: 35–37). Yet Javanese writers insist that it was the Muslim saints and apostles of Java who gave wayang kulit its modern form around the sixteenth century, just as they created the masked theatre (wayang topeng). In Raffles' day Javanese still located the scenes of the *Mahabharata* in the harbour towns of the north coast which had been the cradle of Javanese Islam (Raffles 1817 I: 411–12). Most scholars now accept that the Javanese theatre was transformed, expanded, and popularized in the cosmopolitan coastal cities during the age of commerce, with the language becoming modernized, the leather puppets highly stylized (perhaps to avoid the Islamic ban on human representation), and the beloved (and ancient) indigenous clown figures (*punakawan*) integrated with the Indian epic tales (Ras 1976: 57–61; Pigeaud 1967: 287; Mulyono 1978: 33–86). What is certain is that this was a period of enormous cultural innovation throughout the region, as well as the earliest period of which the historical record enables us to speak with confidence about theatrical developments.

Foreign visitors confirm a rapid expansion in the range of popular theatre at this time. The Chinese accompanying Cheng Ho to Java in the early fifteenth century reported seeing only the *wayang beber*, where the narrator unrolls one section of a painted scroll at a time and chants its story while "the crowd sits around and listens to him, sometimes laughing, sometimes crying" (Ma Huan 1433: 97). Even though the shadow theatre must have had older origins than this drama of scrolls, it was not until Tomé Pires (1515: 177) that it and the masked drama were described as popular entertainments: "The land of Java is [a land] of mummers and masks of various kinds, and both men and women do this. They have entertainments of dancing and stories; they mime; they wear mummers' dresses and all their clothes. They are certainly graceful; they have music of bells—the sound of them playing together is like an organ. . . . At night they make shadows of various shapes, like *beneditos* in Portugal." Although this account contradicts the Javanese belief that Sunan Kalijaga devised the first masks in the Klaten area near Yogyakarta in 1586, Pires' evidence does confirm Pigeaud's argument (1938: 39–52) that the masked drama (like the shadow theatre) was widely enjoyed in the coastal region (the home of Kalijaga) at this period and only later became associated with the rarified courts of central Java. In Banten, too, Scott (1606: 155–56, 161) reported the masked players to be among the popular entertainers for the royal circumcision. By the seventeenth century the dance drama without masks (wayang wong) was making a modest beginning as a kind of interlude, as witnessed by Van Goens (1656: 238) in Mataram.

From the ports of Java many of these forms were taken by Javanese traders to Melaka, Patani, and thence to the Malay world more broadly. Peter Floris (1615: 87) witnessed in Patani "a commedye all by women, to the manner of Java." They also spread (about the sixteenth century) to Banjarmasin in southern Borneo, whose chronicle has the King, Lambung Mangkurat, send an envoy to Giri, the Muslim centre of pilgrimage just outside Gresik, to request that skilled players of the masked drama, the shadow theatre, and various dances be sent across to him "to brighten the place up" (Ras 1968: 41). A different text of the same chronicle relates how the people later celebrated a great royal wedding for forty days and nights: "It was a lively and crowded feast. There were shadow puppet shows in the palace, on the raised platform dance dramas (*wayang wong*) were performed, in the square there was masked drama, in the audience-hall there were *raket* (dance pageant) performances" (*Hikayat Banjar* 314; cf. also 323). Sukadana in southwest Borneo, conquered by Sultan Agung of Mataram in 1622, probably acquired its tradition of wayang kulit at the same time (Barth 1896: 92–93).

The nature of shadow theatre, always lasting through the night and evoking mysteriously the world of gods and spirits, makes clear that its ancient origins were closely linked to religious purposes. Some of those religious associations survived the Islamization of Java, ensuring an important place for wayang kulit even after more spectacular and accessible forms of drama were developed. In Siam the shadow theatre of leather puppets (*nang*) was also very ancient, being mentioned in the Palatine Law conventionally dated 1458 (Nicolas 1927: 105; Dhaninivat 1948: 116). It may be even more ancient in Cambodia, usually regarded as the conduit through which the shadow theatre reached Siam from Java, though there are no early sources to prove it. As Theravada Buddhism gradually deprived its themes of religious relevance, however, it appears to have become an increasingly esoteric ritual activity in Siam, except in the southern provinces bordering the Malay world.

Thai tradition has it that masked drama (*khon*) was developed by King Rama T'ibodi (1491–1529), who had dancers imitate the shadow puppets (Brandon 1967: 65–66). This quickly became the more popular way of enacting the beloved Jataka stories about the Buddha's former incarnations, and it eventually spread to Burma and Cambodia to fulfill the same purpose.

The more purely entertaining dance drama using actors without masks appears to have played a larger role on the Mainland than in Java, either because of the example of Chinese theatre or because there were not the same misgivings about human representation as were posed by Islam. This most secular form of theatre was known in most of the region by the same term, which appears to be derived from the Javanese *lakon* (Thai *lakhon*, Khmer *lkhon*, Malay *lakun*). In Java itself the word was applied to an episode of any theatrical presentation, not necessarily the dance drama. Nevertheless, it is probably in Java that a common Southeast Asian origin for the unmasked drama should be sought.

The relatively full information by French visitors to the court of King Narai (1656–88) includes descriptions of the masked dramas in Ayutthaya played by Mons from Pegu as well as by Thais, and of puppet theatre in which the Lao especially excelled (Tachard 1686: 192, 185; La Loubère 1691: 47). There is, however, no mention of the shadow theatre. As La Loubère (1691: 49) put it:

> The Siamese have three sorts of stage-plays. That which they call Cone [*khon*] is a figure-dance, to the sound of the violin and some other instruments. The dancers are masked and armed, and represent rather a combat than a dance: and tho' every one runs into high motions, and extravagant postures, they cease not continually to intermix some word. Most of their masks are hideous and represent either monstrous beasts, or kinds of devils. The show which they call Lacone [lakhon], is a poem intermixt with epic and dramatic, which lasts three days, from eight in the morning till seven at night. They are histories in verse, serious, and sung by several actors always present, and which do only sing reciprocally. One of them sings the historian's part, and the rest those of the personages which the history makes to speak; but they are all men that sing, and no women. The *rabam* is a double dance of men and women, which is not martial, but gallant. . . . These dancers, both men and women, have all false nails, and very long ones, of copper: They sing some words in their dancing, and they can perform it without much tyring themselves, because their way of dancing is a simple march round, very slow, and without any high motion; but with a great many slow contortions of the body and arms. . . . Mean while two men entertain the spectators with several fooleries. . . . The *khon* and the *rabam* are always call'd at funerals, and sometimes on other occasions. . . . The *Lakhon* serves principally to solemnise the feast of the dedication of a new temple.

This valuable information suggests that at a popular level the masked drama (khon) and the dance drama (lakhon) had already evolved during the culturally innovative reign of King Narai, perhaps both inspired by the more ancient but recondite shadow theatre. At the same time the rabam, which Nicolas (1924: 43) calls a "character dance," had developed out of the ancient sacred dances in a direction which also involved storytelling.

Little is known about Burmese theatre prior to the extensive court-sanctioned borrowing from Thai traditions in the eighteenth century. It never included a shadow theatre, but a similar semisacred role appears to have been played at a popular level by a highly developed art of marionettes (see fig. 40), worked from behind a screen by a large number of strings and pulleys (Pemberton 1830: 31). Prior to the eighteenth-century reforms these marionettes appear to have represented stereotyped animals, or perhaps the spirits of animals, each doing a dance to its own music, followed by stock dances by puppets representing an alchemist or magician and a pair of princely lovers (Htin Aung 1937: 144–49). Another antecedent of the modern Burmese theatre may have been a kind of pageant (*nibhatkin*) played on a bullock cart at festivals to represent scenes from the Jataka cycle (ibid.: 18–20).

Throughout the region there appears to have been a partial con-

Fig. 40 The Burmese "sand pagoda festival" of the twelfth lunar month (March–April), as depicted in a painted manuscript of the mid-nineteenth century. At left is a marionette theatre, before it a Burmese orchestra as accompaniment, and at right various food sellers.

vergence in the age of commerce of two sacral traditions. One derived from predominately female dancers who had originally mediated with spirits or the Hindu gods. This was the tradition of Thai rabam, and of the Burmese development from shamanistic dancing to entertainment which Htin Aung (1937: 21–24) calls the "interlude." Similar origins probably inspired Javanese and Balinese *raket* and *gambuh*, both already present in the fourteenth century—although these appear quite early to have used male dancers (*Wangbang Wideya*: 87, 91; Pigeaud 1938: 345–47; McPhee 1966: 113). The other tradition was the stylized representation of gods and spirits by nonhuman puppets, shadows, and subsequently masked actors. By the seventeenth century these two forms had given rise to an intensely popular theatre which used the *Ramayana*, the *Mahabharata*, Jataka stories, and some events from local history to entertain, to educate, to moralize and at the same time to retain the link between the worlds of men and of gods which was necessary especially at funerals, marriages, and other important rituals.

The urban and cosmopolitan atmosphere of this period made it possible for the theatre to move away to some extent from the purely sacred and conventional, giving rise in Siam and probably Java and

Cambodia to a popular theatre with unmasked human actors, frequently creating new subjects for the stage. That this tradition spread also to the Malay world we know from the *Hikayat Patani* (115–16), which tells of a famous troupe of four men and eight women players who came to Patani in the 1620s. They staged verse dramas set to music (*ikatan*), based on episodes from the *Ramayana* but also on at least two stories from the relatively recent Malay past—one about the Bendahara of Melaka resisting the first Portuguese invasion and the other about the Bendahara of Johor at the time of his attack on Jambi.

Apart from its role as accompaniment to these performances, music played crucial roles in both the theatre of the state and the everyday pleasures of Southeast Asians. Music seemed to be everywhere. The Filipinos, Thais, and Burmese sang as they rowed their boats, harvested their crops, and pounded their rice (Alcina 1668 III: 64; Loarca 1582: 121; Symes 1827 II: 23; Schweisguth 1951: 119–21). The first Dutchmen in Java described how, in the great households of Banten, "dancing goes on all night, so that at night there is a great racket of gongs and instruments" (*Verhael* 1597: 30). A similar comment was made by Bowring (1857 I: 150–51) about the Siam of his day, and the heyday of Ayutthaya is remembered as a period of even more widespread music making (Morton 1976: 13).

No more than with theatre should we seek to distinguish between popular and court music in this period (Kunst 1933 I: 120–21). Prince and peasant were entranced by the same themes and instruments. There was, however, a distinction between the majestic sonorities of the bronze gongs and the more intimate music usually played by women.

It is entirely appropriate that "gong" should be one of the words which Southeast Asia gave to European languages. The word is probably Javanese in origin, but it was borrowed by most Austronesian languages and by Thai (*khong*). Bronze idiophones have played a key role in status and ceremony as well as music, probably ever since the great bronze kettledrums of Dong-son found a market throughout Southeast Asia in the four centuries before Christ. In the age of commerce bronze gongs remained great items of trade, particularly in eastern Indonesia, Borneo, and the Philippines, where they had to be imported from Java or China. They were used, along with wooden slit-drums, to demarcate the hours or sections of the day (Dampier 1697: 231; Yupho 1957: 22); to summon people together or to make important announcements (Lodewycksz 1598: 107; Wilkinson 1903: 374); to add gravity to any important occasion.

As Alcina (1668 III: 722–73) noted, only the rich could afford

Fig. 41 The large Javanese gong carried in military procession, from a relief on the fourteenth century Javanese temple, Candi Panataran, showing Sugriwa's monkey army

these impressive instruments. It was not surprising, therefore, that they were strongly associated with status. When a king or great man went in solemn procession he was accompanied by men beating gongs (fig. 41). "Hanging from wooden poles, they are carried along on the shoulders of two men, while others beat them with wooden mallets; (they produce all) sounds from counterbass to soprano, for some are larger and others smaller" (Galvão 1544: 111; cf. Scott 1606: 155). Royal processions by sea, or naval expeditions, similarly carried a set of bronze instruments to show the king's majesty (Morga 1609: 276; Galvão 1544: 149). On state occasions, such as the tournaments staged by Javanese kings, an assemblage of gongs was always necessary. At Mataram each of the great men had his own stage set up for the tournament, with "their metal instruments, at least 20 to 30, with gongs both large and small, as well as those of the king, who had as many as 200 spread around in five or six places. These gongs are beaten very softly and sweetly before the king's arrival. . . . When the king does arrive in the outer square they begin to beat on all the large and small gongs with such force that there would have been no hope of hearing the beating of ten of our drums" (van Goens 1656: 229–30).

At courts and great houses, gong chimes which consisted of seven or eight gongs of differing sizes and tunings, or more often of a double octave of fourteen or sixteen, were assembled to form an instrument playing octaves of seven pitches. (The exception was the alternative Javanese *slendro* scale of five tones, probably the number intended to be shown in the crude Dutch engravings of north coast ensembles in which only four gongs make up an elementary *bonang*—see fig. 42.) The Portuguese conquerors of Melaka were presented by a ruler of Java with a set of twenty small gongs (perhaps 4 × 5, in slendro scale), as well as two great ones "which they strike in battle" (Albuquerque 1557: 161). In Mindanao, Dampier (1697: 234) found no instruments except an arrangement of sixteen gongs of different sizes. At Ayutthaya the circle of sixteen gongs (*khong wong*), adapted from the Khmer civilization of Angkor and eventually characteristic of Burma, Cambodia, and Siam (see figs. 33 and 40), had already made its appearance in the reign of Narai (La Loubère 1691: 68; Morton 1976: 45–48).

Because gongs were associated with the male concerns of status and warfare, they were usually played outdoors by men. In the Philippines, however (Pigafetta 1524: 36–37), as later in parts of Sumatra, women musicians were in charge of the gong-and-drum orchestra common throughout the region. Women played all but the largest gongs and drums, especially in indoor entertainments to accompany dancing (*Verhael* 1597:30). In Siam two distinct assemblages of instruments began to take shape—the *mahori*, or string ensemble of four or five women, including a singer and drummer (figs. 43a and 43b); and the *pi phat*, usually a male group including a reed instrument (pi), gongs, and drums (Morton 1976: 101–05). The former has been commemorated in painting and carving as part of the inner life of the court and other noble houses, while the latter was used to accompany stage performances and festivals. Kunst (1933: 113–14) has argued that the gamelan of Java developed out of a gradual merging, some time between the fifteenth and eighteenth centuries, of the male pattern of gong-and-drum ensembles and the strings and wind instruments usually played by women (fig. 44). At Mataram there was already something akin to a gamelan, with some stringed instruments and flutes as

Fig. 42 Dutch engraver's impression of the Javanese gongs of Banten, 1596. The contemporary caption, in Lodewycksz 1598, notes their use "to sound the hours, and play all their music . . . and also when they want to summon people in the king's name, as they did when we first arrived there, to show that anyone might buy and sell with us."

well as "many little gongs" (van Goens 1656: 235). In sixteenth-century Patani the typical drum-based ensemble of Malayo-Muslim royalty (*nobat*) had reached the proportions of "four golden trumpets (*nafiri*) and four silver ones, two golden oboes (*serunai*) and two silver ones, twelve royal drums and eight state drums" (Hikayat Patani: 141). What seems certain is that until at least the late seventeenth century there was a great degree of variation and experimentation in the way orchestras were put together.

If bronze instruments and elaborate orchestras were the prerogative of the wealthy, most of the range of simpler Southeast Asian drums, flutes, oboes, and string instruments were within reach of all. For simple villagers, instruments were cheaply made from bamboo, coconut shell, and palm leaf, while even the rhythm of the rice pounder could provide an accompaniment for song. Among the few writers who describe the rural scene, Alcina (1668 III: 64–73; cf. Chirino 1606: 279) revealed the enormous enthusiasm of Filipino villagers for the skilled playing of a simple zither (*kudyape*) by men, or a small lute (*korlong*) by women. For musical dialogues or contests between these

Fig. 43a Female orchestra (*mahori*) from a Thai relief thought to be Sukhothai period

Fig. 43b Another variant of the Thai female orchestra, from a mural in the Buddhaisawan Chapel in Bangkok, c. 1800

Fig. 44 Instruments of the Javanese gamelan in the early nineteenth century, as represented in a Javanese drawing from the north coast

two instruments "so many gather . . . that they fill the house upstairs and down" (ibid.: 67).

The music of Vietnam is better considered as a variant of East than of Southeast Asian musical tradition, despite the many Cham and Cambodian influences upon it. Apart from the similarity of Vietnamese and Chinese instruments, Vietnam used the East Asian pentatonic scale and melodic style in contrast to the dominant polyphony on a seven-tone scale in Southeast Asia (Tran 1967: 19–23; Kunst 1933: 121). The Vietnamese, moreover, wrote down their serious music according to a Chinese-derived notation system (Tran 1967: 64–65). This was a marked departure from the exclusively aural system of transmission elsewhere in Southeast Asia, in which individual musicians looked for variations within a musical repertoire seen as essentially a "steady state" (Sutton 1982: 291–92). In the popular folk music and poetry of Vietnam, on the other hand, the dominant patterns of the region appear to have applied.

Widespread Literacy?

Early European observers of Southeast Asia were surprised by the high level of literacy they found there. Their evidence is most extensive and compelling in just that part of the region where it might be least expected—the Philippines. Even though, as the early Spanish writers recognized, there was no significant written literature in Philippine languages, and writing itself may not have been introduced more than a century or two before the Spanish arrived, both men and women were generally able to incise the seventeen symbols used in Philippine writing on bamboo or strips of palm leaf:

Women commonly know how to write with them [Philippine letters] and when they write do so on certain pieces of bamboo (Dasmariñas 1590A: 424).

So accustomed are all these islanders to writing and reading that there is scarcely a man, still less a woman, who cannot read and write in letters proper to the island of Manila (Chirino 1604: 280).

All the natives, women as well as men, write in this language, and there are very few who do not write well and correctly (Morga 1609: 269).

They all cling fondly to their own method of writing and reading. There is scarcely a man, and still less a woman, who does not know and practice that method (Colin 1660: 51).

Today they [Visayans] use them [Philippine characters] a great deal, and the women much more than the men. The former write them and read them much more fluently than the latter (Alcina 1668 III: 39).

Almost everybody in the Visayas knows how to write in their own characters (Delgado 1751, cited Scott 1968: 58–59).

For no other area are we as well served in the number or quality of firsthand witnesses, especially outside the main trading centres. Nevertheless, the evidence there is from Java and Bali tends in the same direction. Rijklof van Goens, who led five official missions from Batavia to the court of Mataram in the period 1648–54, concluded that the majority of Javanese could read and write (van Goens 1656: 184). Not until the nineteenth century do similarly thorough accounts of Bali appear, though even at that late date Bali probably retained a number of the features of pre-Islamic Java which had been gradually eroded by Islamic or Dutch influence in Java itself. Zollinger (1847: 532), referring to Lombok in the 1840s, observed that "nearly all Balinese can read and write their language, even the people of the lowest condition, as well as the greatest part of the women." In Bali itself four decades later Jacobs (1883: 216) claimed that "almost every adult Balinese can read and write. Most women from the higher classes of Balinese society have also mastered this art."

Such claims to near-universal literacy are surprising, to say the least, in preindustrial societies with no printed literature and no formal system of schools. If they can be accepted, the Southeast Asian achievement would have to be considered unique. Scepticism seems called for, especially when these early statements are compared with the more solid evidence of twentieth-century colonial censuses, which show a depressingly familiar pattern of low literacy, especially among women. The Philippine Census of 1903 revealed that only 20 percent of the population aged ten or more could both read and write, though another 24 percent could read but not write. Taking females alone, only 10.7 percent could both read and write, while 31 percent could read but not write (*Census of the Philippine Islands, 1903* II: 78–79). The 1920 Census of Netherlands India gave even lower figures, with only 6.83 percent of adult males and 0.26 percent of adult females being considered literate in Java, and 8.01 and 0.35 percent, respectively, in Bali and Lombok (*Volkstelling 1920* II: 155, 293).

Western scholars (in contrast to nationalist writers) have tended to resolve this contradiction by dismissing the early witnesses as woefully misled. Moving primarily among the upper classes, European visitors may have generalized from a very small number of elite families to misread the situation of the population as a whole. Yet at least in the Philippines the evidence of the early Spanish missionaries who lived and worked among the people is too strong to be dismissed out of hand.

We could also question the evidence of the colonial censuses, particularly in the Indonesian case. Although literacy was officially defined as the ability to write a letter in any language, the interest of the Netherlands Indies Government and its modern-minded Indonesian census takers—often schoolteachers from other regions (Christian Menadonese and Ambonese were, for example, heavily overrepresented in the teaching profession)—was in the modern education system being established by the colonial government, which taught Malay (Indonesian) or Dutch, both in roman characters. Those attending school in the third class or above were automatically recorded as literate (*Volkstelling 1920* I: 17). The inability of census takers themselves to read the local languages may explain why areas where traditional literacy was in a language and script not taught in school—Java, Bali, and southern Sulawesi—were recorded as having exceptionally low literacy.

In addition to these two factors there is a third possibility—that literacy in Southeast Asia declined between the sixteenth and early twentieth centuries. If this occurred in the island world, it can only have been because the more "modern" and universalist system of monastic education introduced by Islam and Christianity acted to suppress an older pattern of literacy of quite a different type.

The most striking evidence for such an interpretation comes from the 1930 Census of Netherlands India and its less thorough predecessor of 1920. These recorded the highest literacy anywhere in Indonesia not in those provinces where the modern school system was most widespread (North Sulawesi and Ambon) but in the Lampung districts of southern Sumatra. In 1930, 45 percent of adult men and 34 percent of adult women could write, and in contrast to the usual "modern" pattern the older age groups had higher literacy than the younger. The great majority of these literates could write, not in the roman script taught in the government schools, nor yet in the Arabic script learned for reciting the Koran, but in the old Indonesian *ka-ga-nga* alphabet. This was taught in no school and had no value either vocationally or in reading any established religious or secular literature. The explanation given for its persistence was the local custom of *manjau*, a courting game whereby young men and women would gather in the evenings and the youths would fling suggestive quatrains (*pantun*) written in the old script to the young women they fancied (*Volkstelling 1930* IV: 74–75; Loeb 1935: 279–80; personal information from Dr. P. Voorhoeve).[3]

The sources do not reveal how young people learned the script, but since it was not taught in school there must have been a process of transmission in the home, probably from mothers or older siblings, with the very powerful incentive of participation in the mating game. Something of the sort was suggested for Bali by Jacobs (1883: 216), who remarked that the high literacy he observed there was achieved without any schools. "The Balinese learn this [writing] from each other in play, and already small toddlers teach each other to read the Balinese alphabet and to write it on *lontar* leaves."

The Philippines, the writing systems of which were probably derived from those of Sumatra, reveal a pattern strikingly similar to that of Lampung. The detailed Spanish accounts of the Philippines make no mention of schools. They insist that Filipino writing served no religious, judicial, or historical purposes, but was used only "to write missives and notes to one another" (Dasmariñas 1590A: 424; cf. Chirino 1604: 286). One of the few Filipino peoples to retain the old alphabet after the mass Christianization of the seventeenth century were the isolated Mangyan of Mindoro, most of the adults of which are reportedly still literate in it. They still use this writing primarily as an

3. Given the probable bias of census takers mentioned above, it seems likely that Lampung stands out in the census as an exception to the general pattern of low literacy because the old script was too widespread to be ignored, not because it was unique in having survived.

aid for memorizing the love songs which are the central aspect of their culture, especially during the post-harvest *panlūdan* feast in honour of the ancestors. At about the age of puberty their young men and women demand of older relatives a knowledge of the local script to help them cut an impressive figure during the exchanges of love chants at these feasts (Conklin 1949; Conklin 1960: 117–18; Scott 1968: 59).

The exceptionally high rates of female literacy reported for the Philippines, Bali, and Lampung now begin to take on more significance. In the absence of formal schools serving to perpetuate a religious elite, literacy was apparently transmitted by older relatives to children in the home.

South Sulawesi, and the island of Sumbawa influenced by it, form a third area where a ka-ga-nga script related to those of the Philippines and Sumatra was perpetuated without benefit of formal schooling. Adopted only two or three centuries before the region accepted Islam in the early seventeenth century, this script was used in genealogies, histories, literature, and books of divination. At least in Sumbawa it was also used for courting poetry of the Lampung type (Mantja 1984: 37). Islam introduced the Arabic alphabet for religious and other purposes without driving out the old, and one of the reasons for this was explained by Gervaise (1701: 64, 74). Makassarese boys spent an hour in the morning and the evening with the ulama, who taught them "to cast accounts, to explain the Alcoran, to read and to write" in Arabic script. Girls remained in the house, where they were taught by their mothers to read and write. A century and a half later, when a Dutch missionary-scholar scoured South Sulawesi for Bugis and Makassarese manuscripts, he found it was primarily the women who could help him. "In general the Native women, especially the female chiefs, are much more expert in Bugis literature than the men. . . . Finally I looked no longer for the *guru* [religious teachers], but only for the *pasura*, i.e. those who occupy themselves with reading the *sura* or writings. . . . One finds such people only among the chiefly women and similar old women who have been associated with the court for a long time" (Matthes 1856: 184–85). Although the purposes were somewhat different from those in the Philippines and Sumatra, literacy once again was being transmitted by women within the household, and more effectively than in the religious schools, which were overwhelmingly male.

In the countries more influenced by Indian culture the transmission of literacy by male religious specialists through a monastic type of school system is too clear to be denied. Yet even so, in Java and Bali the evidence of the pre-Islamic *kakawin* literature is that writing was also used on a grand scale for love letters and love poems written on palm leaves, pandanus petals, or strips of wood (fig. 45). At least among the court circle, who are the subjects of this classical literature, the skill in composing poems of love appears to have been an essential accomplishment for both sexes (Zoetmulder 1974: 136–53).

Virtually everywhere in Southeast Asia there was a strong tradition of contests in poetry, usually of the four-line pantun type, between men and women as part of the courtship process. Where Islam became established it appears to have prevented or suppressed the habit of writing such poems in letters made of palm leaves. In particular the Arabic script learned in religious schools to read the Koran was not used for such purposes. The tradition of love poetry as part of courtship remained in Islamic areas primarily in oral form—except insofar as older habits were able to survive through the ka-ga-nga alphabet as in Lampung. Islam took with it to Southeast Asia a very different sexual morality which regarded it as not only unnecessary but also dangerous for women to be able to write. The classic Persian *Qabus Nama* (1082: 125) was one of the guides to conduct which made this point explicitly. One Indonesian writer remembered that in his childhood in strongly Islamic West Sumatra "girls were not allowed to go to school, lest their ability to write was used to send love letters to some youth" (Radjab 1950: 17). If this was still the sentiment in relation to government schools in the 1920s, it is easy to imagine that it would have applied even more strongly to the Islamic schools first established in a Sumatra where suggestive love poems were the essence of traditional literature.

In most preindustrial societies in other parts of the world, literacy was kept confined to a male elite in one of two ways. The more common was probably what Goody (1968: 11–20) calls "restricted literacy," where the main purpose of writing was to preserve a sacred literature whose potency was accentuated by its relative inaccessibility. In the European Middle Ages, as in much of the history of India and the Islamic world, literacy appears to have been limited to a very small and exclusively male religious elite and passed on essentially through a monastic tradition. The other, less common, elite were the secular literati of ancient Greece, ancient Rome, and East Asia, whose literacy served civic rather than religious purposes. In China the extreme difficulty of the written language probably discouraged all but the scholar-elite from acquiring it, though in Japan the native phonetic alphabet (*kana*) made possible a wider literacy particularly among women. In Greece most authorities see a remarkable spread of literacy among males of the upper classes, partly because there too there was a

Fig. 45 Panji writing a love poem on palm leaf

phonetic system of writing comparable in its simplicity to the Indonesian and Filipino scripts.

What I am arguing for island Southeast Asia is that although the writing system must originally have been introduced from India in the first Christian millennium to serve a sacred literature, it spread to many parts of Sumatra, South Sulawesi, and the Philippines for quite different, everyday purposes. Prior to the sixteenth-century expansion of Islam and Christianity, writing was being adopted by largely animist cultures where women were more commercially and socially active than in other parts of the world. Women took up writing as actively as men, to use in exchanging notes and recording debts and other commercial matters which were in the female domain. The transmission of literacy was therefore a domestic matter, largely the responsibility of mothers and older siblings, and had nothing to do with an exclusive priestly class. Writing was facilitated by the relative simplicity of alphabets of only fourteen characters for consonantal syllables plus a few vowel markers. Equally important was the universal availability of writing materials suitable for short notes or accounts (but not for long compositions), in the form of palm-leaf and bamboo strips. On this basis we can accept levels of literacy in sixteenth-century Indonesia and the Philippines that were very high by any contemporary standards, and as high as any in the world for women. The closest analogy may be with Japan in the Heian period (Morris 1964: 177–215), where the very high literacy of upper-class women was also rclated to the need to exchange romantic poems as part of the courtship process.

This domestic pattern of literacy does not at first appear relevant to the Theravada Buddhist countries of mainland Southeast Asia, where writing skills had been transmitted through male religious schools since the earliest records. Buddhist monastery schools reached a large proportion of the male population because of the strong belief that a period of time in the monastery would earn essential merit not only for the boy himself but for his parents (Pallegoix 1854 I: 226). About their seventh year Thai and Burmese boys almost universally were consecrated to the monastic life, in which they remained as pupils and servants of the monks for a variable period sometimes ending only with marriage. Young women, by contrast, were reported to have little access to education of any sort, at least in Siam (van Vliet 1636: 89). The Theravada countries, in other words, seem firmly identified with a monastic pattern of literacy quite incompatible with that described for the islands before 1600.

Two factors are common to all the lands below the winds, however. First, the palm leaf and bamboo strips were as readily available for note making in the Mainland as the on islands. More important, the dominant position of women in commerce and the spirited part they took in poetic courting contests were characteristic of the whole of Southeast Asia. Even though almost nothing is known about how literacy was transmitted outside the monasteries (or preceding them), these two factors may explain why Burma had relatively high rates of literacy in comparison even with other Theravada countries.

The early sources (chiefly dating from after 1790) are agreed that Burmese monastic education did produce a literate male population: "there are no mechanics, few of the peasantry, or even the common watermen (usually the most illiterate class), who cannot read and write in the vulgar tongue" (Symes 1827 I: 149; cf. Sangermano 1812: 121; Pemberton 1830: 35; Trant 1827: 259). At the 1901 Census of India, 60.3 percent of Buddhist Burmese men over twenty were shown to be literate (Ireland 1907 I: 381), a figure which contrasts with 10 percent for the whole Indian Empire and may represent as high an achievement by a premodern monastic system as the world knows.

If monastic schools were the only source of literacy, Burmese women might be expected to have been completely illiterate. Yet 5.1 percent of adult Buddhist Burmese women were literate in the 1901 census, far outstripping the rest of the Indian Empire with its overall average of 0.7 percent. In the early nineteenth century Trant (1827: 209) observed that women in Burma "for the most part knew how to read and write," and Malcolm (1840: 59; cf. Kaung 1963: 33–34) that there were private "lay schools" for girls in the major towns. Most girls must, however, have learned at home, where the need for them to conduct commercial operations, which often included the recording of debts, would have provided a motive for learning. I am inclined to infer, in other words, that there must in the Theravada countries have been some interaction between the monastic pattern of "restricted literacy" and a broader Southeast Asian underlay of domestic literacy for everyday purposes.

In Siam and Cambodia monastic education for boys was almost as universal as in Burma, though French missionaries would later claim it was less rigorous, with only 20 percent of Thai boys who went through it really knowing how to read and 10 percent how to write (Pallegoix 1854 I: 226; Chevillard 1889: 147). The better-class boys of Ayutthaya prepared themselves for positions at court by studying Thai writing and literature, some Pali, arithmetic, and astronomy. In the brilliant reign of Narai (1656–88) monastic education was reformed by the introduction of a textbook for the Thai language, the *Chindamani*, which Wyatt (1969: 22) credits with a marked improvement in educational standards.

One might have expected this relatively widespread literacy to have provided the seedbed, with external stimulus, for the development of a brilliant literary culture. The age of commerce did indeed produce remarkable changes in the direction of a cosmopolitan literature, notably in Malay and Thai. At least in the islands this did not, however, grow naturally from the older domestic pattern of literacy. Because both Islam and Christianity introduced a new script along with the new faith, their established pattern of a more restricted, school-based male literacy in most places drove out the old script, which became associated with the pagan past. In the Philippines knowledge of the Indonesian scripts had gone within a century of Christianization; and since they were not used to make permanent records, the existence of most of them is known only through Spanish observers. A similar fate may have overtaken pre-Islamic scripts in Malaya and parts of Sumatra and coastal Borneo. Where the older scripts had not established themselves as a vehicle for sacred writings, they seldom survived the coming of the new.

By the fifteenth century the major systems of writing Southeast Asian languages were established. Apart from Vietnam, where writing had been done in good Chinese since early in the first Christian millennium, all the scripts were ultimately derived and adapted from Indian phonetic systems. Considerable ingenuity was required to adapt these systems to the various Southeast Asian languages, and there seems to have been much experimentation and variety before the stabilization that took place about the twelfth and thirteenth centuries. Burmese began to be written only in that period, in a form which can still be read by a modern Burmese. The five tones of Thai presented special challenges, which appear to have been resolved about the time of the great King Ram Kamheng, who claimed in his famous inscription (1293: 29) to have "sought and desired in his heart, and put into use these strokes of Siamese writing," precisely in 1283. Javanese writing underwent more extensive changes during the period of the spread of Islam, losing much of its earlier adherence to correct Sanskrit orthography and seeking primarily to render Javanese as it sounded (Pigeaud 1967: 29–30).

A radical new development was the spread with Islam of a version of Arabic script already adapted for Persian. Malay, although once written in an Indian-derived script, began to be expressed in the Arabic alphabet at least by the fourteenth century. As the preeminent language of Islam in the region, Malay subsequently became inseparable from the Arabic script, and they spread together into many parts of the Malay Peninsula, Borneo, and the eastern islands where there is little prior evidence of popular writing systems. Other Indonesian languages were often written in Arabic script for religious purposes, but in Java and to a lesser extent in South Sulawesi the pre-Islamic writing system was too well established to give way to Arabic.

A crucial means for the spread of Islam was the school in which boys were taught in the first place to read and recite the Koran in Arabic. There were many such schools in Aceh around 1600 (Davis 1600: 151; Warwijck 1604: 16; Dampier 1699: 95), and the *Hikayat Aceh* (149–50) even recounts how brilliantly the future Sultan Iskandar Muda performed in such a class at age thirteen. Similarly in Banten, Magindanao, and Ternate there are descriptions of the Islamic schools in which the aristocratic and commercial elite learned to read and write in the Arabic script (Lodewycksz 1598: 120; Dampier 1697: 226; Galvão 1544: 123). These schools produced a talented group of Muslim literati in the cities of the lands below the winds, who laid the foundation of a written culture in Malay.

The corollary of this change was to make writing a matter for religious experts, as in Europe and most of the rest of Asia. It is a curious paradox that the growth of a written culture probably reduced the number of people who could write by associating writing with the sacral and the solemn. Van Goens (1656: 184) contrasted his literate

Javanese with other Indonesian peoples who had learned their writing more recently with Islam: "From among a hundred Malays you would scarcely find four who can read, and among the others barely two." There are few ways to check this impression with harder evidence. The Spanish seized a small Brunei vessel in 1579 and demanded to know whether the Malays aboard who claimed to be slaves of the sultan of Brunei could write. Two of the seven could, and each independently read a Malay letter (Brunei expedition 1579: 201–02).

In the larger states of Southeast Asia, as in Europe, it was the male monastic tradition of scholarship which preserved and taught the scriptures and provided the earliest literati serving the state. This tradition, already more widespread in the Mainland than the Islands, would eventually be broadened and developed into the mass culture and school systems of modern times. Preceding and to a limited extent competing with this male monastic tradition, however, there appears to have been a quite different attitude to writing, which regarded it as an ephemeral activity for domestic and economic purposes in which women were as active as men.

Writing Materials

Most writing before the sixteenth century appears to have been done in the more Indianized areas on strips of palm leaf (as in India), and elsewhere on long blades of bamboo (as in China before the development of paper). In the Philippines: "Before they knew anything about paper (and even yet in places where they cannot get it), those people wrote on bamboos or on palm-leaves, using as a pen the point of a knife or other bit of iron, with which they engraved the letters on the smooth side of the bamboo" (Colin 1663: 51; cf. Chirino 1604: 281). In Pegu those submitting petitions to the court had to write them with an iron stylus (fig. 46), on palm leaves about a metre long and five centimetres broad (Fitch 1591: 164). In Java and Bali palm leaves were also the commonest writing material (fig. 47), and books were made by running two strings through the pile of rectangular strips of leaf and through pieces of wood at top and bottom which formed the covers, "very nice and neat" (Lodewycksz 1598: 120, 141–42; cf. Ma Huan 1433: 96; Kratz 1981: 69). The same type of leaf "books" were used in Siam and Burma, but by the 1680s only for more solemn or religious purposes. Twenty-four leaves were usually tied together, their edges gilt in honour of their religious subject (La Loubère 1691: 12; Gerini 1912: 263; Shway Yoe 1882: 130).

In Cambodia, Champa, and Siam some form of parchment made from animal skins appears to have been in use for writing up to about

Fig. 46 Writer of the Burmese *Hlut-daw* (council), 1797, incising records with stylus

Fig. 47 The Balinese ruler of Buleleng, 1865, with his writer preparing to incise a message on a palm leaf

1500, so that both Thai and Khmer incorporate the word for "skin" into their term for a written document (Gerini 1912: 264–65). The thin tree bark noted in Champa by Ma Huan (1433: 83) and in Brunei by Pigafetta (1524: 58) may at first have been a cheaper and more convenient substitute for this parchment.

Given the gradual dispersal of papermaking from China to the rest of the world since its discovery in the second century, it is not surprising that Southeast Asia also learned of this technology. Vietnam was among the first countries to borrow it, perhaps in the third century, and it went on to borrow also the Chinese technique of wood-block printing. In the fifteenth century Vietnamese craftsmen took over from Chinese printers in their country and began to develop different techniques (Tsien 1962: 138–39; Huard and Durand 1954: 158). Dampier (1699: 47) found that they made "indifferent good paper" by soaking tree bark in troughs, pounding, and then drying it.

One Chinese treatise on writing materials, compiled about 1200, conceded that only two countries outside China also made paper—Korea and Java. The paper of Java was "thick and resistant," with leaves about eight metres long (cited Salmon 1983). It may have come to the notice of Chinese because of its use to tell the stories painted on paper scrolls and chanted by a narrator (wayang beber), which Ma Huan observed in the early fifteenth century. It was undoubtedly the Javanese *dluwang*, a coarse paper made by alternately beating and soaking the fibres of the paper mulberry tree, *Broussonetia papyrifera*. This was also one of the materials most used in the first millennium of papermaking in China, and it was being used by Vietnamese and Burmese when their methods were described in the nineteenth century. The same tree, and similar methods of processing it, provided a form of clothing, usually of a semisacred type, for many Southeast Asians and for Polynesians—the well-known tapa cloth. Javanese literary sources since the ninth century have described its making, but as a form of clothing for hermits and ascetics (Guillot 1983). Even if the Javanese did borrow the papermaking technology from China, they used it for clothing, wrapping, and painting rather than for writing, for which the palm-leaf method appeared perfectly satisfactory.

This Javanese paper was "of a yellow colour, strong, tough, but of rather uneven texture" (Crawfurd 1856: 328; cf. Raffles 1817: 175; Pigeaud 1967: 35–36). It was presumably the same paper "made from trees" which the Dutch found in Java in 1596, but which was primarily used "as we use grey paper for wrapping all things in," while serious writing was done on palm leaves (Lodewycksz 1598: 142). Yet the same Dutch expedition probably brought back at least one Javanese text written on it—significantly, an early Muslim treatise

(Drewes 1969: 2). Because of the example of Koranic literature which came to the Archipelago in paper books and the fact that the curves and dots of Arabic script were difficult to cut into fibrous palm leaf, Islam undoubtedly encouraged the use of paper in writing (Pigeaud 1967: 26). In fact, by the time of Raffles (1817 I: 175) the manufacture of dluwang in the Islamic schools of certain districts formed "the principal occupation of the priests, who gain a livelihood by it."

Siam appears to have produced a finer quality of paper than Java, by two methods—one somewhat similar to the Javanese and Chinese but using the indigenous *khoi* tree (*Streblus asper*); the other using old cotton rags as material, in the contemporary European way. The paper thus made was folded like modern computer paper (Varthema 1510: 209; La Loubère 1691: 12; Gerini 1912: 262–66). At Ayutthaya, "all daily happenings (messages, sessions of the court, etc.) are written as open letters on bad paper with a little round pen of soft baked earth" (van Vliet 1636: 97). Burmese also used their own coarse paper for everyday purposes, but blackened it first and then wrote in a white chalk pencil (Trant 1827: 256).

Remarkable as these technical developments were, it was the better-quality imported paper from China, India, and Europe which wrought a more substantial change in writing styles. Large quantities of paper, presumably Chinese, were already being imported to Melaka around 1500 by Ryukyu Islanders (Pires 1515: 130), and Chinese paper was in use in Java, Siam, and Cambodia by around 1600 (Lodewycksz 1598: 120; San Antonio 1604: 98; van Vliet 1636: 98). It is significant, however, that it was the Arabic rather than the Chinese word for paper which was borrowed into Thai (*kradaat*) and into Indonesian languages. The Malay borrowing (*kertas*) had occurred at least by 1520, along with Arabic terms for pen and ink (Pigafetta 1524: 86). The implication of this is that even though papermaking almost certainly reached Southeast Asia from China, it was the importation and local replication of Islamic books which really began the modern era of writing on paper.

Most of the manuscripts which have survived from the seventeenth century were in fact written on European paper, which was one of the relatively few items of European manufacture immediately appreciated in Asia. Following the example of Chinese and Portuguese traders, Gerard Reynst (1615: 60) wrote from Banten to ask the Dutch Company to send out for the Indonesian trade:

> 50 bales [i.e. 500 reams] of paper, including some very fine bales, but it must all be good with no rubbish if sent for these parts.
>
> A dozen great books of large format . . . half journals, half account-books.

Also 1000 books of ordinary format, unlined, some folio and some quarto, bound in fine white parchment, gilt-edged, printed with ornamental foliage without figures, and some bound with red leather, all of best paper.

The English were slower, asking for one hundred reams of "ordinary writing paper" to be sent out as a trial after profitable trading had been observed in Jambi (Court Minutes 1632: 329). By 1660 the Dutch in Java reckoned that they were consuming about 50,000 guilders' worth of paper each year for their own purposes and the trade. They set about building a stone paper mill in Batavia with papermakers sent out from Holland and cotton as the principal raw material (Coolhaas 1968: 351, 368, 449, 460, 471). Although these efforts at local manufacture had very mixed results, relatively inexpensive imported paper certainly became available to Southeast Asians by the mid-seventeenth century, and where palm leaf and bamboo continued to be used this was primarily for reasons of convention or aesthetics.

Literature, Oral and Written

> *Not for [religion]—nor for government and public order—did they make use of their letters. . . . Government and religion are for them founded on tradition . . . and are preserved in songs, which they have committed to memory and learned from childhood, having heard them sung while sailing, while at work, while rejoicing or feasting, and above all while mourning the dead. In these barbarous songs they relate the fabulous genealogies and vain deeds of their gods.*
>
> —*Chirino 1604: 296—on Luzon*

Even though writing was in use for both practical and sacred purposes, most people experienced literature not by reading it but by singing it or hearing it sung. Prose works existed, particularly those dealing with legal and religious matters, and some of them have come to be seen as literature by later generations. There is no doubt, however, that the popular literary heritage which kept Southeast Asian cultures together was in a poetic form that could be recited, chanted, or sung. In the eastern Archipelago, where written texts were relatively scarce, Galvão (1554: 85) believed: "They have no chronicles nor (written) history and they keep no archives. As far as I understand from them, they commit their past to memory by way of aphorisms, songs, and rhyming ballads, of which they are very fond. They make good ones which are handed down from one to another like the Hebrews used to do."

Even where written texts played a larger part in the transmission of literature, most of these were to be heard rather than read. When the sultan of Melaka asked Hang Jebat to "read a story" (*membaca hika-*

yat), he of course meant to chant it from the text to entertain the ruler and his court. The *Hikayat Hang Tuah* (291), which relates this incident, does not mention the content of the story but dwells at length on the beauty of Hang Jebat's voice, which entranced all the ladies of the court, who promptly began to offer betel to him as a token of love. Another Malay source tells of the night before the Portuguese conquest of Melaka, when the Malay war leaders were gathered to prepare their defence. "Why do we sit here idly?" they asked each other. "It would be well for us to read a story so that we may profit from it." They asked the king for the text of the *Hikayat Muhammad Hanafiah*, the Malay version of a Persian epic about a great Shi'ite warrior, so that hearing it sung would inspire their own courage. The sultan eventually obliged, but not before provoking a gratifying declaration of resolve by first sending the *Hikayat Hamzah* in case his warriors' courage was not quite equal to that of the Persian hero (*Sejarah Melayu* 1612: 168). The tradition of chanting "metrical tales of former days" to enthusiastic crowds during the long nights of village feasts continued into the nineteenth century (St. John 1862 II: 260; cf. Newbold 1839 II: 327; Anderson 1826: 50; Sweeney 1973; Pou 1977: 32; L. Andaya 1979).

The Siamese, thought La Loubère (1691: 60), "are born poets." They composed "some historical and moral songs," but especially songs of love. This French informant managed with some difficulty to discover the meaning of the songs which the rowers on the river galleys constantly sang, and declared them "full of smuttiness, and gross immodesty." Later Thai and Lao equivalents of these boat songs were certainly explicitly erotic (Wenk 1968: 95–125; Archaimbault 1972: 29–30). In Burma too this type of antiphonal chant between leader and boatmen never failed to impress (Trant 1827: 217–20). Fortunately a few of the finest seventeenth-century examples of this essentially oral form of literature have been written down and preserved in Thailand as classics:

Leader: As they rush past they glimpse a pretty face, marvellously full and fair, a rounded and gracious figure, curved eyebrows, sleek and lustrous hair;

Chorus: As they pass they glimpse her body, breasts fair and round and firm; they watch closely, the hair is sleek, erect and lissome in bearing, the breasts rounded for love, the eyebrows arched; while a veiled smile of joy and pleasure lurks within . . . (Si Mahasot, cited Schweisguth 1951: 120).

Nothing was more characteristic of Southeast Asian popular literature than this antiphonal form between two singers or groups of singers. Even if outstanding examples of the form were remembered and passed on, its essence was a contest in clever and rapid improvisation. Typically the contest was between a boy and a girl, each taking turns to sing a quatrain which could answer the other, continuing or responding to the theme without losing the rhythm. Alcina (1668 III: 34–35) must often have heard these popular contests on festive nights in the Visayas: "They use it [*bikal* verse] between two persons, either two men or two women. They reply to each other in strict musical time and without hesitation for one or two hours saying anything they wish (in satiric fashion), making public whatever faults they have, either physical (which is the more common), or moral . . . with much laughter and noisy mirth, and with the applause of all who are listening. . . . [*Balak* verse, on the other hand] is always between a man and a woman and most commonly concerns affairs of love." The contests between the sexes were especially popular at the harvest and other festivals, when they provided an opportunity for flirtation and for both boys and girls to show off their wit and grace. This pattern continued until relatively modern times in the villages of Siam and Laos, where the form was known as *lam* (Compton 1979), in Vietnam, where it was *ly* (Tran 1967: 196–99), among Javanese (*parikan*), Sundanese (*sus-uwalan*), Bataks (*umpama*), and Malays (pantun). Verse contests were also a vital part of courtship and popular culture for the Hakka and many smaller minorities in South China.

Contests in alternating verses appear to be very ancient in Southeast Asia, as is already clear from the diversity of vernacular terms for them. Pigeaud (1967: 19) believes them to be the indigenous genre which preceded the written *macapat* and other poetry of the Islamic period in Java. Several good pantun were cited by the *Sejarah Melayu* (1612: 115, 142, 172–73; cf. Roolvink 1966), as if they were current in the fifteenth century. The Thai equivalent was certainly well entrenched at the time of La Loubère's visit (1691: 54): "They do it [raillery] frequently amongst equals, and even in verse; and . . . as well the women as the men."

Because of its nature most oral literature has been either lost or so transformed by the process of transmission and adaptation that we will never know its original form. The creations committed to writing were a small minority, and those that have been preserved a minority smaller still. Even so, the corpus of Southeast Asian written texts which originated in the sixteenth and seventeenth centuries is vastly greater than that from any earlier period. It reveals a literature in process of very rapid change and development, in which the written word played an ever greater role. Spurred partly by the expansion of religious writing, partly by the demands of increasingly sophisticated and wealthy urban centres, more and more texts were written down, copied, translated, and commented upon.

The key to this expansion was certainly the network of wealthy and cosmopolitan trading cities of the age of commerce. Their courts were eager borrowers and innovators in literature as in other fields, and the diversity of foreign merchants and missionaries in their midst provided plenty of stimulus. A number of rulers were themselves writers of note, including Siam's Narai (1656–88) and Mataram's Sultan Agung (1613–46). Even more frequently were the chief religious officials and the ministers in charge of trade men of letters. Some outstanding figures in this category were Raja Laut of Mindanao, who "speaks and writes Spanish . . . and by Spanish books has some knowledge of Europe" (Dampier 1697: 230); Pattengalloang in Makassar, who "had read with curiosity all the chronicles of our European kings [and] always had books of ours in hand, especially those treating with mathematics" (Rhodes 1653: 208); Pangeran Pekik, the prince from the cosmopolitan port of Surabaya who became the chief literary light of Sultan Agung's Mataram (de Graaf 1958: 212–13); and Shamsu'l-din, the chief Islamic authority of Aceh in the period 1600–1630, who was also the leading advisor of rulers, negotiator (in fluent Arabic or Malay) with foreign merchants, and author of several Malay treatises on mysticism which were copied all around the Archipelago (Lancaster 1603: 96–97; Ito 1984: 248–52; Nieuwenhuijze 1945).

The rapidly growing class of literati also included religious scholars and teachers, and some at least of the professional writers and translators attached to courts and other prominent households. One such was the Makassar court writer Ence' Amin (1670: 91), who provided this engaging portrait of himself in his great epic poem *Sya'ir Perang Mengkasar*:

> Ence' Amin was summoned to draw up a letter.
> It was well composed and contained no mistakes;
> it was concisely worded, without any flourishes.
> This Ence' Amin was a clever fellow,
> of rather small stature but well-built . . .
> by birth a Malay of Makassarese descent;
> graceful and attractive in his movements.

Although the literary activity of the region was conducted in a dozen languages, interaction took place through those languages which were also the major common tongues for merchants—Malay, Arabic, and Portuguese. The process of interpretation was not always easy. A Dutch diplomatic letter to the king of Siam was translated first into Portuguese, then Malay, and finally into Thai by the court interpreters, who were "rather slow and punctilious," at least in such formal exchanges (Caen 1632: 222). But once foreigners had mastered Malay they could operate effectively in all the major port cities (except those of Vietnam). The Javanese of Banten, for example, "also use the Malay speech and characters, which is a very effective language, and easy to learn and also to speak, for it is understood not only in India but in all the islands about" (Lodewycksz 1598: 120; cf. Willoughby 1635: fol. 117). Some of its greatest writers had probably learned the language only as adults. Nuruddin ar-Raniri was born in Gujerat and Hamzah Fansuri probably in Ayutthaya, but both enriched what is now called "classical" Malay by writing it beautifully in Aceh—where the native tongue was not Malay at all but Acehnese.

Malay became in this period the major mediator of Arabic, Persian, and Indian ideas and literary styles to the region. First in Pasai, then in Melaka, Patani, Johor, and Makassar, but above all in Aceh during the period 1570–1650, numerous religious and literary classics of western Asia were translated, adapted, and read, in the process inspiring new Malay styles. At the outset of his *Sharabu'l 'Ashiqin* (c. 1590), probably the earliest surviving major prose work in Malay, Hamzah Fansuri stated that he would use that language "in order that all servants of God who do not understand the Arabic and Persian languages may discourse upon it" (cited Al-Attas 1968: 45). Hamzah was also a great poet, who popularized and perhaps created the *sya'ir* four-line verse form in Malay by adapting the Persian *ruba'i* (ibid.; Teeuw 1966). By his deeply mystical writing he also contributed to a fierce debate in Aceh and the Malay world over the ensuing half-century, which brought out some of the most intellectually sophisticated work ever written in Malay. Hamzah's greatest critic, ar-Raniri, who was hounded out of Aceh in 1643 by his numerous enemies after having enjoyed great power under the previous ruler (Ito 1978), wrote numerous tracts against "those who are obstinate . . . identifying God with the Universe" (cited Al-Attas 1966: 99). Ar-Raniri also wrote a considerable corpus of secular prose, including in the *Bustan as-Salatin* a type of historical writing as detached and factual as anything in Malay before modern times.

Similarly dramatic literary developments occurred in other cultures which underwent Islamization, often through the mediation of work in Malay. The port cities of the north coast of Java were also centres of religious polemics about the limits of orthodoxy in Sufi mysticism (Drewes 1969). The same cosmopolitan cities laid the foundation of the Javanese literary tradition later canonized by the courts of the interior (de Graaf and Pigeaud 1974: 165–66; de Graaf 1958: 212–13). In particular, as Ricklefs (1978: 202–22) has pointed out, there was an accurate court tradition of dated chronicles in the first three quarters of the seventeenth century, which declined sharply thereafter. Once again this is evidence of the rise and subsequent decline of a pluralistic and secular urban culture open to the pragmatic needs of a growing cosmopolitan population.

Makassar, where writing in any form seems scarcely to predate the sixteenth century, witnessed perhaps the most rapid flowering of a literary tradition in the seventeenth. Influenced by both Portuguese and Malay literary examples, the Makassarese began to compose matter-of-fact chronicles detailing the rapid rise of Makassar, "only so that these kings are not forgotten by their children, grandchildren and descendants, for there are two dangers of ignorance: either that we think ourselves all great lords, or that others may take us for people of no consequence" (*Sejarah Goa*: 9). This robust tradition of recording the past was undoubtedly encouraged by the extraordinary genius of Karaeng Pattingalloang (1600–1654), known to have commissioned a Malay chronicle of Maluku from an Ambonese refugee in the city. As chancellor of the kingdom he was probably responsible for such remarkable innovations as maps, court diaries, and the translation into Makassarese of Portuguese, Turkish, and Malay texts on military subjects (Reid 1981: 22–23). The Makassar diary (*Lontara'-bilang Gowa*) recorded royal births, deaths, marriages, and divorces, the arrival of ships and envoys, the building of fortifications and palaces, and the outbreak of epidemics, using a double Christian and Muslim dating system. This habit, unmatched below the winds for its "sober conciseness and accuracy," spread to some courts under Makassar's influence, notably those of the Bugis area and Sumbawa (Cense 1966).

In Cambodia, too, the seventeenth was "the most inspired century of literature," according to one of its students (Pou 1977: 41–44). The authors of the period were Buddhist literati who had enthusiastically absorbed the more democratic Theravada outlook without turning their backs on the national heritage of Angkor. Evidently the high degree of foreign (Malay, Spanish, Dutch, Thai) influence which disrupted Khmer politics of this period acted more as a stimulus than a damper in literature.

More confidently can the reign of King Narai be seen as the literary culmination of a process of urbanization and secularization in seventeenth-century Ayutthaya. A distinctive group of talented literati gathered around the king, for the first time independent of the monkish constraints of Buddhist literature written primarily in Pali. Contemporary with similar developments in Aceh, Java, and Makassar, the first court-centred chronicle was written in Thai—"a dry enumeration of facts," but more reliable than many later compilations (Schweisguth 1951: 107; cf. Kasetsiri 1979: 159). Its probable author,

Horathibodi, also produced at royal request a textbook for the correct use of Thai. The great love of the king and his circle, however, was poetry, often in the spontaneous quick-witted form beloved of the people but now also being written down for posterity. Its great themes were themes of love.

In Thai memory the outstanding figure of this circle was a young second-generation writer, Si Prat. The son of the court astrologer and poet, Horathibodi, he became a symbol for Thais of the free poetic spirit. As a boy Si Prat's quick repartee and ability to improvise brilliant verses made him a favourite of the king, but the same qualities kept making him enemies in the court. Reputedly, it was after impishly worsting the favourite royal concubine with cutting verses that he was exiled to Nakhon Sithammarat. There he fell foul of the governor by the suggestive poems he addressed to the women of that court, and was executed while still a young man. The great poem by which he is remembered is a description of his sea voyage to Nakhon Sithammarat, in which each incident reminds him of what he has lost—the splendours of the capital and the beauty of his beloved (Schweisguth 1951: 114–18; Jumsai 1973: 161–69).

The age of commerce was a period of enormous change for the lands below the winds. In cultural and educational forms, as in popular beliefs, legal systems, and even clothing and building styles, the commercial cities were refashioning the communities of which they were the centres. In this respect the period bears comparison with its European analogue, the Renaissance, though this study has sought to make clear that neither the starting point nor the direction of change should be expected to parallel those in other parts of the world.

Southeast Asians remained masters of the commercial expansion which was at the heart of this transformation until the seventeenth century. Commerce had the effect of fertilizing the cities with ideas from elsewhere, strengthening those elites and states which took quickest advantage of them. The mid-seventeenth-century "trade revolution," however, altered the effects of commerce on the region profoundly. The pace of change slowed and even reversed in some respects, as indigenous cities declined, withdrew from international commerce, or were defeated by the Dutch mercantile monopoly. The relative isolation which resulted ensured that the lands below the winds retained into the nineteenth century many of the features forged in the fifteenth and sixteenth. Yet when the high tide of imperialism and capitalism overwhelmed them at the end of the nineteenth century, these countries would no longer be able to compete on equal terms with the intruders as they had in their age of commerce.

Abbreviations
References
Glossary
Index

Abbreviations

ANU	Australian National University
ARA	Algemeen Rijksarchief
BEFEO	*Bulletin de l'Ecole Française d'Extrême Orient*
BKI	*Bijdragen tot de Taal-, Land-, en Volkenkunde van Nederlandsch-Indië*
EFEO	Ecole Française d'Extrême Orient
EIC	East India Company
ENI	*Encyclopaedie van Nederlandsch-Indië*
IOL	India Office Library
JAS	*Journal of Asian Studies*
JBRAS	*Journal of the Burma Research Society*
JMBRAS	*Journal of the Malayan Branch of the Royal Asiatic Society*
JPC	*Jan Pieterz. Coen: bescheiden omtrent zijn bedrijf in Indië*, ed. H. T. Colenbrander. The Hague, M. Nijhoff, 1919–53
JSEAS	*Journal of Southeast Asian Studies*
JSS	*Journal of the Siam Society*
KA	Koloniaal Archief
KITLV	Koninklijk Instituut voor Taal-, Land-, en Volkenkunde
LREIC	*Letters Received by the East India Company . . .*, ed. F. C. Danvers and W. Foster, 6 vols. London, 1896–1901
MBRAS	Malaysian Branch, Royal Asiatic Society
OUP	Oxford University Press
RIMA	*Review of Indonesian and Malaysian Affairs*
SP	*Calendar of State Papers, Colonial Series . . .*, ed. W. N. Sainsbury, 5 vols. London, 1862–95
SPAFA	Seameo Project in Archaelogy and Fine Arts
TBG	*Tijdschrift voor Indische Taal-, Land-, en Volkenkunde*
TNI	*Tijdschrift voor Nederlandsch-Indië*
VBG	*Verhandelingen van het Bataviaasch Genootschap*
VOC	Verenigde Oostindische Compagnie

References

Adat Aceh. Adat Aceh dari satu Manuscript India Office Library, romanized by Teungku Anzib Lamnyong. Banda Aceh, Pusat Latihan Penelitian Ilmu-ilmu Sosial, 1976.

Adatrechtbundels. 45 vols. The Hague, Martinus Nijhoff, 1910–55.

Adriani, N., and A. C. Kruyt 1912–14. *De Bare'e-sprekende Toradja's van Midden-Celebes*, 3 vols. Batavia, Landsdrukkerij.

Al-Attas, Syed Naguib 1966. *Raniri and the Wujudiyyah of Seventeenth Century Acheh*. Singapore, MBRAS.

——— 1968.*The Origin of the Malay Sha'ir*. Kuala Lumpur, Dewan Bahasa dan Pustaka.

Albuquerque, Braz de 1557. *The Commentaries of the Great Alfonso Dalboquerque*, ed. W. de Gray Birch, vol. III. London, Hakluyt Society, 1880.

Alcina, Francisco 1668. "The Munoz Text of Alcina's History of the Bisayan Islands (1668)," preliminary trans. Paul S. Lietz, pt. I, bks. 3 and 4, 1960. Typescript in Department of Anthropology, University of Chicago.

——— 1668A. "Historia de las Islas e Indios de Bisayas," extract in *Readings in Leyte-Samar History*, ed. Ma. Luz C. Vilches. Tacloban, Divine Word University, 1979, pp. 9–29.

Alexander, Jennifer 1984. "Pasar, Pasaran: Trade, Traders, and Trading in Rural Java." Ph.D. diss., Sydney University.

Ali Haji ibn Ahmad, Raja 1866. *The Precious Gift (Tuhfat al Nafis)*, trans. Virginia Matheson and Barbara Andaya. Kuala Lumpur, OUP, 1982.

Amin, Entji 1670. *Sja'ir Perang Mengkasar (The Rhymed Chronicle of the Macassar War)*, trans. C. Skinner. The Hague, Nijhoff for KITLV, 1963.

Andaya, Barbara 1979. *Perak, The Abode of Grace: A Study of an Eighteenth Century Malay State*. Kuala Lumpur, OUP, 1979.

Andaya, Leonard Y. 1979. "A Village Perception of Arung Palakka and the Makassar War of 1666–69," in *Perceptions of the Past in Southeast Asia*, ed. A. Reid and D. Marr. Singapore, Heinemann, pp. 360–78.

——— 1981. *The Heritage of Arung Palakka: A History of South Sulawesi (Celebes) in the Seventeenth Century*. The Hague, Nijhoff for KITLV.

Anderson, John 1826. *Mission to the East Coast of Sumatra in 1823*. London. Reprinted Kuala Lumpur, OUP, 1971.
Anderson, Perry 1978. *Passages from Antiquity to Feudalism*. London, Verso Editions.
Anderson, Wanni Wibulswasdi 1973. "Children's Play and Games in Rural Thailand: A Study in Enculturation and Socialization." Ph.D. diss., University of Pennsylvania; Ann Arbor, University Microfilms.
Appell, G. N. 1968. "The Penis Pin at Peabody Museum, Harvard University." JMBRAS 41, pp. 203–05.
Araujo, Rui de 1510. Letter from Malacca, 6 February 1510, in *Documentação para a historia das missões do padroado portugues do Oriente: Insulindia*, vol. I (1506–1549), ed. Artur de Sá. Lisbon, Agencia Geral do Ultramar, 1954, pp. 20–31.
Archaimbault, Charles 1972. *La course de pirogues au Laos: Un complexe culturel*. Ascona, Artibus Asiae Publishers, 1972.
Artieda, Diego de 1573. "Relation of the Western Islands called Filipinas," in Blair and Robertson 1903–09 III: 190–208.
Aung Thwin, M. 1983. "*Athi, Kyun-Taw, Hpaya-kyun*: Varieties of Commendation and Dependence in Pre-Colonial Burma," in Reid 1983: 64–89.
Aymonier, E. 1891. *Les Tchames et leurs religions*. Paris, Ernest Leroux.
——— 1900. *Le Cambodge: Le royaume actuel*. Paris, Ernest Leroux.
Babad ing Sangkala 1738. Trans. M. C. Ricklefs, in Ricklefs 1978: 16–147.
Babad Tanah Jawa: Poenika serat babad tanah Jawi wiwit saking Nabi Adam doemoegi ing taoen 1647, trans. J. L. Olthof. The Hague, 1941.
Bakhtin, Michael 1940. *Rabelais and His World*, trans. Helene Iswolsky. Bloomington, Indiana University Press, 1984.
Barbosa, Duarte 1518. *The Book of Duarte Barbosa: An Account of the Countries Bordering on the Indian Ocean and Their Inhabitants*, trans. M. Longworth Dames, 2 vols. London, Hakluyt Society, 1918.
Barros, João de 1563. *Da Asia*. 4 Decades in 9 vols. Lisbon, Regia Officina, 1777. Reprinted Lisbon, 1973.
Barrow, John 1806. *A Voyage to Cochinchina in the Years 1792 and 1793*. London, Cadell and Davies. Reprinted Kuala Lumpur, OUP, 1975.
Barth, J. P. J. 1896. "Overzicht der afdeeling Soekadana," *VBG* I, ii.
Battye, Noel A. 1974. "The Military Government and Society in Siam, 1868–1910: Politics and Military Reform during the Reign of King Chulalongkorn." Ph.D. diss., Cornell University.
Bausani, A. 1970. "Indonesia in the Work of Italians," in *Lettera di Giovanni da Empoli*, ed. A. Bausani. Rome, Istituto Italiano per il Medio ed Estremo Oriente, pp. 85–102.
Bayard, D. T. 1979. "The Chronology of Prehistoric Metallurgy in North-east Thailand: *Silabhumi* or *Samrddhabhumi*?" in *Early South East Asia: Essays in Archeology, History, and Historical Geography*, ed. R. B. Smith and W. Watson. Kuala Lumpur, OUP, pp. 15–32.
Beaulieu, Augustin de 1666. "Mémoires du voyage aux Indes Orientales du Général de Beaulieu, dressés par luy-mesme," in *Relations de divers voyages curieux*, ed. Melchisedech Thévenot, vol. II. Paris, Cramoisy.

Beeckman, Daniel 1718. *A Voyage to and from the Island of Borneo in the East Indies*. London. Reprinted London, Dawsons, 1973.
Begin ende Voortgangh 1646. *Begin ende Voortgangh van de Vereenighde Neederlandtsche Geoctroyeerde Oost-Indische Compagnie*, ed. Isaac Commelin. Amsterdam. Reprinted Amsterdam 1974.
Bellwood, Peter 1978. *Man's Conquest of the Pacific: The Pre-History of Southeast Asia and Oceania*. Auckland, Collins.
Bemmelen, R. W. van 1949. *The Geology of Indonesia*, 3 vols. The Hague, Government Printing Office.
Benedict, Paul K. 1942. "Thai, Kadai, and Indonesian: A New Alignment in South-eastern Asia." *American Anthropologist* 44, pp. 576–601.
——— 1975. *Austro-Thai Language and Culture, with Glossary of Roots*. New Haven, HRAF Press.
Berg, Charles 1951. *The Unconscious Significance of Hair*. London.
Best, Thomas 1614. *The Voyage of Thomas Best*, ed. Sir William Foster. London, Hakluyt Society, 1934.
Blair, E. H., and J. A. Robertson (eds.) 1903–09. *The Philippine Islands, 1493–1898*, 55 vols. Cleveland, Arthur H. Clark.
Bobadilla, Diego de 1640. "Relation of the Filipinas Islands by a Religious Who Lived There for Eighteen Years," in Blair and Robertson 1903–09 XXIX: 277–311.
Bontius, James 1629. *An Account of the Diseases, Natural History, and Medicine of the East Indies*. London, 1776.
Boomgaard, Peter 1986. "Morbidity and Mortality in Java, 1820–1880: Changing Patterns of Disease and Death," in Owen 1987: 48–69.
Boon, James A. 1977. *The Anthropological Romance of Bali, 1597–1972: Dynamic Perspectives in Marriage and Caste Politics and Religion*. Cambridge, Cambridge University Press.
Borri, Christoforo 1633. *Cochin-China*, trans. R. Ashley. London, Richard Clutterbuck. Reprinted London, Da Capo Press, 1970 (pagination by letters).
Bosch, F. D. K. 1951. "Guru, Trident, and Spring," trans. in *Selected Studies in Indonesian Archeology by Dr. F. D. K. Bosch*. The Hague, Nijhoff for KITLV, 1961, pp. 153–70.
Boserup, Ester 1965. *The Conditions of Agricultural Growth: The Economics of Agrarian Change under Population Pressure*. New York, Aldine.
——— 1970. *Woman's Role in Agricultural Development*. London, Allen & Unwin.
Bouchon, Geneviève 1979. "Les premiers voyages portugais à Pegou (1512-1520)," *Archipel* 18, pp. 127–58.
Bouhdiba, Abdelwahab 1975. *Sexuality in Islam*, trans. A. Sheridan. London, Routledge & Kegan Paul.
Bouinais, A., and A. Paulus 1885. *L'Indochine française contemporaine*, 2 vols. Paris, Challamel Ainé.
Bowrey, Thomas 1680. *A Geographical Account of Countries round the Bay of Bengal*, ed. R. C. Temple. Cambridge, Hakluyt Society, 1905.
Bowring, Sir John 1857. *The Kingdom and People of Siam*, 2 vols. London. Reprinted Kuala Lumpur, OUP, 1969.

Boxer, C. R. 1967. *Francisco Vieira de Figueiredo: A Portuguese Merchant-Adventurer in South East Asia, 1624–1667*. The Hague, Nijhoff for KITLV.

Boxer Codex. *See* Dasmariñas 1590 A, B, C.

B.P.S. (Biro Pusat Statistik) 1980. *Pola Umur Perkawinan*. Jakarta, B. P. S.

Brakel, L. F. 1975. "State and Statecraft in Seventeenth Century Aceh," in *Pre-Colonial State Systems in Southeast Asia*, ed. A. Reid and L. Castles. Kuala Lumpur, MBRAS, pp. 56–66.

Brandon, James R. 1967. *Theatre in Southeast Asia*. Cambridge, Mass., Harvard University Press.

Braudel, Fernand 1966. *The Mediterranean and the Mediterranean World in the Age of Philip II*, trans. S. Reynolds, 2 vols. New York, Harper Colophon Books, 1976.

——— 1967. *Capitalism and Material Life, 1400–1800*. Glasgow, Fontana/Collins, 1974.

Brink, H. van den 1943. *Dr. Benjamin Frederick Matthes: Zijn Leven en Arbeid in Dienst van het Nederlandsch Bijbelgenootschap*. Amsterdam, Nederlandsch Bijbelgenootschap.

Broecke, Pieter van den 1634. "Journal," in *Pieter van den Broecke in Azië*, ed. W. Ph. Coolhaas, 2 vols. The Hague, Linschoten-Vereeniging, 1962–63.

Brooke, James 1846. *The Expedition to Borneo of H. M. S. Dido for the Suppression of Piracy, with Extracts from the Journal of James Brooke, Esq.*, ed. Henry Keppel. New York, Harper.

——— 1848. *Narrative of Events in Borneo and Celebes down to the Occupation of Labuan: from the Journals of J. Brooke . . . by Captain Rodney Mundy*, 2 vols. London, John Murray.

Brouwer, Henrick, et al. 1633. Letter from Batavia, 15 December 1633, in Coolhaas 1960: 393–432.

Brown, D. E., J. W. Edwards, and Ruth Moore. "Folk Surgery to the Genitals in Southeast Asia." Forthcoming.

Brown, Edward 1861. *A Seaman's Narrative of His Adventures during a Captivity among Chinese Pirates on the Coast of Cochin-China, and Afterwards during a Journey on Foot across That Country, in the Years 1857–58*. London, Charles Westerton.

Brown, R. Grant 1926. *Burma As I Saw It, 1889–1917*. London, Methuen.

Browne, John 1616. Letter from Patani, 30 May 1616, in *LREIC* IV, pp. 106–08.

Brugière 1829. "Notices of the Religion, Manners, and Customs of the Siamese." *Chinese Repository* 13, iv (1844), pp. 169–217.

Brunei expedition 1579. 'Testimony and Proceedings in Regard to the Expeditions to Burney, Jolo, and Mindanao," in Blair and Robertson 1903–09 IV: 148–303.

Burkill, I. H. 1935. *A Dictionary of the Economic Products of the Malay Peninsula*, 2 vols. London, Crown Agents for the Colonies. Reprinted Kuala Lumpur 1966.

Burney, H. 1842. "On the Population of the Burman Empire." *Journal of the Statistical Society of London* 4, iv, pp. 335–47.

Caen, Antonie 1632. "Schriftelijck rapport van seker besendinge gedaen met vijff scheepen . . . aen de Conninginne van Patana ende Coninck van Chiam," in Tiele and Heeres 1886–95 II: 214–31.

Cameron, John 1865. *Our Tropical Possessions in Malayan India.* London, Smith, Elder & Co. Reprinted Kuala Lumpur, OUP, 1965.

Candrasasmita, Uka 1985. "Le rôle de l'architecture et des arts décoratifs dans l'islamisation de l'Indonesia," trans. C. Guillot, *Archipel* 29, pp. 203–12.

Carey, P. B. R. 1981. *Babad Dipanagara: An Account of the Outbreak of the Java War (1825–1830).* Kuala Lumpur, MBRAS.

Carletti, Francesco 1606. *My Voyage around the World,* trans. Herbert Weinstock. New York, Random House, 1964.

Casparis, J. G. de 1975. *Indonesian Palaeography: A History of Writing in Indonesia from the Beginnings to A.D. 1500.* Handbuch der Orientalistik. Leiden and Cologne, E. J. Brill.

——— 1981. "Pour une historie sociale de l'ancienne Java principalement au Xème siècle." *Archipel* 21, pp. 125–51.

Cense, A. A. 1966. "Old Buginese and Makassarese Diaries." *BKI* 122, iv, pp. 416–28.

——— 1979. *Makassaars-Nederlands Woordenboek.* The Hague, Nijhoff for KITLV.

Census of India 1901. Calcutta, Office of the Superintendent of Government Printing, 1903.

Census of the Philippine Islands, 1903. 4 vols. Washington, U. S. Bureau of the Census, 1905.

Chau Ju-Kua c. 1250. *His Work on the Chinese and Arab Trade in the Twelfth and Thirteenth Centuries, entitled Chu-fan-chi,* trans. Friedrich Hirth and W. W. Rockhill. St. Petersburg, 1911. Reprinted Taipei, 1970.

Chevillard, Similien 1889. *Siam et les Siamois.* Paris, Plon & Nourrit.

Chiengmai Chronicle. "Chronique de Xieng Mai," trans. Camille Notton, in *Annales du Siam* III. Paris, Paul Geuthner, 1932.

Chirino, Pedro 1604. *Relación de las Islas Filipinas: The Philippines in 1600,* trans. Ramón Echevarria. Manila, Historical Conservation Society, 1969.

Choisy, Abbé de 1687. *Journal du voyage de Siam fait en 1685 et 1686,* ed. Maurice Garçon. Paris, Duchartre et Van Buggenhoudt, 1930.

Chopra, R. N., S. L. Nayar, and I. C. Chopra 1956. *Glossary of Indian Medicinal Plants.* New Delhi, Council of Scientific and Industrial Research.

Chou Ta-kuan 1297. Translated in Pelliot 1951.

Chung, W. C., and B. C. Ko 1976. "Treatment of Taenia Saginata Infection with Mixture of Areca Nuts and Pumpkin Seeds." *Chinese Journal of Microbiology* 9, pp. 31–35.

Clark, Walter 1643. Letter to Surat, 17 December 1643. IOL, E/3/18, fol. 282.

Cockayne, George 1615. Letter from Makassar, 16 July 1615, in *LREIC* III, pp. 136–47.

Coen, Jan Pieterszoon 1615. Letter to Heren XVII, 22 October 1615, in *JPC* I, pp. 114–46.

——— 1617. Letter to Coromandel Coast, 20 November 1617, in *JPC* II, pp. 291–300.

——— 1619. Letter to Heren XVII, 5 August 1619, in *JPC* I, pp. 445–94.

Colin, Francisco 1663. *Labor Evangelica* (Madrid), trans. in Blair and Robertson 1903–09 XL: 40–98.

Compostel, Jacob 1636. "Origineel daghregister van de voyagie, handel en resconter met 'tschip d'Revengie naer Atchin," in ARA KA 1031 (voc. 1119).

Compton, Carol J. 1979. *Courting Poetry in Laos: A Textual and Linguistic Analysis*. De Kalb, Northern Illinois Center for Southeast Asian Studies.

Conklin, Harold C. 1949. "Bamboo Literacy on Mindoro," *Pacific Discovery II*, 4, pp. 4–11.

——— 1960. "Maling: A Hanunóo Girl from the Philippines," in *In the Company of Man: Twenty Portraits by Anthropologists*, ed. J. B. Casagrande. New York, Harper, pp. 101–25.

Coolhaas, W. Ph. (ed.) 1960. *Generale Missiven van Gouverneurs-Generaal en Raden aan Heren XVII der Verenigde Oostindische Compagnie*, vol. I, 1610–1638. The Hague, Martinus Nijhoff.

——— (ed.) 1964. *General Missiven van Gouverneurs-Generaal en Raden aan Heren XVII der Verenigde Oostindische Compagnie*, vol. II, 1639–1655. The Hague, Martinus Nijhoff.

——— (ed.) 1968. *General Missiven van Gouverneurs-Generaal en Raden aan Heren XVII der Verenigde Oostindische Compagnie*, vol. III, 1655–1674. The Hague, Martinus Nijhoff.

Coolie Budget Commission 1941. *Living Conditions of Plantation Workers and Peasants on Java in 1939–1940*, trans. Robert Van Niel. Ithaca, Cornell University Southeast Asia Program, 1956.

Copland, Patrick 1614. "The Narrative of the Rev. Patrick Copland," in Best 1614: 207–14.

Coté, J. J. P. 1979. "The Colonization and Schooling of the To Pamona of Central Sulawesi, 1894 to 1924." M.Ed. thesis, Monash University.

Coulson and Ivy 1636. Letter to East India Company, 20 December 1636. IOL E/3/15, fols. 293–94.

Court, M. H. 1821. *An Exposition of the Relations of the British Government with the Sultan and State of Palembang.* London, Black, Kingsbury, Parbury, & Allen.

Court Minutes 1632. East India Company Court Minutes, 14 December 1632. *SP 1630–34*: 329.

Couto, Diogo do 1645. *Da Asia.* 9 Decades. Lisbon, Regia Officina Typografica, 1778–88. Reprinted Lisbon, 1974.

Covarrubias, Miguel 1937. *Bali.* New York, Knopf. Reprinted Kuala Lumpur, OUP, 1972.

Cowan, H. K. T. 1938. "Bijdrage tot de kennis der geschiedenis van het rijk Samoedera-Pasé." *TBG* 78, pp. 204–14.

Cox, Hiram 1821. *Journal of a Residence in the Burmhan Empire, and More Particularly at the Court of Amarapoorah.* London, John Warren. Reprinted Gregg International, 1971.

Craen, Hendrik Jansz 1606. "Dagboek gehouden aan boord van het schip Gelderland, gezeild op den 18 December 1603 uit Texel . . . onder bevel van den Admiraal Steven van der Hagen," in de Jonge 1862–88 III: 164–204.

Crawfurd, John 1820. *History of the Indian Archipelago*, 3 vols. Edinburgh, A. Constable.

——— 1828. *Journal of an Embassy from the Governor-General of India to the Courts of Siam and Cochin China*. London. Reprinted Kuala Lumpur, OUP, 1967.

——— 1830. "Evidence of Mr. John Crawfurd, 25 March 1830," in *First Report of the Select Committee on the Affairs of the East India Company*, vol. II (China Trade). Great Britain, Parliamentary Papers, House of Commons, 1830.

——— 1856. *A Descriptive Dictionary of the Indian Islands and Adjacent Countries*. London, Bradbury.

Cressy, David 1980. *Literacy and the Social Order: Reading and Writing in Tudor and Stuart England*. Cambridge, Cambridge University Press.

Croft, Ralph 1613. "A journal kept on board the *Hosiander*, begun by Ralph Standish and continued by Ralph Croft, 3 February 1612 to 29 August 1613," in Best 1614: 93–182.

Crystal Sands. The Crystal Sands: The Chronicles of Nagara Sri Dharrmaraja, trans. David K. Wyatt. Ithaca, Cornell University Southeast Asia Program, 1975.

Cuisinier, Jeanne 1951. *Sumangat: l'âme et son culte en Indochine et en Indonésie*. Paris, Gallimard.

Dagh-Register. Dagh-Register gehouden in 't Casteel Batavia, 1642–1682, 31 vols. Batavia and The Hague, Bataviaasch Genootschap, 1887–1931.

Dampier, William 1697. *A New Voyage round the World*, ed. Sir Albert Gray. London, Argonaut Press, 1927.

——— 1699. *Voyages and Discoveries*, ed. C. Wilkinson. London, Argonaut Press, 1931.

Das Gupta, Ashin 1979. *Indian Merchants and the Decline of Surat, c. 1700–1750*. Wiesbaden, Franz Steiner.

Dasmariñas, Goméz Peréz 1590A. "The manners, customs, and beliefs of the Philippine inhabitants of long ago; being chapters of 'A Late Sixteenth Century Manila Manuscript,'" trans. Carlos Quirino and Mauro Garcia. *The Philippine Journal of Science* 87, iv, 1958, pp. 389–445.

——— 1590B. "Berunai in the *Boxer Codex*," trans. John Carroll. *JMBRAS* 55, ii (1982), pp. 2–16.

——— 1590C. "Relación de las Costumbres del Reyno de Champa," ed. C. R. Boxer, in *Papers Read at the Inauguration of the Scandinavian Institute of Asian Studies, 16-18 September 1968*. Lund, Scandinavian Institute of Asian Studies, 1970, pp. 37–44.

——— 1591. "Account of the Encomiendas in the Philippinas Islands," 31 May 1591, in Blair and Robertson 1903–09 VIII: 96–141.

——— 1592. "Expedition to Tuy," 1 June 1592, in Blair and Robertson 1903–09, VIII: 250–51.

Davis, John 1600. "The Voyage of Captaine John Davis to the Easterne India, Pilot in a Dutch Ship; written by himselfe," in *The Voyages and Works of John Davis the Navigator*, ed. A. H. Markham. London, Hakluyt Society, 1880, pp. 129–89.

Deyell, John 1983. "The China Connection: Problems of Silver Supply in Medieval Bengal," in *Precious Metals in the Later Medieval and Early Modern Worlds*, ed. J. F. Richards. Durham, Carolina Academic Press, pp. 207–27.

Dhaninivat, Prince 1948. "The Shadow-Play as a Possible Origin of the Masked-Play." *JSS* 37. Reprinted in Rutnin 1975: 115–25.

——— 1956. "The Dalang." *JSS* 43, ii. Reprinted in Rutnin 1975: 139–56.

Dias, Balthasar 1559. Letter from Melaka to Antonio de Quadros, S. J., 3 December 1559, in Jacobs 1974: 299–309.

Díaz, Casimiro 1718. *Conquistas*, trans. in Blair and Robertson 1903–09 XLII: 117–312.

Diemen, Antonio van, et al. 1637. Letter from Batavia to Heren XVII, 9 December 1637, in Coolhaas 1960: 596–657.

Diller, A. 1983. "The Thai Epic Romance: From Polysemy to Norm." Unpublished paper, ANU.

Djajadiningrat, Hoesein 1913. *Critische Beschouwing van de Sadjarah Banten*. Haarlem, published dissertation.

Djamour, Judith 1959. *Malay Kinship and Marriage in Singapore*. London, Athlone Press. Reprinted 1965.

Dobbin, Christine 1974. "Islamic Revivalism in Minangkab at the Turn of the Nineteenth Century." *Modern Asian Studies* 8, pp. 319–45.

——— 1983. *Islamic Revivalism in a Changing Peasant Economy: Central Sumatra, 1784–1847*. London and Malmo, Curzon Press for Scandinavian Institute of Asian Studies.

Donselaar, W. M. 1857. "Aanteekeningen over het eiland Saleijer," *Mededeelingen van wege het Nederlandsche Zendelinggenootschap I*, pp. 277–328.

Drake, Francis 1580. "The famous voyage of Sir Francis Drake," in *The Principal Navigations of the English Nation*, ed. Richard Hakluyt. London, Everyman's Library Edition 1907, vol. VIII, pp. 48–75.

Drewes, G. W. J. 1969. *The Admonitions of Seh Bari: A Sixteenth Century Javanese Muslim Text Attributed to the Saint of Bonan*. The Hague, Nijhoff for KITLV.

——— (ed.) 1978. *An Early Javanese Code of Muslim Ethics*. The Hague, Nijhoff for KITLV.

Duff-Cooper, A. 1985. "An Account of the Balinese 'Person' from Western Lombok," *BKI* 141, pp. 67–85.

Dumarçay, J. 1982. "Notes d'architecture javanaise et khmère." *BEFEO* 71, pp. 87–146.

Durand, J. D. 1967. "The Modern Expansion of World Population." *Proceedings of the American Philosophical Society* 3, iii, pp. 136–60.

Earl, G. W. 1837. *The Eastern Seas or Voyages and Adventures in the Indian Archipelago in 1832–33–34*. London, W. H. Allen. Reprinted Singapore, OUP, 1971.

EIC Merchants 1615. Letter of East India Company Merchants at Jambi, 22 October 1615, in *LREIC* III, pp. 201–02.

Ellen, Roy, and I. C. Glover 1974. "Pottery Manufacture and Trade in the

Central Moluccas, Indonesia: The Modern Situation and the Historical Evidence." *Man* 9, pp. 353–79.
Ellis, G. R. 1981. "Arts and Peoples of the Northern Philippines," in *The People and Art of the Philippines*. Los Angeles, Museum of Natural History of the University of California, pp. 183–268.
Empoli, Giovanni da 1514. Letter to Lionardo his father, in *Lettera di Giovanni da Empoli*, ed. A. Bausani. Rome, Istituto Italiano per il Medio ed Estremo Oriente, 1970, pp. 107–61.
Endicott, K. M. 1970. *An Analysis of Malay Magic*. Oxford, Clarendon Press.
——— 1983. "The Effects of Slave Raiding on the Aborigines of the Malay Peninsula," in Reid 1983: 216–45.
Eredia, Manoel Godinho de 1600. "Informação da Auro Chersoneso, ou Peninsula, e das ilhas auriferas, carbunculas, e aromaticas," trans. J. V. Mills. *JMBRAS* 8, i (1930), pp. 228–55.
——— 1613. "Eredia's Description of Malacca, Meridional India, and Cathay," trans. J. V. Mills. *JMBRAS* 8, i (1930), pp. 11–84.
Errington, Shelly 1979. "The Cosmic House of the Buginese." *Asia* January-February 1979, pp. 8-14.
——— 1983. "Embodied *Sumange'* in Luwu," *JAS* XLII, 3, pp. 545–70.
Evans, Ivor H. N. 1923. *Studies in Religion, Folk-Lore, and Customs in British North Borneo and the Malay Peninsula*. Cambridge, Cambridge University Press.
Eveleth, Phyllis B. 1979. "Population Differences in Growth: Environmental and Genetic Factors," in *Human Growth*, ed. F. Falkner and J. M. Tanner, vol. III. New York, Plenum.
Farb, Peter, and George Armelagos 1980. *Consuming Passions: The Anthropology of Eating*. New York, Washington Square Press, 1983.
Finlayson, George 1826. *The Mission to Siam and Hué, the Capital of Cochin-China, in the Years 1821–22*. London, John Murray.
Firth, Raymond 1973. *Symbols, Public and Private*. London. Allen & Unwin.
Fisher, Charles A. 1966. *South-East Asia: A Social, Economic, and Political Geography*. London, Methuen.
Fitch, Ralph 1591. "The voyage of M. Ralph Fitch marchant of London . . . begunne in the yeere of our Lord 1583, and ended 1591," in Hakluyt 1598–1600 III: 287–321.
Floris, Peter 1615. *Peter Floris, His Voyage to the East Indies in the "Globe," 1611–1615*, ed. W. H. Moreland. London, Hakluyt Society, 1934.
Floud, Roderick, and K. W. Wachter 1982. "Poverty and Physical Stature: Evidence on the Standard of Living of London Boys, 1770–1870." *Social Science History* 6, iv, pp. 422–52.
Fogel, R. W., S. L. Engerman, and J. Trussell 1982. "Exploring the Uses of Data on Height: The Analysis of Long-term Trends in Nutrition, Labor Welfare, and Labor Productivity." *Social Science History* 6, iv, pp. 401–21.
Forrest, Thomas 1792. *A Voyage from Calcutta to the Mergui Archipelago Lying on the East Side of the Bay of Bengal*. London, J. Robson.
Forth, G. L. 1981. *Rindi: An Ethnographic Study of a Traditional Domain in Eastern Sumba*. The Hague, Nijhoff for KITLV.

Fox, Robert B. 1959. "The Catalagan Excavations." *Philippine Studies* 7, iii (1959), pp. 325–90.

Frédéric, Louis 1981. *La Vie quotidienne dans la péninsule indochinoise à l'époque d'Angkor, c. 800–1300.* Paris, Hachette.

Frederici, Cesar 1581. "The voyage and travell of M. Caesar Fredericke, Marchant of Venice, into the East India, and beyond the Indies," trans. T. Hickocke, in Hakluyt 1598–1600 III: 198–269.

Fryke, Christopher 1692. "A Relation of a Voyage Made to the East Indies by Christopher Fryke," in *Voyages to the East Indies*, ed. C. Ernest Fayle. London, Casse, 1929.

Galvão, Antonio 1544. *A Treatise on the Moluccas (c. 1544), Probably the Preliminary Version of Antonio Galvão's Lost História das Molucas*, trans. Hubert Jacobs, S. J. Rome, Jesuit Historical Institute, 1971.

Geertz, Clifford 1973. "Deep Play: Notes on the Balinese Cockfight," in *The Interpretation of Cultures: Selected Essays by Clifford Geertz.* New York, Basic Books, pp. 412–53.

——— 1980. *Negara: The Theatre State in Nineteenth Century Bali.* Princeton, Princeton University Press.

Geertz, Hildred 1963. "Indonesian Cultures and Communities," in *Indonesia*, ed. R. T. McVey. New Haven, Yale University Southeast Asia Studies, pp. 24–96.

Gerini, G. E. 1905. "Historical Retrospect of Junkceylon Island." *JSS* 2, ii, pp. 121–267.

——— 1912. *Siam and Its Productions, Arts, and Manufactures: A Descriptive Catalogue of the Siamese Section at the International Exhibition of Industry and Labour Held in Turin April 29–November 19, 1911.* Hertford, Stephen Austin & Sons.

Gervaise, Nicolas 1688. *Histoire naturelle et politique du royaume de Siam.* Paris, Claude Barbin.

——— 1701. *An Historical Description of the Kingdom of Macassar in the East Indies.* London, Tho. Leigh. Reprinted Farnborough, 1971.

Gibb, H. A. R., and J. H. Kramers (eds.) 1961. *Shorter Encyclopedia of Islam.* Leiden, E. J. Brill; London, Luzac.

Gimlette, John D. 1915. *Malay Poisons and Charm Cures.* London. Reprinted Kuala Lumpur, OUP, 1971.

Glass Palace Chronicle. The Glass Palace Chronicle of the Kings of Burma, trans. Pe Maung Tin and G. H. Luce. London, OUP, 1923.

Goens, Rijklof van 1656. "De samenvattende geschriften," in *De Vijf Gezantschapsreizen van Rijklof van Goens naar het Hof van Mataram, 1648–1654*, ed. H. J. de Graaf. The Hague, Nijhoff for Linschoten-Vereeninging, 1956, pp. 173–269.

Goody, Jack (ed.) 1968. *Literacy in Traditional Societies.* Cambridge, Cambridge University Press.

——— 1976. *Production and Reproduction: A Comparative Study of the Domestic Domain.* Cambridge, Cambridge University Press.

Goudswaard, A. 1860. "Brief van Bonthain," 12 October 1854, in *Mededeelingen van wege het Nederlandsche Zendelinggenootschap* IV, pp. 345–66.

Graaf, H. J. de 1958. *De Regering van Sultan Agung, Vorst van Mataram 1613–1645 en die van zijn voorganger Panembahan Séda-ing-Krapjak 1601–1613*. The Hague, Nijhoff for KITLV.

Graaf, H. J. de, and Th. G. Th. Pigeaud 1974. *De Eerste Moslimse Vorstendommen op Java: Studiën over de Staatkundige Geschiedenis van de 15de en 16de Eeuw*. The Hague, Nijhoff for KITLV.

——— 1984.*Chinese Muslims in Java in the Fifteenth and Sixteenth Centuries: The Malay Annals of Semarang and Cerbon*, ed. M. C. Ricklefs. Melbourne, Monash University Papers on Southeast Asia.

Graaff, Nicolaus de 1701. *Reisen van Nicolaus de Graaff naar de Vier Gedeelten des Werelds*, ed. J. C. M. Warnsinck. The Hague, Linschoten-Vereeniging, 1930.

Graham, W. A. 1912. *Siam: A Handbook of Practical, Commercial, and Political Information*, 2nd ed. London, Alexander Moring.

Groeneveldt, W. P. 1880. *Historical Notes on Indonesia and Malaya, Compiled from Chinese Sources*. Batavia, VBG. Reprinted Jakarta, Bhratara, 1960.

Groslier, Bernard P. 1958. *Angkor et le Cambodge au XVle siècle d'après les sources portugaises et espagnoles*. Paris, Presses Universitaires de France.

Guggenheim, Scott 1982. "Cock or Bull: Cockfighting, Social Structure, and Political Commentary in the Philippines." *Pilipinas: A Journal of Philippine Studies* 3, i, pp. 1–35.

Guillot, Claude 1983. "Le *dluwang* ou 'papier javanaise.'" *Archipel* 26, pp. 105–115.

——— 1985. "La symbolique de la mosquée javanaise: A propos de la 'Petite Mosquée de Jatinom.'" *Archipel* 30, pp. 3–20.

Guy, John 1986. "Vietnamese Ceramics and Cultural Identity: Evidence from the Ly and Tran Dynasties," in *Southeast Asia in the Ninth to Fourteenth Centuries*, ed. David G. Marr and A. C. Milner. Singapore, Institute of Southeast Asian Studies, pp. 255–69.

Haan, E. de 1912. *Priangan: De Preanger-Regentschappen onder het Nederlandsche Bestuur tot 1811*, 4 vols. Batavia, Kolff.

——— 1922. *Oud Batavia*, 3 vols. Batavia, Kolff.

Hadimuljono, and C. C. Macknight 1983. "Imported Ceramics in South Sulawesi." *RIMA* 17, pp. 66–91.

Haen, de 1623. "Journael van't gepasseerde op de reyse naer den Mattaram, beginnende den 24 May Anno 1623." Extracts in de Jonge 1862–88 V: 30–39.

Hageman, J. 1859. "Aanteekeningen nopens de Industrie, Handel en Nijverheid van Soerabaja." *Tijdschrift voor Nijverheid en Landbouw in Nederlandsch Indië* 5, pp. 137–52.

——— 1860. "Verslag omtrent de Nijverheid te Soerabaiya." *Tijdschrift voor Nijverheid en Landbouw in Nederlandsch Indië* 6, pp. 139–48.

Hagen, Steven van der 1607. "Oost-Indische Reyse," in *Begin ende Voortgangh* 1646.

Hakluyt, Richard (ed.) 1598–1600. *The Principal Navigations, Voyages, Traffiques, and Discoveries of the English Nation*, Everyman's Edition. London, J. M. Dent, 1907, 8 vols.

Halewijn, M. 1838. "Eenige Reizen in de Binnenlanden van dit Eiland . . . in het jaar 1824." *TNI* I. Partly translated in Ras 1968: 623–24.
Hall, Kenneth R. 1976. "State and Statecraft in Early Srivijaya," in *Explorations in Early Southeast Asian History: The Origins of Southeast Asian Statecraft*, ed. K. R. Hall and J. K. Whitmore. Ann Arbor, University of Michigan Center for South and Southeast Asian Studies, pp. 61–105.
Hamilton, Alexander 1727. *A New Account of the East Indies*. Edinburgh, John Mosman, vol. II. Reprinted London, Argonaut Press, 1930.
Hanks, Lucien M. 1972. *Rice and Man: Agricultural Ecology in Southeast Asia*. Chicago, Aldine-Atherton.
Harahap, F. K. N. 1981. "Catur, Masuk Indonesia lewat Tanah Batak?" *Mutiara* 245 (24 June–27 July 1981).
Harrisson, Tom 1964. "The 'Palang', Its History and Proto History in West Borneo and the Philippines." *JMBRAS* 37, ii, pp. 162–74.
Harrisson, Tom, and Stanley O'Connor 1969. *Excavations of the Prehistoric Iron Industry in West Borneo*, 2 vols. Ithaca, Cornell University Southeast Asia Program.
Hart, Donn V. 1969. *Bisayan Filipino and Malayan Humoral Pathologies: Folk Medicine and Ethnohistory in Southeast Asia*. Ithaca, Cornell University Southeast Asia Program.
Hasell, Jan van 1620. Letter from Singora (Songkhla) to Coen, 4 October 1620, in *JPC* VII, pp. 639–49.
Hauch, D. E. 1972. "The Cai Luong Theatre of Viet Nam, 1915–1970." Ph.D. diss., Southern Illinois University.
Haudricourt, A. G. 1953. "La place du Vietnamien dans les langues austroasiatiques." *Bulletin de la Société de Linguistique* 49, pp. 122–28.
——— 1954. "De l'origine des tons en Vietnamien." *Journal Asiatique* 242, pp. 69–82.
Hawley, Henry 1626. Letter from Batavia to East India Company, 6 February 1626, in *SP 1625–1629*: 145–54.
——— 1627. Letter from Batavia to East India Company, 18 July 1627, in *SP 1625–1629*: 371–72.
Hazeu, G. A. J. 1905. *Tjeribonsch Wetboek (Pepakem Tjerbon) van het jaar 1768*. *VBG* 55.
Heekeren, H. R. van 1958. *The Bronze-Iron Age of Indonesia*. The Hague, Nijhoff for KITLV.
Heemskerck, J. van 1600. "Memorie," in de Jonge 1862–88 II: 448–52.
Hein, Donald 1985. "An Alternative View on the Origins of Ceramic Production at Si Satchanalai and Sukhothai, Central Northern Thailand," in *SPAFA Final Report, Technical Workshop on Ceramics*. Bangkok, SPAFA Co-ordinating Unit, 1985, pp. 259–84.
l'Hermite, Jacob 1612. "Corte Remonstrantie van den tegenwoordigen stant eeniger plaetsen in Indien ende wat remedien vooreerst daertoe dienen gebruyckt." Presented to Heren XVII, Amsterdam, 20 August 1612, in de Jonge 1862–88 III: 380–94.
Hickey, Gerald C. 1982. *Sons of the Mountains: Ethnohistory of the Vietnamese Central Highlands to 1954*. New Haven, Yale University Press.

Hikayat Aceh c. 1630. *De Hikajat Atjéh*, ed. Teuku Iskandar. The Hague, Martinus Nijhoff for KITLV, 1958.
Hikayat Banjar. In Ras 1968: 228–521 (Malay text and English translation).
Hikayat Dewa Mandu. Hikayat Dewa Mandu: Epopée Malaise, vol. I: *Texte et Présentation*, ed. H. Chambert-Loir. Paris, EFEO, 1980, pp. 89–322.
Hikayat Hang Tuah (menurut naskhah Dewan Bahasa dan Pustaka), ed. Kassim Ahmad. Kuala Lumpur, Dewan Bahasa dan Pustaka, 1966.
Hikayat Patani. Hikayat Patani: The Story of Patani, ed. A. Teeuw and D. K. Wyatt. The Hague, KITLV, 1970, vol. I, pp. 68–145.
Hikayat Pocut Muhamat. Hikayat Potjut Muhamat: An Acehnese Epic, trans. G. W. J. Drewes. The Hague, Nijhoff for KITLV, 1979.
Hikayat Raja-Raja Pasai, ed. A. H. Hill. *JMBRAS* 33, ii (1961), pp. 46–107.
Hilton, R. N. 1956. "The Basic Malay House." *JMBRAS* 29, iii, pp. 134–55.
Hoadley, M. C., and M. B. Hooker 1981. *An Introduction to Javanese Law: A Translation of and Commentary on the Agama*. Tucson, University of Arizona Press.
Hoare, William 1620. Letter to East India Company, May 1620, IOL, E/3/7, fols. 167–74.
——— 1630. Letter from Banten, 6 December 1630, in *SP 1630–1634*: 89.
Hooijman, J., 1780. "Berigt omtrent het katoen spinnen en weeven onder de Javanen en Chinesen." *VBG* 2.
Horta 1766. Letter, in *Lettres édifiantes et curieuses, écrites des missions étrangères (de la Compagnie de Jésus)*, 26 vols. Paris, Y. M. M. de Querbeuf, 1780–83, vol. XVI.
Hsia Liang Lin 1937. "Betelnut as a Useful Taeniafuge." *Chinese Medical Journal* 50.
Hsieh Ch'ing-kao 1820. "Hai Lu (A Record of the Seas)," trans. in J. W. Cushman and A. C. Milner, "Eighteenth- and Nineteenth-Century Accounts of the Malay Peninsula." *JMBRAS* 52, i (1979), pp. 12–34.
Htin Aung, Maung 1937. *Burmese Drama: A Study, with Translations, of Burmese Plays*. London, OUP.
Huard, Pierre, and Maurice Durand 1954. *Connaissance du Vietnam*. Paris, Imprimerie Nationale.
Huizinga, Johan 1938. *Homo Ludens: A Study of the Play Element in Culture*. Boston, Beacon Press, 1955.
Hull, Terence H., and Jon E. Rohde 1980. *Prospects for Rapid Decline of Mortality Rates in Java*. Yogyakarta, Gadja Mada University Population Studies Center.
Huntingdon, Richard, and Peter Metcalf 1979. *Celebrations of Death: The Anthropology of Mortuary Ritual*. Cambridge, Cambridge University Press.
Hutterer, Karl 1973. *An Archeological Picture of a Pre-Spanish Cebuano Community*. Cebu City, University of San Carlos.
——— 1977. "Prehistoric Trade and the Evolution of Philippine Societies: A Reconsideration," in *Economic Exchange and Social Interaction in Southeast Asia: Perspectives from Prehistory, History, and Ethnography*, ed. K. L. Hutterer. Ann Arbor, University of Michigan Center for South and Southeast Asian Studies, pp. 177–96.

Huynh Khac Dung, Tuan-Ly 1970. *Hát Bôi: Theatre traditionnel du Vietnam*. Saigon, Kim Lai An Quan.

Hwang Chung 1537. "Hai Yü (Words about the Sea)," in Groeneveldt 1880: 126–28.

Ibn Battuta, Muhammad 1354. *Ibn Battuta: Travels in Asia and Africa 1325–1354*, trans. H. A. R. Gibb. London, Routledge, 1929.

Ibn Majid, Shihab al-Din Ahmad 1462. "al-Mal'aqiya," trans. G. R. Tibbets, in *A Study of the Arabic Texts Containing Material of South-east Asia*. Leiden and London, E. J. Brill, 1979, pp. 99–206.

Ibrahim, ibn Muhammad 1688. *The Ship of Sulaiman*, trans. from the Persian by J. O'Kane. London, Routledge and Kegan Paul, 1972.

"Inlandsche" 1894. "De inlandsche nijverheid ter Westkust van Sumatra." *Tijdschrift voor Nijverheid en Landbouw in Nederlandsch Indië* 49, pp. 301–54.

Innes, Robert L. 1980. "The Door Ajar: Japan's Foreign Trade in the Seventeenth Century." Ph.D. diss., University of Michigan.

Intakosai, Vidya 1984. "The Excavations of Wreck Sites in the Gulf of Thailand." Country Report of Thailand in *SPAFA Final Report, Consultative Workshop on Research on Maritime Shipping and Trade Networks in Southeast Asia, Cisarua, Indonesia, November 20–27, 1984*. Bangkok, SPAFA Co-ordinating Unit, pp. 133–43.

Ireland, Alleyne 1907. *The Province of Burma*, 2 vols. Boston and New York, Houghton Mifflin.

Ishii Yoneo 1971. "Seventeenth Century Japanese Documents about Siam." *JSS* 59, ii, pp. 161–74.

Ito Takeshi 1978. "Why did Nuruddin ar-Raniri Leave Aceh in 1054 A. H.?" BKI 134, pp. 489–91.

——— 1984. "The World of the Adat Aceh: A Historical Study of the Sultanate of Aceh." Ph.D. diss., ANU, Canberra, 1984.

Ivye 1634. Consultation Held in Parranap by Thomas Ivye, Samuel Boys, and George Goldington, 20 December 1634. IOL E/3/15, fols. 78–79.

Jacobs, Hubert (ed.) 1974. *Documenta Malucensia I (1542–1577)*. Rome, Institutum Historicum Societatis Iesu.

Jacobs, Julius 1883. *Eenigen tijd onder de Baliers*. Batavia, Kolff.

——— 1894. *Het familie- en kampong-leven op Groot-Atjeh: eene bijdrage tot de ethnographie van Noord-Sumatra*, 2 vols. Leiden, E. J. Brill.

Jarric, Pierre du 1608. *Histoire des choses plus memorables advenues tant ez Indes Orientales, que autres pais de la descouverte des Portugais*, Vol. I. Bordeaux, Millanges.

Jasper, J. E. 1904. "Inlandsche methoden van hoorn-, been-, schildpad-, en paarlemoer-bewerking." *TBG*, 1904, pp. 1–54.

Jasper, J. E., and M. Pirngadie 1912. *De inlandsche kunstnijverheid in Nederlandsch Indië*, vol. II: *De weefkunst*. The Hague, Mouton.

——— 1916. *De inlandsche kunstnijverheid in Nederlandsch Indië*, vol. III: *De batikkunst*. The Hague, Mouton.

——— 1930. *De inlandsche kunstnijverheid in Nederlandsch Indië*, vol. V: *De bewerking van niet-edele metalen*. The Hague, Mouton.

"Javanese Code [anonymous seventeenth-century Javanese Muslim Code of Ethics]," in Drewes 1978: 14–57.

Jonge, J. K. J. de (ed.) 1862–88. *De Opkomst van het Nederlandsch Gezag in Oost-Indië*, 13 vols. The Hague, Martinus Nijhoff.

Jordaan, R. E., and P. E. de Josselin de Jong 1985. "Sickness as Metaphor in Indonesian Political Myths." *BKI* 141, pp. 253–74.

Jourdain, John 1617. *The Journal of John Jourdain, 1608–1617, describing his experiences in Arabia, India, and the Malay Archipelago*, ed. W. Foster. Cambridge, Hakluyt Society, 1905.

Jumsai, Manich 1973. *History of Thai Literature*. Bangkok, Chalermnit Press.

Juynboll, H. H. 1899. *Catalogus van de Maleische en Sundaneesche handschriften der Leidsche Universiteits-Bibliotheek*. Leiden, E. J. Brill.

Kaempfer, E. 1727. *The History of Japan, Together with a Description of the Kingdom of Siam*, trans. J. G. Scheuchzer, vol. I. Glasgow, James Maclehose, 1906.

Kasetsiri, Charnvit 1979. "Thai Historiography from Modern Times to the Present," in *Perceptions of the Past in Southeast Asia*, ed. A. Reid and D. Marr. Singapore, Heinemann, pp. 156–70.

Kats, J. 1923. *Het Javaansche tooneel*, vol. I: *Wajang Poerwa*. Weltevreden, Commissie voor de Volkslectuur.

Kaudern, Walter 1929. *Games and Dances in Celebes*, vol. IV of *Ethnographical Studies in Celebes*. Göteberg, Elanders Boktryckeri.

Kaung, U. 1963. "History of Education in Burma before the British Conquest and After." *JBRS* 46, ii.

Keeler, Ward 1983. "The Symbolic Dimensions of the Javanese House." Conference Paper, Association of Asian Studies.

Keppel, Henry 1846. *The Expedition to Borneo of H. M. S. Dido for the Suppression of Piracy*. New York, Harper and Brothers.

Kiefer, Thomas M. 1972. *The Tausug: Violence and Law in a Philippine Moslem Society*. New York, Holt, Rinehart and Winston.

Kratz, E. U. 1981. "The Journey to the Far East: Seventeenth and Eighteenth Century German Travel Books as a Source Study." *JMBRAS* 54, i, pp. 65–87.

Kroef, J. M. van der 1956. "Dualism and Symbolic Antithesis in Society," in van der Kroef, *Indonesia in the Modern World*. Bandung, Masa Baru, pp. 138–61.

Kruijt, A. C. 1901. "Het Ijzer in Midden-Celebes." *BKI* 53, pp. 148–60.

Kruyt, A. C. 1932. "De Tol in den Indischen Archipel." *TBG* 72, pp. 415–595.

Kumar, Ann 1980. "Javanese Court Society and Politics in the Late Eighteenth Century: The Record of a Lady Soldier. Pt I: The Religious, Social, and Economic Life of the Court." *Indonesia* 29, pp. 1–46.

Kunst, J. 1933. *Music in Java: Its History, Its Theory, and Its Technique*, trans. E. van Loo, 2 vols. The Hague, Martinus Nijhoff, 1949.

La Bissachère, de 1812. *Etat actuel du Tonkin, de la Cochinchine, et des royaumes de Cambodge, Laos, et Lac-Tho*, 2 vols. Paris, Galignani.

Lach, Donald F. 1965. *Asia in the Making of Europe*, vol I. Chicago, University of Chicago Press.

La Loubère, Simon de 1691. *A New Historical Relation of the Kingdom of Siam*. London, Tho. Horne, 1693. Reprinted Kuala Lumpur, OUP, 1969.

Lancaster, James 1603. *The Voyages of Sir James Lancaster to Brazil and the East Indies, 1591–1603*, ed. Sir William Foster. London, Hakluyt Society, 1940.

Laslett, Peter 1965. *The World We Have Lost: England before the Industrial Age*, 2nd ed. Charles Scribner's Sons, 1973.

——— 1980. "Age at Menarche in Europe since the Eighteenth Century," in *Marriage and Fertility: Studies in Interdisciplinary History*, ed. R. I. Rotberg and T. Robb. Princeton, Princeton University Press, pp. 285–300.

Leach, E. R. 1958. "Magical Hair." *Journal of the Royal Anthropological Institute* 88, ii, pp. 147–64.

Legazpi, Miguel López de 1569. "Relation of the Filipinas Islands, and of the Character and Conditions of Their Inhabitants, July 1569," in Blair and Robertson 1903–09 III: 54–61.

Lennon, W. C. 1796. "Journal of an Expedition to the Molucca Islands under the Command of Admiral Rainier," ed. J. E. Heeres. *BKI* 60 (1908), pp. 249–366.

Le Roy Ladurie, Emmanuel 1979. *Carnival in Romans*, trans. Mary Feeney. New York, George Braziller.

Leur, J. C. van 1934. "On Early Asian Trade," trans. J. S. Holmes and A. van Marle, in van Leur, *Indonesian Trade and Society*. The Hague, Nijhoff, 1955, pp. 1–144.

Liaw Yock Fang 1976. *Undang-undang Melaka: The Laws of Melaka*. The Hague, Nijhoff for KITLV.

Lieban, Richard W. 1967. *Cebuano Sorcery: Malign Magic in the Philippines*. Berkeley, University of California Press.

Lieberman, Victor B. 1984. *Burmese Administrative Cycles: Anarchy and Conquest, c. 1580–1760*. Princeton, Princeton University Press.

Ligtvoet, A. 1880. "Transcriptie van het dagboek der vorsten van Gowa en Tello, met vertaling en aanteekeningen." *BKI* 4, iv, pp. 1–259.

Lijn, Cornelis van der 1648. Letter to Queen of Aceh, 7 May 1648, in Tiele and Heeres 1886–95 III: 430–33.

Lingat, Robert 1952. *Les régimes matrimoniaux du sud-est de l'Asie: Essai de droit comparé indochinois*, vol. I: *Les régimes traditionnels*. Paris and Hanoi, EFEO.

Lintgens, Aernoudt 1597. "Verhael vant tgheenne mij opt eijllandt van Baelle medevaeren is," in *De eerste schipvaart der Nederlanders naar Oost-Indië onder Cornelis de Houtman, 1595–1597*, vol. III, ed. G. P. Rouffaer and J. W. Ijzerman. The Hague, Linschoten-Vereeniging, 1929, pp. 73–103.

Loarca, Miguel de 1582. "Relation of the Filipinas Islands," in Blair and Robertson 1903–09 V: 34–187.

Locsin, Leandro and Cecilia 1967. *Oriental Ceramics Discovered in the Philippines*. Rutland and Tokyo, Charles Tuttle.

Lodewycksz, Willem 1598. "D'eerste Boeck: Historie van Indien vaer inne verhaelt is de avontueren die de Hollandtsche schepen bejeghent zijn," in *De eerste schipvaart der Nederlanders naar Oost-Indië onder Cornelis de*

Houtman, 1595–1597, vol. I, ed. G. P. Rouffaer and J. W. Ijzerman, The Hague, Martinus Nijhoff, 1915.
Loeb, E. M. 1935. *Sumatra: Its History and People*. Vienna, Institut für Völkerkunde.
Lombard, Denys 1967. *Le Sultanat d'Atjéh au temps d'Iskandar Muda, 1607–1636*. Paris, EFEO.
——— 1969. "Jardins à Java." *Arts asiatiques* 9, pp. 136–84.
——— 1974. "La vision de la forêt à Java (Indonésie)." *Etudes rurales* 53, pp. 474–85.
——— 1979. "Regard nouveau sur les 'pirates Malais,' première moitié du XIXe siècle." *Archipel* 18, pp. 231–49.
Lombard, Denys, and Claudine Salmon 1985. "Islam et sinité." *Archipel* 30, pp. 73–94.
Lontara'-bilang Gowa. Translated in Ligtvoet 1880: 1–259.
Loofs-Wissowa, H. H. E. 1983: "The Development and Spread of Metallurgy in Southeast Asia: A Review of the Present Evidence." *JSEAS* 14, i, pp. 1–11.
Lovric, Barbara 1986. "Bali: Myth, Magic, and Morbidity," in Owen 1987: 117–41.
Low, Hugh 1848. *Sarawak: Its Inhabitants and Productions*. London, Richard Bentley.
Luce, G. H. 1940. "Economic Life of the Early Burman." *JBRS* 30, i, pp. 283–335. Reprinted in Burma Research Society, *Fiftieth Anniversary Publications* no. 2, Rangoon, 1960, pp. 323–75.
Luwaran, the Magindanao Code of Laws, trans. Najeeb Saleeby, in Saleeby 1905: 66–78.
Ma Huan 1433. *Ying-yai Sheng-lan: "The Overall Survey of the Ocean's Shores,"* trans. J. V. G. Mills. Cambridge, Hakluyt Society, 1970.
Macartney, Lord 1798. *An Authentic Account of an Embassy from the King of Great Britain to the Emperor of China . . . Taken Chiefly from the Papers of H. E. the Earl of Macartney*, ed. Sir George Staunton, vol. I. London, W. Bulmer.
Macassar factory 1659. Letter to English Presidency, Banten, 9 July 1659. IOL G/10/1, p. 175.
McDonald, Peter 1980. "An Historical Perspective to Population Growth in Indonesia," in *Indonesia: The Making of a Culture*, ed. J. J. Fox. Canberra, ANU, pp. 81–94.
McEvedy, Colin, and Richard Jones 1978. *Atlas of World Population History*. Harmondsworth, Penguin.
MacMicking, Robert 1851. *Recollections of Manilla and the Philippines during 1848, 1849, and 1850*, ed. M. J. Netzorg. Manila, Filipiniana Book Guild.
McNair, J. F. A. 1878. *Perak and the Malays*. London. Reprinted Kuala Lumpur, OUP, 1972.
McNeill, William H. 1976. *Plagues and Peoples*. Harmondsworth, Penguin, 1979.
McPhee, Colin 1966. *Music in Bali: A Study in Form and Instrumental Organization in Balinese Orchestral Music*. New Haven, Yale University Press.

Maetsuyker, Joan, et al. 1657. Letter from Batavia, 31 January 1657, in Coolhaas 1968: 108–46.

——— 1671. Letter from Batavia, 2 September 1671, in Coolhaas 1968: 739–47.

Malcolm, Howard 1840. *Travels in the Burman Empire*. Edinburgh, Chambers.

Mandelslo, Johann Albrecht von 1662. *The Voyages and Travels of J. A. de Mandelslo . . . into the East Indies. Begun in . . . 1638 and finish'd in 1640*, trans. John Davies. London, Dring and Starkey.

Manderson, Lenore 1981. "Roasting, Smoking, and Dieting in Response to Birth: Malay Confinement in Cross-cultural Perspective." *Social Science and Medicine* 15B, pp. 509–20.

Manguin, Pierre-Yves 1980. "The Southeast Asian Ship: An Historical Approach." *JSEAS* 11, ii, pp. 266–76.

——— 1983. "Manpower and Labour Categories in Early Sixteenth Century Malacca," in Reid 1983: 209–15.

Mantja, Lalu 1984. *Sumbawa Pada Masa Lalu*. Surabaya, Rinta.

Marschall, Wolfgang 1968. "Metallurgie und frühe besiedlungsgeschichte Indonesiens," in *Beiträge zur Volkerkunde Südostasiens und Ozeaniens*, ed. W. Fröhlich. Cologne, E. J. Brill, pp. 29–263.

Marsden, William 1783. *The History of Sumatra*, 3rd rev. ed. London, 1811. Reprinted Kuala Lumpur, OUP, 1966.

Mascarenhas, Pero 1564. Letter from Ternate to Fr. Francisco Rodrigues in Goa, December 1563–February 1564, in Jacobs 1974: 431–35.

Masselman, George 1963. *The Cradle of Colonialism*. New Haven, Yale University Press.

Matelief, Cornelis 1608. "Historische verhael vande treffelijcke reyse, gedaen naer de Oost-Indian ende China, met elf schepen, door den Manhasten Admirael Cornelis Matelief de Ionge, inde jaren 1605, 1606, 1607, and 1608," in *Begin ende Voortgangh* 1646.

Matheson, V., and M. B. Hooker 1983. "Slavery in the Malay Texts: Categories of Dependency and Compensation," in Reid 1983: 182–208.

Matthes, B. F. 1852. Letter to Nederlandsch Bijbelgenootschap, 7 October 1852, in van den Brink 1943: 170–76.

——— 1856. "Verslag van een verblijf in de binnenlanden van Celebes, van 24 April tot 24 October 1856," in van den Brink 1943: 178–88.

——— 1864. "Verslag van een uitstapje naar de Ooster-distrikten van Celebes alsmede van verschillende togten in die afdeeling ondernomen, van 25 September tot 22 December 1864," in van den Brink 1943: 242–82.

——— 1875. *Korte verslag aangaande alle mij in Europa bekende Makassaarsche en Boeginesche Handschriften*. Amsterdam, C. A. Spin.

Meilink-Roelofsz, M. A. P. 1962. *Asian Trade and European Influence in the Indonesian Archipelago between 1500 and about 1630*. The Hague, Martinus Nijhoff.

Mendoza, Juan Gonzalez de 1586. "History of the Great Kingdom of China," in Blair and Robertson 1903–09 VI: 88–152.

Meyer, Hans 1890. "A Trip to the Igorots," trans. W. H. Scott, in *German*

Travelers on the Cordillera (1860–1890), ed. W. H. Scott. Manila, Filipiniana Book Guild, pp. 46–103.

Miles, Douglas 1976. *Cutlass and Crescent Moon: A Case Study in Social and Political Change in Outer Indonesia*. Sydney, Sydney University Centre for Asian Studies.

——— 1979. "The Finger-Knife and Ockham's Razor: A Problem in Asian Culture History and Economic Anthropology." *American Ethnologist* 6, ii, pp. 223–43.

Milner, A. C., E. E. McKinnon, and T. Luckman Sinar 1978. "A Note on Aru and Kota Cina." *Indonesia* 26, pp. 1–42.

Mitchell, David 1982. "Endemic Gonorrhoea in Sumba." Paper presented to the Fourth National Conference of the Asian Studies Association of Australia, Melbourne, 10–14 May 1982.

Möller, I. J., J. J. Pindborg, and I. Effendi 1977. "The Relation between Betel Chewing and Dental Caries." *Scandinavian Journal of Dental Research* 85, pp. 64–70.

Morga, Antonio de 1598. "Report of Conditions in the Philippines," 8 June 1598, in Blair and Robertson 1903–09 X: 75–102.

——— 1609. *Sucesos de las Islas Filipinas*, trans. J. S. Cummins. Cambridge, Hakluyt Society, 1971.

Morris, Ivan 1964. *The World of the Shining Prince: Court Life in Ancient Japan*. London, OUP.

Morton, David 1976. *The Traditional Music of Thailand*. Berkeley, University of California Press.

Mouhot, Henri 1864. *Travels in the Central Parts of Indo-China (Siam), Cambodia, and Laos during the Years 1858, 1859, and 1860*. 2 vols. London, John Murray.

Moyer, David S. 1975. *The Logic of the Laws: A Structural Analysis of Malay Language Legal Codes from Bengkulu*. The Hague, Nijhoff for KITLV.

Mulyono, Sri 1978. *Wayang: Asal-usul, Filsafat dan Masa Depannya*. Jakarta, Gunung Agung.

Mundy, Peter 1667. *The Travels of Peter Mundy in Europe and Asia, 1609–1667*, vol. III, ed. R. C. Temple. London, Hakluyt Society, 1919.

Murray, H. J. R. 1913. *A History of Chess*. Oxford, Clarendon. Reprinted 1962.

Nagara-kertagama 1365. "The Nagara-kertagama by *Rakawi* Prapanca of Majapahit, 1365 A.D.," trans. Theodore G. Th. Pigeaud, in *Java in the Fourteenth Century: A Study in Cultural History*, vol. III. The Hague, Nijhoff for KITLV, 1960.

Nash, June, and Manning Nash 1963. "Marriage, Family, and Population Growth in Upper Burma." *Southwestern Journal of Anthropology* 19, pp. 251–66.

Nash, Manning 1965. *The Golden Road to Modernity: Village Life in Contemporary Burma*. Chicago, University of Chicago Press.

Navarrete, Domingo 1676. *The Travels and Controversies of Friar Domingo Navarrete, 1618–1686*, trans. J. S. Cummins, 2 vols. Cambridge, Hakluyt Society, 1962.

Neck, Jacob van 1599. "Reisverhaal," in *De tweede schipvaart der Neder-*

landers naar Oost-Indië onder Jacob Cornelisz van Neck en Wybrant Warwijck, 1598–1600, ed. J. Keuning, vol. I. The Hague, Nijhoff for Linschoten-Vereeniging, 1938, pp. 1–111.

——— 1604. "Journaal van Jacob van Neck," in *De vierde schipvaart der Nederlanders naar Oost-Indië onder Jacob Wilkens en Jacob van Neck (1599–1604)*, ed. H. A. van Foreest and A. de Booy, vol. I. The Hague, Linschoten-Vereeniging, 1980, pp. 166–233.

Newbold, T. J. 1839. *Political and Statistical Account of the British Settlements in the Straits of Malacca*, 2 vols. London, John Murray. Reprinted Kuala Lumpur, OUP, 1971.

Ng Shui Meng 1979. "Demographic Change, Marriage, and Family Formation: The Case of Nineteenth Century Nagcarlan, the Philippines." Ph.D. diss., Sociology, University of Hawaii.

Nguyen Duc Minh. "Medicinal Plants with Anti-Bacterial Properties." *Vietnamese Studies* 50, pp. 51–76.

Nguyen Khac Vien and Huu Ngoc (eds.) 1973. *Anthologie de la littérature vietnamienne*, 2 vols. Hanoi, Editions en Langues Etrangères.

Nguyen Thanh-Nha 1970. *Tableau économique du Vietnam aux XVIIe et XVIIIe siècles*. Paris, Cujas.

Nguyen Van Huyen 1934. *Introduction à l'étude de l'habitation sur pilotis dans l'Asie du Sud-Est*. Paris, Paul Gruthner.

Nicholls, William 1617. Letter from Aceh to Banten, 20 August 1617, in *LREIC* VI, pp. 71–73.

Nicolas, René 1924. 'Le Lakhon Nora ou Lakhon Chatri et les origines du théâtre classique siamois." *JSS* 18, reprinted in Rutnin 1975: 41–61.

——— 1927. "Le théâtre d'ombres au Siam." *JSS* 21, reprinted in Rutnin 1975: 103–114.

Nieuhoff, Johan 1662. "Voyages and Travels into Brasil and the East-Indies," in *A Collection of Voyages and Travels*, 4 vols. London, Awnshawm & John Churchill, 1704, vol. II, pp. 1–369.

Nieuwenhuijze, C. A. O. van 1945. *Samsu 'l-Din van Pasai*. Leiden, published dissertation.

Nitisastro, Widjoyo 1970. *Population Trends in Indonesia*. Ithaca, Cornell University Press.

Noort, Olivier van 1601. "The Voyage of Olivier Noort round about the Globe, being the fourth Circum-Navigation of the same, extracted out of the Latin Diarie," in *Hakluytus Posthumus, or Purchas His Pilgrimes*. Glasgow, James Maclehose for Hakluyt Society, 1905, vol. II, pp. 187–206.

Nyèssen, D. J. H. 1929. *Somatical Investigation of the Javanese, 1929*. Bandung, Anthropological Laboratory of Java, n.d.

Ochse, J. J. 1931. *Vegetables of the Dutch East Indies*. Bogor. New ed., Canberra, ANU Press, 1977.

Oki Akira 1979. "A Note on the History of the Textile Industry in West Sumatra," in *Between People and Statistics: Essays on Modern Indonesian History*, ed. F. van Anrooij, D. H. A. Kolff, J. T. M. van Laanen, and G. J. Telkamp. The Hague, Nijhoff.

Oosterbeek, W. F. Gerdes 1905. "Spelen," in *ENI* IV, pp. 51–63.

Opstall, M. F. van 1985. "From Alkmaar to Ayudhya and Back," *Itinerario IX*, pp. 108–120.
Ortega, Francisco de 1594. "Report concerning Filipinas Islands," in Blair and Robertson 1903–09 IX: 95–105.
Owen, Norman G. 1985. Work in progress on parish registers of Bikol, kindly made available to this author.
——— (ed.) 1987. *Death and Disease in Southeast Asia: Explorations in Social, Medical, and Demographic History*. Singapore, OUP for Asian Studies Association of Australia.
——— 1987A. "The Paradox of Nineteenth Century Population Growth in Southeast Asia," forthcoming.
Pallegoix, J. B. 1854. *Description du royaume Thai ou Siam*, 2 vols. Paris. Reprinted Farnborough, Gregg International, 1969.
Parker, S. R. 1979. "Celadon and Other Related Wares Excavated in Sarawak," in *Chinese Celadons and Other Related Wares in Southeast Asia*, comp. Southeast Asian Ceramic Society. Singapore, Arts Orientalis.
Pedrosa, Ramón 1983. "Abortion and Infanticide in the Philippines during the Spanish Contact." *Philippiniana Sacra* 18, no. 52, pp. 7–37.
Pelliot, Paul 1951. *Mémoires sur les coutumes du Cambodge de Tcheou Ta-Kouan*. Paris, Adrien Maisonneuve.
Pelras, Christian 1981. "Célèbes-Sud avant l'Islam selon les premiers témoignages étrangers." *Archipel* 21, pp. 153–84.
Pemberton, R. B. 1830. "Journey from Munipoor to Ava, and from Thence across the Yooma Mountain to Arracan," ed. D. G. E. Hall. *JBRAS* 63, ii.
Penzer, M. N. 1952. *Poison-Damsels and Other Essays in Folklore and Anthropology*. London, Chas. Sawyer.
Pigafetta, Antonio 1524. *First Voyage around the World*, trans. J. A. Robertson. Manila, Filipiniana Book Guild, 1969, pp. 1–101.
Pigeaud, Th. G. Th. 1938. *Javaanse volksvertoningen: Bijdrage tot de beschrijving van land en volk*. Batavia, Volkslectuur.
——— 1962. *Java in the Fourteenth Century: A Study in Cultural History*, vol IV: *Commentaries and Recapitulations*. The Hague, Nijhoff for KITLV.
——— 1967. *Literature of Java*, vol I. The Hague, Nijhoff for KITLV.
——— 1968. *Literature of Java*, vol II. The Hague, Nijhoff for KITLV.
Pijper, G. F. 1977. *Studiën over de geschiedenis van de Islam in Indonesia, 1900–1950*. Leiden, E. J. Brill.
Pinto, Fernão Mendes 1614. *The Voyages and Adventures of Ferdinand Mendes Pinto, the Portuguese, Done into English by H. Cogan, with an Introduction by A. Vambéry*. London, T. F. Unwin, 1891.
Pires, Tomé 1515. *The Suma Oriental of Tomé Pires*, trans. A. Cortesão, 2 vols. (paginated as one). London, Hakluyt Society, 1944.
Plasencia, Fr. Juan de 1589. "Customs of the Tagalogs," 21 October 1589, in Blair and Robertson 1903–09 VII: 173–85.
Poivre, Pierre 1747. *Les Mémoires d'un voyageur*, ed. L. Malleret. Paris, EFEO, 1968.
Polanco, Fr. Juan Alonso de 1556. "Chronicon," excerpted in Jacobs 1974: 208–10.

Polo, Marco 1298. *The Travels of Marco Polo,* trans. Ronald Latham. Harmondsworth, Penguin Books, 1958.

Pombejra, Dhiravat na 1984. "Okya Sombatthiban and the Verenigde Oost-Indische Compagnie (V. O. C.), c. 1648–1656," in *Relations between Thailand and Other Countries* (Papers of International Conference on Thai Studies). Bangkok, Thai Studies Program, Chulalongkorn University.

Pou, Saveros 1977. *Etudes sur le Ramakerti (XVIe-XVIIe siècles).* Paris, EFEO.

Presidency Bantam 1636. Letter from Presidency Bantam to Court of (English) East India Company, 20 December 1636. IOL, G/10/1, p. 73.

Pretty, Francis 1588. "The admirable and prosperous voyage of the Worshipfull Master Thomas Candish [Cavendish] . . . round about the whole earth, begun in the yeere of our Lord 1586, and finished 1588," in Hakluyt 1598–1600 VIII: 206–55.

Pring 1619. Letter from Sunda Straits, 23 March 1619. IOL E/3/6, fol. 292.

Pyrard, Francis 1619. *The Voyage of Francis Pyrard of Laval to the East Indies, the Maldives, the Moluccas, and Brazil,* trans. A. Gray, 2 vols. London, Hakluyt Society, 1887–89.

Qabus Nama 1082. *A Mirror for Princes: The Qabus Nama by Kai Ka'us ibn Iskandar,* trans. Reuben Levy. London, Cresset Press, 1951.

Rabibhadana, Akin 1969. *The Organization of Thai Society in the Early Bangkok Period.* Ithaca, Cornell University Southeast Asia Program.

Radjab, Muhamad 1950. *Semasa Ketjil Dikampung (1913–1928).* Jakarta, Balai Pustaka.

Raffles, Thomas Stamford 1817. *The History of Java,* 2 vols. London, John Murray. Reprinted Kuala Lumpur, OUP, 1965, 1978.

——— 1818. Letter to Duchess of Somerset, 11 July 1818, in *Memoir of the Life and Public Services of Sir Thomas Stamford Raffles by His Widow.* London, James Duncan, 1837, vol. I, pp. 338–53.

Ram Kamheng 1293. "The Oldest Known Writing in Siamese: The Inscription of Phra Ram Kamhaeng of Sukhothai, 1293 A.D.," trans. C. B. Bradley. *JSS* 6, i (1909), pp. 25–30.

Raniri, Nuru'd-din ar- c. 1644. *Bustanu's-Salatin Bab II, Fasal 13,* ed. T. Iskandar. Kuala Lumpur, Dewan Bahasa dan Pustaka, 1966.

Ras, J. J. 1968. *Hikajat Bandjar: A Study in Malay Historiography.* The Hague, Nijhoff for KITLV.

——— 1976. "The Historical Development of the Javanese Shadow Theatre." *RIMA* 10, ii, pp. 50–76.

Rassers, W. H. 1922. *De Pandji-roman.* Antwerp, de Vos–van Kleef.

Reael, Laurens 1618. Letter from Banda Neira, 7 May 1618, in Coolhaas 1960: 82–84.

Reid, Anthony 1979. "Trade and State Power in Sixteenth and Seventeenth Century Southeast Asia," *Proceedings of the Seventh IAHA Conference, Bangkok, August 1977.* Bangkok, International Association of Historians of Asia, pp. 391–419.

——— 1980. "The Structure of Cities in Southeast Asia: Fifteenth to Seventeenth Centuries." *JSEAS* 11, ii, pp. 235–50.

——— 1981. "A Great Seventeenth Century Indonesian Family: Matoaya and Pattingalloang of Makassar." *Masyarakat Indonesia* 8, i, pp. 1–28.

——— (ed.) 1983. *Slavery, Bondage, and Dependency in Southeast Asia*. St. Lucia, Queensland University Press.

——— 1983A. "The Rise of Makassar." *RIMA* 17, pp. 117–60.

——— 1983B. "Southeast Asian Cities before Colonialism." *Hemisphere* 28, iii, pp. 144–49.

——— 1985. "From Betel-Chewing to Tobacco-Smoking in Indonesia." *JAS* 44, iii, pp. 529–47.

——— 1987. "Low Population Growth and Its Causes in Pre-Colonial Southeast Asia," in Owen 1987: 33–47.

"Relation" 1572. "Relation of the Conquest of the Island of Luzon," 20 April 1572, in Blair and Robertson 1903–09 III: 141–172.

Reynolds, Craig 1979. "A Nineteenth Century Thai Buddhist Defence of Polygamy and Some Remarks on the Position of Women in Thailand," *Proceedings of the Seventh IAHA Conference, Bangkok, August 1977*. Bangkok, International Association of Historians of Asia, pp. 927–70.

Reynst, Gerard 1615. Letter from Banten, 26 October 1615, in Coolhaas 1960: 46–60.

Rhodes, Alexandre de 1653. *Rhodes of Viet Nam: The Travels and Missions of Father Alexander de Rhodes in China and Other Kingdoms of the Orient*, trans. S. Hertz. Westminster, Md., Newman Press, 1966.

Ricklefs, M. C. 1974. *Jogjakarta under Sultan Mangkubumi, 1749–1792: A History of the Division of Java*. London, OUP.

——— 1978. *Modern Javanese Historical Tradition: A Study of an Original Kartasura Chronicle and Related Materials*. London, School of Oriental and African Studies, University of London.

——— 1986. "Some Statistical Evidence on Javanese Social, Economic, and Demographic History in the Later Seventeenth and Eighteenth Centuries." *Modern Asian Studies* 20, i, pp. 1–32.

Ricklefs, M. C., and P. Voorhoeve 1977. *Indonesian Manuscripts in Great Britain: A Catalogue of Manuscripts in British Public Collections*. Oxford, OUP.

Riquel, Hernando 1573. "News from the Western Islands," 1 July 1573, in Blair and Robertson 1903–09 III: 230–49.

Roolvink, R. 1966. "Five-line Songs in the Sejarah Melayu?" *BKI* 122, iv, pp. 454–56.

Rouffaer, G. P. 1904. *De voornaemste industrieën der inlandsche bevolking van Java en Madoera*. The Hague, Nijhoff.

Rumphius, Georg E. 1960. *Ambonsch kruid boek*. Amsterdam, 1741–1750. Extracts trans. E. M. Beekman in *The Poison Tree: Selected Writings of Rumphius on the Natural History of the Indies*, ed. E. M. Beekman. Amherst, University of Massachusets Press, 1981, pp. 41–256.

Rutnin, Mattari (ed.) 1975. *The Siamese Theatre: A Collection of Reprints from the Journals of the Siam Society*. Bangkok, Siam Society.

Rutter, Owen 1929. *The Pagans of North Borneo*. London, Hutchinson.

St. John, Spenser 1862. *Life in the Forests of the Far East*, 2 vols. London, Smith, Elder. Reprinted Kuala Lumpur, OUP, 1974.

Salazar, Domingo de 1590. "The Chinese and the Parian at Manila," 24 June 1590, in Blair and Robertson 1903–09 VII: 212–38.

Salazar, Vincente de 1742. *Historia de el Santissimo Rosario*, trans. in Blair and Robertson 1903–09 XLIII: 27–93.
Saleeby, Najeeb M. 1905. *Studies in Moro History, Law, and Religion*. Manila, Bureau of Public Printing.
Salmon, Claudine 1983. "La fabrication du papier à Java mentionée dans un texte chinois de l'époque des Song du sud." *Archipel* 26, p. 116.
San Agostin, Gaspar de 1720. "Letter on the Filipinos," in Blair and Robertson 1903–09 XL: 183–295.
San Antonio, Gabriel Quiroga de 1604. *Breve y verdadera relación de los successos del Reyno de Camboxa*, in A. Cabaton (ed.), *Brève et véridique relation des événements du Cambodge*. Paris, Ernest Leroux, 1914, pp. 1–83.
Sande, Francisco de 1576. "Relation of the Filipinas Islands," Manila, 7 June 1576, in Blair and Robertson 1903–09 IV: 21–97.
——— 1577. "Relation and Description of the Phelipinas Islands," 8 June 1577, in Blair and Robertson 1903–09 IV: 98–118.
Sangermano, Vincentius 1818. *A Description of the Burmese Empire*, trans. William Tandy, Rome and Rangoon. Reprinted London, Susil Gupta, 1966.
Schamschula, R. G., B. L. Adkins, D. E. Barnes, and G. Charlton 1977. "Betel Chewing and Caries Experience in New Guinea." *Community Dentistry and Oral Epidemiology* 5, vi, pp. 284–86.
Schärer, Hans 1946. *Ngaju religion: The Conception of God among a South Borneo People*, trans. Rodney Needham. The Hague, Nijhoff for KITLV, 1963.
Schoute, D. 1929. *De Geneeskunde in den dienst der Oost-Indische Compagnie in Nederlandsch-Indië*. Amsterdam, J. H. de Bussy.
Schouten, Joost 1636. "A Description of the Government, Might, Religion, Customes, Traffick, and Other Remarkable Affairs in the Kingdom of Siam," trans. R. Manley, in *A True Description of the Mighty Kingdoms of Japan and Siam*, by Francis Caron and Joost Schouten. London, Robert Boulter, 1671, pp. 121–52.
——— 1641. "A report by Commissary Justus Schouten of his visit to Malacca," 7 September 1641, in "The Siege and Capture of Malacca from the Portuguese in 1640–1641," ed. P. A. Leupe, trans. Mac Hacobian. *JMBRAS* 14, i (January 1936), pp. 69–144.
Schrieke, B. 1942. "Ruler and Realm in Early Java," in *Indonesian Sociological Studies: Selected Writings of B. Schrieke*. The Hague and Bandung, Van Hoeve, 1957, vol. II, pp. 1–267.
Schurhammer, Georg 1977. *Francis Xavier: His Life, His Times*, vol. II: *India, 1541–1545*, trans. M. J. Costelloe. Rome, Jesuit Historical Institute.
Schurz, William L. 1939. *The Manila Galleon*. New York, Dutton Paperback, 1959.
Schwaner, C. A. L. M. 1853. *Borneo: Beschrijving van het Stroomgebied van den Barito*, 2 vols. Amsterdam, van Kampen.
Schweisguth, P. 1951. *Etude sur la littérature siamoise*. Paris, A. Maisonneuve.
Scott, Edmund 1606. "An exact discourse of the Subtilties, Fashions, Pollicies,

Religion, and Ceremonies of the East Indians, as well Chyneses as Javans, there abyding and dweling," in *The Voyage of Sir Henry Middleton to the Moluccas*, ed. Sir William Foster. London, Hakluyt Society, 1943, pp. 81–176.

Scott, William H. 1968. *Prehispanic Source Materials for the Study of Philippine History*. Manila, University of Santo Tomas Press.

——— 1974. *The Discovery of the Igorots: Spanish Contacts with the Pagans of Northern Luzon*. Quezon City, New Day.

——— 1982. "Sixteenth Century Tagalog Technology from the *Vocabulario de la Lengua Tagalo* of Pedro de San Buenaventura, O. F. M.," in *Gava': Studies in Austronesian Languages and Cultures*, ed. R. Carle et al. Berlin, Dietrich Reimer, pp. 523–35.

——— 1985. "Boat-Building and Seamanship in Classic Philippine Society." *SPAFA Digest* 6, ii, pp. 15–33.

Sejarah Goa. In Wolhoff and Abdurrahim: 9–78.

Sejarah Melayu 1612. "Sejarah Melayu or 'Malay Annals,'" trans. C. C. Brown. *JMBRAS* 25, ii–iii, 1952 [Malay text in *JMBRAS* 16, iii, 1938].

Sejarah Melayu 1831. *Sejarah Melayu* [The Malay Annals]. Singapore, Mission Press. Romanized ed., Singapore, Malaya Publishing House, 1961.

Semmelink, J. 1885. *Geschiedenis der cholera in Oost-Indië voor 1817*. Utrecht.

Sennett, Richard 1977. *The Fall of Public Man*. New York, Knopf.

Setten van der Meer, N. C. van 1979. *Sawah Cultivation in Ancient Java: Aspects of Development during the Indo-Javanese Period, Fifth to Fifteenth Century*. Canberra, ANU Press.

Shway Yoe [pseud. J. G. Scott] 1882. *The Burman: His Life and Notions*, 2nd ed. London, Macmillan, 1896.

Siegel, James 1979. *Shadow and Sound: The Historical Thought of a Sumatran People*. Chicago, University of Chicago Press.

Skeat, Walter W. 1900. *Malay Magic: Being an Introduction to the Folklore and Popular Religion of the Malay Peninsula*. London, Macmillan. Reprinted New York, Dover Publications, 1967.

——— 1953. "Reminiscences of the Cambridge University Expedition to the North-Eastern Malay States, and to Upper Perak, 1899–1900." *JMBRAS* 26, iv, pp. 9–147.

Skinner, G. W. 1957. *Chinese Society in Thailand: An Analytical History*. Ithaca, Cornell University Press.

Slametmuljana 1976. *A Story of Majapahit*. Singapore, Singapore University Press.

Smith, F. B. 1979. *The People's Health, 1830–1910*. Canberra, ANU Press.

Smith, G. 1974. "The Dutch East India Company in the Kingdom of Ayutthaya, 1604–1694." Ph.D. diss., Northern Illinois University.

Smith, Malcolm 1946. *A Physician at the Court of Siam*. Reprinted Kuala Lumpur, OUP, 1982.

Snouck Hurgronje, C. 1893. *The Achehnese*, trans. A. W. S. O'Sullivan, 2 vols. Leiden, E. J. Brill, 1906.

Sokoloff, K. L., and G. C. Villaflor 1982. "The Early Achievement of Modern Stature in America." *Social Science History* 6, iv, pp. 453–81.

Solheim, W. G. 1968. "Early Bronze in Northeastern Thailand." *Current Anthropology* 9, i, pp. 59–62.

Speelman, Cornelis 1670. "Notitie dienende voor eenen Korten Tijd en tot nader last van de Hooge Regering op Batavia voor den ondercoopman Jan van Oppijnen," 3 vols. Typescript copy at KITLV, Leiden.

——— 1670A. "De handelsrelaties van het Makassaarse rijk volgens de Notitie van Cornelis Speelman uit 1670," ed. J. Noorduyn, in *Nederlandse Historische Bronnen*. Amsterdam, Verloren for Nederlands Historische Genootschap, 1983, vol. III, pp. 96–121.

Spinks, Charles N. 1965. *The Ceramic Wares of Siam*, rev. ed. Bangkok, Siam Society, 1971.

Stapel, F. W. 1922. *Het Bongaais verdrag*. Leiden, Rijksuniversiteit.

Staverton, Thomas 1618. Letter from Makassar, 18 May 1618. IOL, G/10/1, fol. 19.

Stavorinus, J. S. 1798. *Voyage to the East Indies*, trans. S. H. Wilcocke, 3 vols. London. Reprinted London, Dawsons, 1968.

Sternstein, Larry 1984. "The Growth of the Population of the World's Pre-eminent 'Primate City': Bangkok at Its Bicentenary." *JSEAS* 15, i, pp. 43–68.

Stone, Lawrence 1979. *The Family, Sex, and Marriage in England, 1500–1800*. New York, Harper & Row.

Stutterheim, W. I. 1930. *Gids voor de oudheden van Soekoeh en Tjeta*. Surakarta, De Bliksem.

Suchitta, Pornchai 1983. "The History and Development of Iron Smelting Technology in Thailand." Ph.D. diss., Brown University.

Sulaiman, M. Isa 1979. "Dari Gecong hingga ke Rotary: Perkembangan Usaha Kerajinan Pandai Besi Massepe, Kabupaten Sidrap." Ujung Pandang, PLPIIS. Mimeo.

Sulu Code 1878. Trans. Najeeb Saleeby in Saleeby 1905: 89–94.

Sutton, R. Anderson 1982. "Variation in Javanese Gamelan Music: Dynamics of a Steady State." Ph.D. diss., University of Michigan.

——— 1984. "Who is the *Pesindhèn*?" *Indonesia* 37, pp. 119–133.

Sweeney, Amin 1973. "Professional Malay Story-telling: I. Some Questions of Style and Presentation." *JMBRAS* 46, ii, pp. 1–53.

——— 1980. *Authors and Audiences in Traditional Malay Literature*. Berkeley, University of California Center for South and Southeast Asian Studies.

Symes, Michael 1827. *An Account of an Embassy to the Kingdom of Ava in the Year 1795*, 2 vols. Edinburgh, Constable & Co.

Tachard, Guy 1686. *A Relation of the Voyage to Siam Performed by Six Jesuits*, English trans. London, A. Churchill, 1688. Reprinted Bangkok, White Orchid Press, 1981.

Tanner, J. M. 1979. "A Concise History of Growth Studies from Buffon to Boas," in *Human Growth*, ed. Frank Falkner and J. M. Tanner. New York, Plenum, pp. 515–93.

Teeuw, A. 1966. "The Malay Sha'ir: Problems of Origin and Tradition." *BKI* 122, iv, pp. 429–46.

Terwiel, B. J. 1980. *The Tai of Assam and Ancient Tai Ritual*, vol. I: *Life-Cycle Ceremonial*. Gaya, Centre for Southeast Asian Studies.

——— 1983. "Bondage and Slavery in Early Nineteenth Century Siam," in Reid 1983: 118–37.

——— 1987. "Asiatic Cholera in Siam: Its First Occurrence and the 1820 Epidemic," in Owen 1987: 142–61.

Thomas, Keith 1971. *Religion and the Decline of Magic*. Harmondsworth, Penguin Books, 1980.

Throgmorton, Kellum 1617. Letter from Makassar, 12 May 1617, in *LREIC* V, pp. 225–27.

Tiele, P. A., and J. A. Heeres (eds.) 1886–95. *Bouwstoffen voor de geschiedenis der Nederlanders in den Maleischen Archipel*, 3 vols. The Hague, Nijhoff.

Tjan Tjoe Siem 1941. *Javaanse kaartspelen: Bijdrage tot de beschrijving van land en volk. VBG*, no. 75. Bandung, A. C. Nix.

Tobias, J. H. 1857. "Memorie van overgave van het bestuur der Residentie Ternate," in *Ternate*, Penerbitan Sumber Sejarah no. 11. Jakarta, Arsip Nasional Republik Indonesia, 1980, pp. 1–97.

Trager, F. N., and W. J. Koenig 1979. *Burmese Sit-tàns, 1764-1826: Records of Rural Life and Administration*. Tucson, University of Arizona Press.

Traibhumikatha c. 1345. Trans. Frank Reynolds and Mani Reynolds in *Three Worlds according to King Ruang: A Thai Buddhist Cosmology*. Berkeley, University of California Press, 1982.

Tran Van Khe 1967. *Viêtnam: les traditions musicales*. Berlin, Buchet/ Chastel for Institut International d' Etudes Comparatives de la Musique.

[Trant, T. A.] 1827. *Two Years in Ava, from May 1824 to May 1826*. London, John Murray.

Tregonning, K. G. 1965. *A History of Modern Sabah: North Borneo 1881–1963*. Singapore, University of Malaya Press.

True Report 1599. "A True Report of the gainefull, prosperous and speedy voiage to Iava in the East Indies, performed by a fleet of eight ships of Amsterdam." Reprinted in *De tweede schipvaart der Nederlanders naar Oost-Indië onder Jacob Cornelisz van Neck en Wybrant Warwijck, 1598–1600*, ed. J. Keuning. The Hague, Nijhoff for Linschoten-Vereeniging, vol. II, 1940, pp. 27–41.

Turner, William, et al. 1665. Letter from Bantam to Geo. Oxindon in Surat, 28 July 1665. IOL, E/3/29, no. 3061.

Turpin, F. H. 1771. *Turpin's History of Siam*, trans. B. O. Cartwright. Bangkok, 1908.

Turton, Andrew 1978. "Architectural and Political Space in Thailand," in *Natural Symbols in Southeast Asia*, ed. G. B. Milner. London, School of Oriental and African Studies, University of London, pp. 113–32.

"Tweede Boeck" 1601. "Het Tweede Boeck, Journael oft Dagh-Register," pp. 1–186, in *De tweede schipvaart der Nederlanders naar Oost-Indië onder Jacob Cornelisz van Neck en Wybrant Warwijck, 1598–1600*, ed. J. Keuning, vol. III. The Hague, Nijhoff for Linschoten-Vereeniging, 1942.

Undang-undang Melaka: The Laws of Malacca, ed. Liaw Yock Fang. The Hague, Nijhoff for KITLV, 1976.
Valentijn, Francois 1726. *Oud en Nieuw Oost-Indiën*, ed. S. Keijzer. The Hague, H. C. Susan, 1858, 3 vols.
Valeri, Valerio 1985. "Both Nature and Culture: Reflections on Female Impurity in Huaulu (Seram)." Seminar paper, ANU.
Varthema, Ludovico di 1510. *The Travels of Ludovico di Varthema in Egypt, Syria, Arabia Deserta and Arabia Felix, in Persia, India, and Ethiopia,* A.D. *1503 to 1508*, trans. J. W. Jones, ed. G. P. Badger. London, Hakluyt Society, 1863.
Velarde, Pedro Murillo 1749. "Jesuit Missions in the Seventeenth Century," in Blair and Robertson 1903–09 44: 27–119.
Veltman, T. J. 1904. "Nota betreffende de Atjehsche goud- en silversmeedkunst." *TBG* 47, pp. 341–85.
——— 1919. "Geschiedenis van het Landschap Pidië." *TBG* 58, pp. 15–157.
Verhael 1597. "Verhael vande Reyse by de Hollandtsche Schepen gedaen naer Oost-Indien," in *De Eerste Schipvaart der Nederlanders naar Oost-Indië onder Cornelis de Houtman, 1595–1597*, ed. G. P. Rouffaer and J. W. Ijzerman. The Hague, Nijhoff for Linschoten-Vereeniging, vol. II, 1925, pp. 1–76.
Verhoeff, Pieter 1611. "Journael ende Verhael van alle het gene dat ghesien ende voor-ghevallen is op de Reyse, gedaen door . . . Pieter Willemsz Verhoeven, Admirael Generael over 13 Schepen," ed. M. E. van Opstall, in *De Reis van de Vloot van Pieter Willemsz Verhoeff naar Azië 1607–1612*. The Hague, Nijhoff for Linschoten-Vereeniging, vol. I, 1972, pp. 191–298.
Vlamingh van Oudtshoorn, A. de 1644. "Journael of Daghregister gehouden geduijrent sijn aenwijs in Aitchien." ARA KA 1059 bis (VOC 1157), fols. 567–610.
Vliet, Jeremias van 1636. "Description of the Kingdom of Siam," trans. L. F. van Ravenswaay. *JSS* 7, i (1910).
——— 1640. *The Short History of the Kings of Siam*, trans. Leonard Andaya. Bangkok, Siam Society, 1975.
Volkstelling 1920. Uitkomsten der in de maand 1920 gehouden volkstelling, 2 vols. Batavia, Ruygrok, 1922.
Volkstelling 1930. 8 vols. Batavia, Department van Economische Zaken, 1933–38.
Vollenhoven, C. van 1918. *Van Vollenhoven on Indonesian Adat Law: Selections from Het Adatrecht van Nederlandsch-Indië*, trans. J. F. Holleman. The Hague, Nijhoff for KITLV, 1981.
Wales, H. G. Quaritch 1931. *Siamese State Ceremonies: Their History and Function*. London, Bernard Quaritch.
——— 1934. *Ancient Siamese Government and Administration*. London, Bernard Quaritch. Reprinted New York, Paragon, 1965.
——— 1952. *Ancient South-East Asian Warfare*. London, Bernard Quaritch.
Wallace, Alfred R. 1869. *The Malay Archipelago*. London, Macmillan. Reprinted New York, Dover, 1962.
Wangbang Wideya. In *Wangbang Wideya: A Javanese Panji Romance*, trans. S. O. Robson. The Hague, Martinus Nijhoff for KITLV, 1971, pp. 57–241.

Warwijck, Wybrant van 1604. "Historische Verhael vande Reyse gedaen inde Oost-Indien, met 15 Schepen voor Reeckeningh vande vereenichde Gheoctroyeerde Oost-Indische Compagnie," in *Begin ende Voortgangh* 1646.
Wenk, Klaus 1968. *Die Ruderlieder—kap hē rüö—in der literatur Thailands.* Wiesbaden, Franz Steiner.
Wessing, Robert 1978. *Cosmology and Social Behaviour in a West Javanese Settlement.* Athens, Ohio University Center for International Studies.
West, John 1617. Letter from Makassar, 10 August 1617, in *LREIC* VI, pp. 62–64.
Westby, Richard 1615. "Journal of a Voyage from Bantam to Jambi, 11 September–25 October 1615," in *LREIC* III, pp. 160–69.
Wheatley, Paul 1959. "Geographical Notes on Some Commodities Involved in Sung Maritime Trade." *JMBRAS* 32, ii.
——— 1961. *The Golden Khersonese: Studies in the Historical Geography of the Malay Peninsula before A. D. 1500.* Kuala Lumpur, University of Malaya Press.
——— 1964. *Impressions of the Malay Peninsula in Ancient Times.* Singapore, Eastern Universities Press.
White, George 1678. "Report on the Trade of Siam," in John Anderson, *English Intercourse with Siam in the Seventeenth Century.* London, 1890. Reprinted Bangkok, Chalermnit, 1981, pp. 421–28.
White, John 1824. *A Voyage to Cochin-China.* London, Longman. Reprinted Kuala Lumpur, Oxford University Press, 1972.
Whitmore, J. K. 1983. "Vietnam and the Monetary Flow of Eastern Asia, Thirteenth to Eighteenth Centuries," in *Precious Metals in the Later Medieval and Early Modern Worlds*, ed. J. F. Richards. Durham, Carolina Academic Press, pp. 363–93.
Wilkinson, R. J. 1903. *A Malay-English Dictionary (Romanised)*, 2 vols. Mytilene, Salavopoulos, and Kinderlis, 1932. Reprinted London, Macmillan, 1959.
——— 1908. "Law: Introductory Sketch," in *Papers on Malay Subjects*, ed. R. J. Wilkinson. Kuala Lumpur, F. M. S. Government Press, reprinted 1922.
——— 1908A. "The Incidents of Malay Life," in *Papers on Malay Subjects*, ed. R. J. Wilkinson. Kuala Lumpur, F. M. S. Government Press, reprinted 1920.
——— 1910. "Malay Amusements," in *Papers on Malay Subjects*, ed. R. J. Wilkinson. Kuala Lumpur, F. M. S. Government Press.
Willemsz, Pieter 1642. "Atchins dachregister," 26 September–27 November 1642, ARA KA 1051 bis (VOC 1143) fols. 499–527.
Willoughby, G., et al. 1635. Letter from Banten, 31 January 1634. IOL, E/3/15, fols. 113–18.
——— 1636. Letter from Banten, 1 January 1636. IOL E/3/15, fol. 154.
Winstedt, R. O. 1935. *History of Malaya*, rev. ed. Singapore, Marican and Sons, 1962.
——— 1940. *A History of Classical Malay Literature.* Reprint of 2nd (1960) ed., Kuala Lumpur, OUP, 1972.
Wolff, J. O. 1976. "Malay Borrowings in Tagalog," in *Southeast Asian History*

and Historiography: Essays Presented to D. G. E. Hall, ed. C. D. Cowan and J. M. Echols. Ithaca, Cornell University Press, pp. 345–67.

Wolhoff, G. J., and Abdurrahim. *Sedjarah Goa*. Makassar, Jajasan Kebudajaan Sulawesi Selatan dan Tenggara, n. d.

Wonderaer, Jeronimus 1602. Letter from Tachem (Tatchim, Cochin-China), 5 April 1602, in *De vierde schipvaart der Nederlanders naar Oost-Indië onder Jacob Wilkens en Jacob van Neck (1599–1604)*, ed. H. A. van Foreest and A. de Booy. The Hague, Linschoten-Vereniging, 1981, vol. II, pp. 67–91.

Wood, W. A. R. 1924. *A History of Siam*. London. Reprinted Bangkok, 1959.

Woodard, David 1796. *The Narrative of Captain David Woodard and Four Seamen*. London, J. Johnson, 1805. Reprinted London, Dawsons of Pall Mall, 1969.

Woodside, Alexander B. 1971. *Vietnam and the Chinese Model: A Comparative Study of Vietnamese and Chinese Government in the First Half of the Nineteenth Century*. Cambridge, Harvard University Press.

Wrigley, E. A., and R. S. Schofield 1981. *The Population History of England: A Reconstruction*. London, Edward Arnold.

Wurm, S. A., and B. Wilson 1983. *English Finderlist of Reconstructions in Austronesian Languages (Post-Brandstetter)*, rev. ed. Canberra, ANU Department of Linguistics.

Wyatt, David K. 1969. *The Politics of Reform in Thailand: Education in the Reign of King Chulalongkorn*. New Haven, Yale University Press.

——— 1984. *Thailand: A Short History*. New Haven, Yale University Press.

Yu, Insun, 1978. "Law and Family in Seventeenth and Eighteenth Century Vietnam." Ph.D. diss., University of Michigan.

Yupho, Dhanit 1957. *Thai Musical Instruments*, trans. David Morton. Bangkok, Siva Phorn, 1960.

Zoetmulder, P. J. 1974. *Kalangwan: A Survey of Old Javanese Literature*. The Hague, Nijhoff for KITLV.

Zollinger, H. 1847. "The Island of Lombok" (trans. from *TNI* 1847). *Journal of the Indian Archipelago and Eastern Asia* 5 (1851), pp. 323–44.

Glossary

Abbreviations: (A) Arabic; (B) Burmese; (J) Javanese; (K) Khmer; (M) Malay; (T) Tagalog; (Th)Thai; (V) Vietnamese

alun-alun(J): Square to north of Javanese palace
amok(M): Frenzied attack
anito(T): Spirit
arak(A/M): Distilled liquor
bahar(M): Variable unit of weight, equivalent to 3 *pikul* or approx. 180 kg when weighing pepper, but only 7.25 kg when weighing gold
baju(M): Tunic
balon(Anglo-Indian): Galley
batik(J): Wax-resist process of cloth dyeing
belacan(M): Pickled fish or prawn paste
cash(Anglo-Indian): Chinese copper-lead coin of lowest value (from Portuguese *caixa*)
datu(M/T): Elder, patriarch, chief; but in Toba Batak a magical healer
gambuh(J): Dance pageant
gamelan(J): Javanese orchestra consisting chiefly of bronze percussion
gantang(M): Measure of volume, equivalent to about 3.1 kg for rice
gudang(M): Storehouse
hat boi(V): Dance drama of Vietnam
hikayat(M): Story (often historical)
ikat(M): Process of cloth dyeing by tying warp threads
ka-ga-nga(Redjang, etc.): First three syllabic letters of Sumatran alphabets; hence alphabet
kakawin(J): Old-Javanese poetic form
kampung(M): Urban compound or quarter

kauman(A/J): Islamic quarter of Javanese city
kebaya(M): Loose-fitting, long-sleeved woman's garment
kendi(M): Water jug, with narrow spout
khon(Th): Masked dance
khong(Th): Gong
kora-kora(Ternate): War galley (like Filipino *caracao*)
koyang(M): Measure of weight; 40 *pikul* or approx. 2400 kg
kris(J/M): Dagger
krom(Th): Administrative department; service division
lakhon(Th): Dance drama
lontar(M): Palm tree (*Borassus sundaicus Becc.*), the sap of which is used for sugar and wine, and the leaves for writing material
lurik(J): Striped cotton cloth
macapat(J): Form of sung poetry in Java of the Islamic period
mas(M): Gold; small gold coin
nang(Th): Shadow puppet theatre
nat(B): Powerful spirit
nipah(M): Palm (*Nipa fruticans*) used for roof thatch
orangkaya(M): Aristocrat, usually with wealth from trade
pamor(J): Damask formed on iron-nickel alloy in *kris* blade
pantun(M): Quatrains, usually improvized orally, in which first half rhymes with second (abab)
parang(M): Machete
phrai luang(Th): Commoner owing corvée to the crown
pikul(M): A man's load, taken as 100 *kati*(approx. 60 kg)
rabam(Th): Dance pageant
raja(M): King
raket(J): Dance pageant
sangha(Pali/Th/K): Theravada Buddhist monkhood
sarung(M): Sarong, wraparound lower garment for both sexes
sepak raga(M): Game of kicking basketwork ball
shari'a(A/M): Islamic law code
slendro(J): Five-tone scale (as opposed to seven-tone *pelog*)
songket(M): Silk cloth embroidered with gold or silver thread
suasa(M): Gold-copper alloy
sya'ir(M): Four-line verse form, rhyming aaaa
tahil(M): Unit of weight for silver (580 gr) and unit of account (1000 *cash*)
talak(A): Repudiation of wife by husband in Islamic law
tembaga(M): Copper; brass
tuak(M): Palm wine
tumakkajannangngang(Makassarese): Overseer of service obligations of a particular craft group
ulama(A/M): Islamic scholars (plural in Arabic, but here used also for singular)
wayang(J): Theatre
wayang kulit(J): Shadow puppet theatre
zina'(A): Fornication

Index

ALSO AVAILABLE IN PAPERBACK

Southeast Asia in the Age of Commerce, 1450–1680
Volume Two: Expansion and Crisis
Anthony Reid

This book completes Reid's vivid exploration of everyday life in the various societies of Southeast Asia (highly praised in Volume One) by moving on to the economic, political, and religious changes that determined the region's place in the early modern world. If the first volume defined Southeast Asia as a place, the second defines the age of commerce as a period. Between the fifteenth and the mid-seventeenth centuries, Southeast Asia became a crucial part of a global commercial system, embraced the scriptural world religions (Islam, Christianity, and Theravada Buddhism), and experimented with centralized states and commercial cosmopolitan cities. *Expansion and Crisis* explains why in the mid-seventeenth century Southeast Asia diverged from the capitalist path taken by Europe and began a process of disengagement from world commerce and economic growth.

"A most impressive piece of work which rests upon a vast range of evidence. . . . Reid's two volumes together set a new standard for the historical study of Southeast Asia as a region."
—M. C. Ricklefs, *Economic History of Southeast Asia*

"Reid offers a large, broad-brushed, brightly colored canvas of carefully gleaned and finely honed detail. . . . Reid's comparative perspective lends considerable explanatory power to his treatment of the multifaceted changes in Southeast Asia. He masterfully synthesizes the broad theses of comparative economic history with his detailed portrait of the lands of Southeast Asia most influenced by the age of commerce."
—Robert J. Donia, *Journal of Economic History*